interchange

FIFTH EDITION

intro

Teacher's Edition

Jack C. Richards

CAMBRIDGE
UNIVERSITY PRESS

CAMBRIDGE
UNIVERSITY PRESS

University Printing House, Cambridge CB2 8BS, United Kingdom

One Liberty Plaza, 20th Floor, New York, NY 10006, USA

477 Williamstown Road, Port Melbourne, VIC 3207, Australia

314–321, 3rd Floor, Plot 3, Splendor Forum, Jasola District Centre, New Delhi – 110025, India

79 Anson Road, #06–04/06, Singapore 079906

Cambridge University Press is part of the University of Cambridge.

It furthers the University's mission by disseminating knowledge in the pursuit of education, learning and research at the highest international levels of excellence.

www.cambridge.org
Information on this title: www.cambridge.org/9781108406055

First published 1995
Second edition 2000
Third edition 2005
Fourth edition 2013

20 19 18 17 16 15 14 13 12 11 10 9 8 7 6 5 4 3

Printed in the United Kingdom by Latimer Trend

A catalogue record for this publication is available from the British Library

ISBN 9781316620113 Intro Student's Book with Online Self-Study
ISBN 9781316620120 Intro Student's Book A with Online Self-Study
ISBN 9781316620137 Intro Student's Book B with Online Self-Study
ISBN 9781316620144 Intro Student's Book with Online Self-Study and Online Workbook
ISBN 9781316620151 Intro Student's Book A with Online Self-Study and Online Workbook
ISBN 9781316620168 Intro Student's Book B with Online Self-Study and Online Workbook
ISBN 9781316622377 Intro Workbook
ISBN 9781316622391 Intro Workbook A
ISBN 9781316622407 Intro Workbook B
ISBN 9781108406055 Intro Teacher's Edition
ISBN 9781316622216 Intro Class Audio CDs
ISBN 9781316623855 Intro Full Contact with Online Self-Study
ISBN 9781316623862 Intro Full Contact A with Online Self-Study
ISBN 9781316623879 Intro Full Contact B with Online Self-Study
ISBN 9781108403047 Presentation Plus Intro

Additional resources for this publication at www.cambridge.org/interchange

Contents

Plan of Intro book

Titles/Topics	Speaking	Grammar
 **UNIT 1** PAGES 2–7 **What's your name?** Alphabet; greetings and leave-takings; names and titles of address; numbers 0–10, phone numbers, and email addresses	Introducing yourself and friends; saying hello and good-bye; asking for names and phone numbers	Possessive adjectives *my, your, his, her*; the verb *be*; affirmative statements and contractions
 **UNIT 2** PAGES 8–13 **Where are my keys?** Possessions, classroom objects, personal items, and locations in a room	Naming objects; asking for and giving the locations of objects	Articles *a, an,* and *the*; *this/these, it/they*; plurals; yes/no and *where* questions with *be*; prepositions of place: *in, in front of, behind, on, next to,* and *under*
PROGRESS CHECK PAGES 14–15		
 **UNIT 3** PAGES 16–21 **Where are you from?** Cities and countries; adjectives of personality and appearance; numbers 11–103 and ages	Talking about cities and countries; asking for and giving information about place of origin, nationality, first language, and age; describing people	The verb *be*: affirmative and negative statements, yes/no questions, short answers, and Wh-questions
 **UNIT 4** PAGES 22–27 **Is this coat yours?** Clothing; colors; weather and seasons	Asking about and describing clothing and colors; talking about the weather and seasons; finding the owners of objects	Possessives: adjectives *our* and *their*, pronouns, names, and *whose*; present continuous statements and yes/no questions; conjunctions *and, but,* and *so*; placement of adjectives before nouns
PROGRESS CHECK PAGES 28–29		
 **UNIT 5** PAGES 30–35 **What time is it?** Clock time; times of the day; everyday activities	Asking for and telling time; asking about and describing current activities	Time expressions: *o'clock,* A.M., P.M., *noon, midnight, in the morning/afternoon/evening, at 7:00/night/midnight*; present continuous Wh-questions
 **UNIT 6** PAGES 36–41 **I ride my bike to school.** Transportation; family relationships; daily routines; days of the week	Asking for and giving information about how people go to work or school; talking about family members; describing daily and weekly routines	Simple present statements with regular and irregular verbs; simple present yes/no and Wh-questions; time expressions: *early, late, every day, on Sundays/weekends/weekdays*
PROGRESS CHECK PAGES 42–43		
 **UNIT 7** PAGES 44–49 **Does it have a view?** Houses and apartments; rooms; furniture	Asking about and describing houses and apartments; talking about the furniture in a room	Simple present short answers; *there is, there are; there's no, there isn't a, there are no, there aren't any*
 **UNIT 8** PAGES 50–55 **Where do you work?** Jobs and workplaces	Asking for and giving information about work; giving opinions about jobs; describing workday routines	Simple present Wh-questions with *do* and *does*; placement of adjectives after *be* and before nouns
PROGRESS CHECK PAGES 56–57		

Pronunciation/Listening	Writing/Reading	Interchange Activity
Linked sounds Listening for the spelling of names, phone numbers, and email addresses	Writing a list of names, phone numbers, and email addresses	"Celebrity classmates": Introducing yourself to new people PAGE 114
Plural *-s* endings Listening for the locations of objects	Writing the locations of objects	"Find the differences": Comparing two pictures of a room PAGE 115
Syllable stress Listening for countries, cities, and languages; listening to descriptions of people	Writing questions requesting personal information	"Let's talk!": Finding out more about your classmates PAGE 118
The letters *s* and *sh* Listening for descriptions of clothing and colors	Writing questions about what people are wearing	"Celebrity fashions": Describing celebrities' clothing PAGES 116–117
Rising and falling intonation Listening for times of the day; listening to identify people's actions	Writing times of the day "Message Me!": Reading an online chat between two friends	"What's wrong with this picture?": Describing what's wrong with a picture PAGE 119
Third-person singular *-s* endings Listening for activities and days of the week	Writing about your weekly routine "What's Your Schedule Like?": Reading about someone's daily schedule	"Class survey": Finding out more about classmates' habits and routines PAGE 120
Words with *th* Listening to descriptions of homes; listening to people shop for furniture	Writing about your dream home "Unique Hotels": Reading about two interesting hotels	"Find the differences": Comparing two apartments PAGE 121
Reduction of *do* Listening to people describe their jobs	Writing about jobs "Dream Jobs": Reading about two unusual jobs	"The perfect job": Figuring out what job is right for you PAGE 122

Pronunciation/Listening	Writing/Reading	Interchange Activity
Sentence stress Listening for people's food preferences	Writing about mealtime habits "It's a Food Festival!": Reading about foods people celebrate	"Planning a party": Choose snacks for a party and compare answers PAGE 123
Pronunciation of *can* and *can't* Listening for people's favorite sports to watch or play; listening to people talk about their abilities	Writing questions about sports "Awesome Sports Records": Reading about fitness records from around the world	"Hidden talents": Finding out more about your classmates' hidden talents PAGE 124
Reduction of *going to* Listening to people talk about their holiday plans	Writing about weekend plans "Happy Birthday to You!": Reading about birthday customs in different places	"Take a guess": Making guesses about a classmate's plans PAGE 125
Sentence intonation Listening to people talk about health problems; listening for medications	Writing advice for health problems "Do You Know Your Body?": Reading interesting facts about your body	"Problems, problems": Giving advice for some common problems PAGE 126
Compound nouns Listening to people talk about shopping; listening to directions	Writing directions "A Tour of Palermo, Buenos Aires": Reading about popular tourist attractions in Buenos Aires, Argentina	"Giving directions": Asking for directions in a neighborhood PAGE 127, 128
Simple past *-ed* endings Listening to people talk about their past summer activities	Writing about last weekend "Did You Have a Good Weekend?": Reading about four people's weekend experiences	"Past activities": Comparing your classmates' childhoods PAGE 129
Negative contractions Listening for places and dates of birth	Writing questions about a person's life "Who is Marina Chapman?": Reading about a woman's life	"This is your life": Finding out more about your classmates' lives PAGE 130
Reduction of *want to* and *have to* Listening to phone conversations about making and changing plans	Writing about weekend plans "Austin City Limits!": Reading about events at a festival	"The perfect weekend": Making plans with your classmates PAGE 131

Informed by teachers

Teachers from all over the world helped develop *Interchange Fifth Edition*. They looked at everything – from the color of the designs to the topics in the conversations – in order to make sure that this course will work in the classroom. We heard from 1,500 teachers in:

- Surveys
- Focus Groups
- In-Depth Reviews

We appreciate the help and input from everyone. In particular, we'd like to give the following people our special thanks:

Jader Franceschi, **Actúa Idiomas,** Bento Gonçalves, Rio Grande do Sul, Brazil

Juliana Dos Santos Voltan Costa, **Actus Idiomas,** São Paulo, Brazil

Ella Osorio, **Angelo State University,** San Angelo, TX, US

Mary Hunter, **Angelo State University,** San Angelo, TX, US

Mario César González, **Angloamericano de Monterrey, SC,** Monterrey, Mexico

Samantha Shipman, **Auburn High School,** Auburn, AL, US

Linda, **Bernick Language School,** Radford, VA, US

Dave Lowrance, **Bethesda University of California,** Yorba Linda, CA, US

Tajbakhsh Hosseini, **Bezmialem Vakif University,** Istanbul, Turkey

Dilek Gercek, **Bil English,** Izmir, Turkey

erkan kolat, **Biruni University, ELT,** Istanbul, Turkey

Nika Gutkowska, **Bluedata International,** New York, NY, US

Daniel Alcocer Gómez, **Cecati 92,** Guadalupe, Nuevo León, Mexico

Samantha Webb, **Central Middle School,** Milton-Freewater, OR, US

Verónica Salgado, **Centro Anglo Americano,** Cuernavaca, Mexico

Ana Rivadeneira Martínez and Georgia P. de Machuca, **Centro de Educación Continua – Universidad Politécnica del Ecuador,** Quito, Ecuador

Anderson Francisco Guimerães Maia, **Centro Cultural Brasil Estados Unidos,** Belém, Brazil

Rosana Mariano, **Centro Paula Souza,** São Paulo, Brazil

Carlos de la Paz Arroyo, Teresa Noemí Parra Alarcón, Gilberto

Bastida Gaytan, Manuel Esquivel Román, and Rosa Cepeda Tapia, **Centro Universitario Angloamericano,** Cuernavaca, Morelos, Mexico

Antonio Almeida, **CETEC,** Morelos, Mexico

Cinthia Ferreira, **Cinthia Ferreira Languages Services,** Toronto, ON, Canada

Phil Thomas and Sérgio Sanchez, **CLS Canadian Language School,** São Paulo, Brazil

Celia Concannon, **Cochise College,** Nogales, AZ, US

Maria do Carmo Rocha and CAOP English team, **Colégio Arquidiocesano Ouro Preto – Unidade Cônego Paulo Dilascio,** Ouro Preto, Brazil

Kim Rodriguez, **College of Charleston North,** Charleston, SC, US

Jesús Leza Alvarado, **Coparmex English Institute,** Monterrey, Mexico

John Partain, **Cortazar,** Guanajuato, Mexico

Alexander Palencia Navas, **Cursos de Lenguas, Universidad del Atlántico,** Barranquilla, Colombia

Kenneth Johan Gerardo Steenhuisen Cera, Melfi Osvaldo Guzman Triana, and Carlos Alberto Algarín Jiminez, **Cursos de Lenguas Extranjeras Universidad del Atlantico,** Barranquilla, Colombia

Jane P Kerford, **East Los Angeles College,** Pasadena, CA, US

Daniela, **East Village,** Campinas, São Paulo

Rosalva Camacho Orduño, **Easy English for Groups S.A. de C.V.,** Monterrey, Nuevo León, Mexico

Adonis Gimenez Fusetti, **Easy Way Idiomas,** Ibiúna, Brazil

Eileen Thompson, **Edison Community College,** Piqua, OH, US

Ahminne Handeri O.L Froede, **Englishouse escola de idiomas,** Teófilo Otoni, Brazil

Ana Luz Delgado-Izazola, **Escuela Nacional Preparatoria 5, UNAM,** Mexico City, Mexico

Nancy Alarcón Mendoza, **Facultad de Estudios Superiores Zaragoza, UNAM,** Mexico City, Mexico

Marcilio N. Barros, **Fast English USA,** Campinas, São Paulo, Brazil

Greta Douthat, **FCI Ashland,** Ashland, KY, US

Carlos Lizárraga González, **Grupo Educativo Anglo Americano, S.C.,** Mexico City, Mexico

Hugo Fernando Alcántar Valle, **Instituto Politécnico Nacional, Escuela Superior de Comercio y Administración-Unidad Santotomás, Celex Esca Santo Tomás,** Mexico City, Mexico

Sueli Nascimento, **Instituto Superior de Educação do Rio de Janeiro,** Rio de Janeiro, Brazil

Elsa F Monteverde, **International Academic Services,** Miami, FL, US

Laura Anand, **Irvine Adult School,** Irvine, CA, US

Prof. Marli T. Fernandes (principal) and Prof. Dr. Jefferson J. Fernandes (pedagogue), **Jefferson Idiomas,** São Paulo, Brazil

Herman Bartelen, **Kanda Gaigo Gakuin,** Tokyo, Japan

Cassia Silva, **Key Languages,** Key Biscayne, FL, US

Sister Mary Hope, **Kyoto Notre Dame Joshi Gakuin,** Kyoto, Japan

Nate Freedman, **LAL Language Centres,** Boston, MA, US

Richard Janzen, **Langley Secondary School,** Abbotsford, BC, Canada

Christina Abel Gabardo, **Language House,** Campo Largo, Brazil
Ivonne Castro, **Learn English International,** Cali, Colombia
Julio Cesar Maciel Rodrigues, **Liberty Centro de Línguas,** São Paulo, Brazil
Ann Gibson, **Maynard High School,** Maynard, MA, US
Martin Darling, **Meiji Gakuin Daigaku,** Tokyo, Japan
Dax Thomas, **Meiji Gakuin Daigaku,** Yokohama, Kanagawa, Japan
Derya Budak, **Mevlana University,** Konya, Turkey
B Sullivan, **Miami Valley Career Technical Center International Program,** Dayton, OH, US
Julio Velazquez, **Milo Language Center,** Weston, FL, US
Daiane Siqueira da Silva, Luiz Carlos Buontempo, Marlete Avelina de Oliveira Cunha, Marcos Paulo Segatti, Morgana Eveline de Oliveira, Nadia Lia Gino Alo, and Paul Hyde Budgen, **New Interchange-Escola de Idiomas,** São Paulo, Brazil
Patrícia França Furtado da Costa, Juiz de Fora, Brazil
Patricia Servín
Chris Pollard, **North West Regional College SK,** North Battleford, SK, Canada
Olga Amy, **Notre Dame High School,** Red Deer, Canada
Amy Garrett, **Ouachita Baptist University,** Arkadelphia, AR, US
Mervin Curry, **Palm Beach State College,** Boca Raton, FL, US
Julie Barros, **Quality English Studio,** Guarulhos, São Paulo, Brazil
Teodoro González Saldaña and Jesús Monserrrta Mata Franco, **Race Idiomas,** Mexico City, Mexico
Autumn Westphal and Noga La`or, **Rennert International,** New York, NY, US
Antonio Gallo and Javy Palau, **Rigby Idiomas,** Monterrey, Mexico Tatiane Gabriela Sperb do Nascimento, **Right Way,** Igrejinha, Brazil
Mustafa Akgül, **Selahaddin Eyyubi Universitesi,** Diyarbakır, Turkey
James Drury M. Fonseca, **Senac Idiomas Fortaleza,** Fortaleza, Ceara, Brazil
Manoel Fialho S Neto, **Senac – PE,** Recife, Brazil
Jane Imber, **Small World,** Lawrence, KS, US
Tony Torres, **South Texas College,** McAllen, TX, US
Janet Rose, **Tennessee Foreign Language Institute,** College Grove, TN, US
Todd Enslen, **Tohoku University,** Sendai, Miyagi, Japan
Daniel Murray, **Torrance Adult School,** Torrance, CA, US
Juan Manuel Pulido Mendoza, **Universidad del Atlántico,** Barranquilla, Colombia
Juan Carlos Vargas Millán, **Universidad Libre Seccional Cali,** Cali (Valle del Cauca), Colombia
Carmen Cecilia Llanos Ospina, **Universidad Libre Seccional Cali,** Cali, Colombia
Jorge Noriega Zenteno, **Universidad Politécnica del Valle de México,** Estado de México, Mexico
Aimee Natasha Holguin S., **Universidad Politécnica del Valle de México UPVM,** Tultitlàn Estado de México, Mexico
Christian Selene Bernal Barraza, **UPVM Universidad Politécnica del Valle de México,** Ecatepec, Mexico
Lizeth Ramos Acosta, **Universidad Santiago de Cali,** Cali, Colombia
Silvana Dushku, **University of Illinois Champaign,** IL, US
Deirdre McMurtry, **University of Nebraska – Omaha,** Omaha, NE, US
Jason E Mower, **University of Utah,** Salt Lake City, UT, US
Paul Chugg, **Vanguard Taylor Language Institute,** Edmonton, Alberta, Canada
Henry Mulak, **Varsity Tutors,** Los Angeles, CA, US
Shirlei Strucker Calgaro and Hugo Guilherme Karrer, **VIP Centro de Idiomas,** Panambi, Rio Grande do Sul, Brazil
Eleanor Kelly, **Waseda Daigaku Extension Centre,** Tokyo, Japan
Sherry Ashworth, **Wichita State University,** Wichita, KS, US
Laine Bourdene, **William Carey University,** Hattiesburg, MS, US
Serap Aydın, Istanbul, Turkey
Liliana Covino, Guarulhos, Brazil
Yannuarys Jiménez, Barranquilla, Colombia
Juliana Morais Pazzini, Toronto, ON, Canada
Marlon Sanches, Montreal, Canada

Additional content contributed by Kenna Bourke, Inara Couto, Nic Harris, Greg Manin, Ashleigh Martinez, Laura McKenzie, Paul McIntyre, Clara Prado, Lynne Robertson, Mari Vargo, Theo Walker, and Maria Lucia Zaorob.

The Fifth Edition of *Interchange*

Interchange, the world's favorite English course, has a long tradition of teaching students how to speak confidently. Millions of people all over the world attest to its effectiveness.

What Makes *Interchange* Special?

Jack C. Richards' communicative methodology: Refined over years and in countless classrooms, the *Interchange* approach is rooted in solid pedagogy.

Flexible units: Instructors can change the order of the activities in each unit, keeping lessons fresh and students engaged. Additional photocopiable activities and a full video program give teachers even more freedom to make *Interchange* their own.

Students speak right from the start: The solid research and winning content give students the confidence to speak early and often.

What's New in the Fifth Edition?

50% new content: Readings, listenings, conversations, and Snapshots have been updated throughout the books.

Improved exercises for listenings and readings: We listened to teachers' requests for greater variety in the activities that accompany the listenings and readings.

New digital tools: Self-study for every student available online. An online workbook with fun games.

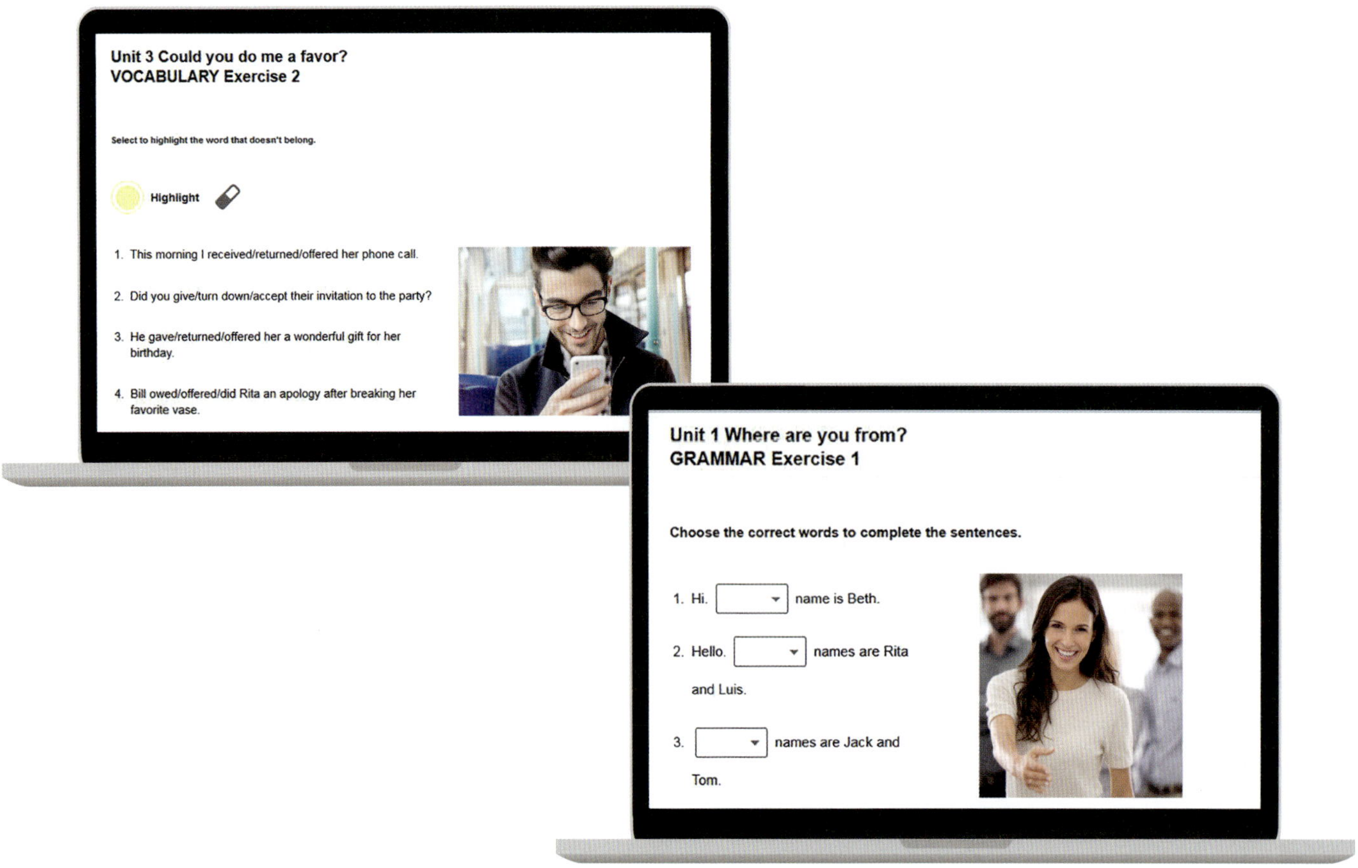

Student's Book overview

Every unit in *Interchange Fifth Edition* contains two cycles, each of which has a specific topic, grammar point, and function. The units in Level Intro contain a variety of exercises, including a Snapshot, Conversation, Grammar focus, Pronunciation, Discussion (or Speaking), Word power, Listening, Writing, Reading, and Interchange activity. The sequence of these exercises differs from unit to unit. Here is a sample unit from Level Intro.

Cycle 1 (Exercises 1–5)

Topic: sports
Grammar: simple present Wh-questions
Function: discuss sports students watch and play

10 What sports do you like?

▸ Discuss sports to watch and play
▸ Discuss skills, abilities, and talents

1 SNAPSHOT

Listen and practice.

SPORTS QUIZ

Brazil's favorite sport is soccer. Their second favorite is . . .
- [ ] tennis
- [ ] volleyball
- [ ] swimming

Mexico's favorite sport is soccer. Their second favorite sport is . . .
- [ ] football
- [ ] hockey
- [ ] baseball

Canada's favorite sport is ice hockey. Their second favorite sport is . . .
- [ ] basketball
- [ ] ice-skating
- [ ] snowboarding

South Korea's favorite sport is basketball. Their second favorite sport is . . .
- [ ] bike riding
- [ ] hiking
- [ ] soccer

Brazil: volleyball; Mexico: baseball; Canada: basketball; South Korea: soccer

Can you guess what sports are the second favorite in each country? Check (✓) the sports.
Do you like sports? What sports are popular in your country?

2 CONVERSATION When do you play all these sports?

Listen and practice.

TARA So, Victor, what do you do in your free time?
VICTOR Well, I really like sports.
TARA Cool! What sports do you like?
VICTOR My favorite sports are basketball, soccer, and tennis.
TARA Wow! You're a really good athlete. When do you play all these sports?
VICTOR Oh . . . I don't play them very often.
TARA What do you mean?
VICTOR I just watch them on TV!

64

Snapshot

- Introduces the unit or cycle topic
- Presents vocabulary for discussing the topic
- Uses real-world information
- Provides personalized guided discussion questions

Conversation

- Provides structured listening and speaking practice
- Introduces the meaning and use of Cycle 1 grammar in context
- Uses pictures to set the scene and illustrate new vocabulary
- Provides follow-up listening tasks

Grammar focus

- Includes audio recordings of the grammar
- Provides controlled grammar practice in realistic contexts, such as short conversations
- Provides freer, more personalized speaking practice

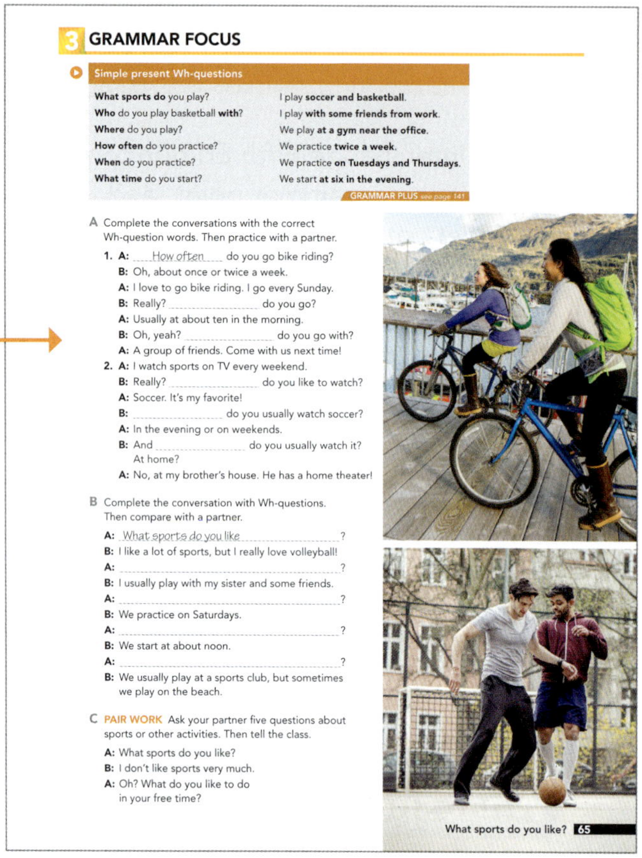

3 GRAMMAR FOCUS

Simple present Wh-questions

What sports do you play?	I play **soccer and basketball**.
Who do you play basketball **with**?	I play **with some friends from work**.
Where do you play?	We play **at a gym near the office**.
How often do you practice?	We practice **twice a week**.
When do you practice?	We practice **on Tuesdays and Thursdays**.
What time do you start?	We start **at six in the evening**.

GRAMMAR PLUS see page 141

A Complete the conversations with the correct Wh-question words. Then practice with a partner.

1. A: *How often* do you go bike riding?
B: Oh, about once or twice a week.
A: I love to go bike riding. I go every Sunday.
B: Really? ________ do you go?
A: Usually at about ten in the morning.
B: Oh, yeah? ________ do you go with?
A: A group of friends. Come with us next time!
2. A: I watch sports on TV every weekend.
B: Really? ________ do you like to watch?
A: Soccer. It's my favorite!
B: ________ do you usually watch soccer?
A: In the evening or on weekends.
B: And ________ do you usually watch it? At home?
A: No, at my brother's house. He has a home theater!

B Complete the conversation with Wh-questions. Then compare with a partner.

A: *What sports do you like* ?
B: I like a lot of sports, but I really love volleyball!
A: ________?
B: I usually play with my sister and some friends.
A: ________?
B: We practice on Saturdays.
A: ________?
B: We start at about noon.
A: ________?
B: We usually play at a sports club, but sometimes we play on the beach.

C PAIR WORK Ask your partner five questions about sports or other activities. Then tell the class.

A: What sports do you like?
B: I don't like sports very much.
A: Oh? What do you like to do in your free time?

What sports do you like? 65

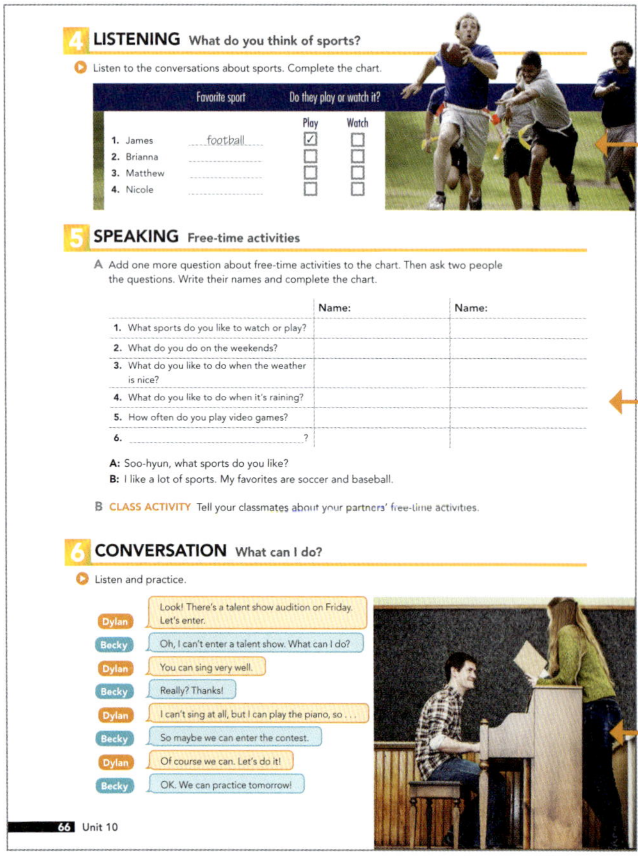

4 LISTENING What do you think of sports?

Listen to the conversations about sports. Complete the chart.

	Favorite sport	Do they play or watch it? Play	Watch
1. James	*football*	☑	☐
2. Brianna		☐	☐
3. Matthew		☐	☐
4. Nicole		☐	☐

5 SPEAKING Free-time activities

A Add one more question about free-time activities to the chart. Then ask two people the questions. Write their names and complete the chart.

	Name:	Name:
1. What sports do you like to watch or play?		
2. What do you do on the weekends?		
3. What do you like to do when the weather is nice?		
4. What do you like to do when it's raining?		
5. How often do you play video games?		
6. ________?		

A: Soo-hyun, what sports do you like?
B: I like a lot of sports. My favorites are soccer and baseball.

B CLASS ACTIVITY Tell your classmates about your partners' free-time activities.

6 CONVERSATION What can I do?

Listen and practice.

Dylan: Look! There's a talent show audition on Friday. Let's enter.
Becky: Oh, I can't enter a talent show. What can I do?
Dylan: You can sing very well.
Becky: Really? Thanks!
Dylan: I can't sing at all, but I can play the piano, so . . .
Becky: So maybe we can enter the contest.
Dylan: Of course we can. Let's do it!
Becky: OK. We can practice tomorrow!

66 Unit 10

Listening

- Provides pre-listening focus tasks or questions
- Develops a variety of listening skills, such as listening for main ideas and details

Speaking

- Provides communicative tasks that help develop oral fluency
- Includes pair work, group work, and class activities

Conversation

- Provides structured listening and speaking practice
- Introduces the meaning and use of Cycle 2 grammar, useful expressions, and discourse
- Uses pictures to set the scene and illustrate new vocabulary

Cycle 2 (Exercises 6–12)

Topic: skills and abilities
Grammar: *Can* for ability
Function: discuss skills, abilities, and talents

Grammar focus

- Presents examples from the previous conversation
- Provides controlled grammar practice in realistic contexts, such as short conversations

Pronunciation

- Provides controlled practice in recognizing and producing sounds linked to the cycle grammar
- Promotes extended or personalized pronunciation practice

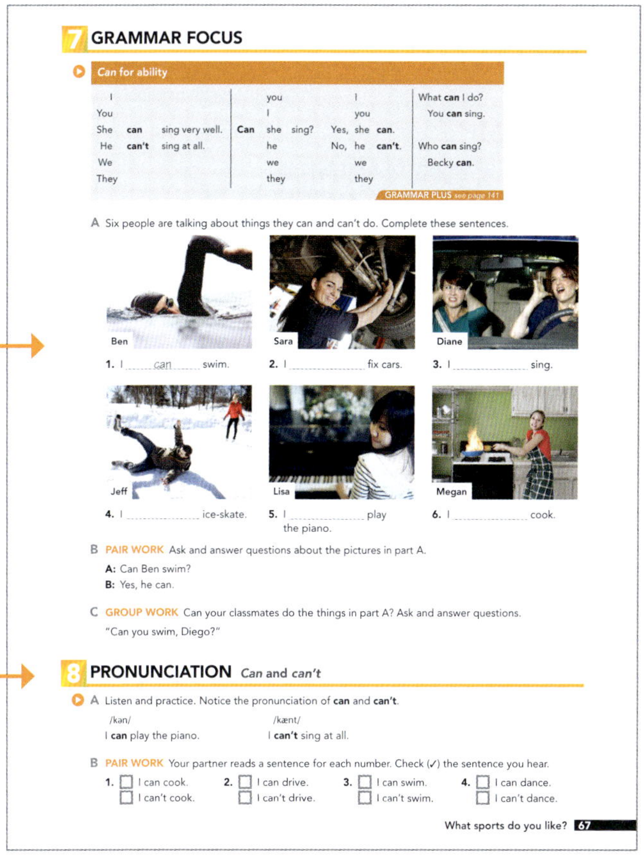

7 GRAMMAR FOCUS

Can for ability

I				you			I		What **can** I do?
You				I			you		You **can** sing.
She	**can**	sing very well.	**Can**	she	sing?	Yes,	she	**can**.	
He	**can't**	sing at all.		he		No,	he	**can't**.	Who **can** sing?
We				we			we		Becky **can**.
They				they			they		

GRAMMAR PLUS see page 141

A Six people are talking about things they can and can't do. Complete these sentences.

Ben
1. I ___can___ swim.
Sara
2. I ______ fix cars.
Diane
3. I ______ sing.
Jeff
4. I ______ ice-skate.
Lisa
5. I ______ play the piano.
Megan
6. I ______ cook.

B PAIR WORK Ask and answer questions about the pictures in part A.
A: Can Ben swim?
B: Yes, he can.

C GROUP WORK Can your classmates do the things in part A? Ask and answer questions.
"Can you swim, Diego?"

8 PRONUNCIATION *Can* and *can't*

A Listen and practice. Notice the pronunciation of **can** and **can't**.
/kən/ I **can** play the piano.
/kænt/ I **can't** sing at all.

B PAIR WORK Your partner reads a sentence for each number. Check (✓) the sentence you hear.
1. ☐ I can cook. ☐ I can't cook.
2. ☐ I can drive. ☐ I can't drive.
3. ☐ I can swim. ☐ I can't swim.
4. ☐ I can dance. ☐ I can't dance.

What sports do you like? 67

9 LISTENING Are you good at sports?

Listen to three people talk about their abilities. Write J (Joshua), M (Monica), or A (Anthony) on the things they can do well.

1 2 3 4 5 6 7 8

10 WORD POWER Talents and abilities

A Complete the word map with talents and abilities from the list. Then listen and practice.

✓ bake cookies
build a robot
design a website
do math in your head
edit a video
fix a computer
make electronic music
play chess
ride a horse
run a marathon
skateboard
take good photos
tell good jokes

MUSICAL OR ARTISTIC
ATHLETIC
TALENTS AND ABILITIES
TECHNICAL
OTHER
bake cookies

B GROUP WORK Who can do the things in part A? Make a list of guesses about your classmates.
A: Who can bake cookies?
B: I think Melanie can.
C: Who can design . . . ?

bake cookies - Melanie
design a website

C CLASS ACTIVITY Go around the room and check your guesses.
A: Melanie, can you bake cookies?
B: Yes, I can.

11 INTERCHANGE 10 Hidden talents and abilities

Learn more about your classmates' hidden talents and abilities. Go to Interchange 10 on page 124.

68 Unit 10

Listening

- Provides pre-listening focus tasks or questions
- Develops a variety of listening skills, such as listening for main ideas and details

Word power

- Presents vocabulary related to the unit topic
- Provides practice with collocations and categorizing vocabulary
- Promotes freer, more personalized practice

Reading

- Presents a variety of text types
- Introduces the text with a pre-reading task
- Develops a variety of reading skills, such as reading for main ideas, reading for details, and inferencing
- Promotes discussion that involves personalization and analysis

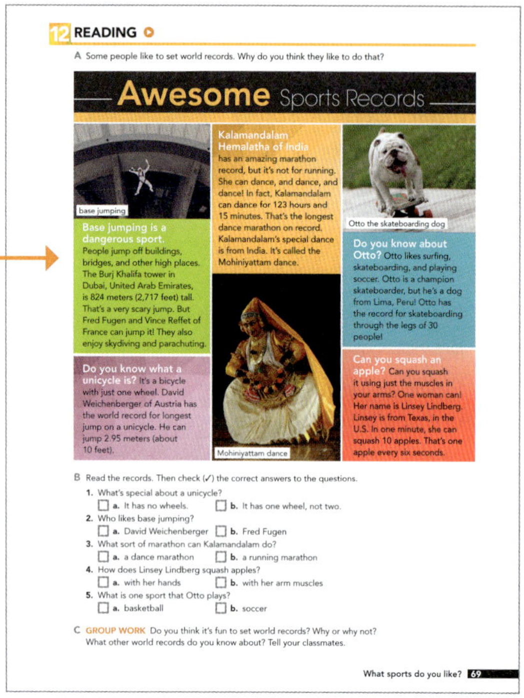

12 READING

A Some people like to set world records. Why do you think they like to do that?

Awesome Sports Records

base jumping

Base jumping is a dangerous sport. People jump off buildings, bridges, and other high places. The Burj Khalifa tower in Dubai, United Arab Emirates, is 824 meters (2,717 feet) tall. That's a very scary jump. But Fred Fugen and Vince Reffet of France can jump it! They also enjoy skydiving and parachuting.

Kalamandalam Hemalatha of India has an amazing marathon record, but it's not for running. She can dance, and dance, and dance! In fact, Kalamandalam can dance for 123 hours and 15 minutes. That's the longest dance marathon on record. Kalamandalam's special dance is from India. It's called the Mohiniyattam dance.

Otto the skateboarding dog

Do you know about Otto? Otto likes surfing, skateboarding, and playing soccer. Otto is a champion skateboarder, but he's a dog from Lima, Peru! Otto has the record for skateboarding through the legs of 30 people!

Do you know what a unicycle is? It's a bicycle with just one wheel. David Weichenberger of Austria has the world record for longest jump on a unicycle. He can jump 2.95 meters (about 10 feet).

Mohiniyattam dance

Can you squash an apple? Can you squash it using just the muscles in your arms? One woman can! Her name is Linsey Lindberg. Linsey is from Texas, in the U.S. In one minute, she can squash 10 apples. That's one apple every six seconds.

B Read the records. Then check (✓) the correct answers to the questions.

1. What's special about a unicycle?
   - ☐ a. It has no wheels.
   - ☐ b. It has one wheel, not two.
2. Who likes base jumping?
   - ☐ a. David Weichenberger
   - ☐ b. Fred Fugen
3. What sort of marathon can Kalamandalam do?
   - ☐ a. a dance marathon
   - ☐ b. a running marathon
4. How does Linsey Lindberg squash apples?
   - ☐ a. with her hands
   - ☐ b. with her arm muscles
5. What is one sport that Otto plays?
   - ☐ a. basketball
   - ☐ b. soccer

C GROUP WORK Do you think it's fun to set world records? Why or why not? What other world records do you know about? Tell your classmates.

What sports do you like? 69

In the back of the book

Interchange activity

- Expands on the unit topic, vocabulary, and grammar
- Provides opportunities to consolidate new language in a creative or fun way
- Promotes fluency with communicative activities such as discussions, information gaps, and games

Grammar plus

- Explores the unit grammar in greater depth
- Practices the grammar with controlled exercises
- Can be done in class or assigned as homework

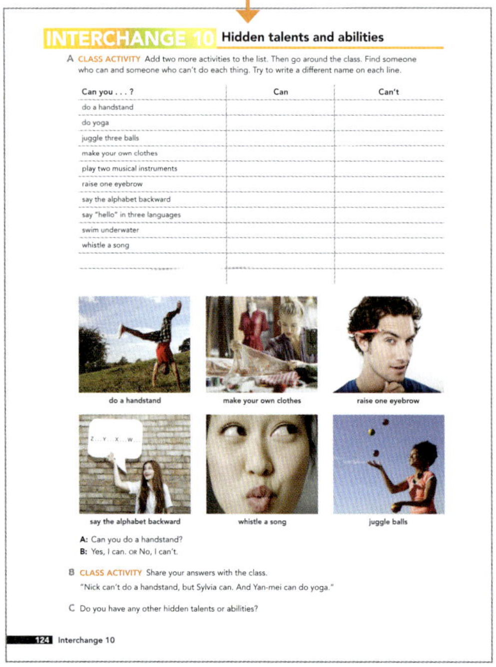

INTERCHANGE 10 Hidden talents and abilities

A CLASS ACTIVITY Add two more activities to the list. Then go around the class. Find someone who can and someone who can't do each thing. Try to write a different name on each line.

Can you . . . ?	Can	Can't
do a handstand		
do yoga		
juggle three balls		
make your own clothes		
play two musical instruments		
raise one eyebrow		
say the alphabet backward		
say "hello" in three languages		
swim underwater		
whistle a song		

do a handstand · make your own clothes · raise one eyebrow · say the alphabet backward · whistle a song · juggle balls

A: Can you do a handstand?
B: Yes, I can. or No, I can't.

B CLASS ACTIVITY Share your answers with the class.
"Nick can't do a handstand, but Sylvia can. And Yan-mei can do yoga."

C Do you have any other hidden talents or abilities?

124 Interchange 10

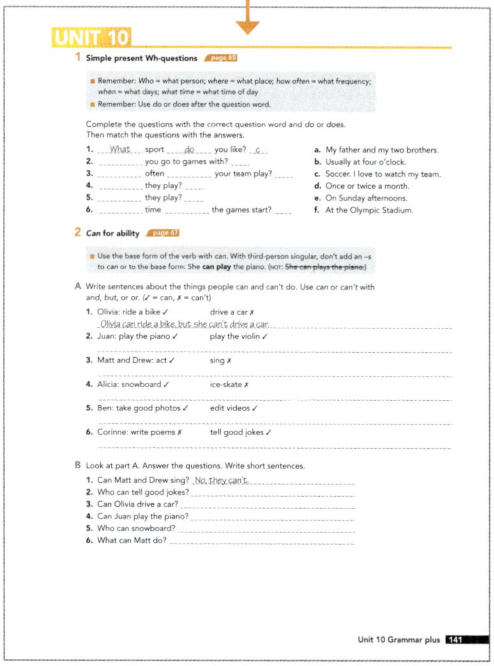

UNIT 10

1 Simple present Wh-questions page 65

- Remember: Who = what person; where = what place; how often = what frequency; when = what days; what time = what time of day
- Remember: Use do or does after the question word.

Complete the questions with the correct question word and do or does. Then match the questions with the answers.

1. What sport do you like? c
2. ______ you go to games with? ____
3. ______ often ______ your team play? ____
4. ______ they play? ____
5. ______ they play? ____
6. ______ time ______ the games start? ____

a. My father and my two brothers.
b. Usually at four o'clock.
c. Soccer. I love to watch my team.
d. Once or twice a month.
e. On Sunday afternoons.
f. At the Olympic Stadium.

2 Can for ability page 67

- Use the base form of the verb with can. With third-person singular, don't add an -s to can or to the base form: She can play the piano. (NOT: ~~She can plays the piano.~~)

A Write sentences about the things people can and can't do. Use can or can't with and, but, or or. (✓ = can, ✗ = can't)

1. Olivia: ride a bike ✓ drive a car ✗
   Olivia can ride a bike, but she can't drive a car.
2. Juan: play the piano ✓ play the violin ✓
3. Matt and Drew: act ✓ sing ✗
4. Alicia: snowboard ✓ ice-skate ✗
5. Ben: take good photos ✓ edit videos ✓
6. Corinne: write poems ✗ tell good jokes ✓

B Look at part A. Answer the questions. Write short sentences.

1. Can Matt and Drew sing? No, they can't.
2. Who can tell good jokes?
3. Can Olivia drive a car?
4. Can Juan play the piano?
5. Who can snowboard?
6. What can Matt do?

Unit 10 Grammar plus 141

Online Self-study overview

Interchange Fifth Edition online Self-study provides students with hundreds of additional exercises to practice the language taught in the Student's Book on their own, in the classroom, or in the lab.

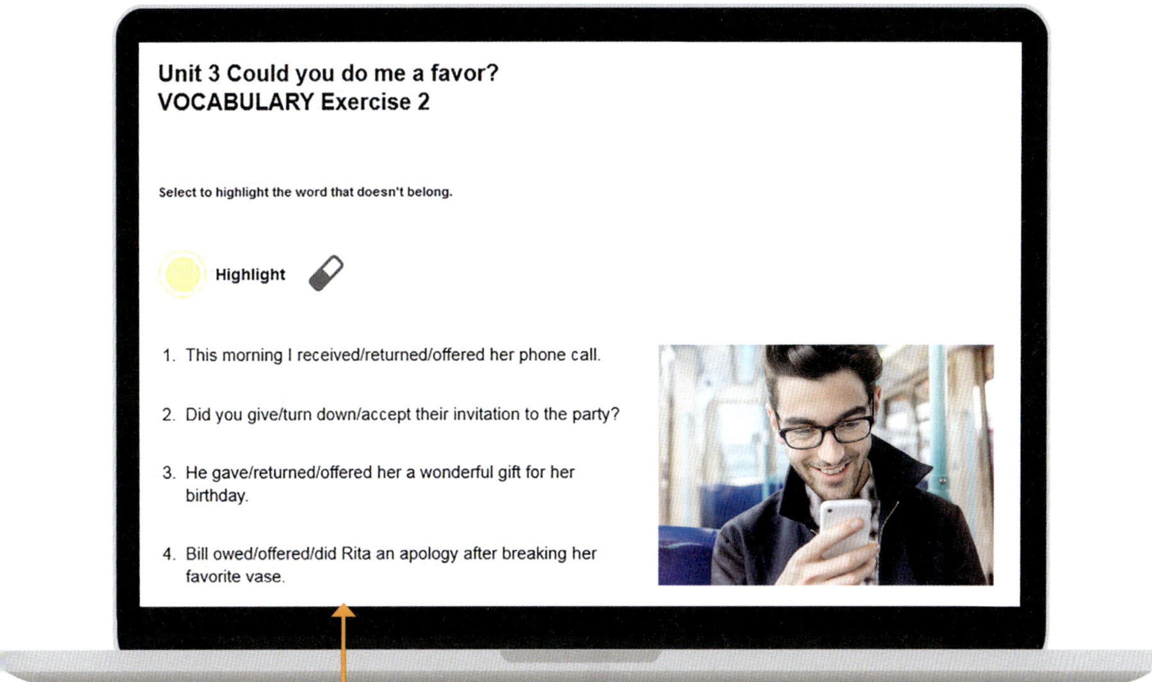

Interactive exercises

Hundreds of interactive exercises provide hours of additional:

- vocabulary practice
- grammar practice
- listening practice
- speaking practice
- reading practice

The complete *Interchange* video program

The entire *Interchange* video program for this level is included online with exercises that allow the students to watch and check comprehension themselves.

Online Workbook overview

The *Interchange Fifth Edition Online Workbook* provides additional activities to reinforce what is presented in the corresponding Student's Book. Each *Online Workbook* includes:

- A variety of interactive activities which correspond to each Student's Book lesson, allowing students to interact with workbook material in a fresh, lively way.
- Instant feedback for hundreds of activities, challenging students to focus on areas for improvement.
- Simple tools for teachers to monitor students' progress such as scores, attendance, and time spent online, providing instant information.

The *Interchange Fifth Edition Online Workbooks* can be purchased in two ways:

- as an institutional subscription,
- as part of a Student's Book with Online Workbook Pack.

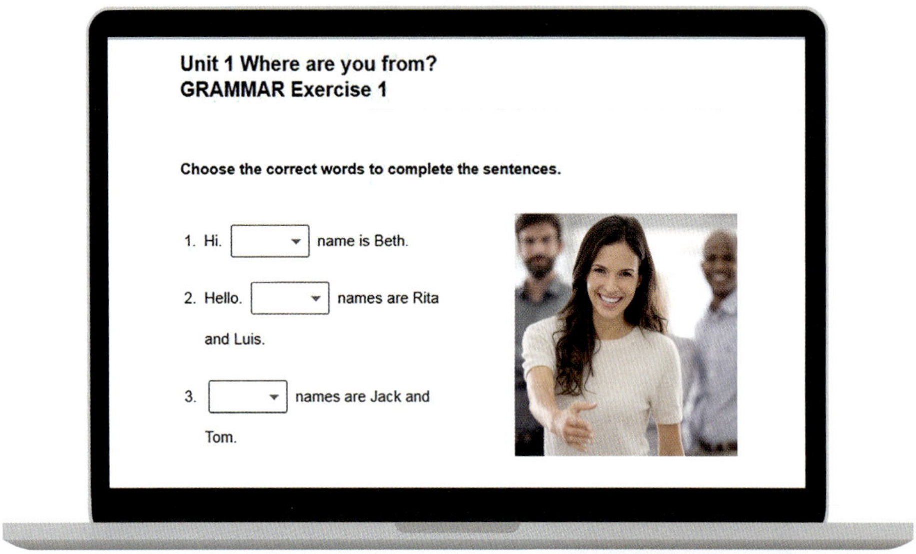

Games

- Fun, interactive, self-scoring activities in the Online Workbooks offer a fresh change of pace.

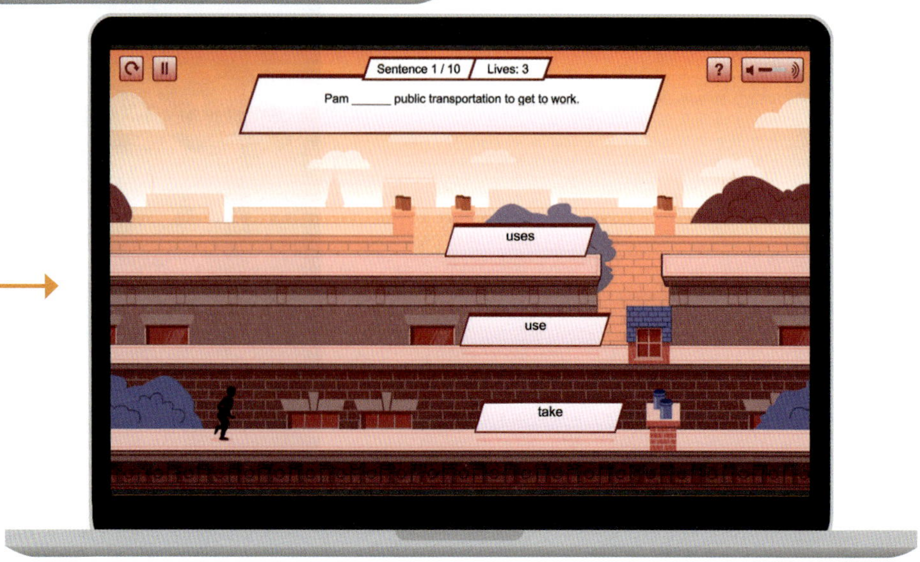

Workbook overview

Interchange Fifth Edition provides students with additional opportunities to practice the language taught in the Student's Book outside of the classroom by using the Workbook that accompanies each level.

7 Does it have a view?

1 Label the parts of the house.

1. bedroom
2.
3.
4.
5.
6.
7.
8.

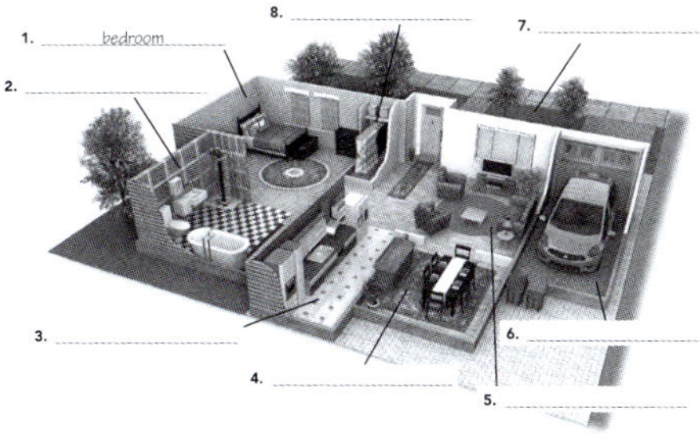

2 Complete the conversation. Use the sentences in the box.

- [ ] No, I don't. I live with my sisters.
- [x] No, I live in an apartment.
- [ ] Yes, it has three bedrooms.
- [ ] Yes, it has a great view of the city.

Ji-hye: Do you live in a house, Fernanda?
Fernanda: No, I live in an apartment.
Ji-hye: Well, is it very big?
Fernanda:
Ji-hye: Does it have a view?
Fernanda:
Ji-hye: Oh, that's great! And do you live alone?
Fernanda:

37

Vocabulary

- Provides vocabulary practice based on the unit topic

9 Choose the correct responses.

1. A: My apartment has a view of the park.
   B: You're lucky.
   - Guess what!
   - You're lucky.
2. A: Do you need living room furniture?
   B:
   - Yes, I do. I need a sofa and a coffee table.
   - No, I don't. I need a sofa and a coffee table.
3. A: I really need a new desk.
   B:
   - So let's go shopping this weekend.
   - That's great!
4. A: Do you have chairs in your kitchen?
   B:
   - Yes, I do. I need six chairs.
   - Yes, I do. I have six chairs.

10 Draw a picture of your home. Then write a description. Use the questions in the box for ideas.

Do you live in a house or an apartment?
What furniture do you have?
What rooms does your home have?
Who lives with you?

42 Unit 7

Grammar

- Reinforces the unit grammar through controlled practice

Writing

- Promotes freer, more personalized practice
- Reinforces the vocabulary and grammar in the unit

Teacher's Edition overview

The Teacher's Editions provide complete support for teachers who are using *Interchange Fifth Edition*. They contain Supplementary Resources Overview charts to help teachers plan their lessons (for more information see page xx), Language summaries, Workbook answer keys, Audio scripts, Fresh ideas, and Games. They also include detailed teaching notes for the units and Progress checks in the Student's Books.

Teaching notes

- Learning objectives for each exercise
- Step-by-step lesson plans
- Audio scripts
- Answers and Vocabulary definitions
- Stimulating and fun Games to review or practice skills such as grammar and vocabulary
- Alternative ways to present and review exercises in the Fresh ideas
- Tips that promote teacher training and development
- Options for alternative presentations or expansions
- Suggestions for further practice in other *Interchange Fifth Edition* components and online
- Suggestions for regular assessment using quizzes and tests

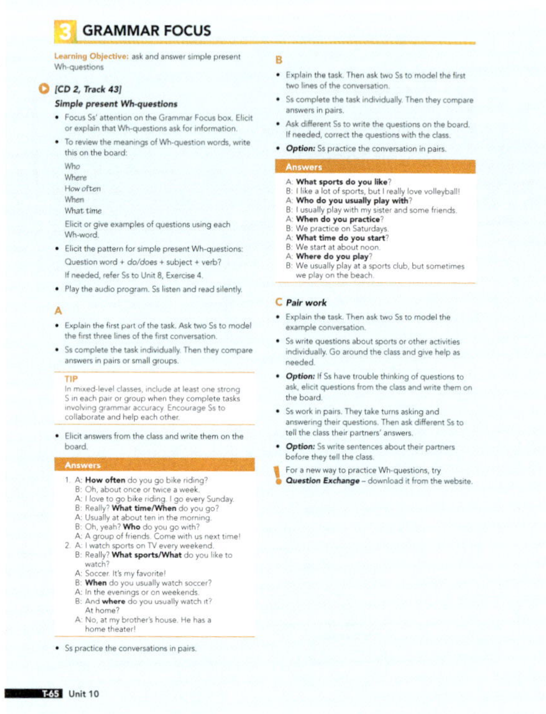

3 GRAMMAR FOCUS

Learning Objective: ask and answer simple present Wh-questions

[CD 2, Track 43]

Simple present Wh-questions

- Focus Ss' attention on the Grammar Focus box. Elicit or explain that Wh-questions ask for information.
- To review the meanings of Wh-question words, write this on the board:

  Who
  Where
  How often
  When
  What time

  Elicit or give examples of questions using each Wh-word.
- Elicit the pattern for simple present Wh-questions:

  Question word + *do/does* + subject + verb?

  If needed, refer Ss to Unit 8, Exercise 4.
- Play the audio program. Ss listen and read silently.

A

- Explain the first part of the task. Ask two Ss to model the first three lines of the first conversation.
- Ss complete the task individually. Then they compare answers in pairs or small groups.

TIP
In mixed-level classes, include at least one strong S in each pair or group when they complete tasks involving grammar accuracy. Encourage Ss to collaborate and help each other.

- Elicit answers from the class and write them on the board.

Answers

1. A: **How often** do you go bike riding?
   B: Oh, about once or twice a week.
   A: I love to go bike riding. I go every Sunday.
   B: Really? **What time/When** do you go?
   A: Usually at about ten in the morning.
   B: Oh, yeah? **Who** do you go with?
   A: A group of friends. Come with us next time!
2. A: I watch sports on TV every weekend.
   B: Really? **What sports/What** do you like to watch?
   A: Soccer. It's my favorite!
   B: **When** do you usually watch soccer?
   A: In the evenings or on weekends.
   B: And **where** do you usually watch it? At home?
   A: No, at my brother's house. He has a home theater!

- Ss practice the conversations in pairs.

B

- Explain the task. Then ask two Ss to model the first two lines of the conversation.
- Ss complete the task individually. Then they compare answers in pairs.
- Ask different Ss to write the questions on the board. If needed, correct the questions with the class.
- ***Option:*** Ss practice the conversation in pairs.

Answers

A: **What sports do you like**?
B: I like a lot of sports, but I really love volleyball!
A: **Who do you usually play with**?
B: I usually play with my sister and some friends.
A: **When do you practice**?
B: We practice on Saturdays.
A: **What time do you start**?
B: We start at about noon.
A: **Where do you play**?
B: We usually play at a sports club, but sometimes we play on the beach.

C ***Pair work***

- Explain the task. Then ask two Ss to model the example conversation.
- Ss write questions about sports or other activities individually. Go around the class and give help as needed.
- ***Option:*** If Ss have trouble thinking of questions to ask, elicit questions from the class and write them on the board.
- Ss work in pairs. They take turns asking and answering their questions. Then ask different Ss to tell the class their partners' answers.
- ***Option:*** Ss write sentences about their partners before they tell the class.

! For a new way to practice Wh-questions, try ***Question Exchange*** – download it from the website.

T-65 Unit 10

Complete Assessment Program

The complete assessment program contains oral and written quizzes and tests. It includes PDF and Microsoft Word versions of all quizzes, mid-term and final tests, the placement test program, audio, audio scripts, and answer keys.

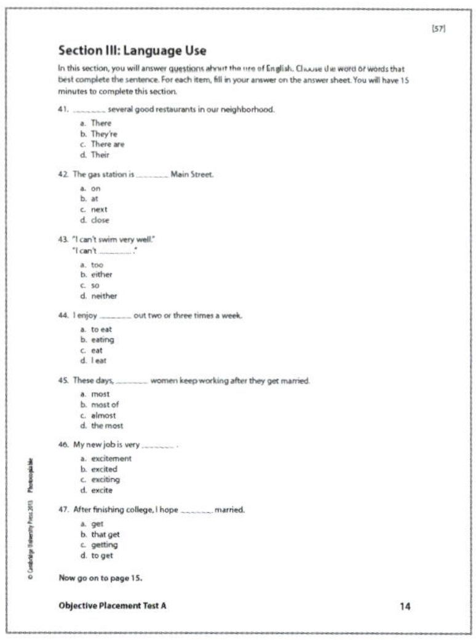

[57]

Section III: Language Use

In this section, you will answer questions about the use of English. Choose the word or words that best complete the sentence. For each item, fill in your answer on the answer sheet. You will have 15 minutes to complete this section.

41. _______ several good restaurants in our neighborhood.
    a. There
    b. They're
    c. There are
    d. Their

42. The gas station is _______ Main Street.
    a. on
    b. at
    c. next
    d. close

43. "I can't swim very well."
    "I can't _______."
    a. too
    b. either
    c. so
    d. neither

44. I enjoy _______ out two or three times a week.
    a. to eat
    b. eating
    c. eat
    d. I eat

45. These days, _______ women keep working after they get married.
    a. most
    b. most of
    c. almost
    d. the most

46. My new job is very _______.
    a. excitement
    b. excited
    c. exciting
    d. excite

47. After finishing college, I hope _______ married.
    a. get
    b. that get
    c. getting
    d. to get

Now go on to page 15.

Objective Placement Test A 14

Presentation Plus overview

Interchange Presentation Plus is a complete classroom presentation package, combining the contents of the Student's Book, the class audio, and the video program for each level of the series into a convenient one-stop presentation solution. It can be used with all types of interactive whiteboards or with just a projector and a computer to present *Interchange* core materials in the classroom in a lively and engaging way.

Presentation Plus simplifies several of the teaching tasks that take place in the classroom.

You can use Presentation Plus to display the answers for the exercises in an uncomplicated way, zoom in on a page to more efficiently focus students' attention on an activity or image, and even annotate pages for future lessons.

cambridge.org/interchange

Go online for a variety of materials to assist with your teaching of the series. Here you will find practical articles, correlations, language summaries, overviews of supplementary materials, ideas for games and extra activities, as well as a number of downloadable worksheets for projects and extra practice of vocabulary, grammar, listening, writing, and speaking.

Supplementary Resources Overviews

Indicate all the activities available in the various ancillary components that can be used after each exercise in the Student's Book units for extra practice, review, and assessment.

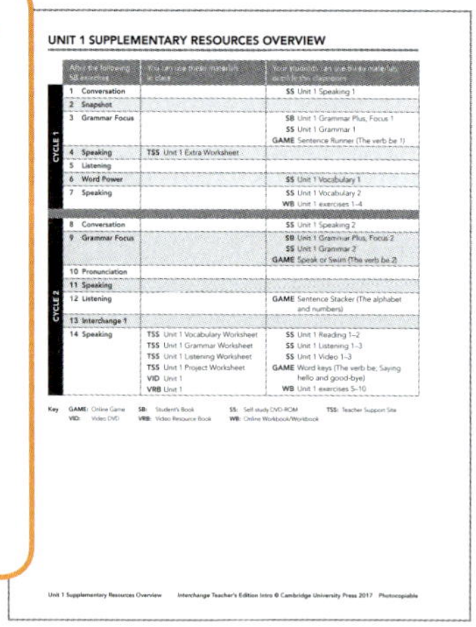

Downloadable worksheets

- Offer extra speaking opportunities
- Provide guidance for projects and extra practice of grammar, vocabulary, listening, and writing

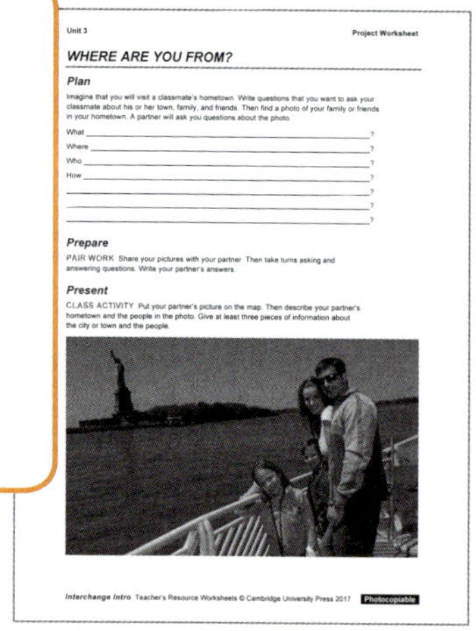

Video Program overview

The *Interchange* Video Program is designed to complement the Student's Books. Each video provides further practice related to the topics, language, and vocabulary introduced in the corresponding unit of the Student's Book.

PROGRAM COMPONENTS

Video

The sixteen videos in each level's video program complement Units 1 through 16 of the corresponding Student's Book. There are a variety of genres: dramatized stories, documentaries, interviews, profiles, and travelogues.

Video Resource Book

The Video Resource Book contains the following:

- engaging **photocopiable worksheets** for students
- detailed **teaching notes** for teachers
- answer keys for the student worksheets
- complete video transcripts

TEACHING A TYPICAL VIDEO SEQUENC

The **worksheets** and **teaching notes** for each video are organized into four sections: *Preview, Watch the video, Follow-up*, and *Language close-up*. The unit-by-unit teaching notes in the Video Resource Book give detailed suggestions for teaching each unit.

Preview

The *Preview* activities build on each other to provide student with relevant background information and key vocabulary tha will assist them in better understanding the video.

Watch the video

The carefully sequenced *Watch the video* activities first help students focus on gist and then guide them in identifying important details and language. These tasks also prepare them for *Follow-up* speaking activities.

Follow-up

The *Follow-up* speaking activities encourage students to extend and personalize information by voicing their opinions or carrying out communicative tasks.

Language close-up

Students finish with the *Language closeup*, examining and practicing the particular language structures and functions presented in the video.

Introduction to the CEFR

Introduction to the Common European Framework of Reference (CEFR)

The overall aim of the Council of Europe's Common European Framework of Reference (CEFR) is to provide objective criteria for describing and assessing language proficiency in an internationally comparable manner. The Council of Europe's work on the definition of appropriate learning objectives for adult language learners dates back to the '70s. The influential Threshold series (J. A. van Ek and J. L. M. Trim, Cambridge University Press, 1991) provides a detailed description in functional, notional, grammatical, and sociocultural terms, of what a language user needs to be able to do in order to communicate effectively in the sort of situations commonly encountered in everyday life. Three levels of proficiency are identified, called Waystage, Threshold, and Vantage (roughly corresponding to Elementary, Intermediate, and Upper Intermediate).

The Threshold series was followed in 2001 by the publication of the Common European Framework of Reference, which describes six levels of communicative ability in terms of competences or "can do" statements: A1 (Breakthrough), A2 (Waystage), B1 (Threshold), B2 (Vantage), C1 (Effective Operational Proficiency), and C2 (Mastery). Based on the CEFR descriptors, the Council of Europe also developed the European Language Portfolio, a document that enables learners to assess their language ability and to keep an internationally recognized record of their language learning experience.

Interchange Fifth Edition and the Common European Framework of Reference

The table below shows how *Interchange Fifth Edition* correlates with the Council of Europe's levels and with some major international examinations.

	CEFR	Council of Europe	Cambridge ESOL	IELTS	TOEFL iBT	TOEIC
Interchange						
Level Intro	A1	Breakthrough				120+
Level 1	A2	Waystage				225+
Level 2	B1	Threshold	KET (Key English Test)	4.0–5.0	57–86	550+
Level 3			PET (Preliminary English Test)			
Passages						
Level 1	B2	Vantage	FCE (First Certificate in English)	5.5–6.5	87–109	785+
Level 2	C1	Effective Operational Efficiency	CAE (Certificate in Advanced English)	7.0–8.0	110–120	490+ (Listening) 445+ (Reading)

Source: http://www.cambridgeesol.org/about/standards/cefr.html

Essential teaching tips

Classroom management

Error correction

- During controlled practice accuracy activities, correct students' wrong use of the target language right away, either by correcting the error yourself or, whenever possible, having the student identify and / or correct the error. This way, the focus is on accuracy, and students can internalize the correct forms, meaning, and use of the language.
- During oral fluency activities, go around the room and take notes on errors you hear. Do not interrupt students. Instead, take notes of their errors in the use of target language and write these errors on the board. Encourage students to correct them first. Be sure to point out and praise students for language used correctly as well.

Grouping students

It is good to have students work in a variety of settings: individually, in pairs, in groups and as a class. This creates a more student-centered environment and increases student talking time.

- The easiest and quickest way to put students in pairs is to have two students sitting close to one another work together. This is good for when students need to have a quick discussion or check answers.
- To ensure students don't always work with the same partner and / or for longer activities, pair students by name, e.g., Maria work with Javier.
- One way to put students in groups is to give them a number from 1 to 4, and then have all number 1s work together, all number 2s work together, and so forth.

Instructions

- Give short instructions and model the activity for the students.
- Check your instructions, but avoid asking, Do you understand? Instead ask concept questions such as, Are you going to speak or write when you do this activity?

Monitoring

- Make sure you go around the room and check that the students are doing the activity and offer help as necessary.
- Monitor closely during controlled practice, but don't make yourself too accessible during fluency activities; otherwise, students may rely on you to answer questions rather than focus on communicating their ideas to their partner or group.

Teaching lower-level students

- Teach the Classroom Language on page xxiii and put useful language up in the classroom, so the students get used to using English.
- Don't rush. Make sure all the students have had enough time to practice the material.
- Do a lot of repetition and drilling of the new target language.
- Encourage students to practice and review target language by doing activities in the Workbook and Self-study.
- Elicit answers from your students and involve them in the learning process. Even though they are beginners, they may have a passive knowledge of English. Find out what they already know by asking them questions.
- Use the optional activities within the Teaching Notes and the Supplementary Resources Overview charts at the beginning of each unit in this Teacher's Edition to add variety to your lessons.

Teaching reading and listening

- Reading and Listening texts are meant to help the students become better readers / listeners, not to test them. Explain to your students why they need to read or listen to a text several times.
- Adapt the reading speed to the purpose of the reading. When the students read for gist, encourage them to read quickly. When students read for detail, give them more time.

Classroom Language Teacher instructions

Unit 1 Supplementary Resources Overview

	After the following SB exercises	You can use these materials in class	Your students can use these materials outside the classroom
CYCLE 1	**1 Conversation**		**SS** Unit 1 Speaking 1
	2 Snapshot		
	3 Grammar Focus		**SB** Unit 1 Grammar Plus, Focus 1 **SS** Unit 1 Grammar 1 **GAME** Sentence Runner (The verb *be* 1)
	4 Speaking	**TSS** Unit 1 Extra Worksheet	
	5 Listening		
	6 Word Power		**SS** Unit 1 Vocabulary 1
	7 Speaking		**SS** Unit 1 Vocabulary 2 **WB** Unit 1 exercises 1–4
CYCLE 2	**8 Conversation**		**SS** Unit 1 Speaking 2
	9 Grammar Focus		**SB** Unit 1 Grammar Plus, Focus 2 **SS** Unit 1 Grammar 2 **GAME** Speak or Swim (The verb *be* 2)
	10 Pronunciation		
	11 Speaking		
	12 Listening		**GAME** Sentence Stacker (The alphabet and numbers)
	13 Interchange 1		
	14 Speaking	**TSS** Unit 1 Vocabulary Worksheet **TSS** Unit 1 Grammar Worksheet **TSS** Unit 1 Listening Worksheet **TSS** Unit 1 Project Worksheet **VID** Unit 1 **VRB** Unit 1	**SS** Unit 1 Reading 1–2 **SS** Unit 1 Listening 1–3 **SS** Unit 1 Video 1–3 **GAME** Word keys (The verb *be*; Saying hello and good-bye) **WB** Unit 1 exercises 5–10

Key **GAME:** Online Game **SB:** Student's Book **SS:** Online Self-study **TSS:** Teacher Support Site
VID: Video DVD **VRB:** Video Resource Book **WB:** Online Workbook/Workbook

My Plan for Unit 1

Use the space below to customize a plan that fits your needs.

With the following SB exercises	I am using these materials in class	My students are using these materials outside the classroom

With or instead of the following SB section	I am using these materials for assessment

1 What's your name?

- Say hello and make introductions
- Say good-bye and exchange contact information

1 CONVERSATION My name is Joshua Brown.

A Listen and practice.

Joshua: Hello. My name is Joshua Brown.
Isabella: Hi. My name is Isabella Martins.
Joshua: It's nice to meet you, Isabella.
Isabella: Nice to meet you, too.
Joshua: I'm sorry. What's your last name again?
Isabella: It's Martins.

First names	Last names
↓	↓
Joshua	Brown
Isabella	Martins

B **PAIR WORK** Introduce yourself to your partner.

2 SNAPSHOT

Listen and practice.

Nicholas Hoult

Names and nicknames

Nicholas (Nick)	Madison (Maddie)	Jennifer (Jen)
Emily (Em)	Joshua (Josh)	Isabella (Izzy)
Michael (Mike)	William (Will)	Elizabeth (Liz)

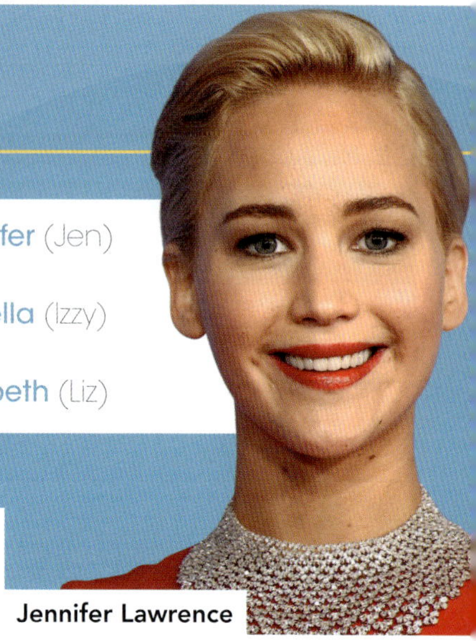

Jennifer Lawrence

What are some popular names and nicknames in your country?
Do you have a nickname? What is it?

1 What's your name?

Cycle 1, Exercises 1–7

In Unit 1, students say hello, make introductions, and say good-bye and exchange contact information. By the end of Cycle 1, students will be able to say hello and make introductions using *my, your, his,* and *her.* By the end of Cycle 2, students will be able to say good-bye and exchange contact information using subject pronouns and the verb *be.*

1 CONVERSATION

Learning Objective: use *my* and *your* while saying hello and making introductions

TIP
To learn your Ss' names, have them make name cards. Each S folds a piece of paper in thirds and writes his or her name on one side. Then they place the name cards on their desks.

A *[CD 1, Track 1]*

- Books closed. Introduce yourself. Shake hands with a S and say: "Hi. My name is . . ." or "I'm . . ." Encourage Ss to respond using their own names (e.g., *My name is* . . . or *I'm* . . .) When Ss respond, say: "It's nice to meet you."
- Books open. Focus Ss' attention on the picture and the names in the conversation.
- Play the audio program. Ss listen and read silently.
- Write these sentences on the board:

  I'm Isabella Martins.
  My name is Joshua Brown.
- Explain that *I'm* . . . and *My name is* . . . have the same meaning. Change *Isabella Martins* to *Joshua Brown* (and vice versa) in the sentences on the board.
- Play the audio program again. Ss listen and read silently. Explain that *Nice to meet you* means "It's nice to meet you," and *I'm sorry. What's your last name again?* means "Please repeat your last name."
- To explain the meaning of *too,* draw two female stick figures on the board. Label each figure *Isabella.* Point to one and say: "My name is Isabella." Then point to the other and say: "My name is Isabella, too."
- Write this sentence on the board:

  It's nice to meet you.

  Ask a S to read the sentence. Respond: "It's nice to meet you, too."
- Play the audio program again. Ss listen and read silently. Then they practice the conversation in pairs.

! For a new way to practice this conversation, try ***Look Up and Speak!*** – download it from the website.

- Focus Ss' attention on the first names and last names in the box. Model with your own name. Say: "My first name is . . . My last name is . . ." Ask a few Ss: "What's your first name? What's your last name?"

B *Pair work*

- Explain the task. Then model it with a few Ss, using your own names and the conversation as a model.
- Ss stand up and practice the conversation in pairs. When they finish, they practice the conversation with a different partner.
- Ss change roles and partners several times. Go around the class and encourage Ss to shake hands and smile while introducing themselves.
- ***Option:*** Ask one or two pairs of Ss to role-play the conversation for the class.

! For a new way to practice this conversation, try ***Moving Dialog*** – download it from the website.

2 SNAPSHOT

Learning Objective: talk about popular names in the U.S. and their own countries

[CD 1, Track 2]

- Focus Ss' attention on the Snapshot. Explain that these are popular names in English. A *nickname* is an informal name for a person, place, or thing.
- Play the audio program. Ss listen and repeat.
- Write this on the board:

  Michael

  Ask: "What is the nickname for Michael?" Elicit the answer. (Answer: Mike). Circle the first part of the name: "Mich." Explain that we change the spelling for the nickname "Mike." Repeat with the name Madison (Maddie).
- Read the focus questions.
- Elicit popular names and nicknames and list them under the Ss' countries. Then elicit any nicknames the Ss have and add them to the lists.

3 GRAMMAR FOCUS

Learning Objective: ask and answer questions with *What's . . . name?* and *my, your, his,* and *her*

[CD 1, Track 3]

- Play the audio program for the Grammar Focus box. Ss listen and read silently.

A

- Focus Ss' attention on the pictures. Ask Ss what the people are doing. (Answer: shaking hands/meeting each other/introducing themselves)
- Read the example aloud. Ss complete the task individually. Elicit the answers.

Answers

1. A: Hello. What's **your** name?
   B: Hi. **My** name is Carlos.
   What's **your** name?
   A: **My** name is Akina.
2. A: What's **his** name?
   B: **His** name is Ethan.
   A: And what's **her** name?
   B: **Her** name is Caroline.

B *Pair work*

- Ss practice in pairs using their own names and the names of other Ss. Then have each partner stand and find a new partner and practice again. Repeat until each S has spoken to three or four partners.

4 SPEAKING

Learning Objectives: identify letters and their sounds; spell people's names

A *[CD 1, Track 4]*

- Play the first part of the audio program. Ss listen and read silently. Then play the first part of the audio program again. Ss listen and repeat.
- ***Option:*** Ss practice the alphabet in pairs, taking turns reading the letters.

B Class activity *[CD 1, Track 5]*

- Explain the task and focus Ss' attention on the example list of classmates' names.
- Play the second part of the audio program. Ss listen and read silently. Then play the second part again, pausing after each line. Ss listen and repeat.
- Model the task with a S. Then Ss go around the class with their notebooks and complete the task.

5 LISTENING

Learning Objective: listen for correct spelling

[CD 1, Track 6]

- Read the four pairs of names aloud. Point out that the names in each pair have the same pronunciation.
- Play the first conversation in the audio program and model the task. Then play the rest of the audio program, pausing after each conversation. Ss listen and complete the task.
- Ss compare their answers in pairs. Then write the answers on the board.

Audio script

1.
Woman Is your name Cate Lopez?
Cate That's right.
Woman And how do you spell your first name?
Cate It's C-A-T-E.
Woman OK. Thank you.

2.
Woman Eric Russo. Is your first name spelled E-R-I-C?
Erick No. My name is spelled E-R-I-C-*K*.
Woman I'm sorry. Could you repeat that?
Erick Yes. It's E-R-I-C-*K*.
Woman Oh, so it's Erick with a C-*K*. Got it.

3.
Sophia My name is Sophia Peters.
Woman Thank you. Sophia . . . that's S-O-F-I-A?
Sophia No. It's spelled S-O-*P*-*H*-I-A.
Woman Oh, excuse me. S-O-P-H-I-A.
Sophia That's right.

4.
Woman Your name, please?
Zachary It's Zachary Tanaka.
Woman Is your first name Z-A-C-K-A-R-Y?
Zachary No, it's Z-A-C-*H*-A-R-Y.
Woman Oh, so it's Z-A-C-*H*-A-R-Y. Thank you, Mr. Tanaka.

Answers

1. Cate 2. Erick 3. Sophia 4. Zachary

3 GRAMMAR FOCUS

My, you, his, her

What's **your** name?	**My** name's Carlos.	What**'s** = What **is**
What's **his** name?	**His** name's Joshua.	
What's **her** name?	**Her** name's Isabella.	

GRAMMAR PLUS *see page 132*

A Complete the conversations. Use *my*, *your*, *his*, or *her*.

1. **A:** Hello. What's ___*your*___ name?
   B: Hi. __________ name is Carlos.
   What's __________ name?
   A: __________ name is Akina.

2. **A:** What's __________ name?
   B: __________ name is Ethan.
   A: And what's __________ name?
   B: __________ name is Caroline.

B **PAIR WORK** Practice the conversations with a partner.

4 SPEAKING Spelling names

A Listen and practice.

A	B	C	D	E	F	G	H	I	J	K	L	M	N	O	P	Q	R	S	T	U	V	W	X	Y	Z
a	b	c	d	e	f	g	h	i	j	k	l	m	n	o	p	q	r	s	t	u	v	w	x	y	z

B **CLASS ACTIVITY** Listen and practice. Then practice with your own names. Make a list of your classmates' names.

A: What's your name?
B: My name is Akina Hayashi.
A: Is that A-K-I-N-A?
B: Yes, that's right.
A: How do you spell your last name? H-A-Y-A-S-H-Y?
B: No, it's H-A-Y-A-S-H-I.

My classmates
Akina Hayashi
Ethan Reed

5 LISTENING Your name, please?

How do you spell the names? Listen and check (✓) the correct answers.

1. ☐ Kate
   ☐ Cate
2. ☐ Erick
   ☐ Eric
3. ☐ Sophia
   ☐ Sofia
4. ☐ Zackary
   ☐ Zachary

6 WORD POWER Titles

A Listen and practice.

Miss Kato (single females)
Mrs. Jones (married females)
Ms. Yong (single or married females)
Mr. Rodriguez (single or married males)

B Listen and write the titles.

1. ________ Santos 2. ________ Wilson 3. ________ Park 4. ________ Rossi

7 SPEAKING Saying hello

A Listen and practice.

B **CLASS ACTIVITY** Go around the class. Greet your classmates formally (with titles) and informally (without titles).

6 WORD POWER

Learning Objective: use titles for men and women

A *[CD 1, Track 7]*

- Focus Ss' attention on the box with titles. Read each title aloud and ask Ss to repeat.
- Explain that we use titles with last names. Remind Ss of the meanings of *male* and *female*.
- Ask the class: "Who uses the title *Miss*? *Mrs.*? *Ms.*? *Mr.*?" Ss raise their hands. Explain that the end punctuation for *Mrs.*, *Ms.*, and *Mr.* is a *period*.
- Play the audio program. Ss listen and repeat.
- ***Option:*** To help Ss recognize the difference between *Miss* and *Ms.*, ask them to put their hands on their throats and say the words. The sound /s/ in *Miss* has no vibration, but the sound /z/ in *Ms.* has a vibration.

B *[CD 1, Track 8]*

- Play the audio program. Ss listen and read silently. Play the audio program again. Ss complete the task.
- Call on Ss to say the names and titles. Write the answers on the board.

Answers

1. Mr.
2. Mrs.
3. Miss
4. Ms.

- ***Option:*** Ss work in pairs. S1 spells out the names on his or her list, and S2 writes them down. Then they change roles. The pairs check answers by comparing lists.

7 SPEAKING

Learning Objective: use formal and informal greetings for different times of day

A *[CD 1, Track 9]*

- Focus Ss' attention on the pictures.
- Play the audio program once or twice. Ss listen and read silently.
- Elicit the expressions that mean "hello" and write them on the board. (Answers: Hi, Good morning, Good afternoon, Good evening, Hello) Encourage Ss to use the pictures to guess the meanings of *morning*, *afternoon*, and *evening*.
- Check Ss' understanding of when to use titles. Point to picture 2 and invent full names for the woman (e.g., *Paula Rodriguez*) and the girl (e.g., *Taylor Conner*). Write the names on the board.

T: (*point to the woman's speech bubble*) Good morning, Mrs. Conner. How are you? (*ask Ss*) OK?
Ss: No!
T: (*point to the girl's speech bubble*) I'm just fine, Paula. Thank you. (*ask Ss*) OK?
Ss: No!

- Play the audio program again, pausing after each short conversation. Ss listen and repeat.

TIP
To encourage Ss to learn the Classroom Language on page v of the Student's Book, write the expressions on cards. Then put the cards on the walls.

B *Class activity*

- Books closed. Explain and model the first task. Write *formal greetings* on the board. Then greet several Ss using titles. For example:

T: Good evening, (Mr. Chen).
S1: Good evening, (your title and last name).
T: Hello, (Ms. Ramirez).
S2: Hello, (your title and last name).

- ***Option:*** If Ss don't know each other's names yet, have them wear name tags during the activity.
- Ss go around the class and greet four or five classmates. Go around the room and check their use of titles and last names.
- When each S has greeted four or five others, stop the activity.
- Explain and model the second task. Write *informal greetings* on the board. Ask two Ss to greet each other using first names only. For example:

S1: Hi, (Alicia).
S2: Hi, (Mariko).

- Ss go around the class and greet four or five classmates. Go around the room and check their use of first names only.

! For a new way to practice greetings, try ***Musical Dialog*** – download it from the website.

End of Cycle 1

See the Supplementary Resources chart at the beginning of this unit for additional teaching materials and student activities related to this Cycle.

Cycle 2, Exercises 8–14

8 CONVERSATION

Learning Objective: use subject pronouns and *be* in short conversations about introductions and greetings

A *[CD 1, Track 10]*

- Books open. Focus Ss' attention on the pictures. Point to the picture of Lena Garza and ask: "What's her name?" (Answer: Her name is Lena Garza.)
- Play the audio program once or twice. Ss listen and read silently.
- If needed, explain any new vocabulary. For *excuse me*, tap a S on the shoulder and say: "Excuse me" to get his or her attention. For *over there*, put a S's book on the other side of the classroom. Stand next to the S, point to the book, and say: "Your book is over there." For *history*, write an historic date and event Ss might know on the board (e.g., *April 12, 1961: first person in space*).
- Ss cover the text. Play the audio program again. Ss listen and look at the pictures.
- Ss work in groups of three. They practice the conversations three times, changing roles.
- ***Option:*** Ask one or two groups to role-play the conversations for the class.

TIP
To keep Ss interested in role plays, ask no more than two pairs or groups to role-play conversations for the class. Keep a record of who role-played the conversations and choose different Ss each time.

! For a new way to practice this conversation, try ***Disappearing Dialog*** – download it from the website.

B *Group work*

- Books closed. Explain the task. Write this conversation on the board:

  S1: Hi, (S2).
  S2: Hi, (S1).
  S1: (S2), this is (S3).
  S2: Hi, (S3).
  S3: Hi, (S2). Nice to meet you.

  Then ask three Ss to model the conversation.
- Ss take turns introducing each other in groups of three. Remind Ss to look at each other as they speak.

9 GRAMMAR FOCUS

Learning Objective: use subject pronouns and *be* in short conversations

[CD 1, Track 11]

- Focus Ss' attention on the Grammar Focus box. Ss read silently.
- Play the audio program for the Grammar Focus box. Ss listen and read silently.
- Focus Ss' attention on the contractions. Contrast the pronunciation of *I am* and *I'm*, *you are* and *you're*, and so on. Point out that we use contractions in statements and negative short answers. We do not use them in yes/no questions or positive short answers.
- Play the audio program again. Ss listen and repeat.
- ***Option:*** Ss underline the contractions in the conversations in Exercise 8. Then they compare answers in pairs. (Answers: I'm, She's, I'm, You're, I'm, He's)

A

- Books closed. Write the first two lines of the conversation on the board. Do not fill in the example.
- Explain and model the task. Point out the choices in parentheses. Elicit the correct answers and write them on the board.
- Books open. Ss complete the task individually. As they work, copy the rest of the conversation on the board.
- Ask different Ss to write the correct answers on the board. Go over answers with the class.

Answers

Ben:	Hello, Christy. How **are** you?
Christy:	**I'm** fine, thanks. **I'm** sorry – what's your name again?
Ben:	**It's** Ben – Ben Durant.
Christy:	That's right! Ben, this **is** Joshua Brown. **He's** in our history class.
Ben:	**It's** nice to meet you.
Joshua:	Hi, Ben. I think **you're** in my English class, too.
Ben:	Oh, right! Yes, I **am**.

- Ss practice the conversation in groups of three. Then they change roles and practice again.

8 CONVERSATION Are you Andrea Clark?

A Listen and practice.

Daniel Excuse me. Are you Andrea Clark?
Sheila No, I'm not. She's over there.
Daniel Oh, I'm sorry.

Lena Matt? This is your book.
Matt Oh, thank you. You're in my math class, right?
Lena Yes, I am. I'm Lena Garza.

Jack Hey, Christy, this is Ben. He's in our history class.
Christy Hi, Ben.
Ben Hi, Christy. Nice to meet you.

B **GROUP WORK** Greet a classmate. Then introduce him or her to another classmate.

"Hey, Eduardo, this is . . ."

9 GRAMMAR FOCUS

The verb *be*

I'm Lena Garza.	**Are you** Andrea Clark?	**I'm** = I am
You're in my class.	Yes, **I am**. (~~Yes, I'm.~~)	You**'re** = You are
She's over there. (**Andrea is** over there.)	No, **I'm not**.	He**'s** = He is
He's in our class. (**Ben is** in our class.)		She**'s** = She is
It's Garza. (**My last name is** Garza.)	How **are you**?	It**'s** = It is
	I'm fine, thanks.	

GRAMMAR PLUS see page 132

A Complete the conversation with the correct words in parentheses. Then practice with a partner.

Ben Hello, Christy. How ___*are*___ (are / is) you?
Christy __________ (I'm / It's) fine, thanks. __________ (I'm / It's) sorry – what's your name again?
Ben __________ (Is / It's) Ben – Ben Durant.
Christy That's right! Ben, this __________ (is / it's) Joshua Brown. __________ (He's / She's) in our history class.
Ben __________ (I'm / It's) nice to meet you.
Joshua Hi, Ben. I think __________ (I'm / you're) in my English class, too.
Ben Oh, right! Yes, I __________ (am / 'm).

B Complete the conversations. Then practice in groups.

Cara Excuse me. ___Are___ you Alex Lane?
James No, ________ not. My name ________ James Harris. Alex ________ over there.
Cara Oh, sorry.

Cara ________ you Alex Lane?
Alex Yes, I ________.
Cara Hi. ________ Cara Ruiz.
Alex Oh, ________ in my history class, right?
Cara Yes, I ________.
Alex ________ nice to meet you, Cara.

C **CLASS ACTIVITY** Write your name on a piece of paper. Put the papers in a bag. Then take a different paper. Find the other student.

A: Excuse me. Are you Min-ji Cho?
B: No, I'm not. She's over there.
A: Hi. Are you Min-ji Cho?
C: Yes, I am.

10 PRONUNCIATION Linked sounds

Listen and practice. Notice the linked sounds.

I'm Isabella. She's over there. You're in my class.

11 SPEAKING Personal information

A Listen and practice.

0	1	2	3	4	5	6	7	8	9	10
zero (oh)	one	two	three	four	five	six	seven	eight	nine	ten

B **PAIR WORK** Practice these phone numbers and email addresses. Then listen and check your answers.

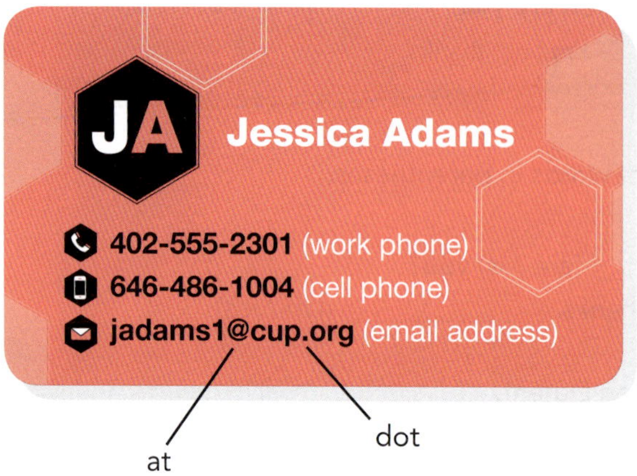

"Her name is Jessica Adams. Her work phone number is four-oh-two, five-five-five, two-three-oh-one. Her cell . . ."

B

- Books closed. Write the first conversation on the board. Do not fill in the example.
- Explain the task. Then elicit the correct answers for the first conversation and write them on the board.
- Books open. Ss complete the task for the second conversation individually. Then they compare answers in pairs.
- Ask Ss to write the second conversation on the board. Then ask the class to correct any errors.

Answers

Cara:	Excuse me. **Are** you Alex Lane?
James:	No, **I'm** not. My name **is** James Harris. Alex **is** over there.
Cara:	Oh, sorry.
Cara:	**Are** you Alex Lane?
Alex:	Yes, I **am**.
Cara:	Hi. **My name is/I'm** Cara Ruiz.
Alex:	Oh, **you're** in my history class, right?
Cara:	Yes, I **am.**
Alex:	**It's** nice to meet you, Cara.

- Read the conversations aloud, pausing after each line. Ss listen, look up, and repeat.
- Ss practice the conversations in groups of three. Go around the class and encourage Ss to look at each other when speaking.

C *Class activity*

- Explain the first part of the activity. Ss write their first and last names on pieces of paper and put them in a bag.
- Explain and model the second part of the activity. Take a paper from the bag and ask a few Ss whose names are not on the paper:

  T: Excuse me. Are you (*name on paper*)?
  S1: No, I'm not. He's/She's over there.

  Then ask the S whose name is on the paper:

  T: Excuse me. Are you (*name on paper*)?
  S2: Yes, I am.
- Have Ss take papers, go around the room, and complete the activity. If Ss know each other well, ask them to imagine they are meeting for the first time.

10 PRONUNCIATION

Learning Objective: sound more natural by using linked sounds

[CD 1, Track 12]

- Explain that there are five vowels in English: *a*, *e*, *i*, *o*, and *u*. The other letters are consonants.
- Focus Ss' attention on the examples. Point out that *Isabella*, *over*, and *in* begin with vowels. The words before them end in consonants. In relaxed speech, people link these sounds together.
- Play the audio program. Ss listen and read silently.
- Play the audio program again. Ss listen and practice.
- ***Option:*** Ss underline the linked sounds in the conversations in Exercise 8 on page 5. Elicit answers from the class. (Answers: She**'s o**ver there. Thi**s i**s your book. You**'re i**n my math class, right? Ye**s, I a**m**. I'm** Lena Garza. Hey, Christy, thi**s i**s Ben. He**'s i**n our history class.) Then play the audio program for Exercise 8 again and ask Ss to listen for the linked sounds.

TIP
Ss often don't understand native English speakers because they seem to talk quickly. Teaching Ss to be aware of linked sounds can greatly increase listening comprehension.

11 SPEAKING

Learning Objective: use the numbers from zero to 10 in phone numbers and email addresses

A *[CD 1, Track 13]*

- Books open. Play the audio program. Ss listen and read silently.
- Play the audio program again. Ss listen and repeat.

B *Pair work [CD 1, Track 14]*

- Explain the task and read the example aloud. Write the phone number 402-555-2301 on the board. Read each digit and have Ss repeat it. Then read the complete phone number. Ask different Ss to read the phone number aloud.
- Point out that we say "zero" when *0* is alone. However, we can say "zero" or "oh" when it is with other numbers. For example, we can say *505* as "five-zero-five" or "five-oh-five."
- Focus Ss' attention on Jessica's email address and read it aloud. Write the @ symbol on the board and point out that it's pronounced "at." Tell Ss that the period in an email address is pronounced "dot."
- Focus Ss' attention on Ryan's email address and read it aloud. Write a dash and an underscore on the board and explain that they look similar, but the dash is higher up than the underscore.
- Have Ss practice reading the information on the business cards.
- Play the audio program. Ss listen and read silently.

12 LISTENING

Learning Objective: listen for correct names, phone numbers, and email addresses

A ***[CD 1, Track 15]***

- Focus Ss' attention on the contact list. Ask: "Do you remember these people? Who are they?" If Ss don't remember, focus their attention on Exercises 3, 4, 8, and 9.
- Play the audio program. Ss listen and complete the list. Then they go over their answers in pairs. Play the audio program again as needed.

Audio script

Isabella What's Ben Durant's phone number, Joshua?
Joshua It's seven-one-eight, five-five-five, eight-two-four-one.
Isabella Seven-one-eight, five-five-five, eight-two-four-one?
Joshua Yes, that's it.
Isabella And his email address?
Joshua It's Ben Durant at C-U-P dot org. . . . OK. Cara Ruiz. What's her phone number?
Isabella Hmm. Cara. Her number is three-four-seven, five-five-five, seven-six-four-five.
Joshua Three-four-seven, five-five-five, seven-six-four-five?
Isabella That's right. Her email is Cara R at cambridge dot org. That's C-A-R-A-R at cambridge dot org. Now, let's see. Andrea Clark. Her phone number is two-one-two, six-four-five, five-nine-six-zero. Right?
Joshua Yes, that's right. Two-one-two, six-four-five, five-nine-six-zero.
Isabella Her email address is A Clark one-three-four at C-U-P dot org.
Joshua So that's A-C-L-A-R-K one-three-four at C-U-P dot org?
Isabella Yes.
Joshua And Akina Hayashi's number and email?
Isabella Oh, Akina is my roommate. Our number is nine-one-seven, five-five-five, two-eight-oh-seven. Her email address is Akina H at cambridge dot org.
Joshua I'm sorry. Can you spell that?
Isabella Her email address?
Joshua Yeah.
Isabella Sure. It's A-K-I-N-A-H at cambridge dot org.
Joshua OK. Got it. Thanks.

Answers

Name	Phone number	Email address
Ben Durant	718-555-8241	bendurant@cup.org
Cara Ruiz	347-555-7645	carar@cambridge.org
Andrea Clark	212-645-5960	aclark134@cup.org
Akina Hayashi	917-555-2807	akinah@cambridge.org

B ***Class activity***

- Explain the task and model the conversation with a S. Then Ss take their notebooks, go around the class, and complete the task.

13 INTERCHANGE 1

See page T-114 for teaching notes.

14 SPEAKING

Learning Objective: use formal and informal ways to say good-bye for different times of the day

A ***[CD 1, Track 16]***

- Focus Ss' attention on the pictures in Exercise 7 on page 4. Then focus their attention on Exercise 14. Say: "Now they are saying good-bye."
- Play the audio program once or twice. Ss listen and read silently.
- Elicit the expressions that mean "good-bye" and write them on the board. (Answers: See you later, Bye-bye, Bye, See you tomorrow, Good-bye, Have a good evening, Good night) Point out that *good night* means "good-bye."
- Play the audio program again, pausing after each short conversation. Ss listen and repeat.

B ***Class activity***

- Explain the activity. Then model it with several Ss in different ways. For example: "Good night, Juan. Have a good evening, Kumiko. See you later, Nadia."
- Ss go around the class and complete the activity. Remind Ss to use different expressions.

End of Cycle 2

See the Supplementary Resources chart at the beginning of this unit for additional teaching materials and student activities related to this Cycle.

12 LISTENING Contact information

A Isabella and Joshua are making a list of classmates' phone numbers and email addresses. Listen and complete the list.

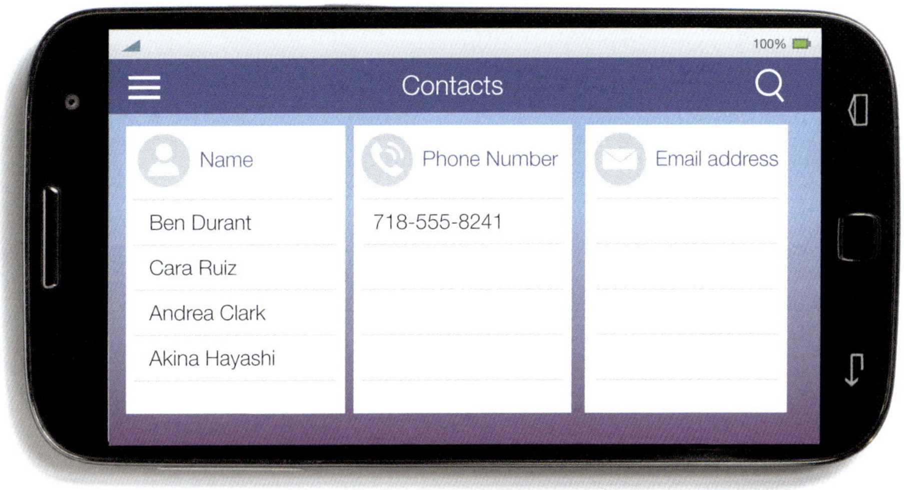

B **CLASS ACTIVITY** Make a list of your classmates' names, phone numbers, and email addresses.

A: What's your name?
B: I'm Maria Ventura.

A: And what's your phone number?
B: It's 323-555-7392.

13 INTERCHANGE 1 Celebrity classmates

Meet some "famous classmates." Go to Interchange 1 on page 114.

14 SPEAKING Saying good-bye

A Listen and practice.

B **CLASS ACTIVITY** Go around the room. Say good-bye to your classmates and teacher.

Unit 2 Supplementary Resources Overview

	After the following SB exercises	You can use these materials in class	Your students can use these materials outside the classroom
CYCLE 1	**1 Snapshot**		
	2 Articles		**SS** Unit 2 Vocabulary 1
	3 Conversation		**SS** Unit 2 Speaking 1
	4 Pronunciation		**GAME** Name the Picture (Common Objects)
	5 Grammar Focus		**SB** Unit 2 Grammar Plus, Focus 1 **SS** Unit 2 Grammar 1 **GAME** Say the Word (*This/these, it/they;* plurals)
	6 Speaking		**WB** Unit 2 exercises 1–4
CYCLE 2	**7 Conversation**		**SS** Unit 2 Speaking 2
	8 Grammar Focus		**SB** Unit 2 Grammar Plus, Focus 2 **SS** Unit 2 Grammar 2 **GAME** Speak or Swim (Yes/No and *where* questions with *be*)
	9 Word Power	**TSS** Unit 2 Vocabulary Worksheet **TSS** Unit 2 Grammar Worksheet **TSS** Unit 2 Extra Worksheet	**SS** Unit 2 Vocabulary 2 **GAME** Sentence Runner (Prepositions; article *the*)
	10 Listening	**TSS** Unit 2 Listening Worksheet	
	11 Speaking		
	12 Interchange 2	**TSS** Unit 2 Project Worksheet **VID** Unit 2 **VRB** Unit 2	**SS** Unit 2 Reading 1–2 **SS** Unit 2 Listening 1–3 **SS** Unit 2 Video 1–3 **WB** Unit 2 exercises 5–9

With or instead of the following SB section	You can also use these materials for assessment
Units 1–2 Progress Check	**ASSESSMENT PROGRAM** Units 1–2 Oral Quiz **ASSESSMENT PROGRAM** Units 1–2 Written Quiz

Key **GAME:** Online Game **SB:** Student's Book **SS:** Online Self-study **TSS:** Teacher Support Site
VID: Video DVD **VRB:** Video Resource Book **WB:** Online Workbook/Workbook

My Plan for Unit 2

Use the space below to customize a plan that fits your needs.

With the following SB exercises	I am using these materials in class	My students are using these materials outside the classroom

With or instead of the following SB section	I am using these materials for assessment

2 Where are my keys?

- Identify and discuss personal and classroom objects
- Discuss the location of items

1 SNAPSHOT

Listen and practice.

Check (✓) the things in your bag.
What is one other thing in your bag?

2 ARTICLES Classroom objects

A Listen. Complete the sentences with *a* or *an*.

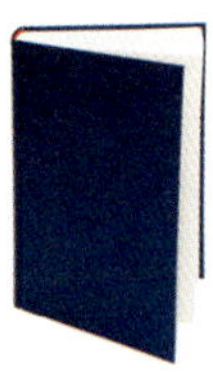

1. This is ________ book.

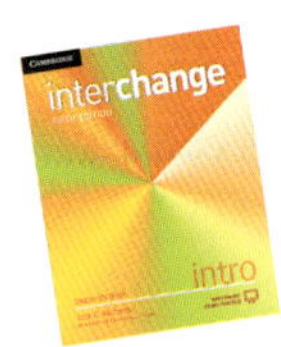

2. This is ________ English book.

3. This is ________ eraser.

4. This is ________ notebook.

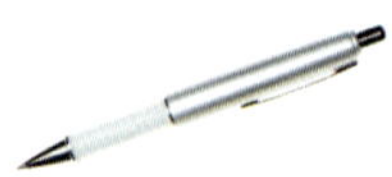

5. This is ________ pen.

6. This is ________ clock.

articles

an + vowel sound
a + consonant sound

B PAIR WORK Find and spell these things in your classroom.

backpack	chair	eraser	pen	notebook
board	desk	pencil	wall	wastebasket
poster	door	outlet	book	window

A: This is a chair.
B: How do you spell *chair*?
A: C-H-A-I-R.

2 Where are my keys?

Cycle 1, Exercises 1–6

In Unit 2, students identify and discuss personal and classroom objects and discuss the location of items. By the end of Cycle 1, students will be able to identify and discuss personal and classroom objects using the articles *a/an*, plurals, *this/these*, and *it/they*. By the end of Cycle 2, students will be able to discuss the location of items using yes/no and *where* questions with *be*, the article *the*, and prepositions of place.

1 SNAPSHOT

Learning Objective: discuss common personal items

[CD 1, Track 17]

- Focus Ss' attention on the pictures. Then play the audio program. Ss listen and read silently.
- Play the audio program again. Ss listen and repeat.
- Write the words *wallet* and *hairbrush* on the board. Then explain and model the first task. Take a wallet from your bag and say: "What's in my bag? A wallet. It's a wallet." Check (✓) the word *wallet* on the board.
- Ss complete the first task individually.
- To check comprehension, ask: "Who has a wallet?" Take out your wallet. Repeat with the remaining items.
- Say: "Take out one thing from your bag. What is it?" Elicit Ss' answers and write them on the board. Help Ss name any objects they show.

For more practice with this vocabulary, play ***Kim's Game*** – download it from the website.

2 ARTICLES

Learning Objective: use *a* and *an* in short statements about common classroom objects

A ***[CD 1, Track 18]***

- Focus Ss' attention on the pictures. Elicit or say the names of the objects. Ss repeat.
- Focus Ss' attention on the *articles* box. Explain that we use *an* before vowel sounds and *a* before consonant sounds. Write examples from Exercise 1 on the board (e.g., *an umbrella, a wallet*). Then elicit examples of vowel sounds and consonant sounds.
- Focus Ss' attention on the pictures again. Ask: "Which words start with vowel sounds? Which words start with consonant sounds?"
- Explain the task. Then play the audio program. Ss listen and complete the task. Play the audio program again if needed.
- Elicit the answers and write them on the board. Ss check their answers. Then they practice reading the sentences in pairs.

Answers

1. This is **a** book.
2. This is **an** English book.
3. This is **an** eraser.
4. This is **a** notebook.
5. This is **a** pen.
6. This is **a** clock.

For more practice listening for *a* and *an*, try ***Run for It!*** – download it from the website. Put signs with *a* and *an* on the walls. Then read out phrases with these articles (e.g., *a cell phone, an eraser*).

B ***Pair work***

- Explain the task. Then say the words one by one. Ss listen and repeat. Explain any new vocabulary.
- Model the example conversation with the class. Point to a chair and say: "This is a chair." The class asks: "How do you spell *chair*?" Say: "C-H-A-I-R." Then change roles with the class.
- Ss complete the task in pairs. They go around the class, find the classroom objects, and practice the conversation. Circulate and help Ss identify and spell objects as needed.
- ***Option***: Ask: "What other things are in the class?" Ask Ss to point to them and elicit the names. Ask: "How do you spell . . . ?" Elicit the spellings of these words and write them on the board.

TIP
To help Ss remember the names of classroom objects, have them make labels in English and attach the labels to the objects.

3 CONVERSATION

Learning Objective: use *this, these*, and plurals in a short conversation

[CD 1, Track 19]

- Focus Ss' attention on the picture. Ask: "What things are in the picture?" Elicit or explain any new vocabulary (e.g., *flash drives, tablet, tablet case*).
- Ask: "Who is Brandon? Christina?" Play the audio program. Ss listen for the answers. Then elicit the answers by asking Ss to identify the people in the picture.
- Explain that people say: *They're cool., Wow!*, and *It's great!* to show pleasure. Play the audio program again. Ss listen for these expressions.
- Ss practice the conversation in groups of three. Go around the classroom and encourage Ss to look at each other and use intonation.
- ***Option***: Ask one or two groups to role-play the conversation for the class.

! For a new way to practice this conversation, try ***Substitution Dialog*** – download it from the website. Substitute the words *flash drives* with *wallets, tablet* with *cell phone*, and *tablet case* with *eraser*.

4 PRONUNCIATION

Learning Objective: identify different pronunciations of plural *-s* endings and sound more natural when saying plural nouns

A ***[CD 1, Track 20]***

- Books closed. Demonstrate the meaning of *singular* and *plural*. Hold up three pens. Point to one and say: "One pen. *Pen* is singular." Point to two pens and say: "Two pens. *Pens* is plural." Point to all three pens and say: "Three pens. *Pens* is plural."
- Write these words on the board and underline the plural *-(e)s* endings:

  pens books sunglasses

  Say each word slowly so Ss can hear the endings. Ss repeat.
- Write the phonetic symbols above each word:

/z/	/s/	/ɪz/
pens	books	sunglasses

  Pronounce the symbols and the words. Ss repeat.
- Books open. Focus Ss' attention on the chart. Then play the audio program. Ss listen and read silently.
- Play the audio program again. Ss listen and repeat.
- ***Option***: Explain these pronunciation rules:
  1. When nouns end in vowel sounds or voiced consonant sounds (e.g., /n/, /r/), we pronounce the plural -s as /z/ (e.g., *pencils, cell phones*).
  2. When nouns end in voiceless consonant sounds (e.g., /p/, /t/, /k/), we pronounce the plural -s as /s/ (e.g., *laptops*).
  3. When nouns end in sibilant consonant sounds (e.g., /s/, /tʃ/), we pronounce the plural -s as /ɪz/ (e.g., *classes*).

B

- Say the singular nouns one by one. Ss repeat.
- Copy the pronunciation chart on the board.
- Explain and model the task. Say: "Phone case phone cases." Then write it in the chart on the board.
- Ss complete the task individually. Go around the class and give help as needed.
- Ask different Ss to complete the chart on the board.

Answers

/z/	/s/	/ɪz/
student IDs	paper clips	phone cases
newspapers	tablets	purses
televisions	tickets	boxes

C ***[CD 1, Track 21]***

- Play the audio program again. Ss listen and check their answers. Then correct the answers on the board as a class.
- ***Option***: Ss add more words to the chart in small groups. Go around the class and help with vocabulary, pronunciation, and spelling. Then elicit words from the class and add them to the chart on the board.

For more practice with pronouncing words with plural -s endings, play ***Tic-Tac-Toe*** – download it from the website. Ss have to say and spell the words correctly.

3 CONVERSATION What are these?

Listen and practice.

Brandon Excuse me. What are these?
Christina They're flash drives.
Brandon Oh, they're cool. And what's this?
Christina It's a tablet.
Brandon A tablet? Really? Wow! It's great!
Christina Yes, it is. It's a new model.
Brandon Huh . . . and what's this?
Christina It's a tablet case.
Brandon Oh. It's . . . interesting . . . and different.

4 PRONUNCIATION Plural –s endings

A Listen and practice. Notice the pronunciation of the plural **–s** endings.

s = /z/		***s*** = /s/		***(e)s*** = /ɪz/	
flash drive	flash drive**s**	desk	desk**s**	tablet case	tablet case**s**
cell phone	cell phone**s**	laptop	laptop**s**	class	class**es**
pencil	pencil**s**	backpack	backpack**s**	hairbrush	hairbrush**es**

B Say the plural form of these nouns. Then complete the chart.

phone case

student ID

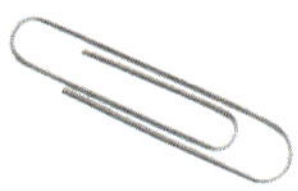
paper clip

newspaper

purse

tablet

television

ticket

box

/z/	/s/	/ɪz/
		phone cases

C Listen and check your answers.

5 GRAMMAR FOCUS

This/these, it/they; plurals

This is a laptop.

What**'s this**?
It's a flash drive.

These are laptop**s**.

What **are these**?
They're flash drive**s**.

It**'s** = It is
They**'re** = They are

GRAMMAR PLUS *see page 133*

Complete these conversations. Then practice with a partner.

1. **A:** What _are these_ ?
   B: ________________.
2. **A:** What ________________?
   B: ________________.
3. **A:** What ________________?
   B: ________________.

4. **A:** What ________________?
   B: ________________.
5. **A:** What ________________?
   B: ________________.
6. **A:** What ________________?
   B: ________________.

6 SPEAKING What's this called?

A Listen and practice.

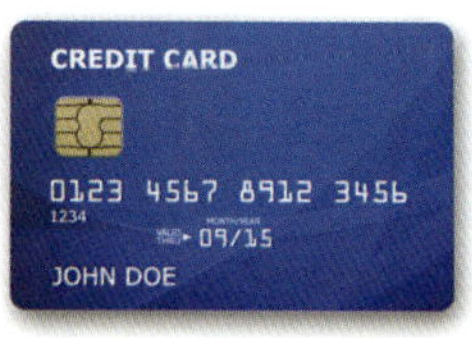

A: What's this called in English?
B: I don't know.
C: It's a credit card.
A: How do you spell that?
C: C-R-E-D-I-T C-A-R-D.

A: What are these called in English?
B: I think they're called headphones.
A: How do you spell that?
B: H-E-A-D-P-H-O-N-E-S.

B **GROUP WORK** Choose four things. Put them on a desk. Then ask about the name and spelling of each thing.

5 GRAMMAR FOCUS

Learning Objective: ask and answer questions with *this/these*, *it/they*, and plurals

TIP
Write the learning objectives on the board. When you finish each exercise, check (✓) the objectives you covered.

[CD 1, Track 22]

- Books closed. Write *this* and *these* on the board. Hold up a pen and say: "This is a pen." Then hold up two pens and say: "These are pens."
- Contrast the pronunciation of *this* and *these*. Ss repeat. If needed, point out that the /ɪ/ in *this* is a short sound, but the /iː/ in *these* is a long sound.
- Books open. Focus Ss' attention on the Grammar Focus box. Play the audio program. Ss listen and read silently.
- Elicit or explain that *this* and *it* are singular and *these* and *they* are plural.
- Explain the task. Model the first conversation with a S.
- Ss complete the task individually.
- Go over the answers by asking different pairs of Ss to read the conversations. Check Ss' use of apostrophes and capital letters.
- Then Ss practice the conversations in pairs.

Answers

1. A: What **are these**?
   B: **They're keys**.
2. A: What **are these**?
   B: **They're backpacks**.
3. A: What**'s this**?
   B: **It's an umbrella**.
4. A: What **are these**?
   B: **They're sunglasses**.
5. A: What**'s this?**
   B: **It's a wallet**.
6. A: What**'s this**?
   B: **It's a window**.

- ***Option:*** Write this model conversation on the board:

  A: What's ______________?
  B: It's ______________.
  A: What are ______________?
  B: They're ______________.

  Ss go around the classroom in pairs. They practice asking and answering questions about classroom objects. Go around the class and help Ss with the use of *this/these* and *it/they*.

6 SPEAKING

Learning Objectives: ask and answer questions about the names of things using *this/that*, *these/they*; practice spelling

A *[CD 1, Track 23]*

- Focus Ss' attention on the pictures. Then play the audio program. Ss listen and read silently.
- Play the audio program again. Ss listen and repeat.
- Ss practice the conversations in groups of three. They take turns with each role.

B *Group work*

- Explain and model the task. Put four objects on your desk, including some you haven't taught yet.
- Point to one object and ask: "What's this/What are these called in English?" Elicit the answer. Then ask: "How do you spell that?" Elicit the answer. If Ss don't know the answers, tell them to ask you the questions.
- Ss complete the task in groups of three or four. Go around the class and help with vocabulary and spelling as needed.
- ***Option***: To review vocabulary and spelling, make a list of five to 10 words and scramble the letters (e.g., *drcite drac* for *credit card*, *neohhapsde* for *headphones*). Ss unscramble the words in pairs.

TIP
To make it easy for Ss to record new vocabulary, keep a Vocabulary List on one side of the board. Add new words to it throughout the lesson.

For more practice with vocabulary, play ***Picture It!*** – download it from the website. Ss draw pictures and ask: "What is this?" or "What are these?"

End of Cycle 1

See the Supplementary Resources chart at the beginning of this unit for additional teaching materials and student activities related to this Cycle.

7 CONVERSATION

Learning Objective: use yes/no and *where* questions with *be* in short conversations about lost items

[CD 1, Track 24]

- Books closed. Play the audio program. Ask: "What are the man and woman looking for?" Elicit the answer. (Answer: car keys)
- Books open. Focus Ss' attention on the picture.
- Play the audio program again. Ss listen and read silently. Ask the class: "Who has the car keys and the wallet?" Elicit the answer. (Answer: the server)
- Elicit or explain any new vocabulary. To explain *pocket*, point to an article of clothing with a pocket.
- Play the audio program again. Ss listen and repeat. Point out the stress on the italicized word *is* in the last line.
- Ss practice the conversation in groups of three. They take turns reading each role.
- ***Option:*** Ask one or two groups to role-play the conversation for the class. Encourage them to role-play it without their books if possible.

! For a new way to practice this conversation, try ***Say It With Feeling!*** – download it from the website.

8 GRAMMAR FOCUS

Learning Objective: ask and answer yes/no and *where* questions with *be*

[CD 1, Track 25]

- Books open. Focus Ss' attention on the Grammar Focus box. Then play the audio program. Ss listen and read silently.
- Write *it's* and *they're* on the board. Circle the apostrophes. Explain that we use apostrophes in contractions.
- ***Option***: Ask Ss to find and underline the contractions *it's* and *they're* in Exercise 7.
- Point out that we use capital letters for the first letter in a question or statement.
- Play the audio program again. Ss listen and read silently.

A

- Explain the task. Model the example conversation with a S.
- Ss complete the conversations individually.
- Elicit the answers from the class. Ask Ss to spell the answers, using the words *apostrophe* and *capital* when needed. Write the answers on the board.
- Go over the answers on the board and correct them as a class.

Answers

1. A: **Is** this your cell phone?
   B: No, **it's** not.
   A: **Are** these your car keys?
   B: Yes, **they** are. Thanks!
2. A: Where **are** my glasses?
   B: Are **these** your glasses?
   A: No, they're **not**.
   B: Look! **Are** they in your pocket?
   A: Yes, **they are**. Thanks!
3. A: Where **are** your headphones?
   B: **They're** on the table.
   A: No, **they're** not. They're *my* headphones!
   B: You're right. My headphones **are** in my backpack.
4. A: **Is** this my umbrella?
   B: No, **it's** not. It's my umbrella.
   A: Sorry. **Where** is my umbrella?
   B: **It's/It is** on your chair.
   A: Oh, you're right!

- Ss practice the conversations in pairs. Encourage Ss to use props if possible.

B *Group work*

- Explain the activity. Then hold up a pen and model the conversations. Ss repeat.
- Use mime to demonstrate the meaning of *Let me see*. Pick up a S's pen and say: "Let me see." Examine the pen and then say: "No, it's not my pen."
- Model the activity. Put an object in a bag. Then ask three Ss to put objects in the bag. Take out one object and ask a S: "Is this your . . . ?" Continue until you find the owner. Then ask each S to take an object from the bag and find the owner.
- Ss work in groups of four. Give each group a bag or box. Ss complete the activity. Go around the class and give help as needed.

7 CONVERSATION Where are my car keys?

Listen and practice.

Lauren: Oh, no! Where are my car keys?

Matt: I don't know. Are they in your purse?

Lauren: No, they're not.

Matt: Maybe they're on the table in the restaurant.

Server: Excuse me. Are these your keys?

Lauren: Yes, they are. Thank you!

Server: You're welcome. And is this your wallet?

Lauren: Hmm. No, it's not. Where's your wallet, Matthew?

Matt: It's in my pocket. . . . Wait a minute! That *is* my wallet!

8 GRAMMAR FOCUS

Yes/No and *where* questions with *be*

Is this your wallet?	**Where's** your wallet?
Yes, **it is**. / No, **it's not**.	**It's** in my pocket.
Are these your keys?	**Where are** my keys?
Yes, **they are**. / No, **they're not**.	**They're** on the table.

GRAMMAR PLUS *see page 133*

A Complete these conversations. Then practice with a partner.

1. **A:** ___Is___ this your cell phone?
   B: No, ________ not.
   A: ________ these your car keys?
   B: Yes, ________ are. Thanks!

2. **A:** Where ________ my glasses?
   B: Are ________ your glasses?
   A: No, they're ________.
   B: Look! ________ they in your pocket?
   A: Yes, ________. Thanks!

3. **A:** Where ________ your headphones?
   B: ________ on the table.
   A: No, ________ not. They're *my* headphones!
   B: You're right. My headphones ________ in my backpack.

4. **A:** ________ this my umbrella?
   B: No, ________ not. It's my umbrella.
   A: Sorry. ________ is my umbrella?
   B: ________ on your chair.
   A: Oh, you're right!

B GROUP WORK Choose one of your things and put it in a bag. Then choose something from the bag that is not your object. Find the owner of this object.

A: Is this your pen, Akiko?
B: No, it's not.

C: Are these your keys, Marcos?
D: Let me see. Yes, they are.

9 WORD POWER Prepositions; article *the*

A Listen and practice.

Where is **the** cell phone?
The cell phone is in **the** box.

in

in front of

behind

on

next to

under

B Complete these sentences. Then listen and check your answers.

1. The books are *in the backpack*.

2. The flash drives are ______________.

3. The newspaper is ______________.

4. The chair is ______________.

5. The wallet is ______________.

6. The glasses are ______________.

C **PAIR WORK** Ask and answer questions about the pictures in part B.

A: Where are the books?
B: They're in the backpack.

10 LISTENING Emily's things

Listen. Where are Emily's things? Check (✓) the correct locations.

1. sunglasses	☐ on the table	☐ in her purse
2. ID	☐ in her wallet	☐ in front of the clock
3. headphones	☐ on the chair	☐ next to the television
4. tablet	☐ on the table	☐ under the table

9 WORD POWER

Learning Objective: describe where items are using prepositions of place and the definite article *the*

A *[CD 1, Track 26]*

- Focus Ss' attention on the pictures and the prepositions of place. Play the audio program. Ss listen and read silently.
- Play the audio program again. Ss listen and repeat.
- To check Ss' understanding of the prepositions, put a cell phone on a box. Ask: "Where is the cell phone?" Elicit the answer. Put the cell phone in different positions around the box and ask the question again.

B *[CD 1, Track 27]*

- Focus Ss' attention on the pictures. If needed, review the names of the objects and their pronunciations.
- Explain the task and read the first example. Ss complete the task individually.
- Ask different Ss to write their answers on the board. Play the audio program. Ss listen and check their answers. Correct any errors on the board as a class.

Answers

1. The books are **in the backpack**.
2. The flash drives are **next to the laptop**.
3. The newspaper is **on the tablet**.
4. The chair is **behind the desk**.
5. The wallet is **on the notebook**.
6. The glasses are **in front of the television**.

C *Pair work*

- Explain the task. Model the conversation with a S.
- Ss complete the activity in pairs. Go around the class and encourage Ss to ask two questions when possible. For example, for item 2 they can ask: "Where are the flash drives?" and "Where is the laptop?"
- ***Option***: Before the next class, put objects in unusual places around the classroom. Then have Ss find the objects and write down their locations.

10 LISTENING

Learning Objective: listen for the location of objects discussed using yes/no and *where* questions with *be*

[CD 1, Track 28]

- Ask Ss to read out the objects and the locations.
- Explain the task. Then play the audio program as many times as needed. Ss complete the exercise.

TIP
To reduce Ss' anxiety, point out that they will hear the audio program several times. Also, assure them that they don't have to understand everything in order to answer correctly.

Audio script

Emily	Where are my sunglasses?
Kevin	Are they on the table?
Emily	No. . . . Oh, here they are – in my purse. Now, where's my ID? Hmm . . . it's not in my wallet. Where . . . ?
Kevin	There it is! In front of the clock!
Emily	Oh, of course! Thanks, Kevin. Let's see. My headphones. Where are they? Next to the television? No. . . .
Kevin	Are they behind your purse?
Emily	No, they aren't. Oh, they're on the chair. Great! Now, I just need one more thing: my tablet. . . . Maybe it's on the table.
Kevin	No, it's not. . . . It's *under* the table.

- Ss go over their answers in pairs. Then go over the answers with the class.

Answers

1. sunglasses – in her purse
2. ID – in front of the clock
3. headphones – on the chair
4. tablet – under the table

- ***Option***: Ss make statements about Emily's things from memory (e.g., *Emily's sunglasses are in her purse.*)

! For a new way to practice listening for locations, try ***Stand Up, Sit Down*** – download it from the website. Ss stand up and sit down whenever they hear a location (e.g., *on the table*).

TIP
To encourage Ss to develop learning strategies for the Grammar Plus section, hold a class discussion. Ask the class: "When do you do the Self-study exercises? What helps you to do them?" Encourage Ss to share information. If helpful, give your own suggestions.

11 SPEAKING

Learning Objective: ask and answer questions about the location of personal items

Pair work

- Explain the activity and read the list of Kevin's things.
- Focus Ss' attention on the picture. Review vocabulary, if needed. Then model the example conversation with a S.
- Ss complete the activity in pairs. Go around the class and give help as needed. Make sure Ss take turns.

TIP
To make sure you help all Ss equally during pair and group work, vary your routine. For example, sometimes start at the front of the class; other times start at the back.

- To elicit the answers, ask different pairs to ask and answer questions about each thing. If possible, encourage Ss to give alternate answers.

Questions and possible answers

Where's his cell phone?
It's under the chair.
Where's his hairbrush?
It's on the table.
Where's his laptop?
It's on the table/under the magazine.
Where's his umbrella?
It's in the wastebasket.
Where are his glasses?
They're on the table/next to the magazine.
Where are his keys?
They're next to the umbrella.
Where's his tablet?
It's in front of the television.
Where's his credit card?
It's in front of the clock.

- ***Option:*** Ss work in pairs. S1 studies the picture for two minutes and then closes the book. S2 looks at the picture and asks *where* questions (e.g., *Where is Kevin's cell phone?*). S1 answers from memory. Then they change roles.

12 INTERCHANGE 2

See page T-115 for teaching notes.

End of Cycle 2

See the Supplementary Resources chart at the beginning of this unit for additional teaching materials and student activities related to this Cycle and for assessment tools.

11 SPEAKING Where are Kevin's things?

PAIR WORK Help Kevin find his things. Ask and answer questions.

cell phone	hairbrush	laptop	umbrella	glasses	keys	tablet	credit card

A: Where's his cell phone?
B: It's under the chair.

12 INTERCHANGE 2 Find the differences

Compare two pictures of a room. Go to Interchange 2 on page 115.

Units 1–2 Progress check

SELF-ASSESSMENT

How well can you do these things? Check (✓) the boxes.

I can . . .	Very well	OK	A little
Introduce myself and other people (Ex. 1)	☐	☐	☐
Say hello and good-bye (Ex. 1)	☐	☐	☐
Exchange contact information (Ex. 2)	☐	☐	☐
Understand names for everyday objects and possessions (Ex. 3)	☐	☐	☐
Ask and answer questions about where things are (Ex. 4, 5)	☐	☐	☐

1 SPEAKING How are you?

A Complete the conversation. Use the sentences and questions in the box.

Francisco *Hi. How are you?*
Nicole I'm fine, thanks. ____________
Francisco Pretty good, thanks. ____________
Nicole And I'm Nicole White.
Francisco ____________
Nicole Nice to meet you, too. ____________
Francisco Yes, I am.
Nicole ____________
Francisco See you in class.

> My name is Francisco Diaz.
> Oh, are you in my English class?
> How about you?
> ✓ Hi. How are you?
> It's nice to meet you, Nicole.
> Well, have a good day.

B **PAIR WORK** Practice the conversation from part A. Use your own information. Then introduce your partner to a classmate.

"Monica, this is my friend. His name is Kenta. . . ."

2 SPEAKING Is your phone number . . . ?

CLASS ACTIVITY Write your phone number on a piece of paper. Then put the papers in a bag. Take a different paper and find the owner. Write his or her name on the paper.

A: Kamal, is your phone number 781-555-1532?
B: No, it's not. Sorry!
A: Bruna, is your . . . ?

Units 1–2

Progress check

SELF-ASSESSMENT

Learning Objectives: reflect on one's learning; identify areas that need improvement

- Ask: "What did you learn in Units 1 and 2?" Elicit Ss' answers.
- Ss complete the Self-assessment. Explain to Ss that this is not a test; it is a way for them to evaluate what they've learned and identify areas where they need additional practice. Encourage them to be honest, and point out they will not get a bad grade if they check (✓) *A little*.
- Ss move on to the Progress check exercises. You can have Ss complete them in class or for homework, using one of these techniques:
  1. Ask Ss to complete all the exercises.
  2. Ask Ss: "What do you need to practice?" Then assign exercises based on their answers.
  3. Ask Ss to choose and complete exercises based on their Self-assessment.

1 SPEAKING

Learning Objectives: demonstrate one's ability to introduce oneself and another person and to say hello and good-bye

A

- Explain the task. Focus Ss' attention on the conversation.
- Read the sentences and questions in the box aloud. Ss listen and repeat.
- Ss complete the conversation individually.
- Ss compare answers in pairs. Then elicit the correct answers from the class.
- ***Option:*** Ss practice the conversation in pairs.

Answers

Francisco: **Hi. How are you?**
Nicole: I'm fine, thanks. **How about you?**
Francisco: Pretty good, thanks. **My name is Francisco Diaz.**
Nicole: And I'm Nicole White.
Francisco: **It's nice to meet you, Nicole.**
Nicole: Nice to meet you, too. **Oh, are you in my English class?**
Francisco: Yes, I am.
Nicole: **Well, have a good day.**
Francisco: See you in class.

B *Pair work*

- Explain the task. Then model the example sentences.
- Model the introduction with two Ss, using your name.
- Ss complete the task in pairs. Then each pair joins another pair and introduces each other. Go around the class and encourage Ss to look at each other when they speak.
- Continue until all Ss meet each other.

TIP
If you don't have enough class time for the speaking activities, assign each S a speaking partner. Then have Ss complete the activities with their partners for homework.

2 SPEAKING

Learning Objectives: demonstrate one's ability to exchange personal information; demonstrate one's ability to use numbers 0–10

Class Activity

- Explain the task and model the example conversation with a S.
- Each S writes his or her phone number on a piece of paper. Go around the class and give help as needed.
- Model the task. Ask three Ss to put their papers in a bag. Take a paper from the bag and ask the different Ss: "Is your phone number . . . ?" When a S says: "Yes, it is," ask: "How do you spell your name?" Then pretend to write the S's name on the paper.
- Collect the papers from all the Ss and put them in a bag.
- Each S takes a paper from the bag. Then Ss go around the class and complete the task. When they make a match, they write the S's name and sit down.
- ***Option:*** Elicit names and phone numbers from the class.

3 LISTENING

Learning Objective: demonstrate one's ability to listen for and understand names of personal items

[CD 1, Track 29]

- Explain the task and focus Ss' attention on the pictures.
- Play the audio program once or twice. Ss complete the task individually.

Audio script

1. *Man* What's this?
   Woman It's a purse.
2. *Woman* What's this?
   Man It's a cell phone.
3. *Man* What are these?
   Woman They're cell phones.
4. *Woman* What's this?
   Man It's a wallet.
5. *Man* What are these?
   Woman They're purses.
6. *Woman* What are these?
   Man They're wallets.

- To check answers, ask: "What's (number 1)?" Ask different Ss to answer. If needed, play the audio program again.

Answers

2, 3, 1, 5, 4, 6

4 SPEAKING

Learning Objective: demonstrate one's ability to ask and answer questions about where things are

A

- Explain the task and focus Ss' attention on the picture. Ask a S to model the example sentence. Point out that each sentence should have the verb *be* and a preposition.
- Ss complete the task individually. Go around the class and help with vocabulary as needed (e.g., *wall, window*).
- Ss compare their lists in pairs. They take turns reading their sentences aloud. Go around the class and help with pronunciation as needed.

Possible answers

The chair is on the desk.
The cell phone is under the desk.
The backpack/The bag is in the wastebasket.
The umbrella is behind the picture.
The chairs are under the table.
The newspaper is on the wall.
The television is on/in front of the window.
The clock is in front of the television./The television is behind the clock.
The laptop is on the clock.
The air conditioner is on the table.

B *Pair work*

- Explain the task and ask two Ss to model the example conversation. Then Ss complete the task in pairs. Go around the class and check Ss' use of grammar.

5 SPEAKING

Learning Objective: demonstrate one's ability to ask and answer questions about where things are

- Explain the first part of the task. Ask a S the first example question, and elicit the answer. (Answer: No, it isn't.) Ask a different S the second example question and elicit the answer. (Answer: Yes, it is.)
- Ss complete the first part of the task individually. Go around the class and make sure Ss write three questions with "yes" answers and two questions with "no" answers.
- Explain the second part of the task. Ss take turns asking and answering the questions. Go around the class and check Ss' use of grammar.

WHAT'S NEXT?

Learning Objective: become more involved in one's learning

- Focus Ss' attention on the Self-assessment again. Ask: "How well can you do these things now?"
- Ask Ss to underline one thing they need to review. Ask: "What did you underline? How can you review it?"
- If needed, plan additional instruction, activities, or reviews based on Ss' answers.

3 LISTENING What's this? What are these?

Listen to the conversations. Number the pictures from 1 to 6.

☐

☐

☐

☐

☐

☐

4 SPEAKING What's wrong with this room?

A What's wrong with this room? Make a list. Find 10 things.

B **PAIR WORK** Ask and answer *Where* questions about the picture.

A: Where's the chair?
B: It's on the desk.

5 SPEAKING Yes or No game

Write five yes/no questions about the picture in Exercise 4. Make three questions with "yes" answers and two questions with "no" answers. Then ask a partner the questions.

A: Is the chair behind the clock?
B: No, it isn't.

A: Is the clock in front of the television?
B: Yes, it is.

Unit 3 Supplementary Resources Overview

	After the following SB exercises	You can use these materials in class	Your students can use these materials outside the classroom
CYCLE 1	1 Snapshot		
	2 Conversation		**SS** Unit 3 Speaking 1
	3 Grammar Focus		**SB** Unit 3 Grammar plus, Focus 1 **SS** Unit 3 Grammar 1 **GAME** Sentence Runner (Yes/No questions with *be* and Wh-questions with *be*)
	4 Pronunciation		**GAME** Spell or Slime (Languages and nationalities)
	5 Speaking		**WB** Unit 3 exercises 1–3
CYCLE 2	6 Conversation		**SS** Unit 3 Speaking 2
	7 Speaking		**SS** Unit 3 Vocabulary 1 **GAME** Name the Picture (Numbers and ages)
	8 Grammar Focus	**TSS** Unit 3 Grammar Worksheet **TSS** Unit 3 Listening Worksheet **TSS** Unit 3 Extra Worksheet	**SB** Unit 3 Grammar plus, Focus 2 **SS** Unit 3 Grammar 2 **GAME** Sentence Runner (Yes/no questions with be and Wh-questions with *be*)
	9 Word Power	**TSS** Unit 3 Vocabulary Worksheet	**SS** Unit 3 Vocabulary 2 **GAME** Sentence Stacker (Descriptions)
	10 Listening		
	11 Interchange 3	**TSS** Unit 3 Project Worksheet **VID** Unit 3 **VRB** Unit 3	**SS** Unit 3 Reading 1–2 **SS** Unit 3 Listening 1–3 **SS** Unit 3 Video 1–3 **WB** Unit 3 exercises 4–8

Key
GAME: Online Game **SB:** Student's Book **SS:** Online Self-study **TSS:** Teacher Support Site
VID: Video DVD **VRB:** Video Resource Book **WB:** Online Workbook/Workbook

My Plan for Unit 3

Use the space below to customize a plan that fits your needs.

With the following SB exercises	I am using these materials in class	My students are using these materials outside the classroom

With or instead of the following SB section	I am using these materials for assessment

3 Where are you from?

- Discuss cities, countries, nationalities, and languages
- Discuss people's appearances, personalities, and ages

1 SNAPSHOT

Listen and practice.

THE TEN LARGEST CITIES IN THE WORLD

CITIES

1. Tokyo
2. Delhi
3. Shanghai
4. Mexico City
5. Mumbai
6. São Paulo
7. Osaka
8. Beijing
9. New York
10. Cairo

COUNTRIES

a. Brazil
b. China
c. Egypt
d. India
e. Japan
f. Mexico
g. the U.S.

(based on population)

Answers: 1. e 2. d 3. b 4. f 5. d 6. a 7. e 8. b 9. g 10. c

Match the cities with the countries. Then check your answers at the bottom of the Snapshot.
What other large cities are in each country? What large cities are in your country?

2 CONVERSATION Are you from Rio?

A Listen and practice.

Alexis: Are you from Florida, Felipe?

Felipe: Well, my family is in Florida now, but we're from Brazil originally.

Alexis: Really? My father is Brazilian – from Rio de Janeiro!

Felipe: So, is your first language Portuguese?

Alexis: No, it's English. Are you from Rio?

Felipe: No, we're not. We're from São Paulo.

B Listen to Alexis and Felipe talk to Fernando, Nanami, and Sophia. Check (✓) True or False.

	True	False
1. Fernando is from Spain.	☐	☐
2. Nanami is from Japan.	☐	☐
3. Sophia's first language is French.	☐	☐

3 Where are you from?

Cycle 1, Exercises 1–5

In Unit 3, students discuss cities, countries, nationalities, and languages, and people's appearances, personalities, and ages. By the end of Cycle 1, students will be able to discuss cities, countries, nationalities, and languages using yes/no questions with *be*. By the end of Cycle 2, students will be able to discuss people's appearances, personalities, and ages using Wh-questions with *be*.

1 SNAPSHOT

Learning Objective: identify and name cities and countries

[CD 1, Track 30]

- Focus Ss' attention on the lists of cities and countries. Play the audio program. Ss listen and read silently. Then play the audio program again. Ss repeat.
- Explain the first task.
- Ss complete the task individually. Then they check their answers at the bottom of the Snapshot.
- Ask the class: "What other large cities are in each country? What large cities are in your country?" Ss discuss the questions in small groups and list the answers.
- Write the names of the countries in the Snapshot as headings on the board. Add the names of any other countries the Ss are from. Then elicit answers from the class and ask Ss to write them on the board.

Possible answers

Brazil: Rio (de Janeiro), Salvador
China: Beijing, Guangzhou
Egypt: Alexandria, Giza
India: Chennai (Madras), Kolkata (Calcutta)
Japan: Yokohama, Osaka
Mexico: Guadalajara, Monterrey
the U.S.: Chicago, Los Angeles

2 CONVERSATION

Learning Objective: use yes/no questions and answers with *be* in a short conversation about where someone is from

A *[CD 1, Track 31]*

- Books closed. Ss listen to the audio program. Ask: "What places do they talk about?" (Answer: Florida, Brazil, Rio de Janeiro, São Paulo)
- Books open. Focus Ss' attention on the picture and set the scene. These people work together.
- Play the audio program again. Ss listen and read silently. Elicit or explain any new vocabulary (e.g., *originally*: first; in the beginning).
- Play the audio program again. Ss listen and repeat. Then they practice the conversation in pairs.

B *[CD 1, Track 32]*

- Explain the task and set the scene. Explain that they will hear Alexis and Felipe talking to three other co-workers: Fernando, Nanami, and Sophia.
- Go over the statements in the chart. Explain that *True* means "correct" and *False* means "incorrect."
- Play the audio program. Ss listen and complete the task individually.

Audio script

1.
Alexis So where are you from, Fernando?
Fernando I'm from Spain.
Alexis Oh, what part of Spain are you from?
Fernando I'm from Madrid.

2.
Felipe Is your name Japanese, Nanami?
Nanami Yes, it is. But I'm from the U.S. – from New York.
Felipe So you're American.
Nanami Yes, I am. But my parents are from Japan originally.

3.
Felipe By the way, Alexis, this is Sophia.
Alexis Nice to meet you, Sophia. Are you from Brazil, too?
Sophia No, I'm from Montreal.
Alexis So you're Canadian. Is your first language English?
Sophia No, it's not. My first language is French.

- Elicit answers from the class and write them on the board. Encourage Ss to correct the false answer.

Answers

1. True
2. False (She's from the U.S./New York.)
3. True

3 GRAMMAR FOCUS

Learning Objectives: use negative statements and yes/no questions with *be*

[CD 1, Track 33]

Statements with be

- Books closed. Write these statements on the board:

  Sophia's from Canada. She's not from Brazil.
  Fernando's from Spain. He's not from Mexico.

  Point out that we use *not* in negative statements.
- Books open. Focus Ss' attention on the negative statements in the Grammar Focus box. Play the audio program. Ss listen and read silently. Then play the audio program again. Ss listen and repeat.

Yes/No questions and short answers with be

- Write this on the board:

I am early.	*He is from Chile.*
Am I early?	*Is he from Chile?*

- Elicit or explain the pattern for statements and yes/no questions with *be*:

  Statements: Subject + verb + complement.
  Questions: Verb + subject + complement?

  If needed, explain that a *complement* follows the verb at the end of a sentence. Then go over the examples in the Grammar Focus box.
- Focus Ss' attention on the short answers. Point out that we use contractions with negative short answers, but not with positive short answers. Go over the negative and positive short answers.
- Play the audio program for the Grammar Focus box. Ss listen and read silently. Then play the audio program again. Ss listen and repeat.
- Note: To avoid confusion, this Grammar Focus presents only one negative form of be (i.e., *you're not, he's not*). The Grammar Focus in Unit 4, Cycle 2 presents the alternate form (*you aren't, he isn't*).

A

- Explain the task and model the first conversation with the class.
- Ss complete the task individually.
- Write lines on the board for each conversation. For example:

  1. A: ________________
     B: ________________ ________________
     A: ________________
     B: ________________
     A: ________________
     B: ________________

- Ask different Ss to write the answers on the board. Then go over the answers with the class.

Answers

1. A: **Are** Diana and Mario from Ecuador?
   B: No, **they're/they are** not. **They're/They are** from Mexico.
   A: **Are** you from Mexico, too?
   B: No, **I'm/I am** not. I'm from Colombia.
   A: So, **is** your first language Spanish?
   B: Yes, it **is**.
2. A: **Is** Meera from England?
   B: No, **she's/she is** not. She's from Australia.
   A: **Is** she from Sydney?
   B: Yes, she **is.** But her parents are from India. **They're/They are** not from Australia originally.
   A: **Is** Meera's first language Hindi?
   B: No, **it's/it is** not. **It's/It is** English.
3. A: Ji-hye, **are** you and Kwang-ho from South Korea?
   B: Yes, we **are**.
   A: And **are you** from Seoul?
   B: No, **we're/we are** not. **We're/We are** from Busan.

- Ss practice the conversations in pairs. Go around the class and help with pronunciation.

B

- Explain the task and model the first example.
- Ss complete the task individually. Then they go over their answers in pairs. Ask different pairs to read the questions and answers for the class.

Answers

1. d 2. c 3. e 4. a 5. b

- Ss practice the questions and answers in pairs.

C *Pair work*

- Explain the first part of the task and elicit an example question from the class. Encourage Ss to use the questions in part B as models and the information about countries, nationalities, and languages in the appendix in the back of the book.
- Ss complete the task individually. Go around the class and help with grammar and spelling as needed.
- Explain the second part of the task. Ss ask each other their questions in pairs. Go around the class and encourage Ss to give additional information in their answers.
- ***Option***: Ss change partners and ask the questions again.

For more practice making positive and negative statements with *be*, play ***True or False?*** – download it from the website.

3 GRAMMAR FOCUS

Negative statements and yes/no questions with *be*

I'm not	from Rio.	**Are you**	from São Paulo?		I **am.**		**I'm not.**
You're not	late.	**Am I**	early?		**you are.**		**you're not.**
She's not	from Japan.	**Is she**	from the U.S.?		**she is.**		**she's not.**
He's not	from Chile.	**Is he**	from Mexico?	Yes,	**he is.**	No,	**he's not.**
It's not	English.	**Is it**	French?		**it is.**		**it's not.**
We're not	from China.	**Are you**	from South Korea?		**we are.**		**we're not.**
You're not	early.	**Are we**	late?		**you are.**		**you're not.**
They're not	in India.	**Are they**	in Egypt?		**they are.**		**they're not.**

We**'re** = we are

GRAMMAR PLUS *see page 134*

For a list of countries, nationalities, and languages, see the appendix at the back of the book.

A Complete the conversations. Then practice with a partner.

1. **A:** ___Are___ Diana and Mario from Ecuador?
   B: No, ________ not. ________ from Mexico.
   A: ________ you from Mexico, too?
   B: No, ________ not . I'm from Colombia.
   A: So, ________ your first language Spanish?
   B: Yes, it ________.

2. **A:** ________ Meera from England?
   B: No, ________ not. She's from Australia.
   A: ________ she from Sydney?
   B: Yes, she ________. But her parents are from India. ________ not from Australia originally.
   A: ________ Meera's first language Hindi?
   B: No, ________ not. ________ English.

3. **A:** Ji-hye, ________ you and Kwang-ho from South Korea?
   B: Yes, we ________.
   A: And ________ from Seoul?
   B: No, ________ not. ________ from Busan.

Bogotá, Colombia

Busan, South Korea

B Match the questions with the answers. Then practice with a partner.

1. Are Liam and Grace from England? __d__
2. Is your first language Mandarin? ____
3. Are you Egyptian? ____
4. Is Mr. Lau from Beijing? ____
5. Is your mother from the U.K.? ____

a. No, he's not. He's from Shanghai.
b. Yes, she is. She's from London.
c. No, it's not. It's Cantonese.
d. No, they're not. They're from New Zealand.
e. Yes, we are. We're from Cairo.

C **PAIR WORK** Write five questions about your classmates. Then ask and answer your questions with a partner.

4 PRONUNCIATION Syllable stress

A Listen and practice. Notice the syllable stress.

● •	• ●	● • •	• ● •
China	Brazil	Canada	Malaysia
Turkey	Japan	Mexico	Morocco

B What is the syllable stress in these words? Add the words to the chart in part A. Then listen and check.

English	Spanish	Arabic	Korean
Mexican	Honduras	Chinese	Peru

C **GROUP WORK** Are the words in part A countries, nationalities, or languages? Make a chart and add more words.

Countries	Nationalities	Languages
Brazil	Brazilian	Portuguese
Mexico	Mexican	Spanish

5 SPEAKING Is Bruno Mars from Italy?

A Where are these people from? Check (✓) your guesses.

1

Bruno Mars
- ☐ Italy
- ☐ the Philippines
- ☐ the U.S.

2

Morena Baccarin
- ☐ Argentina
- ☐ Brazil
- ☐ the U.S.

3

Gael García Bernal
- ☐ Brazil
- ☐ Mexico
- ☐ Spain

4

Mao Asada
- ☐ China
- ☐ Japan
- ☐ South Korea

5

Chris Hemsworth
- ☐ Australia
- ☐ Canada
- ☐ England

B **PAIR WORK** Compare your guesses. Then check your answers at the bottom of the page.

A: Is Bruno Mars from Italy?
B: No, he's not.
A: Is he from the Philippines?

Answers: 1. the U.S. 2. Brazil 3. Mexico 4. Japan 5. Australia

4 PRONUNCIATION

Learning Objective: sound more natural by using correct syllable stress

A *[CD 1, Track 34]*

- Play the audio program once or twice. Ss listen and read silently. Point out that the stressed syllables are pronounced slightly stronger than unstressed syllables.
- ***Option***: Play the audio program and clap on the stressed syllables. Then play the audio program again. Ss clap on the stressed syllables.
- Play the audio program again. Ss listen and repeat.
- ***Option***: Ask Ss to find the countries on a world map.

B *[CD 1, Track 35]*

- Explain the task. Then Ss complete the task individually or in pairs. Go around the class and encourage Ss to read the words aloud.
- Play the audio program once or twice. Ss check their answers. Then play the audio program again. Ss listen and repeat.

O o	o O	O o o	o O o
China	Brazil	Canada	Malaysia
Turkey	Japan	Mexico	Morocco
English	Chinese	Mexican	Honduras
Spanish	Peru	Arabic	Korean

C *Group work*

- Write these headings on the board:

  Countries *Nationalities* *Languages*
- Explain the task. Read a few words from part B and elicit the answers. Write them under the correct headings.
- Ss complete the task in groups of three or four. Go around the class and help with spelling as needed.
- Ss check their answers in the appendix in the back of the book. Then elicit Ss' answers. Ask different Ss to add their words to the board.
- ***Option***: Write these questions on the board:
  1. *Where do people speak English?*
  2. *Where do people speak Arabic?*
  3. *Where do people speak Spanish?*
  4. *Where do people speak Chinese?*
- Ss work in teams. They list as many countries as possible in five minutes. The team with the most correct countries wins.

! For a new way to teach syllable stress, try ***Walking Stress*** – download it from the website.

5 SPEAKING

Learning Objective: discuss people's nationalities using yes/no questions with *be*

A

- Explain the task. Ss complete the task individually. Go around the class and encourage Ss to guess.

B *Pair work*

- Explain the task. Then ask two Ss to model the example conversation.
- Ss complete the task in pairs. Go around the class and help Ss with grammar and pronunciation as needed.

TIP
To determine if Ss need additional controlled grammar practice or explanation, check their performance in the speaking activities. If Ss make a lot of errors, plan a follow-up lesson for a later class.

- Ss check their answers at the bottom of the page.
- ***Option***: Ss work in pairs or small groups. For homework, they write a similar exercise about five different famous people, using part A as a model. In class, the pairs or groups exchange exercises. Then they repeat the activity with the new exercises.

End of Cycle 1

See the Supplementary Resources chart at the beginning of this unit for additional teaching materials and student activities related to this Cycle.

Cycle 2, Exercises 6–11

6 CONVERSATION

Learning Objective: use Wh-questions with *be* in a conversation describing people

[CD 1, Track 36]

- Focus Ss' attention on the picture and set the scene. Nadia is talking to Ben about other guests at a wedding party.
- Text covered. Ask: "Who else is at the party?" Play the audio program and have Ss listen for the answer. Then elicit the answer. (Answer: Ben's sister Madison (Maddie) and her daughter Mia.)
- Text uncovered. Write these questions on the board:

  1. Is Madison 20 years old?
  2. Is she shy?
  3. Is Mia six years old?

  Play the audio program again. Ss listen and read silently. Then elicit the answers. (Answers: 1. No 2. Yes 3. Yes)
- ***Option:*** Elicit the corrected answer from Ss: 1. She's 28.
- Elicit or explain any new vocabulary.

Vocabulary
cute: attractive, especially in a youthful way
What's she like?: Tell me about her personality and appearance.
smart: intelligent

- Ss practice the conversation in pairs. Go around the class and give help as needed.
- ***Option***: Ask one or two pairs of Ss to role-play the conversation for the class.

7 SPEAKING

Learning Objective: say people's ages using numbers from 11 to 103

A *[CD 1, Track 37]*

- Play the audio program. Ss listen and read silently.
- Play the audio program again. Ss repeat. Help Ss with any numbers they have difficulty pronouncing.

B *[CD 1, Track 38]*

- Play the audio program. Ss listen and read silently.
- Point out the differences in stress. In numbers that end with *-teen*, the last syllable is stressed. In numbers that end with *-ty*, the first syllable is stressed.
- Play the audio program again. Ss listen and repeat.
- ***Option:*** Write these number pairs on the board:

12, 20	14, 40	16, 60	18, 80
13, 30	15, 50	17, 70	19, 90

  Point to number pairs and ask different Ss to say the pairs.

TIP
It is difficult to hear which Ss are using correct pronunciation or stress during choral repetition; therefore, ask Ss to repeat the numbers, words, or phrases individually.

- ***Option***: Ss write a list of 10 numbers ending with *-ty* or *-teen*. Then they work in pairs. S1 reads the numbers aloud and S2 listens and writes them down. Then they change roles. The pairs check answers by comparing lists.

C *Pair work*

- Write the names from Part C on the board. Focus Ss' attention on the pictures. Tell Ss that they have one minute to memorize each person's age. Call time and have Ss close their books.
- Model the pair work with a S. Ask: "How old is Carol?" Then Ss ask and answer questions about Ben's family from memory.
- Call on Ss to ask and answer questions about each person. Write the answers. Then have Ss open their books and check.

For more practice with numbers, play ***Bingo*** – download it from the website.

6 CONVERSATION Who's that?

A Listen and practice.

Nadia Who's that?

Ben She's my sister.

Nadia She's really pretty. What's her name?

Ben Madison. We call her Maddie.

Nadia Madison . . . that's a beautiful name. How old is she?

Ben She's twenty-eight.

Nadia And what's she like? Is she nice?

Ben Well, she's shy, but she's really kind.

Nadia And who's that little girl?

Ben That's her daughter Mia. She's six years old.

Nadia She's cute!

Ben Yes, she is – and she's very smart, too.

7 SPEAKING Numbers and ages

A Listen and practice.

11 eleven	**21** twenty-one	**40** forty
12 twelve	**22** twenty-two	**50** fifty
13 thirteen	**23** twenty-three	**60** sixty
14 fourteen	**24** twenty-four	**70** seventy
15 fifteen	**25** twenty-five	**80** eighty
16 sixteen	**26** twenty-six	**90** ninety
17 seventeen	**27** twenty-seven	**100** one hundred
18 eighteen	**28** twenty-eight	**101** one hundred (and) one
19 nineteen	**29** twenty-nine	**102** one hundred (and) two
20 twenty	**30** thirty	**103** one hundred (and) three

B Listen and practice. Notice the word stress.

thirteen – thirty   fourteen – forty   fifteen – fifty   sixteen – sixty

C **PAIR WORK** Look at the people in Ben's family for one minute. How old are they? Close your books and tell your partner.

A. Carol – 76

B. Richard – 50

C. Karen – 49

D. Amber – 17

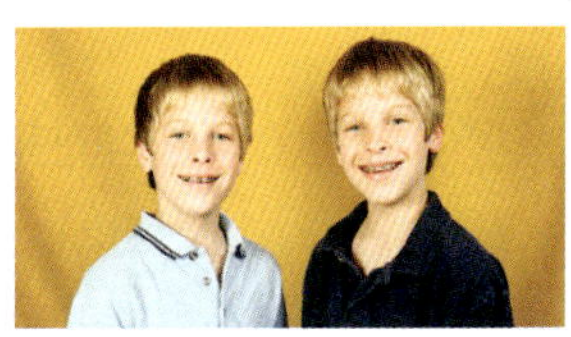

E. Jay and Joe – 10

8 GRAMMAR FOCUS

Wh-questions with *be*

What's your name?	**Who's that?**	**Who are they?**
My name is Sophia.	She's my sister.	They're my classmates.
Where are you from?	**How old is she?**	**Where are they from?**
I'm from Canada.	She's twenty-eight.	They're from San Francisco.
How are you today?	**What's she like?**	**What's San Francisco like?**
I'm fine, thanks.	She's very nice.	It's very beautiful.
	Who**'s** = Who **is**	

GRAMMAR PLUS *see page 134*

A Complete the conversations with Wh-questions. Then practice with a partner.

1. **A:** Look! Who's that ________________?
   B: Oh, she's a new student.
   A: ________________________?
   B: I think her name is Yoo-jin.
   A: Yoo-jin? ________________________?
   B: She's from South Korea.

2. **A:** Hi, Brittany. ________________________?
   B: I'm fine, thanks. My friend Leandro is here this week – from Argentina.
   A: Oh, cool. ________________________?
   B: He's really friendly.
   A: ________________________?
   B: He's twenty-five years old.

3. **A:** Azra, ________________________?
   B: I'm from Turkey. From Ankara.
   A: ________________________?
   B: Well, Ankara is the capital of Turkey. It's very old.
   A: ________________________?
   B: My last name is Ganim.

4. **A:** Good morning, Luke.
   ________________________?
   B: I'm great, thanks.
   A: Cool. ________________________?
   B: They're my friends from school.
   A: ________________________?
   B: They're from Miami, like me.

B **PAIR WORK** Write six Wh-questions about your partner and six Wh-questions about your partner's best friend. Then ask and answer the questions.

Your partner	Your partner's best friend
Where are you from?	Who's your best friend?

8 GRAMMAR FOCUS

Learning Objective: ask and answer Wh-questions with *be*

[CD 1, Track 39]

- Books closed. Write these questions and answers on the board:

  What's this? It's my tablet.
  Where are you from? I'm from Brazil.
  Who's that? She's my sister.
  How old is she? She's 28.

  Use these examples to review the meanings of the Wh-words.
- Books open. Focus Ss' attention on the Grammar Focus box. Play the audio program. Ss listen and read silently.
- Play the audio program again. Ss listen and repeat.

A

- Explain the task and focus Ss' attention on the four pictures. Point out that each picture goes with a different short conversation.
- Copy the first four lines of the first conversation on the board. Elicit the missing question and write it on the blank line.
- Ss complete the task individually. Go around the class and give help as needed. Encourage Ss to use the Grammar Focus box and to use contractions.
- Elicit the answers from the class and write them on the board.

Answers

1. A: Look! **Who's that**?
   B: Oh, she's a new student.
   A: **What's/What is her name**?
   B: I think her name is Yoo-jin.
   A: Yoo-jin? **Where's/Where is she from**?
   B: She's from South Korea.
2. A: Hi, Brittany. **How are you**?/**How are you doing**?
   B: I'm fine, thanks. My friend Leandro is here this week – from Argentina.
   A: Oh, cool. **What's/What is he like**?
   B: He's really friendly.
   A: **How old is he**?
   B: He's twenty-five years old.
3. A: Azra, **where are you from**?
   B: I'm from Turkey. From Ankara.
   A: **What's/What is Ankara/it like**?
   B: Well, Ankara is the capital of Turkey. It's very old.
   A: **What's/What is your last name**?
   B: My last name is Ganim.
4. A: Good morning, Luke. **How are you**?/**How are you doing**?
   B: I'm great, thanks.
   A: Cool. **Who are they**?
   B: They're my friends from school.
   A: **Where are they from**?
   B: They're from Miami, like me.

- Model the first conversation line by line. Ss listen and repeat. Then they practice it in pairs. Repeat with the other three conversations.

B *Pair work*

- Explain the first part of the task. Then read the example questions. To explain *best friend*, draw three stick figures on the board and write My friends over them. Circle one figure and write #1 under it. Say: "This is my best friend."
- Elicit one or two more questions from the class.
- ***Option***: Ss write two or three additional Wh-questions.

TIP
If higher-level Ss finish early or want to do more, give them an extra task.

- Ss write their questions individually. Go around the class and give help as needed. Write an ✗ next to the questions that have grammar mistakes. Encourage Ss to correct the mistakes themselves or with help from their classmates.

TIP
To help Ss become actively engaged in their learning, encourage them to correct their own mistakes.

- Elicit questions from the class and write them on the board.
- Explain the second part of the task and model it with a S. Ask the questions on the board. The S answers them.
- Ss complete the task in pairs. Go around the class and give help as needed.
- ***Option***: Ss exchange questions. Then they ask a new partner the questions.

9 WORD POWER

Learning Objective: use adjectives to describe people's personalities and appearance

A ***[CD 1, Track 40]***

- Focus Ss' attention on the picture and the words. Elicit or explain any new vocabulary. Point out that we usually use *pretty* for women and *handsome* for men. We use the other adjectives for men or women.
- Play the audio program. Ss repeat.

B ***Pair work***

- Explain the first part of the task. Elicit other words that describe personality (e.g., *smart*) and appearance (e.g., *beautiful*, *cute*).
- Ss complete the chart individually. Then ask two Ss to write their answers on the board.

Answers

Personality

talkative	quiet
friendly	serious
kind	shy
funny	

Appearance

pretty	tall
handsome	heavy
good-looking	thin
short	

- Explain and model the second part of the task. Ask a S to read the example sentence. Then describe your own personality and appearance.
- Ss describe their personality and appearance in pairs.

10 LISTENING

Learning Objective: develop skills listening for context clues

[CD 1, Track 41]

- Explain the task. Ss listen to three short conversations. They check (✓) the words that describe each person.
- Play the audio program once or twice. Ss listen and complete the chart individually.
- Ss check their answers in pairs. Go around the class and encourage them to use complete sentences (e.g., *Nora's not talkative. She's quiet.*)
- Go over the answers with the class. Play the audio program again if needed.

Audio script

1.
Man 1 Wow! Who's that?
Woman 1 Who? The tall guy?
Man 1 No. The very good-looking girl over there.
Woman 1 Oh, that's Nora.
Man 1 Is she talkative?
Woman 1 No, she isn't. She's really quiet. But she's very nice.

2.
Woman 2 My new classmate's name is Taylor.
Man 2 Oh, cool. What's Taylor like?
Woman 2 Oh, very funny.
Man 2 Nice. And is she good-looking?
Woman 2 Yes, *he* is.
Man 2 *He*? Is Taylor a guy?
Woman 2 Yes, he is. Sorry!

3.
Woman 3 Who's that short guy over there?
Woman 4 That's my brother, Austin.
Woman 3 He's very talkative.
Woman 4 Yes, he really is.
Woman 3 Is he serious?
Woman 4 Austin? Oh, no. But he's really funny.

Answers

1. Nora: pretty, quiet
2. Taylor: funny, handsome
3. Austin: short, talkative

11 INTERCHANGE 3

See page T-118 for teaching notes.

End of Cycle 2

See the Supplementary Resources chart at the beginning of this unit for additional teaching materials and student activities related to this Cycle.

9 WORD POWER Describing people

A Listen and practice.

a. pretty
b. handsome
c. good-looking
d. talkative
e. friendly
f. kind
g. funny
h. quiet
i. serious
j. shy
k. short
l. tall
m. heavy
n. thin

B **PAIR WORK** Complete the chart with words from part A. Add two more words to each list. Then describe your personality and appearance to a partner.

Personality			Appearance		
talkative			pretty		

"I'm tall, friendly, and very talkative."

10 LISTENING Wow! Who's that?

Listen to three descriptions. Check (✓) the two correct words for each description.

1. Nora is . . .	2. Taylor is . . .	3. Austin is . . .
☐ tall	☐ funny	☐ short
☐ pretty	☐ pretty	☐ serious
☐ quiet	☐ handsome	☐ talkative
☐ talkative	☐ serious	☐ tall

11 INTERCHANGE 3 Let's talk!

Talk to your classmates. Go to Interchange 3 on page 118.

Unit 4 Supplementary Resources Overview

	After the following SB exercises	You can use these materials in class	Your students can use these materials outside the classroom
CYCLE 1	1 **Word Power**	**TSS** Unit 4 Extra Worksheet	**GAME** Spell or Slime (Clothes)
	2 **Speaking**		**SS** Unit 4 Vocabulary 1 **GAME** Name the Picture (Colors and clothes)
	3 **Pronunciation**		
	4 **Conversation**		**SS** Unit 4 Speaking 1
	5 **Grammar Focus**		**SB** Unit 4 Grammar plus, Focus 1 **SS** Unit 4 Grammar 1 **GAME** Sentence Runner (Possessives)
	6 **Listening**		**WB** Unit 4 exercises 1–4
CYCLE 2	7 **Snapshot**		**SS** Unit 4 Vocabulary 2
	8 **Conversation**		**SS** Unit 4 Speaking 2
	9 **Grammar Focus**	**TSS** Unit 4 Vocabulary Worksheet **TSS** Unit 4 Grammar Worksheet	**SB** Unit 4 Grammar plus, Focus 2 **SS** Unit 4 Grammar 2–4 **GAME** Say the Word (Present continuous statements; conjunctions)
	10 **Listening**	**TSS** Unit 4 Listening Worksheet	
	11 **Interchange 4**	**TSS** Unit 4 Project Worksheet **VID** Unit 4 **VRB** Unit 4	**SS** Unit 4 Reading 1–2 **SS** Unit 4 Listening 1–3 **SS** Unit 4 Video 1–3 **WB** Unit 4 exercises 5–8

With or instead of the following SB section	You can also use these materials for assessment
Units 3–4 Progress Check	**ASSESSMENT PROGRAM** Units 3–4 Oral Quiz **ASSESSMENT PROGRAM** Units 3–4 Written Quiz

Key **GAME:** Online Game **SB:** Student's Book **SS:** Online Self-study **TSS:** Teacher Support Site
VID: Video DVD **VRB:** Video Resource Book **WB:** Online Workbook/Workbook

My Plan for Unit 4

Use the space below to customize a plan that fits your needs.

With the following SB exercises	I am using these materials in class	My students are using these materials outside the classroom

With or instead of the following SB section	I am using these materials for assessment

4 Is this coat yours?

- Discuss work and free-time clothes; colors
- Discuss the weather and what people are wearing

1 WORD POWER Clothes

A Listen and practice.

B Complete the chart with words from part A.

Clothes for warm weather	Clothes for cold weather

C **PAIR WORK** Look around the classroom. What clothes do you see? Tell a partner.

"I see jeans, a sweater, boots, and . . ."

4 Is this coat yours?

Cycle 1, Exercises 1–6

In Unit 4, students discuss work and free-time clothes, colors, and the weather and what people are wearing. By the end of Cycle 1, students will be able to discuss work and free-time clothes and colors using possessive adjectives, possessive pronouns, and possessives with names. By the end of Cycle 2, students will be able to discuss the weather and what people are wearing using the present continuous and conjunctions.

1 WORD POWER

Learning Objective: identify and describe clothes

A *[CD 1, Track 42]*

- Focus Ss' attention on the pictures.
- Play the audio program. Ss listen and read silently. Elicit or explain the meaning of *clothes for work* and *clothes for free time*. Point out which clothes are usually worn by women, which clothes are usually worn by men, and which clothes can be worn by both men and women.
- Play the program again. Ss listen and repeat.
- Read out the names of different clothes in the pictures. Ss point to the clothes.
- ***Option:*** Elicit names of other clothes from the class and write the words on the board. Model the pronunciation. Ss repeat.

TIP
To avoid overwhelming Ss with too much new vocabulary, present the words on the page and limit the number of extra words you teach each day.

- ***Option***: Books closed. Ask: "Who is wearing (a blouse)?" Ss wearing (a blouse) stand up or raise their hands.

B

- Explain the task. Elicit the names of one or two clothing items for warm weather. Then elicit the names of one or two clothing items for cold weather.
- Point out that some clothes can go in both columns.
- Ss complete the chart individually. Then they compare answers in pairs or small groups.
- Elicit answers from the class. Ask two Ss to write the answers on the board.

Possible answers

Clothes for warm weather	Clothes for cold weather
cap	hat
T-shirt	scarf
shorts	sweater
sneakers	coat
swimsuit	gloves
	boots

C *Pair work*

- Demonstrate the activity by indicating several clothing items that Ss are wearing.
- Ss complete the task in pairs. Then elicit answers from the class.

TIP
To regularly review vocabulary, make it part of your teaching routine. For example, start each class with a vocabulary game or warm-up activity.

For more practice with clothing vocabulary, play ***Kim's Game*** – download it from the website. Ss look at pictures of people wearing different clothes. Then they list the clothes from memory.

2 SPEAKING

Learning Objective: identify colors

A [CD 1, Track 43]

- Focus Ss' attention on the colors. Then play the audio program. Ss listen and read silently.
- Play the audio program again. Ss listen and repeat.
- ***Option***: Point to different clothes and other objects in the classroom. Ask: "What color is this? What color are these?" Elicit answers from the class.

B *Group work*

- Explain the task and model the example conversation with a S. Ss repeat. Then ask different pairs of Ss to model the conversation.
- Ss complete the task in small groups.
- Elicit names of Ss who like different colors. Ask: "Is your favorite blue? green?"

C *Group work*

- Focus Ss' attention on Exercise 1 on page 22. Explain the task. Hold up your book and point to the suit. Read the first statement. Then point to the socks and read the second statement.
- Read the statements again. Ss repeat.
- Ss complete the task in small groups. Go around the class and give help as needed.
- Elicit descriptions from the class.
- Option: Write 10 colors on the board. Ss work in teams to find two items of each color. They can look in the Student's Book or in the classroom. The first team to find two objects of each color wins.

3 PRONUNCIATION

Learning Objective: sound more natural when saying words with *s* and *sh*

A [CD 1, Track 44]

- Elicit words that begin with *s* or *sh*. Write them in two columns on the board.
- Play the audio program. Ss listen and read silently.
- Play the audio program again. Ss listen and repeat.

B

- Explain the task. Read the sentences slowly. Ss listen and repeat. Then ask different Ss to read the sentences aloud.
- ***Option:*** Ss write their own sentences with the letters *s* and *sh*. Then they read their sentences in pairs.
- ***Option:*** Write this tongue twister on the board:

  She sells seashells by the seashore.

  Explain the meaning of any new words. Point out that this sentence is difficult for native English speakers to say quickly. Then Ss practice reading the tongue twister in pairs.

4 CONVERSATION

Learning Objective: use possessive adjectives and pronouns in a conversation about clothing and colors

[CD 1, Track 45]

- Focus Ss' attention on the picture and set the scene. Ashley and Jessica are doing laundry at home.
- Write these focus questions on the board:

  1. *What clothes are they talking about?*
  2. *What colors are the clothes?*
- Play the audio program. Then elicit answers to the focus questions. (Answers: 1. a blouse, jeans 2. blue)
- Elicit or explain any new vocabulary.

Vocabulary
dry: not wet
disaster: a very bad event
problem: something that causes difficulty

- Ask the class: "What's the disaster? What's the problem?" Play the audio program. Ss listen and read silently. Then elicit the answers. (Answers: All their clothes are blue. The problem is the blue jeans.)
- Play the audio program again. Ss listen and repeat, line by line. Then they practice the conversation in pairs. Go around the class and give help as needed.
- ***Option:*** Ask one or two pairs to role-play the conversation for the class.

2 SPEAKING Colors

A Listen and practice.

white	light gray	gray
dark gray	beige	light brown
brown	dark brown	black

B **GROUP WORK** Ask about favorite colors.

A: What are your favorite colors?
B: My favorite colors are orange and dark blue.

C **GROUP WORK** Describe the clothes in Exercise 1.

A: The suit is black.
B: The socks are dark blue.

3 PRONUNCIATION The letters *s* and *sh*

A Listen and practice. Notice the pronunciation of **s** and **sh**.

suit	**s**ocks	**s**wimsuit
shirt	**sh**orts	**sh**oes

B Read the sentences. Pay attention to the pronunciation of **s** and **sh**.

1. This is Jo**sh**ua's new **s**uit.
2. These are **S**arah's purple **sh**oes!
3. Where are my **sh**oes and **socks**?
4. My **sh**orts and T-**sh**irts are blue!

4 CONVERSATION Whose jeans are these?

Listen and practice.

Ashley Great! Our clothes are dry.

Jessica Hey, where is my new blouse?

Ashley What color is your blouse? Is this yours?

Jessica No, this blouse is blue. Mine is white. Wait! It *is* mine. My white blouse is . . . blue!

Ashley Oh, no! Look. It's a disaster! *All* our clothes are blue . . .

Jessica Here's the problem. It's these blue jeans. Whose jeans are these? Are they yours?

Ashley Uh, yes, they're mine. Sorry.

5 GRAMMAR FOCUS

Possessives

Adjectives	Pronouns	Names	
my	**mine.**	**Jack's** tie.	s = /s/
your	**yours.**	**Taylor's** shoes.	s = /z/
These are **his** shoes.	These shoes are **his.**	**Alex's** coat.	s = /ɪz/
her	**hers.**		
our	**ours.**	**Whose** tie is this? It's **Greg's.**	
their	**theirs.**	**Whose** shoes are these? They're **Taylor's.**	

GRAMMAR PLUS *see page 135*

A Complete the conversations with the correct words in parentheses. Then practice with a partner.

1. **A:** This isn't ___my___ (my / mine) raincoat. Is it ________ (your / yours)?
   B: No, it's not ________ (my / mine). Ask Emma. Maybe it's ________ (her / hers).
2. **A:** Hey! These aren't ________ (our / ours) sneakers!
   B: You're right. ________ (Our / Ours) are over there.
3. **A:** Are these ________ (your / yours) gloves, Erin?
   B: No, they're not ________ (my / mine). Maybe they are Logan's. ________ (His / Your) gloves are gray.
4. **A:** ________ (Whose / Yours) T-shirts are these? Are they Hayley's and Brad's?
   B: No, they're not ________ (their / theirs) T-shirts. ________ (Their / Theirs) are white, not blue.

B **CLASS ACTIVITY** Put one of your things in a box. Then choose a different thing from the box. Go around the class and find the owner.

A: Laura, are these sunglasses yours?
B: No, they're not mine. Maybe they're Joon-ho's.

C: Wei, is this your pen?
D: Yes, it is.

6 LISTENING Her sneakers are purple.

A Listen to someone describe six people. Number the pictures from 1 to 6 in the order you hear them.

☐ Alicia

☐ 1 Sarah

☐ Andrea

☐ Amanda

☐ Cody

☐ Kyle

B **PAIR WORK** Now talk about the people. What colors are their clothes?

A: What color is Alicia's jacket?
B: It's beige.

5 GRAMMAR FOCUS

Learning Objective: use possessive adjectives, possessive pronouns, and possessives with names

[CD 1, Track 46]

Possessives

- Focus Ss' attention on the possessive adjectives in the first column of the Grammar Focus box.
- Hold up your book and say: "This is *my* book." Indicate a nearby S's book and say: "This is *your* book." Continue with the remaining possessive adjectives.
- Focus Ss' attention on the possessive pronouns in the second column of the Grammar Focus box. Hold up your book and say: "This book is *mine*." Continue with the remaining possessive pronouns.
- Play the audio program for the first and second columns. Ss listen and read silently.
- Focus Ss' attention on the third column. Point out that names are made possessive by adding *'s*. The pronunciation follows the same pronunciation rules as plural -s endings. Refer Ss to Unit 2, Exercise 4. Point out that *whose* means "what person's."
- Play the audio program for the third column.

A

- Explain the first part of the task and model the first short conversation with a S.
- Ss complete the task individually or in pairs. Then ask different Ss to write the short conversations on the board. Go over the answers as a class.

Answers

1. A: This isn't **my** raincoat. Is it **yours**?
   B: No, it's not **mine**. Ask Emma. Maybe it's **hers**.
2. A: Hey! These aren't **our** sneakers!
   B: You're right. **Ours** are over there.
3. A: Are these **your** gloves, Erin?
   B: No, they're not **mine**. Maybe they are Logan's. **His** gloves are gray.
4. A: **Whose** T-shirts are these? Are they Haley's and Brad's?
   B: No, they're not **their** T-shirts. **Theirs** are white, not blue.

- Explain the second part of the task. Ss practice the conversations in pairs.

B *Class activity*

- Explain the task. Then ask four Ss to read the example conversation.
- Ss put things (e.g., a watch, glasses, a pen) in a box or bag. Then they choose a different thing.
- Ss go around the class and find the owners. When they find the owner, they sit down.

6 LISTENING

Learning Objective: listen for details in a short conversation about clothing and colors

A *[CD 1, Track 47]*

- Explain the task. Play the first part of the audio program. Ask Ss to identify number 1 (Answer: Sarah)
- Play the audio program. Ss number the boxes.
- Go over answers with the class.

Audio script

Announcer Welcome to Fashion Week Fashion. Let's see some cool fashion!
Number one is in a beautiful black blouse. Her skirt is blue, and her black high heels are from Italy. Thank you, number one.
And here's number two. Her skirt is black, her blouse is blue, and her blue high heels are Japanese. Looking good!
Say hello to number three. His suit is light gray, his tie is dark green, and his shoes are brown.
Now for number four, handsome in a dark gray suit. He has a light green tie, and his shoes are black. Well done!
Let's welcome number five. Her cap is green, and she has a beige jacket. Her jeans are blue, and her sneakers are purple. Very nice!
Last up is pretty number six with purple sneakers and blue jeans. Her jacket is dark brown, and her cap is red. Wonderful, number six!

Answers

1. Sarah	3. Kyle	5. Alicia
2. Amanda	4. Cody	6. Andrea

B *Pair work*

- Explain the task and model the example conversation with a S.
- Ss complete the task in pairs.

End of Cycle 1

See the Supplementary Resources chart at the beginning of this unit for additional teaching materials and student activities related to this Cycle.

7 SNAPSHOT

Learning Objective: discuss the seasons and the weather

[CD 1, Track 48]

- Focus Ss' attention on the pictures.
- Play the audio program. Ss listen and read silently.
- Play the audio program again. Ss listen and repeat.
- ***Option:*** Focus Ss' attention on the thermometers. Elicit or explain the difference between *Fahrenheit* and *Celsius*. Elicit the temperatures in each picture.
- Read the focus questions aloud. Ss discuss the questions in small groups. If possible, put Ss from different countries and/or cities in each group.
- Elicit answers from the class. Write their answers on the board.

TIP
If your writing is hard to read, use capital letters or draw lines on the board to keep your writing straight.

- ***Option:*** If Ss come from countries with seasons that don't match the photos in the Snapshot, elicit or teach words that do (e.g., *rainy season, monsoon season*).
- ***Option:*** Ss work in pairs. They label the colors and objects in the pictures. Set a five-minute time limit. Then elicit the answers. Ss get one point for each correct answer.

! For a new way to practice seasons and weather, try ***Vocabulary Steps*** – download it from the website. Ss rank their favorite seasons and weather.

8 CONVERSATION

Learning Objective: use the present continuous in a short conversation about clothing and weather

[CD 1, Track 49]

- Focus Ss' attention on Exercise 4 on page 23. Write these questions on the board:

  1. Who are they?
  2. Where are they?

  Elicit the answers. (Answers: Ashley and Jessica; at home)
- Focus Ss' attention on Exercise 8 on page 25. Set the scene. Ashley and Jessica are leaving a store. Ask these questions and write them on the board:

  1. Which one is Ashley? What is she wearing?
  2. Which one is Jessica? What is she wearing?
  3. What's the weather like?
  4. What season is it?

  Elicit answers from the class. (Possible answers: 1. She's the woman on the right. She's wearing pants, shoes, and a jacket. 2. She's the woman on the left. She's wearing a hat, gloves, a scarf, a coat, jeans, and boots. 3. It's snowing. It's cold and windy. 4. It's winter.)
- Play the audio program. Ss listen and read silently. Elicit or explain the meaning of any new vocabulary. Point out that *What's the matter?* means "What's the problem?"
- Play the audio program again. Ss listen and repeat. Encourage Ss to try to copy the speakers' intonation.
- Ss practice the conversation in pairs. Go around the class and give help as needed.

TIP
If some Ss find practicing the conversation too easy, make the task more challenging. For example, they can role-play the conversation from memory, continue the conversation, or focus on their pronunciation.

- ***Option***: Ask one or two pairs to role-play the conversation for the class.

! For a new way to practice this conversation, try ***Moving Dialog*** – download it from the website.

7 SNAPSHOT

Listen and practice.

WEATHER AND SEASONS AROUND THE WORLD

It's spring in São Paulo, Brazil.
It's warm. It's very sunny.

It's summer in Seoul, South Korea.
It's raining. It's hot and humid.

It's fall in Chicago in the U.S.
It's cool. It's cloudy and windy.

It's winter in Toronto, Canada.
It's snowing. It's very cold.

What season is it now in your town or city? What's the weather like today?
What's your favorite season?

8 CONVERSATION Are you wearing your gloves?

Listen and practice.

Ashley Oh, no!
Jessica What's the matter?
Ashley It's snowing! Wow, it's so cold and windy!
Jessica Are you wearing your gloves?
Ashley No, I'm not. They're at home.
Jessica What about your scarf?
Ashley It's at home, too.
Jessica Well, you're wearing your coat.
Ashley But my coat isn't very warm. And I'm not wearing boots!
Jessica OK. Let's take a taxi.
Ashley Good idea!

9 GRAMMAR FOCUS

Present continuous statements; conjunctions

I**'m**	I**'m not**	OR:
You**'re**	You**'re not**	You **aren't**
She**'s wearing shoes.**	She**'s not**	She **isn't wearing boots.**
We**'re**	We**'re not**	We **aren't**
They**'re**	They**'re not**	They **aren't**
It**'s snowing.**	It**'s not**	It **isn't raining.**

Conjunctions

It's snowing, **and** it's windy.
It's sunny, **but** it's cold.
It's windy, **so** it's very cold.

GRAMMAR PLUS *see page 135*

A Complete these sentences from a travel show on TV. Then compare with a partner.

1

My name is Dylan Jones. I *'m wearing* a new gray suit. I ______________ new black shoes, too. It's raining, but I ______________ ______________ a raincoat.

2

It's very hot and sunny today. Michael ______________ light blue shorts and white sneakers. He ______________ a white T-shirt, but he ______________ a cap.

3

Adriana Fuentes is from Mexico. She ______________ a pretty yellow dress and a brown belt. She ______________ high heels and a light brown jacket, but she ______________ a coat. Wow, it's really windy!

4

Hee-sun and Kun-woo are here with me today. They're 10 years old. It's really cold, so they ______________ winter clothes. They ______________ boots, gloves, hats, and scarves. And they ______________ heavy coats!

9 GRAMMAR FOCUS

Learning Objectives: use present continuous statements and the conjunctions *and*, *but*, and *so*; use present continuous yes/no questions and adjective + noun

[CD 1, Track 50]

Present continuous statements

- Focus Ss' attention on the left side of the Grammar Focus box. Explain that we use the present continuous to talk about actions that are happening now.
- Focus Ss' attention on the first column in the Grammar Focus box. Elicit or explain the pattern for positive present continuous statements: Subject + *be* + verb + *-ing*.
- Focus Ss' attention on the second column in the Grammar Focus box. Elicit or explain the pattern for negative present continuous statements: Subject + *be* + *not* + verb + *-ing*.
- Point out that the contractions in the second column have the same meaning as the contractions in the first column.
- Play the audio program for the left side of the Grammar Focus box. Ss listen and read silently.
- ***Option:*** Ask Ss to underline the present continuous statements in the Conversation on page 25. Then elicit the answers. (Answers: It's snowing. Well, you're wearing your coat. And I'm not wearing boots!)

Conjunctions

- Focus Ss' attention on the right side of the Grammar Focus box. Point out that we use the conjunction *and* to join two similar sentences. We use the conjunction *but* to join two contrasting sentences. We use *so* to indicate that we're adding a consequence or result. Elicit or explain that we use a comma in these sentence.
- Play the audio program for the right side of the Grammar Focus box. Ss listen and read silently.

TIP

To help explain general grammar concepts, teach your Ss common terms such as *subjects*, *verbs*, and *contractions*.

A

- Explain the first part of the task. Read the first two sentences in item 1 to model the task.
- ***Option:*** For lower-level classes, point out that the verb for all answers is *wear*.
- Ss complete the task individually. Go around the class to give help and encourage Ss to use contractions.
- Ss compare their sentences in pairs. Then ask different Ss to write the answers on the board. Go over the answers with the class.

Answers

1. My name is Dylan Jones. I**'m wearing** a new gray suit. I**'m wearing** new black shoes, too. It's raining, but I**'m not wearing** a raincoat.
2. It's very hot and sunny today. Michael **is wearing** light blue shorts and white sneakers. He**'s wearing** a white T-shirt, but he **isn't wearing** a cap.
3. Adriana Fuentes is from Mexico. She**'s wearing** a pretty yellow dress and a brown belt. She**'s wearing** high heels and a light brown jacket, but she **isn't wearing** a coat. Wow, it's really windy!
4. Hee-sun and Kun-woo are here with me today. They're 10 years old. It's really cold, so they**'re wearing** winter clothes. They**'re wearing** boots, gloves, hats, and scarves. And they**'re wearing** heavy coats!

- ***Option:*** Ss work in pairs. They take turns reading the sentences aloud. Go around the class and help Ss with pronunciation.

For more practice with clothing and the present continuous, play ***Change Chairs*** – download it from the website.

[CD 1, Track 51]

Present continuous yes/no questions

- Focus Ss' attention on the Grammar Focus box. Explain the pattern for present continuous yes/no questions:

  Be + subject + verb + *-ing*?

  Point out that the contractions *she's not* and *she isn't* and *they're not* and *they aren't* have the same meaning.
- Play the audio program for the Grammar Focus box. Ss listen and read silently.

Adjective + noun

- Focus Ss' attention on the Adjective + noun box. Point out the positions of the adjectives and nouns in the sentences. Read the text aloud. Ss listen and read silently.

B *Pair work*

- Explain the task and model the example conversation with a S. Then Ss complete the task in pairs.
- Ask different pairs of Ss to read the questions and answers. Correct any incorrect answers as a class.

Answers

1. Yes, he is.
2. No, he's not./No, he isn't.
3. Yes, he is.
4. No, he is not./No, he isn't.
5. Yes, he is.
6. No, he's not./No, he isn't.
7. No, she's not./No, she isn't.
8. Yes, she is.
9. Yes, she is.
10. No, they're not./No, they aren't.
11. Yes, they are.
12. No, they're not./No, they aren't.

C

- Ss write four new questions individually. Then they ask and answer the questions in pairs.

10 LISTENING

Learning Objective: listen for main ideas about what people are wearing

A *[CD 1, Track 52]*

- Set the scene. Kayla and John are at a party. They are talking about other people's clothes. Then explain the task and go over the pronunciation of the names.
- Play the audio program once or twice. Ss listen and complete the task. Then elicit the answers.

Audio script

John	Hi, Kayla! Great to see you!
Kayla	Hi, John.
John	That's a beautiful dress. You look great in pink.
Kayla	Thanks. You look good, too. Your brown jacket is really nice. And that's a cool cap.
John	Thanks!
Kayla	So, who's here?
John	Hmm. Let's see. Well, there's Ryan. He's really nice.
Kayla	Where's Ryan?
John	He's over there. He's wearing black jeans and a light green T-shirt.
Kayla	Who's Ryan with?
John	The woman in the orange blouse and white skirt? That's Amber.
Kayla	Amber?
John	Yeah. She's very funny. She's friends with Robert.
Kayla	Where's Robert?
John	He's wearing a shirt and tie. He's talking to Brittany. She's wearing . . .
Kayla	What's the matter, John?
John	Well, she's wearing a pink dress, too. Um, it looks like yours.

Answers

Kayla, John, Robert, Brittany, Ryan, Amber

B *Group work*

- Explain the task and model the conversation with two Ss. Then Ss ask questions in small groups.

C *Group work*

- Ss write five questions individually. Then they ask and answer the questions in small groups.

11 INTERCHANGE 4

See pages T-116 and T-117 for teaching notes.

End of Cycle 2

See the Supplementary Resources chart at the beginning of this unit for additional teaching materials and student activities related to this Cycle and for assessment tools.

Present continuous yes/no questions

Are you **wearing** gloves?	Yes, I **am**.	No, I**'m not**.
Is she **wearing** boots?	Yes, she **is**.	No, she**'s not**./No, she **isn't**.
Are they **wearing** sunglasses?	Yes, they **are**.	No, they**'re not**./No, they **aren't**.

B PAIR WORK Ask and answer these questions about the people in part A.

1. Is Dylan wearing a gray suit?
2. Is he wearing a raincoat?
3. Is he wearing black shoes?
4. Is Michael wearing jeans?
5. Is he wearing a T-shirt?
6. Is he wearing a cap?
7. Is Adriana wearing a skirt?
8. Is she wearing a jacket?
9. Is she wearing high heels?
10. Are Hee-sun and Kun-woo wearing swimsuits?
11. Are they wearing gloves and hats?
12. Are they wearing sneakers?

A: Is Dylan wearing a gray suit?
B: Yes, he is. Is he wearing a raincoat?
A: No, he's not. OR No, he isn't.

adjective + noun

My suit is **black**.
I'm wearing **a black suit**.

C Write four more questions about the people in part A. Then ask a partner the questions.

10 LISTENING You look great in pink.

A Listen. What are their names? Write the names **Brittany**, **Ryan**, **John**, **Robert**, **Kayla**, and **Amber** in the correct boxes.

B GROUP WORK Ask questions about the people in the picture.

A: Is John wearing a brown jacket?
B: Yes, he is.
C: Is he wearing a cap?

C GROUP WORK Write five questions about your classmates. Then ask and answer the questions.

Are Maria and Bruno wearing jeans?
Is Bruno wearing a red shirt?

11 INTERCHANGE 4 Celebrity fashions

What are your favorite celebrities wearing? Go to Interchange 4 on pages 116–117.

Units 3–4 Progress check

SELF-ASSESSMENT

How well can you do these things? Check (✓) the boxes.

I can . . .	Very well	OK	A little
Ask and answer questions about countries of origin, nationalities, and languages (Ex. 1)	☐	☐	☐
Understand descriptions of people (Ex. 2)	☐	☐	☐
Ask and answer questions about people's appearance and personality (Ex. 2, 5)	☐	☐	☐
Ask and answer questions about people's possessions (Ex. 3)	☐	☐	☐
Talk and write about my and other people's favorite things (Ex. 4)	☐	☐	☐
Ask and answer questions about what people are wearing (Ex. 5)	☐	☐	☐

1 SPEAKING Interview with my classmates

Match the questions with the answers. Then ask and answer the questions with a partner. Answer with your own information.

1. Are you from Argentina? __h__
2. Where are you and your family from? _____
3. What is your hometown like? _____
4. Is English your first language? _____
5. Who is your best friend? _____
6. How old is your best friend? _____
7. Is our teacher from the U.S.? _____
8. Are our classmates friendly? _____

a. It's very beautiful.
b. Yes, she is.
c. We're from Montevideo.
d. My best friend is Takuya.
e. Yes, they are.
f. No, it's not. It's Spanish.
g. He's nineteen.
h. No, I'm not. I'm from Uruguay.

2 LISTENING Where's your friend Jacob?

A Listen to four conversations. Check (✓) the correct description for each person. You will check more than one adjective.

1. Jacob
- ☐ tall
- ☐ short
- ☐ funny
- ☐ serious
- ☐ nice
- ☐ shy

2. Monica
- ☐ tall
- ☐ talkative
- ☐ pretty
- ☐ shy
- ☐ nice
- ☐ friendly

3. Hannah
- ☐ thin
- ☐ short
- ☐ quiet
- ☐ shy
- ☐ serious
- ☐ funny

4. Ki-nam
- ☐ tall
- ☐ short
- ☐ funny
- ☐ friendly
- ☐ talkative
- ☐ quiet

B Write five yes/no questions about the people in part A. Then ask a partner the questions.

Is Jacob tall?
Is Monica thin?

Units 3–4

Progress check

SELF-ASSESSMENT

Learning Objectives: reflect on one's learning; identify areas that need improvement

- Ask: "What did you learn in Units 3 and 4?" Elicit Ss' answers.
- Ss complete the Self-assessment. Explain to Ss that this is not a test; it is a way for them to evaluate what they've learned and identify areas where they need additional practice. Encourage them to be honest, and point out they will not get a bad grade if they check (✓) *A little*.
- Ss move on to the Progress check exercises. You can have Ss complete them in class or for homework, using one of these techniques:
  1. Ask Ss to complete all the exercises.
  2. Ask Ss: "What do you need to practice?" Then assign exercises based on their answers.
  3. Ask Ss to choose and complete exercises based on their Self-assessment.

1 SPEAKING

Learning Objective: demonstrate one's ability to ask and answer questions about countries of origin, nationalities, and languages

- Explain the first part of the task. Ask two Ss to read question 1 and the answer.
- Ss match the questions and answers individually. Then they compare answers in pairs.
- To check answers, ask different pairs of Ss to read the questions and answers.

Answers

1. h	3. a	5. d	7. b
2. c	4. f	6. g	8. e

- Explain the second part of the task. Ask a S to read question 1 to you. Then answer with your own information.
- Ss complete the task in pairs. Go around the class and give help as needed.

2 LISTENING

Learning Objective: demonstrate one's ability to understand descriptions of people

A *[CD 1, Track 53]*

- Explain the task. Then play the audio program. Ss complete the task.
- Play the audio program again. Ss listen and check their answers.
- Ss compare their answers in pairs. Play the audio program as many times as needed.
- To check answers, ask: "What's (Jacob) like?" Continue with the remaining names.

Audio script

1.
Woman Where's your friend Jacob?
Man He's over there.
Woman Is he that tall man?
Man No, Jacob is the short man with glasses.
Woman What's he like?
Man He's a little serious, but he's very nice.
2.
Woman What's Monica like?
Man Hmm. She's a little tall, and she's very talkative.
Woman Is she pretty?
Man Oh, yes. And she's very friendly.
3.
Woman What's your friend Hannah like?
Man She's very quiet and shy. And she's a little short.
Woman Is she really serious?
Man No, she's actually very funny.
4.
Woman Who's that?
Man Oh. That's my friend Ki-nam.
Woman Wow! He's really tall.
Man Yes. And he's very friendly and talkative.

Answers

1. Jacob: short, serious, nice
2. Monica: tall, talkative, pretty, friendly
3. Hannah: short, quiet, shy, funny
4. Ki-nam: tall, friendly, talkative

B

- Explain the task and model the example questions.
- Ss write their questions individually. Go around the class and give help as needed.
- Ss take turns asking and answering their questions in pairs.

3 SPEAKING

Learning Objective: demonstrate one's ability to discuss clothes and possessions

Class activity

- Set the scene. Ss imagine they are roommates with a messy room. They are looking for their clothes.
- Explain the first part of the task and focus Ss' attention on the pictures. Point out that the Ss' pictures can be very simple. If needed, draw very simple sketches on the board as examples.
- Ss draw pictures individually. Go around the class and make sure each picture is on a different piece of paper.
- Collect the pictures and put them in a bag or box. Then each S takes three pictures from the bag or box. Make sure Ss don't take their own pictures.
- Explain the second part of the task. Then ask two pairs of Ss to model the example conversations. Point out that when Ss find the owners, they should return the pictures.
- Ss perform the second part of the task. They continue until all Ss have their own pictures.

4 SPEAKING

Learning Objective: demonstrate one's ability to discuss and compare favorite seasons, colors, and clothes

A

- Explain the first part of the task and focus Ss' attention on the chart.
- Ss complete the *Me* column of the chart individually. Go around the class and help with vocabulary as needed.
- Explain the second part of the task.
- ***Option:*** For lower-level classes, elicit questions Ss can ask their partners:
  1. *What's your favorite season?*
  2. *What's your favorite color?*
  3. *What are your favorite clothes?*

  If needed, write them on the board.
- Ss complete the task in pairs. Go around the class and make sure Ss complete the *My partner* column of the chart.
- ***Option:*** Each pair joins another pair. Ss compare answers in small groups.

B

- Explain the task. Ask different Ss to model the example sentences. Remind Ss that *and* joins similar sentences, *but* joins contrasting sentences, and *so* adds a consequence or result.
- Ss write sentences individually. Go around the class and give help as needed.
- Elicit sentences from the class. Ask different Ss to write them on the board.

5 SPEAKING

Learning Objective: demonstrate one's ability to ask and answer questions about people's appearance and clothes

Group work

- Focus Ss' attention on the picture and explain the task. Ask four Ss to model the example conversation. Point out that Ss ask: "Is it . . . ?" when they don't know if the person is male or female.
- Ss play the game in small groups. Go around the class and encourage Ss to use short answers. The S who guesses correctly thinks of the next classmate.
- ***Option:*** For small classes, play this game as a class.

WHAT'S NEXT?

Learning Objective: become more involved in one's learning

- Focus Ss' attention on the Self-assessment again. Ask: "How well can you do these things now?"
- Ask Ss to underline one thing they need to review. Ask: "What did you underline? How can you review it?"
- If needed, plan additional instruction, activities, or reviews based on Ss' answers.

3 SPEAKING Are these your clothes?

CLASS ACTIVITY Draw three pictures of clothes on different pieces of paper. Then put the papers in a bag. Take three different papers, go around the class, and find the owners.

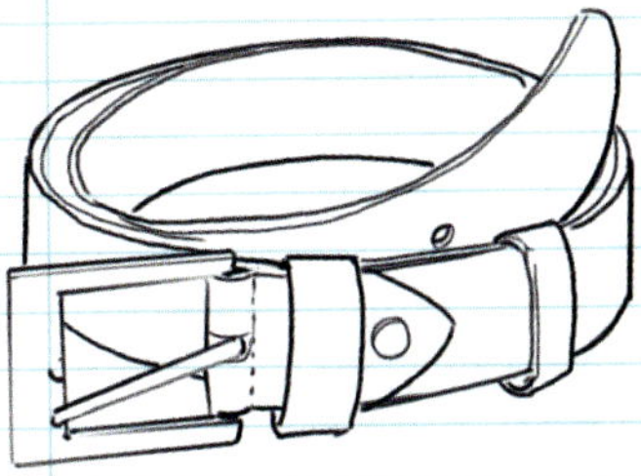

A: Anna, is this your belt?
B: No, it's not mine. Maybe it's Miki's.

A: Ji-hun, are these your sneakers?
C: Yes, they're mine. Thanks!

4 SPEAKING Similar or different?

A Write your favorite things in the chart. Then ask a partner about his or her favorite things. Write them in the chart.

Favorite	Me	My partner
1. season		
2. color		
3. clothes		

B Compare answers. What's the same? What's different? Write sentences.

Spring is my favorite season, and it's Mariana's favorite season. That's the same.
My favorite color is green, but Mariana's favorite color is red, so that's different.

5 SPEAKING I'm thinking of . . .

GROUP WORK Think of a student in the class. Your classmates ask yes/no questions to guess the student.

A: I'm thinking of a student in this class.
B: Is it a woman?
A: Yes, it is.
C: Is she short?
A: No, she isn't.
D: Is she wearing blue jeans?

WHAT'S NEXT?

Look at your Self-assessment again. Do you need to review anything?

Unit 5 Supplementary Resources Overview

	After the following SB exercises	You can use these materials in class	Your students can use these materials outside the classroom
CYCLE 1	1 Snapshot		**SS** Unit 5 Vocabulary 1
	2 Conversation		**SS** Unit 5 Speaking 1
	3 Grammar Focus		**SB** Unit 5 Grammar plus, Focus 1 **SS** Unit 5 Grammar 1–2 **GAME** Name the Picture (Time) **GAME** Sentence Stacker (Present continuous and time expressions)
	4 Listening		**WB** Unit 5 exercises 1–4
CYCLE 2	5 Conversation		**SS** Unit 5 Speaking 2
	6 Pronunciation		
	7 Grammar Focus		**SB** Unit 5 Grammar plus, Focus 2 **SS** Unit 5 Grammar 3 **GAME** Speak or Swim (Present continuous Wh-questions) **GAME** Sentence Runner (Present continuous questions)
	8 Word Power	**TSS** Unit 5 Vocabulary Worksheet **TSS** Unit 5 Grammar Worksheet **TSS** Unit 5 Listening Worksheet **TSS** Unit 5 Extra Worksheet	**SS** Unit 5 Vocabulary 2
	9 Interchange 5		
	10 Reading	**TSS** Unit 5 Project Worksheet **VID** Unit 5 **VRB** Unit 5	**SS** Unit 5 Reading 1–2 **SS** Unit 5 Listening 1–3 **SS** Unit 5 Video 1–3 **WB** Unit 5 exercises 5–9

Key **GAME:** Online Game **VID:** Video DVD **SB:** Student's Book **VRB:** Video Resource Book **SS:** Online Self-study **WB:** Online Workbook/Workbook **TSS:** Teacher Support Site

My Plan for Unit 5

Use the space below to customize a plan that fits your needs.

With the following SB exercises	I am using these materials in class	My students are using these materials outside the classroom

With or instead of the following SB section	I am using these materials for assessment

5 What time is it?

- Discuss cities and time zones
- Discuss people's activities

1 SNAPSHOT

Listen and practice.

Time Zones

Mexico City 10:00 A.M. | New York 11:00 A.M. | Dubai 7:00 P.M. | Seoul 12:00 A.M.

Is your city or town in the same time zone as one of these cities?
What other events or shows are on television in different time zones?

2 CONVERSATION It's two o'clock in the morning!

A Listen and practice.

Amar: Hello?

Brian: Hi, Amar! This is Brian. I'm calling from New York.

Amar: Brian? Wait. . . . Where are you?

Brian: I'm home on vacation, remember? I'm calling about the soccer game. Great game!

Amar: Oh, that's good. But what time is it there?

Brian: It's 2:00 P.M. And it's two o'clock in Australia, too. Right?

Amar: That's right – it's two o'clock in the morning!

Brian: 2:00 A.M.? Oh, of course! I'm really sorry.

Amar: That's OK. Congratulations on the game!

2:00 A.M.

2:00 P.M.

5 What time is it?

Cycle 1, Exercises 1–4

In Unit 5, students discuss cities, time zones, and people's activities. By the end of Cycle 1, students will be able to discuss cities and time zones using time expressions. By the end of Cycle 2, students will be able to discuss people's activities using the present continuous.

1 SNAPSHOT

Learning Objective: discuss cities and international time zones

[CD 1, Track 54]

- Focus Ss' attention on the pictures. Then play the audio program. Ss listen and repeat.
- Ask the first question. Elicit answers from the class.

TIP
To give all Ss a chance to answer questions, don't always call on the first Ss who raise their hands. Instead, give Ss time to think and wait until more Ss raise their hands.

- Ask the second question. Elicit answers from the class.
- ***Option:*** Bring atlases, world maps, or globes to class. Ss use them to answer the questions. Go over the pronunciation of additional cities as needed.
- ***Option:*** Ask: "Where are these cities?" Ss list the country for each city in pairs or small groups. Then elicit the answers. Ss get one point for each correct answer. (Answers: Mexico City, Mexico; New York, the United States; Dubai, United Arab Emirates; Seoul, South Korea)
- ***Option:*** Based on the time of day in each picture, have Ss guess what other types of television programs might be on in each city.

2 CONVERSATION

Learning Objective: use time expressions and times of day in a short conversation

[CD 1, Track 55]

- Books closed. Write these questions on the board:
  1. *Where is Brian?*
  2. *Where is Amar?*
- Play the audio program. Ss listen for the answers. Then elicit the answers from the class. (Answers: 1. New York 2. Australia)
- ***Option:*** Ask Ss to find New York and Australia on a world map or globe.
- Books open. Focus Ss' attention on the picture. Set the scene. Brian is at home on vacation in New York. Amar is in Australia. He's sleeping. Brian is calling Amar.
- Write these focus questions on the board:
  1. *Is it 2:00 P.M. in New York?*
  2. *Is it 2:00 A.M. in Australia?*

  Then play the audio program again. Ss listen for the answers. Elicit the answers. (Answers: 1. Yes 2. Yes)
- Elicit the meaning of any new vocabulary. Encourage Ss to guess.

Vocabulary
vacation: time off of work
Right?: Is this correct?
Congratulations: what you say when you are happy for someone's success

- Play the audio program again. Ss listen and repeat.
- Ss practice the conversation in pairs.
- ***Option:*** Ask one or two pairs to role-play the conversation for the class.

! For a new way to practice this conversation, try the ***Onion Ring*** technique – download it from the website.

3 GRAMMAR FOCUS

Learning Objectives: ask and answer questions using time expressions; use times of day

What time is it?

[CD 1, Track 56]

- Focus Ss' attention on the clocks. Play the audio program. Ss listen and read silently.
- Point out that *o'clock* is for exact hours only, not hours + minute. Point out the uses of *after* and *to*. Explain that five *after two* means "five minutes after two," and *a quarter after two* means "fifteen minutes after two."
- Play the audio program again. Ss listen and repeat.
- ***Option:*** Draw more clocks on the board with different times. Ask: "What time is it?" and elicit the answers. Elicit different ways of saying each time when possible.

A *Pair work*

- Explain the task and model the example conversation with a S.
- Ss complete the task in pairs. Encourage Ss to answer in different ways when possible.
- Elicit answers from the class.

TIP
To encourage quiet Ss to speak more loudly, don't walk closer to them and repeat their answers. Instead, move away from the Ss slowly and encourage them to speak louder so everyone can hear them.

Answers

1. It's ten (minutes) after ten./It's ten-ten.
2. It's one (minute) after six./It's six-oh-one.
3. It's ten (minutes) to six./It's five-fifty.
4. It's eight-thirty.
5. It's five (minutes) after nine./It's nine-oh-five.
6. It's twelve forty-five./It's a quarter to one.

- ***Option:*** Ask Ss to draw 10 clock faces on a piece of paper and number them. Then read a list of 10 different times aloud (e.g., *3:10, 6:30, 12:15, 4:40, 1:05, 2:25, 5:35, 11:50, 8:20, 5:30*). Ss draw the times on the clock faces. Then ask different Ss to draw the clocks on the board. Go over the answers as a class.

For more practice with times, play ***Concentration*** – download it from the website. Ss match cards with times (e.g., *4:00*) and cards with clock faces.

Is it A.M. or P.M.?

[CD 1, Track 57]

- Focus Ss' attention on the pictures. Point out that the place is the same, but the time of day is different. (Students may recognize the Golden Gate Bridge of San Francisco, in the U.S.)
- Play the audio program. Ss listen and read silently.
- Point out that *noon* is 12:00 P.M. and *midnight* is 12:00 A.M. Explain these guidelines for using the time expressions:

  1. in the morning = 1:00 A.M. to noon
  2. in the afternoon = noon to about 5:00 P.M.
  3. in the evening = about 5:00 P.M. to about 9:00 P.M.
  4. at night = about 7:00 P.M. to after midnight

- Tell Ss that *afternoon* has stress on the last syllable (after**noon**), but *morning* and *evening* have stress on the first syllable (**mor**ning, **eve**ning).
- Play the audio program again. Ss listen and repeat.

B *Pair work*

- Explain the task and model the example with a S:

  S: It's eight o'clock in the morning.
  T: It's 8:00 A.M.

- Ss complete the task in pairs. Then they change roles. Go around the class and check Ss' use of time expressions.

Answers

2. It's 3:00 P.M.
3. It's 6:00 P.M.
4. It's midnight.
5. It's ten (o'clock) in the morning.
6. It's four (o'clock) in the afternoon.
7. It's seven (o'clock) in the evening.
8. It's noon.

- ***Option:*** Ss underline the time expressions in the Conversation on page 30. Then elicit the answers. (Answers: But what time is it there?, It's <u>2:00 P.M.</u> / And it's <u>two o'clock</u> in Australia, too. / That's right - it's <u>two o'clock</u> in the morning! / <u>2:00 A.M.</u>?)

TIP
To raise Ss' awareness of a grammar structure's meaning and use, connect the Grammar Focus to the previous Conversation.

For more practice with A.M. and P.M., play ***Run For It!*** – download it from the website. Put signs with A.M. and P.M. on the walls and read out sentences with different time expressions.

3 GRAMMAR FOCUS

What time is it?

It's two **o'clock**.

It's two-oh-five.
It's five **after** two.

It's two-fifteen.
It's **a quarter after** two.

It's two-thirty.

It's two-forty.
It's twenty **to** three.

It's two forty-five.
It's **a quarter to** three.

GRAMMAR PLUS *see page 136*

A PAIR WORK Look at these clocks. What time is it?

1 

2 

3 

4 

5 

6 

A: What time is it?
B: It's ten after ten. OR It's ten-ten.

Is it A.M. or P.M.?

It's six (o'clock) **in the morning**.
It's 6:00 A.M.

It's twelve (o'clock).
It's 12:00 P.M.
It's **noon**.

It's four (o'clock) **in the afternoon**.
It's 4:00 P.M.

It's six (o'clock) **in the evening**.
It's 6:00 P.M.

It's nine (o'clock) **at night**.
It's 9:00 P.M.

It's twelve (o'clock) **at night**.
It's 12:00 A.M.
It's midnight.

GRAMMAR PLUS *see page 136*

B PAIR WORK Say each time a different way.

1. It's eight o'clock in the morning. *"It's 8:00 A.M."*
2. It's three o'clock in the afternoon.
3. It's six o'clock in the evening.
4. It's twelve o'clock at night.
5. It's 10:00 A.M.
6. It's 4:00 P.M.
7. It's 7:00 P.M.
8. It's 12:00 P.M.

4 LISTENING What time is it in Tokyo?

A Lauren and John are calling friends in different parts of the world. Listen. What time is it in these cities?

City	Time
Vancouver	4:00 P.M.
Bangkok	
London	
Tokyo	
São Paulo	

B Listen again. Check (✓) the correct answers.

1. Tanawat is . . . ☐ getting married. ☐ in São Paulo. ☐ sleeping.
2. Richard is . . . ☐ in London. ☐ in Bangkok. ☐ late.
3. Misaki is . . . ☐ in Tokyo. ☐ in Vancouver. ☐ watching TV.

5 CONVERSATION What are you doing?

Listen and practice.

JAY Hey, Kate!

KATE What are you doing?

JAY I'm cooking.

KATE I know, but why are you cooking now? It's three o'clock in the morning!

JAY I'm sorry, but I'm really hungry.

KATE Hmm . . . What are you making?

JAY Spaghetti.

KATE With tomato sauce?

JAY With tomato sauce and cheese.

KATE I love spaghetti! Uh . . . I'm getting hungry, too.

JAY Good. Let's eat!

6 PRONUNCIATION Rising and falling intonation

A Listen and practice. Notice the intonation of the yes/no and Wh-questions.

Is he cooking? ↗	What's he making? ↘
Are they sleeping?	What are they doing?

B Listen to the questions. Draw a rising arrow (↗) for rising intonation and a falling arrow (↘) for falling intonation.

1. ↗ 2. ______ 3. ______ 4. ______ 5. ______ 6. ______

4 LISTENING

Learning Objective: listen for specific information about times in a short conversation

A ***[CD 1, Track 58]***

- Explain the task and set the scene. Lauren and John are calling friends in different cities around the world.
- Play the audio program once or twice. Ss listen and complete the chart.

Audio script

Lauren	What time is it now, John?
John	It's four o'clock.
Lauren	OK. It's 4:00 P.M. here in Vancouver, so it's 7:00 A.M. in Bangkok. I'm calling Tanawat.
John	Now? He's sleeping!
Lauren	Oh, you're right. Well, let's call your friend Richard. What time is it in London?
John	It's 1:00 A.M.
Lauren	Oh, that's late. What time is it in Tokyo?
John	9:00 A.M.
Lauren	Great. I'm calling Misaki.
John	Wait a minute. She's in São Paulo this week. Remember?
Lauren	Oh, right. Well, I have her phone number in São Paulo.
John	What time is it there?
Lauren	Um . . . it's nine in the evening. . . . She's watching television, of course. She does that every evening.
John	So are you calling her?
Lauren	Sure. We have to tell someone we're getting married!

- Ss compare their answers in pairs. Elicit the answers and write the correct answers on the board. (Answers: Vancouver: 4:00 P.M., Bangkok: 7:00 A.M., London: 1:00 A.M., Tokyo: 9:00 A.M., São Paulo: 9:00 P.M.)

B ***[CD 1, Track 59]***

- Explain that Ss will listen to the conversation again and check the correct answers in the chart.
- ***Option:*** Have Ss try to complete the chart from memory. Then play the audio to check their answers.
- Play the audio program once or twice. Ss listen and complete the chart.
- Ss read the answers aloud: 1. Tanawat is **sleeping**. 2. Richard is in **London**. 3. Misaki is **watching TV**.

End of Cycle 1

See the Supplementary Resources chart at the beginning of this unit for additional teaching materials and student activities related to this Cycle.

Cycle 2, Exercises 5–10

5 CONVERSATION

Learning Objective: use present continuous Wh-questions in a conversation about someone's activities

[CD 1, Track 60]

- Books closed. Ask these focus questions: "What time is it? What is Jay doing?"
- Play the audio program. Then elicit the answers from the class. (Answers: 3:00 A.M., cooking)
- Books open. Focus Ss' attention on the picture and elicit or explain any new vocabulary.
- Play the audio program again. Ss listen and read silently.
- Play the audio program again. Ss listen and repeat. Then they practice the conversation in pairs.

6 PRONUNCIATION

Learning Objective: sound more natural when asking yes/no and Wh-questions with rising and falling intonation

A ***[CD 1, Track 61]***

- Explain the task and focus Ss' attention on the arrows. Point out that yes/no questions have rising intonation and Wh-questions have falling intonation.
- Play the audio program. Ss listen and read silently. Play the audio program again. Ss listen and repeat.

B ***[CD 1, Track 62]***

- Play the first question and model the task.
- Play the audio program. Ss complete the task individually.

Audio script

1. Are you wearing a coat?
2. What are you doing now?
3. What time is it?
4. Is it midnight?
5. What color is his T-shirt?
6. Are you from Thailand?

- Play the audio program again to check answers.

Answers

1. ↗ 2. ↘ 3. ↘ 4. ↗ 5. ↘ 6. ↗

7 GRAMMAR FOCUS

Learning Objectives: ask and answer present continuous Wh-questions; use the conjunction *so*

[CD 1, Track 63]

- Focus Ss' attention on the pictures and the labels. Point out that when it is 4:00 A.M. in San Diego, it is 6:00 A.M. in Guadalajara.
- Ask Ss about the time in different cities. For example:

  T: What time is it in Washington, D.C.?
  Ss: It's 7:00 A.M.

Present continuous Wh-questions

- Play the audio program. Ss listen and read silently.
- Elicit or explain the pattern for present continuous Wh-questions:

  Wh-word + *be* + subject + verb + *-ing*?

TIP
To help Ss remember how to form a new structure, write it on the board using different colors for important features. For example:
What's Victoria doing?
She's sleeping.

- ***Option:*** Ss underline the present continuous Wh-questions in the Conversation on page 32. Then elicit the answers. (Answers: What are you doing? … why are you cooking now? What are you making?)
- Review the meaning of *so*. Read the statement about Leticia: "It's 6:00 A.M., so she's getting up." Ask: "Why is Leticia getting up?" Elicit the answer. (Answer: It's 6:00 A.M.)
- Play the audio program for the questions and answers again. Ss listen and repeat.
- For the last picture, ask Ss: "What time is it? What are you doing now?" Elicit Ss' answers. (Possible answers: I'm studying English. I'm talking.)
- ***Option:*** Ss imagine it is a different time of the day. Ask: "What time is it? What are you doing?" Elicit answers with *so*. For example:

  T: What are you doing, John?
  S: It's 5:00, so I'm cooking dinner.

A *Pair work*

- Explain the task and model the first two questions with different Ss.
- Ss complete the task in pairs. Go around the class and help Ss with grammar as needed.
- Ask different pairs to ask and answer the questions. If Ss make any errors, encourage them to try to correct them.

Answers

1. Lya and Erin are having breakfast.
2. Tamara is eating dinner.
3. She's working in Cairo.
4. He's checking his messages in Osaka.
5. He's sleeping.
6. He's wearing a suit and tie.
7. It's 6:00 A.M./It's six (o'clock) in the morning.
8. It's noon.

B *Group work*

- Focus Ss' attention on the spelling box. Read the text in the spelling box aloud. Ss listen and read silently.
- Explain these spelling rules for present continuous verbs:
  1. For most verbs, add *-ing* to the base form (e.g., *sleeping*).
  2. If the base form ends with a vowel + a consonant, double the final consonant and add *-ing* (e.g., *getting*).
  3. If the base form ends with a silent *e*, drop the *e* and add *-ing* (e.g., *having*).
- Explain the first part of the task. Write *who*, *what*, *where*, *when*, and *why* on the board, and elicit example questions for each Wh-word. Point out that Ss should use each Wh-word at least once.
- Ss work individually. Go around the class and help with grammar and spelling as needed.
- Explain the second part of the task. Then Ss ask and answer their questions in small groups.

TIP
To help Ss avoid common errors, write the target feature on a card. For example, if your Ss forget the *-ing* ending when practicing the present continuous, write *-ing* on a card. When a S forgets to use the *-ing* ending, hold up the card.

- ***Option:*** Elicit questions from each group. Ss ask different groups their questions.

For more practice asking and answering present continuous Wh-questions, play ***Hot Potato*** – download it from the website.

7 GRAMMAR FOCUS

Present continuous Wh-questions

San Diego 4:00 A.M.

What's Daniel **doing**?

He**'s sleeping** right now.

Guadalajara 6:00 A.M.

What's Leticia **doing**?

It's 6:00 A.M., so she**'s getting up**.

Washington, D.C. 7:00 A.M.

What are Lya and Erin **doing**?

They're having breakfast.

Brasilia 9:00 A.M.

What's Tiago **doing**?

He**'s going** to work.

Edinburgh noon

What are Kim and Paul **doing**?

It's noon, so they**'re eating** lunch.

Cairo 3:00 P.M.

What's Amina **doing**?

She**'s working**.

Jakarta 7:00 P.M.

What's Tamara **doing**?

She**'s eating** dinner right now.

Osaka 9:00 P.M.

What's Kento **doing**?

He**'s checking** his messages.

Your city 00:00

What are you **doing**?

It's . . . I**'m** . . .

GRAMMAR PLUS *see page 136*

A PAIR WORK Ask and answer the questions about the pictures.

1. Who's having breakfast?
2. Who's eating dinner?
3. Where's Amina working?
4. Where's Kento checking his messages?
5. What's Daniel doing?
6. What's Tiago wearing?
7. Why is Leticia getting up?
8. Why are Kim and Paul having lunch?

spelling

sleep → slee**ping**

get → get**ting** (+ *t*)

have → hav**ing** (– *e*)

B GROUP WORK Write five more questions about the pictures. Then ask and answer your questions in groups.

8 WORD POWER What are they doing?

A Listen and practice. *"They're dancing."*

dance

drive

listen to music

play basketball

read

ride a bike

run

shop

study

swim

take a walk

watch a movie

B **PAIR WORK** Ask and answer questions about the pictures in part A.

A: Are they running?
B: No, they're not.

A: What are they doing?
B: They're dancing.

C **GROUP WORK** Make two teams. Write an activity on a piece of paper. Give the paper to the other team. Two members act out each activity. Their team guesses. Can they guess the activity?

A: Are you running?
B: No, we're not.

C: Are you riding bikes?
D: Yes, we are!

9 INTERCHANGE 5 What's wrong with this picture?

What's wrong with this picture? Go to Interchange 5 on page 119.

8 WORD POWER

Learning Objective: describe people's activities

A *[CD 1, Track 64]*

- Focus Ss' attention on the pictures. Play the audio program. Ss listen and repeat.
- Say the verbs or phrases under the pictures in random order. Ask different Ss to find the matching picture and form a complete sentence. For example:

  T: watch a movie
  S1: They're watching a movie.
  T: read
  S2: She's reading.
- ***Option:*** Ss write complete sentences about each picture.

B *Pair work*

- Explain the task. Point to the first picture and model the example conversation with a S.
- Ss complete the task in pairs. Go around the class and check Ss' use of grammar and rising or falling intonation.
- ***Option:*** Ss look through Units 1–5 in pairs or small groups. They ask and answer present continuous questions about the people in the pictures. Go around the class and give help as needed.

C *Group work*

- Explain the task. Point to the activity (riding bikes) and to the conversation in the book. Model the example with some Ss.
- Divide the class into two teams. Each team writes an activity on a piece of paper.
- Each team gives their paper to a pair of Ss on the other team. The pair reads the activity silently so their team doesn't know what it is. Then the pair acts out the activity. Their team asks yes/no questions to guess what they are doing.
- Then a pair from the other team acts out their activity. Their team guesses.
- Repeat until everyone has had a chance to mime an activity.
- ***Option***: For added challenge, set a time limit.

9 INTERCHANGE 5

See page T-119 for teaching notes.

10 READING

Learning Objectives: skim and read for details in messages between friends

A *[CD 1, Track 65]*

- Focus Ss' attention on the title and pictures. Explain that this conversation is taking place on social media between two women, Eva and Pam.
- Focus Ss' attention on the names *Eva35* and *PamL*. Elicit or explain that these are Eva's and Pam's screen names or online IDs.
- Explain the task. Explain that *skim* means "to read quickly to find general information."
- Write these questions on the board:

  1. *Where are they?*
  2. *What are they doing?*

  Point out that Ss can complete the task quickly by finding the answers to these questions.
- Ss complete the task individually. Go over the answers by pointing to each picture and asking "What's her name?"

Answers

top picture: Pam
bottom picture: Eva

B

- Explain the task. Ss read the text more carefully. Point out that they can find the answers quickly by looking for the phrases from the list. Ask: "Who is watching a movie?" Ss look through the conversation to find the answer. (Answer: Eva)
- Ss complete the task individually.
- Ss compare their answers in pairs. Then go over the answers with the class.

Answers

1. **Eva** is watching a movie.
2. **Eva** is visiting friends.
3. **Pam** is working in an office.
4. **Lety** is making coffee.
5. **Paul** is calling Eva on her cell phone.
6. **Pam's** boss is calling Pam.

- Ss read the conversation again. Elicit or explain any new vocabulary.

Vocabulary

message: to communicate online, especially by text or through a website
social media: websites/online communities where people share ideas, personal messages, and photos or videos
report: information about a subject, written or spoken

C *Pair work*

- Explain the task. Take a piece of paper and model having an online conversation with a S. Pass the paper back and forth as you ask and answer written questions. Read them aloud on each turn.
- Ss write an online conversation in pairs. They take turns writing questions and answers on one piece of paper. Go around the class and give help with grammar, vocabulary, and spelling as needed.

TIP

To encourage Ss to write conversations using their own ideas, have them close their Student's Books.

- *Option:* Ask one or two pairs to read their online chats aloud.

End of Cycle 2

See the Supplementary Resources chart at the beginning of this unit for additional teaching materials and student activities related to this Cycle.

10 READING

A Skim the conversation. Write the name of the correct person on each picture.

MESSAGE ME!

Eva and Pam are friends. They message on social media every day. Pam lives in Atlanta, in the United States. Eva is visiting friends in Puebla, Mexico.

Profile | Photos | Share | Find Friends

Eva35 Hey! How are you today, Pam?

PamL Hi, Eva! I'm fine, thanks. What are you doing?

Eva35 I'm sitting on the couch watching a movie. It's great!

PamL Lucky you! I'm writing a report. It's for my job.

Eva35 Oh, really? Are you at your office?

PamL Yeah. My friend Lety is making me coffee. She's helping me with the report.

Eva35 Cool. I'm . . . Oh, wait. My cell phone is ringing. Be right back. Sorry. It's my friend, Paul. He's making lunch.

PamL Right. I have to go, Eva. Sorry. My boss is calling me.

Eva35 OK. Good luck with the report! Have a good evening!

PamL Thanks, Eva. Enjoy your movie!

B Read the conversation. Who is doing these things? Choose the correct answers.

1.	Pam	Eva	. . . is watching a movie.
2.	Eva	Pam	. . . is visiting friends.
3.	Pam	Eva	. . . is working in an office.
4.	Lety	Paul	. . . is making coffee.
5.	Paul	Pam	. . . is calling Eva on her cell phone.
6.	Eva	Pam's boss	. . . is calling Pam.

C **PAIR WORK** Think about online conversations you have with friends. What do you say? What do you ask about? Write a short conversation.

Unit 6 Supplementary Resources Overview

	After the following SB exercises	You can use these materials in class	Your students can use these materials outside the classroom
CYCLE 1	1 Snapshot		**SS** Unit 6 Vocabulary 1
	2 Conversation		**SS** Unit 6 Speaking 1
	3 Word Power	**TSS** Unit 6 Vocabulary Worksheet	**SS** Unit 6 Vocabulary 2 **GAME** Spell or Slime (Family)
	4 Grammar Focus		**SB** Unit 6 Grammar plus, Focus 1 **GAME** Sentence Runner (Simple present statements 1) **GAME** Sentence Stacker (Simple present statements 2)
	5 Pronunciation	**TSS** Unit 6 Extra Worksheet	**WB** Unit 6 exercises 1–4
CYCLE 2	6 Conversation		**SD** Unit 6 Speaking 2
	7 Grammar Focus	**TSS** Unit 6 Grammar Worksheet **TSS** Unit 6 Listening Worksheet	**SB** Unit 6 Grammar plus, Focus 2 **SS** Unit 6 Grammar 1–2 **GAME** Work Keys (Simple present questions)
	8 Listening		
	9 Speaking		
	10 Interchange 6		
	11 Reading	**TSS** Unit 6 Project Worksheet **VID** Unit 6 **VRB** Unit 6	**SS** Unit 6 Reading 1–2 **SS** Unit 6 Listening 1–2 **SS** Unit 6 Video 1–3 **WB** Unit 6 exercises 5–10

With or instead of the following SB section	You can also use these materials for assessment
Units 5–6 Progress Check	**ASSESSMENT PROGRAM** Units 5–6 Oral Quiz **ASSESSMENT PROGRAM** Units 5–6 Written Quiz

Key
GAME: Online Game **SB:** Student's Book **SS:** Online Self-study **TSS:** Teacher Support Site
VID: Video DVD **VRB:** Video Resource Book **WB:** Online Workbook/Workbook

My Plan for Unit 6

Use the space below to customize a plan that fits your needs.

With the following SB exercises	I am using these materials in class	My students are using these materials outside the classroom

With or instead of the following SB section	I am using these materials for assessment

6 I ride my bike to school.

- Discuss transportation and family
- Discuss daily and weekly routines

1 SNAPSHOT

Listen and practice.

Check (✓) the kinds of transportation you use.
What are some other kinds of transportation?

2 CONVERSATION They use public transportation.

Listen and practice.

Yuto: Nice car, Austin! Is it yours?

Austin: No, it's my sister's. She has a new job and she drives to work.

Yuto: Is her job here in the suburbs?

Austin: No, it's downtown.

Yuto: My parents work downtown, but they don't drive to work. They use public transportation.

Austin: The bus or the train?

Yuto: The bus doesn't stop near our house, so they take the train.

6 I ride my bike to school.

Cycle 1, Exercises 1–5

In Unit 6, students discuss transportation, family, and daily and weekly routines. By the end of Cycle 1, students will be able to discuss transportation and family using simple present statements. By the end of Cycle 2, students will be able to discuss daily and weekly routines using simple present questions.

1 SNAPSHOT

Learning Objective: describe kinds of transportation

[CD 2, Track 1]

- Focus Ss' attention on the title and pictures. Elicit or explain any new vocabulary.

Vocabulary
transportation: ways of going to different places
get around: go from place to place

- Play the audio program. Ss listen and read silently.
- Play the audio program again. Ss listen and repeat.
- Explain the first task. Ss check the kinds of transportation they use individually. Then they compare answers in groups. Write this model conversation on the board:

  A: I walk and I take the bus. How about you, Joe?
  B: I take the subway. How about you, Maria?

- Ss complete the task in groups. Elicit their answers.
- Explain the second task. Ss make a list of other kinds of transportation in groups. Point out that they can list unusual kinds of transportation.
- Elicit answers from each group and write them on the board. (Possible answers: boat, ship, plane, helicopter, truck, horse, camel) Explain or draw pictures of any new vocabulary

TIP
To collect vocabulary for future warm-ups, reviews, and games, make a Vocabulary box. As you present new words, ask different Ss to write them on pieces of paper and put them in the box.

For more practice with transportation vocabulary, play ***Sculptures*** – download it from the website.

2 CONVERSATION

Learning Objective: use simple present statements in a conversation about transportation

[CD 2, Track 2]

- Books closed. Write this focus question on the board:

  What three kinds of transportation do the speakers talk about?

  Play the audio program and Ss listen for the answer. Elicit the answer. (Answer: a car, the bus, the train)
- Books open. Use the picture to set the scene. Yuto and Austin are in front of Austin's house.
- Ask these questions:
  1. What are Austin and Yuto wearing?
  2. What are they looking at?
  3. What color is the car?
  4. Whose car is it?

  Then elicit the answers. (Answers: 1. T-shirts and jeans 2. a car 3. blue 4. Austin's sister's)
- Play the audio program again. Ss listen and read along silently.
- Elicit or explain any new vocabulary.

Vocabulary
suburbs: area outside of a city where many people live
downtown: the business center of a city
public transportation: transportation everyone can use, such as buses, trains, and subways

- Play the audio program again. Ss listen and repeat.
- Ss practice the conversation in pairs. Go around the class and give help as needed.
- ***Option:*** Ask one or two pairs to role-play the conversation for the class.

For a new way to practice this conversation, try ***Moving Dialog*** – download it from the website.

3 WORD POWER

Learning Objective: describe family relationships

A *[CD 2, Track 3] Pair work*

- Focus Ss' attention on the pictures. Point out that this is the family of Austin from Exercise 2.
- Ss study the family. Read the names (e.g., *Tom, Lisa*) aloud. Ss repeat. Then read the words for family relationships (e.g., *husband, wife*). Ss listen and repeat.
- Focus Ss' attention on the words in the box. Explain that the words on the left (i.e., *kids, mom, dad*) are informal ways to say the words on the right. Read the words. Ss repeat.
- Explain the task and read the first sentence. Ss complete the sentences in pairs.
- Play the audio program again. Ss listen and check their answers.

Answers

Lisa is Tom's **wife**.
Megan and Austin are their **children/kids**.
Tom is Lisa's **husband**.
Austin is Lisa's **son**.
Megan is Tom's **daughter**.
Austin is Megan's **brother**.
Megan is Austin's **sister**.
Tom and Lisa are Austin's **parents**.

- ***Option:*** Play the audio program again. Ss listen and repeat.

B *Pair work*

- Explain the task and ask a S to model the example sentences aloud. Then tell the class about your family.
- Ss talk about their families in pairs.
- ***Option:*** Ask Ss to bring pictures of their families to class to show their classmates.

4 GRAMMAR FOCUS

Learning Objective: use simple present statements with regular and irregular verbs

[CD 2, Track 4]

Simple present statements

- Focus Ss' attention on the Grammar Focus box.
- Explain that we use the simple present for things that happen regularly (e.g., *I walk to school.*) We also use the simple present for things that are permanent (e.g., *I come from New York.)*
- Play the audio program. Ss listen and read silently.
- Point out the *-s* ending on the verbs that follow *he* and *she*. Explain that regular simple present verbs with *he*, *she*, and *it* end in *-s*.
- Point out *don't* and *doesn't* in the negative sentences. Explain that *don't* and *doesn't* are contractions of *do not* and *does not*.
- Elicit or explain the meaning of *use, far, near, alone,* and *need*.

A

- Focus Ss' attention on the verb endings box. Point out that *study* changes to *studies* because it ends in consonant + *y*, and *watch* changes to *watches* because it ends in *ch*.
- Read the text in the verb endings box aloud. Ss listen and repeat.
- Set the scene for the exercise. Tom Mitchell from Exercise 3 is talking about his family.
- Elicit or explain any new vocabulary.

Vocabulary
retired: not working because of age

- Explain the first part of the task and model the first sentence. Point out that the pronoun for *my family and I* is *we*. Elicit or explain that simple present verbs with *we* don't end in *-s*.
- Ss complete the task individually. Go around the class and give help as needed.
- Explain the second part of the task. Ss compare answers in pairs. Then elicit answers from the class and write them on the board.

Answers

1. My family and I **live** in the suburbs. My wife and I **work** near here, so we **walk** to work. Our daughter Megan **works** downtown, so she **drives** to work. Our son **doesn't** drive. He **rides** his bike to school.
2. My parents **live** in the city. My mother **takes** the subway to work. My father is retired, so he **doesn't** work now. He also **uses** public transportation, so they **don't** need a car.

3 WORD POWER Family members

A **PAIR WORK** Complete the sentences about the Mitchell family. Then listen and check your answers.

1. Lisa is Tom's ___wife___.
2. Megan and Austin are their ________.
3. Tom is Lisa's ________.
4. Austin is Lisa's ________.
5. Megan is Tom's ________.
6. Austin is Megan's ________.
7. Megan is Austin's ________.
8. Tom and Lisa are Austin's ________.

kids = children
mom = mother
dad = father

B **PAIR WORK** Who are the people in your family? What are their names?

"My father's name is Arthur. My sisters' names are Emilia and Sabrina."

4 GRAMMAR FOCUS

Simple present statements

I	**walk**	to school.	I	**don't live**	far from here.	**don't** = do not
You	**ride**	your bike to school.	You	**don't live**	near here.	**doesn't** = does not
He	**works**	near here.	He	**doesn't work**	downtown.	
She	**takes**	the bus to work.	She	**doesn't drive**	to work.	
We	**live**	with our parents.	We	**don't live**	alone.	
They	**use**	public transportation.	They	**don't need**	a car.	

GRAMMAR PLUS *see page 137*

A Tom Mitchell is talking about his family. Complete the sentences with the correct verb forms. Then compare with a partner.

1. My family and I ___live___ (live / lives) in the suburbs. My wife and I ________ (work / works) near here, so we ________ (walk / walks) to work. Our daughter Megan ________ (work / works) downtown, so she ________ (drive / drives) to work. Our son ________ (don't / doesn't) drive. He ________ (ride / rides) his bike to school.

2. My parents ________ (live / lives) in the city. My mother ________ (take / takes) the subway to work. My father is retired, so he ________ (don't / doesn't) work now. He also ________ (use / uses) public transportation, so they ________ (don't / doesn't) need a car.

verb endings: *he, she, it*

walk → walk**s**
ride → ride**s**
study → stud**ies**
watch → watch**es**

Simple present statements with irregular verbs

I/you/we/they	*he/she/it*
I **have** a bike.	My mother **has** a car.
We **do** our homework every day.	My father **does** a lot of work at home.
My parents **go** to work by train.	The train **goes** downtown.

GRAMMAR PLUS *see page 137*

B Yuto is talking about his family and his friend Austin. Complete the sentences. Then compare with a partner.

1. My parents ___*have*___ (have / has) a house in the suburbs. My mom and dad ________ (go / goes) downtown to work. My parents are very busy, so I ________ (do / does) a lot of work at home.
2. My brother doesn't live with us. He ________ (have / has) an apartment in the city. He ________ (go / goes) to school all day, and he ________ (do / does) his homework at night.
3. I ________ (have / has) a new friend. His name is Austin. We ________ (go / goes) to the same school, and sometimes we ________ (do / does) our homework together.

C **PAIR WORK** Tell your partner about your family.

"I have one brother and two sisters. My brother is a teacher. He has a car, so he drives to work."

5 PRONUNCIATION Third-person singular *–s* endings

Listen and practice. Notice the pronunciation of the **–s** endings.

s = /s/		s = /z/		(e)s = /ɪz/		*irregular*	
take	tak**es**	drive	driv**es**	dance	danc**es**	do	do**es**
sleep	sleep**s**	study	studi**es**	watch	watch**es**	have	ha**s**

6 CONVERSATION What time do you get up?

Listen and practice.

Paige: Let's go to the park Sunday morning.

Adam: Good idea, but let's go in the afternoon. I sleep late on weekends.

Paige: What time do you get up?

Adam: I get up at noon.

Paige: Really? That's late. Do you eat breakfast at noon?

Adam: Yeah. What time do *you* get up?

Paige: At ten o'clock.

Adam: Oh, that's early for a Sunday.

Paige: Hey, I have an idea! Let's eat at Park Café. They serve breakfast all day!

[CD 2, Track 5]

Simple present statements with irregular verbs

- Focus Ss' attention on the Grammar Focus box. Remind Ss that regular simple present verbs with *he*, *she*, and *it* end in *-s*.
- Point out that irregular simple present verbs change in different ways. Elicit or explain that *have*, *do*, and *go* change to *has*, *does*, and *goes* with *he*, *she*, and *it*.
- Play the audio program. Ss listen and read silently.

B

- Set the scene. Yuto is Austin's friend from Exercise 2 on page 36. He is talking about his family and Austin.
- Explain the first part of the task and model the first sentence.
- Ss complete the task individually. Then they compare answers in pairs.
- Elicit answers from the class and write them on the board.

Answers

1. My parents **have** a house in the suburbs. My mom and dad **go** downtown to work. My parents are very busy, so I **do** a lot of work at home.
2. My brother doesn't live with us. He **has** an apartment in the city. He **goes** to school all day, and he **does** his homework at night.
3. I **have** a new friend. His name is Austin. We **go** to the same school, and sometimes we **do** our homework together.

C *Pair work*

- Explain the task and model the example sentences. Point out that Ss should try to use the verbs *have*, *do*, and *go*.
- Ss complete the task in pairs. Go around the class and write down any grammar errors you hear. Then write them on the board and correct them as a class.
- ***Option:*** Ss take notes about their partner's family. Then they tell the class. For example: "My partner has one brother and two sisters. They . . ."

5 PRONUNCIATION

Learning Objectives: differentiate between third-person singular *-s* endings and use them correctly to sound more natural

[CD 2, Track 6]

- Point out that the pronunciation of third-person singular *-s* endings in the simple present follows the same rules as the pronunciation of *-s* endings for plural nouns.
- Play the audio program. Ss listen and read silently.
- Play the audio program again. Ss listen and repeat.
- ***Option:*** If Ss have trouble pronouncing /s/ and /z/ correctly, tell them to say the sounds with their fingers on their throats. The sound /z/ causes a vibration, but the sound /s/ does not.

End of Cycle 1

See the Supplementary Resources chart at the beginning of this unit for additional teaching materials and student activities related to this Cycle.

Cycle 2, Exercises 6–11

6 CONVERSATION

Learning Objective: use simple present questions in a conversation about daily routines

[CD 2, Track 7]

- Text covered. Focus Ss' attention on the picture. Ask the class: "Where are the speakers? What are they wearing? What do you think they're talking about?" Encourage Ss to make guesses.
- Play the audio program. Ss listen. Then ask them if their guesses were correct.
- Text uncovered. Ask the class: "What time does Adam get up on Sundays? What time does Paige get up?" Play the audio program again. Ss listen for the answers. Elicit the answers. (Answers: Adam gets up at noon. Paige gets up at ten o'clock.)
- Elicit or explain the meaning of any new vocabulary.

Vocabulary
Let's . . . : I suggest that we . . .

- Play the audio program again. Ss listen and repeat.
- Ss practice the conversation in pairs.

! For a new way to practice this conversation, try the ***Onion Ring*** technique – download it from the website.

7 GRAMMAR FOCUS

Learning Objective: use simple present questions and time expressions

[CD 2, Track 8]

Simple present questions

- Focus Ss' attention on the left column of the Grammar Focus box. Elicit or explain the pattern for simple present yes/no questions:

  Do/Does + subject + verb?
- Focus Ss' attention on the right column of the Grammar Focus box. Elicit or explain the pattern for simple present Wh-questions:

  Wh-word + *do/does* + subject + verb?
- Play the audio program for the Grammar Focus box. Ss listen and read silently. Point out that yes/no questions have rising intonation and Wh-questions have falling intonation.

Time expressions

- Focus Ss' attention on the time expressions box. Elicit or explain the meaning of any new words. Explain the following rules:
  1. Use *at* with specific times (e.g., *9:00, noon, midnight*) and with *night*.
  2. Use *in the* with *morning, afternoon,* and *evening*.
  3. Use *on* with specific days of the week (e.g., *Sundays, weekends, weekdays*).
- Read the time expressions aloud.
- ***Option:*** Ss underline the time expressions in the Conversation in Exercise 6. Elicit the answers. (Answers: Sunday morning, in the afternoon, late, on weekends, at noon, late, at noon, at ten o'clock, early, a Sunday)

For more practice with time expressions, play ***Tic-Tac-Toe*** – download it from the website.

A

- Explain the task and model the first question.
- Ss complete the task individually. Go around the class and give help as needed.
- Elicit answers from the class.

Answers

1. **Do** you get up late on Sundays?
2. **Do** you have lunch at home every day?
3. What time **does** your father leave work on Fridays?
4. **Does** your mother cook on weekdays?
5. **Does** your father shop on Saturdays?
6. **Do** you take a walk in the evening?
7. When **do** you listen to music?
8. What time **do** you check your email?
9. What time **do** your parents have dinner?
10. When **do** you study English?
11. **Does** your best friend ride a bike on weekends?
12. **Does** your father drive to work every morning?

B *Pair work*

- Explain the task. Ask two Ss to model the example conversation.
- Ss complete the task in pairs.

For more practice with simple present Wh-questions and time expressions, try ***Line Up!*** – download it from the website. Ask questions such as: "What time do you get up?"

C

- Explain the first part of the task. Explain that *unscramble* means "to put in the correct order."
- Write the first question on the board and demonstrate how to unscramble it. Point out that every question begins with a capital letter and ends with a question mark.
- Ss complete the task individually. Go around the class and check Ss' use of capital letters.
- Ss compare their answers in pairs. Then ask different pairs of Ss to read the conversations.

Answers

1. What time do you eat dinner?
2. Do you check your messages every morning?
3. Does this class start at seven o'clock?
4. When do you listen to music?
5. Do you and your friends play sports on weekends?

- Explain the second part of the task. Ss ask and answer the questions in pairs. This time, they use their own information. Remind Ss to use rising intonation for yes/no questions and falling intonation for Wh-questions.
- Ss complete the task in pairs. Go around the class and check their use of intonation.
- ***Option:*** Ss write three scrambled questions individually. Then they exchange scrambled questions with a partner and unscramble them.

7 GRAMMAR FOCUS

Simple present questions

Do you **get up** early on Sundays?	**What time do** you **get up**?
No, I **get up** late.	At noon.
Does he **eat** breakfast at seven o'clock?	**What time does** she have dinner?
No, he **eats** breakfast at seven-thirty.	At eight o'clock.
Do they **take** a taxi to class?	**When do** they **take** the subway?
No, they **take** the bus.	On Mondays and Wednesdays.

GRAMMAR PLUS *see page 137*

A Complete the questions with *do* or *does*.

1. ___Do___ you get up late on Sundays?
2. ________ you have lunch at home every day?
3. What time ________ your father leave work on Fridays?
4. ________ your mother cook on weekdays?
5. ________ your father shop on Saturdays?
6. ________ you take a walk in the evening?
7. When ________ you listen to music?
8. What time ________ you check your email?
9. What time ________ your parents have dinner?
10. When ________ you study English?
11. ________ your best friend ride a bike on weekends?
12. ________ your father drive to work every morning?

time expressions

early	**in** the morning
late	**in** the afternoon
every day	**in** the evening
at 9:00	**on** Sundays
at noon/midnight	**on** weekdays
at night	**on** weekends

B PAIR WORK Ask and answer the questions from part A. Use time expressions from the box.

A: Do you get up late on Sundays?
B: No, I don't. I get up at eight o'clock. I play basketball on Sunday mornings.

C Unscramble the questions to complete the conversations. Then ask a partner the questions. Answer with your own information.

1. **A:** What time do you eat dinner?
   you / what time / dinner / do / eat
   B: At 7:00 P.M.
2. **A:** ________________________?
   you / every morning / check your messages / do
   B: Yes, I check my messages on the bus every morning.
3. **A:** ________________________?
   at / start / does / seven o'clock / this class
   B: No, this class starts at eight o'clock.
4. **A:** ________________________?
   listen to music / you / do / when
   B: I listen to music in the evening.
5. **A:** ________________________?
   on weekends / you and your friends / do / play sports
   B: Yes, we play volleyball on Saturdays.

8 LISTENING Kayla's weekly routine

Listen to Kayla talk about her weekly routine. Check (✓) the days she does each thing.

	Monday	Tuesday	Wednesday	Thursday	Friday	Saturday	Sunday
get up early	☐	☐	☐	☐	☐	☐	☐
go to work	☐	☐	☐	☐	☐	☐	☐
play tennis	☐	☐	☐	☐	☐	☐	☐
go shopping	☐	☐	☐	☐	☐	☐	☐
see friends	☐	☐	☐	☐	☐	☐	☐
dinner with family	☐	☐	☐	☐	☐	☐	☐
study	☐	☐	☐	☐	☐	☐	☐

9 SPEAKING My weekly routine

A What do you do every week? Write your routine in the chart.

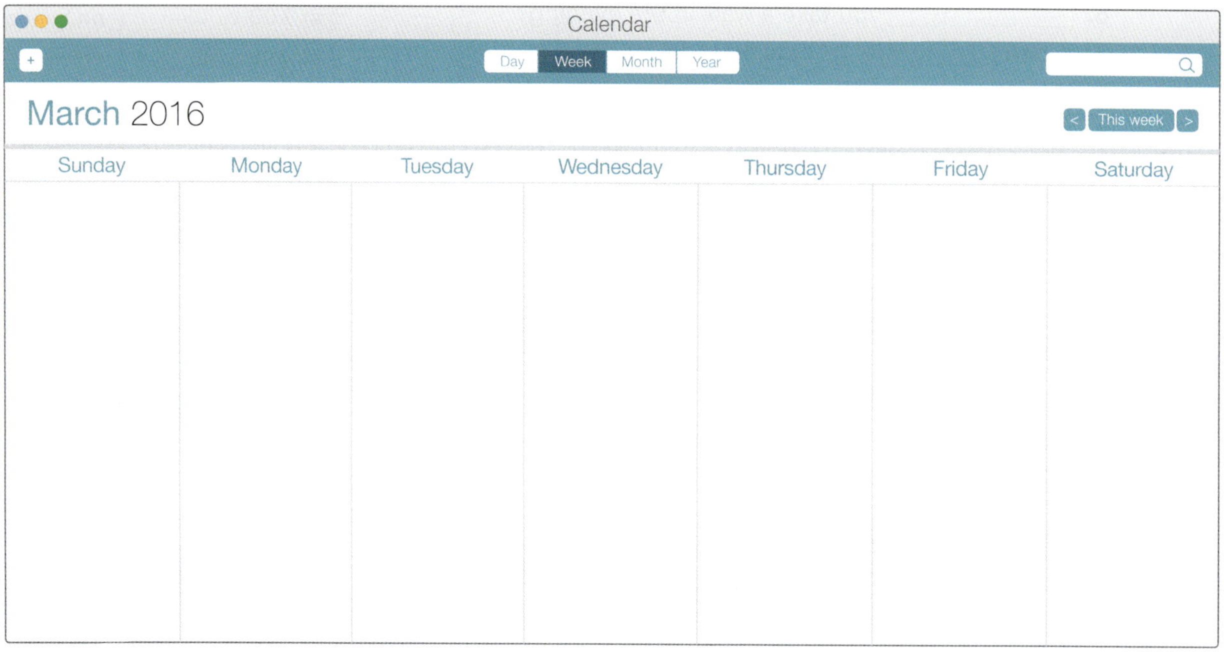

B **GROUP WORK** Discuss your weekly routines. Ask and answer questions.

A: I play tennis on Sunday mornings.
B: What do you do on Sunday afternoons?
A: I see my friends. We watch movies or play games. What about you?
C: On Sundays, I have lunch with my parents. In the afternoon, we talk or take a walk.

10 INTERCHANGE 6 Class survey

Find out more about your classmates.
Go to Interchange 6 on page 120.

8 LISTENING

Learning Objective: listen for details about someone's weekly routine

[CD 2, Track 9]

- Focus Ss' attention on the days of the week. Read each one aloud. Ss repeat.
- Explain the task. Then go over the activities in the chart. Elicit or explain any new vocabulary. Ensure Ss understand that a *routine* is a "usual pattern of activities."
- Play the audio program. Ss listen for any activities Kayla talks about. Then elicit the activities they hear.
- Play the audio program again. Ss listen and check the days she does each thing.
- Ss compare answers in small groups. Play the audio program again for Ss to check their answers. Then elicit the answers from the class.

TIP
If Ss feel nervous about listening to audio recordings or have difficulty answering questions when they listen, have them work together in pairs or small groups. Explain that they can help each other.

Audio script

Man Do you get up early every day, Kayla?
Kayla Well, I get up early on weekdays and on Saturdays. I go to school from Monday to Friday, and I work on Saturdays, so I get up around seven o'clock.
Man How about on Sundays?
Kayla Sundays? That's the day I sleep late.
Man What else do you do? I mean, what do you do for fun during the week?
Kayla I love tennis. I play three times a week – on Mondays, Tuesdays, and Thursdays. Oh, and I also go shopping on Saturdays after work.
Man What about the rest of the weekend? When do you see your friends?
Kayla Let's see. I see friends on Fridays and Saturdays. That's in the evening. But not on Sunday evenings. My family always eats dinner together then.
Man When do you study?
Kayla Every day!
Man Wow! You're really busy!

Answers

get up early: Monday, Tuesday, Wednesday, Thursday, Friday, Saturday
go to work: Saturday
play tennis: Monday, Tuesday, Thursday
go shopping: Saturday
see friends: Friday, Saturday
dinner with family: Sunday
study: Monday, Tuesday, Wednesday, Thursday, Friday, Saturday, Sunday

9 SPEAKING

Learning Objectives: write and discuss weekly routines

A

- Explain the task. Ss write their weekly activities in the chart. Ask three Ss to share things they will write in the chart.
- Ss complete the task individually. Go around the class and give help as needed.

B *Group work*

- Explain the task. Then ask three Ss to read the example conversation.
- List these words on the board: Mondays, Tuesdays, Wednesdays, Thursdays, Fridays, Saturdays, Sundays, weekdays, weekends. Point out that we use *on* and the plural form of days of the week to talk about routine activities (e.g., *on Mondays*).
- Ss complete the task in small groups. Go around the class and give help as needed. Encourage Ss to talk about all their routines.
- Ask different groups to share their information with the class.

TIP
To make sure that all Ss participate, tell them they will share information or answers with the class.

10 INTERCHANGE 6

See page T-120 for teaching notes.

11 READING

Learning Objectives: scan and read for details in an article; sequence events in daily schedules

A *[CD 2, Track 10]*

- Read the title aloud. Explain that a *schedule* is a list of planned activities.
- Ss cover the interview and focus their attention on the picture.
- Read the question. Encourage Ss to use the picture to make predictions. Elicit predictions from the class, and ask for their reasons. (Possible prediction: Mike travels for his job.)
- Ss uncover the text. Tell them to scan the interview to check their predictions. Explain that *scan* means "to read quickly to find specific information." Encourage Ss to look for words like *early, late, in the morning/ afternoon/evening*, and for clock times.

TIP
To encourage Ss to scan, set a time limit. This helps Ss focus on finding the words that will help them complete the task.

- Elicit the answer. (Answer: Mike's job is sleeping in different hotels.)

B

- Explain the first part of the task. Ss read the article individually and underline any words they don't know.
- Ss share information about the words they underlined in small groups. Elicit or explain the meaning of any remaining words.

Vocabulary
strange: not the way things usually are
travel blog: a website with information about travel
lights: lamps, etc.
noise: sounds, especially unwanted sounds
tourist: a person who travels and visits places for fun
travel agency: a company that plans travel for people

- Explain the second part of the task. Ss number the events in Mike's schedule individually. Then they compare answers in pairs.
- Elicit the answers from the class.

Answers

a. 3
b. 1
c. 4
d. 5
e. 2
1. 2:00 P.M. – 4:00 P.M.
2. 6:00 A.M.
3. 7:00 P.M.
4. 10:00 P.M.
5. 8:00 A.M.

C

- Elicit or explain the meanings of *early bird* and *night owl*. Give examples (e.g., Mike gets up at 6:00 A.M., so he's an early bird. I go to bed at one o'clock in the morning, so I'm a night owl.).

Vocabulary
early bird: a person who gets up early
night owl: a person who stays up late

- Explain the first part of the task. Model the task by writing five sentences about your schedule on the board. Ask: "Am I an early bird or a night owl?"
- Ss complete the task individually. Go around the class and give help as needed.
- Explain the second part of the task. Ss read their sentences in pairs. They take turns reading their sentences aloud.
- Ask: "Who is an early bird? Who is a night owl?" Elicit answers from the class.
- ***Option:*** Ss tell the class about their partner's schedule.

End of Cycle 2

See the Supplementary Resources chart at the beginning of this unit for additional teaching materials and student activities related to this Cycle and for assessment tools.

11 READING

A Scan the interview. What's unusual about Mike's job?

What's your schedule like?

Every week, we interview someone with an unusual schedule. In this week's interview, we meet Mike Watts, a professional "sleeper." Yes, that's correct. Mike's job pays him to sleep! Here, Mike talks to us about his schedule.

News Now: Hi Mike, thanks for talking to us. What's your schedule like?

Mike: Hi there! My schedule's strange, but I love it. I go to bed at 10:00 P.M. in a different hotel room every night.

News Now: Wow! That's cool! Do you get up early?

Mike: Yes, I get up at 6:00 A.M. I'm an early bird! I like the morning. At 8:00 A.M., I have a big breakfast in the hotel restaurant.

News Now: So, who pays you to do that?

Mike: I work for a travel blog. They pay me to stay in different hotels and write about them. People read the blog and go to the hotels. Right now, I'm at a hotel in Finland, Hotel Finn.

News Now: And what do you do before you go to bed?

Mike: Every afternoon, from 2:00 P.M. to 4:00 P.M., I write about each room. I talk about the bed, the lights, the noise . . .

News Now: Who reads the blog?

Mike: Lots of different people read it. Business people, tourists, travel agencies . . . people who want to know about hotels, really!

News Now: What do you do in the evening?

Mike: At 7:00 P.M., I talk to the hotel manager. Then I go to my new room and go to bed.

News Now: Do you like sleeping?

Mike: Yes, I do! I'm very good at it!

B Read the article. Number the activities in Mike's schedule from 1 to 5. Then answer the questions. Write the times.

_____ **a.** Mike writes about each room.
__1__ **b.** He gets up.
_____ **c.** He talks to the hotel manager.
_____ **d.** He goes to his new room.
_____ **e.** He has a big breakfast.

1. What time does Mike write about each room? __________
2. What time does he get up? __________
3. What time does he talk to the hotel manager? __________
4. What time does he go to bed? __________
5. What time does he have breakfast? __________

C Are you an "early bird," like Mike? Or are you a "night owl"? Write five sentences about your schedule. Compare with a partner.

early bird

night owl

Units 5–6 Progress check

SELF-ASSESSMENT

How well can you do these things? Check (✓) the boxes.

I can . . .	Very well	OK	A little
Understand times and descriptions of activities (Ex. 1)	☐	☐	☐
Ask and answer questions about present activities (Ex. 2)	☐	☐	☐
Talk about personal routines (Ex. 3)	☐	☐	☐
Ask and answer questions about routines (Ex. 4)	☐	☐	☐
Ask and answer questions about celebrities' appearances and activities (Ex. 5)	☐	☐	☐

1 LISTENING I'm calling from Los Angeles.

It's 9:00 A.M. in Los Angeles. Stephanie is calling friends around the world. Listen to the conversations and complete the chart.

	1. Chelsea	2. Carlos	3. Nicholas
City	New York		
Time			
Activity			

2 SPEAKING We're on vacation!

Student A: Imagine your classmates are on vacation. Student B calls you. Ask questions about your classmates.

Student B: Imagine you are on vacation with your classmates. Call Student A. Answer Student A's questions about your classmates.

A: Hello?
B: Hi, it's . . . . I'm on vacation in . . .
A: In . . . ? Wow! What are you doing?
B: . . .
A: Who are you with?
B: . . .
A: What's he/she doing?
B: . . .
A: Well, have fun. Bye!

Units 5–6

Progress check

SELF-ASSESSMENT

Learning Objectives: reflect on one's learning; identify areas that need improvement

- Ask: "What did you learn in Units 5 and 6?" Elicit Ss' answers.
- Ss complete the Self-assessment. Explain to Ss that this is not a test; it is a way for them to evaluate what they've learned and identify areas where they need additional practice. Encourage them to be honest, and point out they will not get a bad grade if they check (✓) *A little*.
- Ss move on to the Progress check exercises. You can have Ss complete them in class or for homework, using one of these techniques:
  1. Ask Ss to complete all the exercises.
  2. Ask Ss: "What do you need to practice?" Then assign exercises based on their answers.
  3. Ask Ss to choose and complete exercises based on their Self-assessment.

1 LISTENING

Learning Objective: demonstrate one's ability to understand times and descriptions of activities

[CD 2, Track 11]

- Explain the task. Focus Ss' attention on the chart and read the names of the people aloud.
- Play the audio program once or twice. Ss listen and complete the chart individually.
- Ss compare answers in small groups. Play the audio program again if needed.
- To check answers, ask: "Where is (Chelsea)? What time is it there? What is (she) doing?"

Audio script

1.
Chelsea Hello?
Stephanie Hey, Chelsea! It's Stephanie. I'm calling from Los Angeles!
Chelsea Stephanie! How's it going?
Stephanie I'm good. So, how are things in New York?
Chelsea Oh, everything's great.
Stephanie What time is it there?
Chelsea It's about twelve o'clock.
Stephanie It's noon? Oh, I'm sorry. Are you having lunch now?
Chelsea No, no it's OK. I'm just watching television.
2.
Carlos Hello?
Stephanie Hi, Carlos. It's Stephanie, in Los Angeles. How are you doing?
Carlos I'm not sure, Stephanie. It's a little early for me.
Stephanie Really? What time is it in Mexico City?
Carlos Well, it's a quarter after eleven in the morning here.
Stephanie 11:15 A.M.?
Carlos Yeah. I'm having breakfast right now.
Stephanie You're having breakfast?
Carlos Yeah. I always get up late on Saturdays.
3.
Nicholas Hello?
Stephanie Hi, Nicholas!
Nicholas Um, hi, uh, is this Madison?
Stephanie No! It's Stephanie.
Nicholas Oh, hi, Stephanie.
Stephanie So, Nicholas, how are things in Sydney?
Nicholas Things are fine, but . . . do you know it's three-thirty in the morning here?
Stephanie Oh, I'm sorry!
Nicholas It's OK. I'm not sleeping.
Stephanie What are you doing?
Nicholas I'm playing a new video game. It's really fun! That's why I'm not sleeping.

Answers

	1. Chelsea	2. Carlos	3. Nicholas
City	New York	Mexico City	Sydney
Time	12:00 noon	11:15 A.M.	3:30 A.M.
Activity	watching television	having breakfast	playing a new video game

2 SPEAKING

Learning Objective: demonstrate one's ability to ask and answer questions about current activities

- Set the scene and explain the task.
- Focus Ss' attention on the pictures. Ask: "Who is on vacation: the man or the woman? What is she doing?" Elicit Ss' answers.
- Elicit vacation places and activities and write them on the board.
- Ss role-play the conversation in pairs. Then they change roles and role-play the conversation again.

3 SPEAKING

Learning Objective: demonstrate one's ability to discuss personal routines

A

- Explain the task and focus Ss' attention on the chart. Point out that Ss should choose one day of the week and write activities for *in the morning*, *in the afternoon*, *in the evening*, and *at night*. If needed, elicit activities from the class.
- Ss complete the chart individually. Go around the class and give help with vocabulary as needed.

B *Pair work*

- Explain the task. Ask two Ss to model the example conversation.
- Ss discuss their routines in pairs. Go around the class and give help as needed.
- ***Option:*** Ss take notes on their partner's activities.
- ***Option:*** Ss write sentences about their partner's routines. Go around the class and encourage Ss to use sentences with *and* and *but*. Then have them tell the class about their partner's routines.

4 SPEAKING

Learning Objective: demonstrate one's ability to ask and answer questions about routines and lifestyles

A

- Explain the task and focus Ss' attention on the chart.
- Ask different Ss to read the questions aloud.
- Ss complete the task individually. Go around the class and make sure Ss check only *Yes* or *No*.

B *Class activity*

- Explain the task. Point out that Ss try to find classmates whose answers are the same as their own. Ss should find a different classmate to answer each question and write his or her name on the line.
- Ss go around the class and complete the task. Go around the class and encourage Ss to look at each other when they talk and to change partners often.
- Elicit answers from the class. Ask: "Do you live with your parents? Who says yes? Who says no?" Elicit names of Ss from the class. Continue with the remaining questions.

5 SPEAKING

Learning Objective: demonstrate one's ability to ask and answer questions about people's appearance and habits and routines

Group work

- Explain the task and model the example questions.
- To model the activity, choose a famous living person. The class asks yes/no questions to guess the person.
- Ss play the game in small groups. Go around the class and make sure Ss take turns and ask yes/no questions.
- ***Option:*** Ss can ask only 10 questions for each famous person. If no one guesses correctly after 10 questions, the S who chose the person gets one point.

WHAT'S NEXT?

Learning Objective: become more involved in one's learning

- Focus Ss' attention on the Self-assessment again. Ask: "How well can you do these things now?"
- Ask Ss to underline one thing they need to review. Ask: "What did you underline? How can you review it?"
- If needed, plan additional instruction, activities, or reviews based on Ss' answers.

3 SPEAKING One day in my week

A Choose one day of the week and write it in the blank. What do you do on this day? Complete the chart.

	Day:
In the morning	
In the afternoon	
In the evening	
At night	

B PAIR WORK Tell your partner about your routine on the day from part A.

A: On Saturdays, I exercise in the morning. I run in the park with my friends.
B: What time do you run?
A: We run at 9:00.

4 SPEAKING Lifestyle survey

A Answer the questions in the chart. Check (✓) Yes or No.

	Yes	No	Name
1. Do you live with your parents?	☐	☐	
2. Do both your parents work?	☐	☐	
3. Do you play video games at night?	☐	☐	
4. Do you eat dinner with your family?	☐	☐	
5. Do you stay at home on weekends?	☐	☐	
6. Do you work on Saturdays?	☐	☐	

B CLASS ACTIVITY Go around the class and find classmates with the same answers. Write their names in the chart. Try to write a different name on each line.

5 SPEAKING Guess who!

GROUP WORK Think of a famous person. Your classmates ask yes/no questions to guess the person.

Is it a man? a woman?
Does he/she live in . . . ?
Is he/she a singer? an actor?
Does he/she speak English?
Does he/she play soccer? basketball?
Does he/she wear glasses?

WHAT'S NEXT?

Look at your Self-assessment again. Do you need to review anything?

Unit 7 Supplementary Resources Overview

	After the following SB exercises	You can use these materials in class	Your students can use these materials outside the classroom
CYCLE 1	1 **Snapshot**		**SS** Unit 7 Vocabulary 1
	2 **Conversation**		**SS** Unit 7 Speaking 1
	3 **Grammar Focus**		**SB** Unit 7 Grammar plus, Focus 1 **SS** Unit 7 Grammar 1 **GAME** Say the Word (Simple present short answers)
	4 **Listening**		**WB** Unit 7 exercises 1–4
CYCLE 2	5 **Word Power**	**TSS** Unit 7 Vocabulary Worksheet **TSS** Unit 7 Listening Worksheet **TSS** Unit 7 Extra Worksheet	**SD** Unit 7 Vocabulary 2 **GAME** Spell or Slime (Furniture) **GAME** Sentence Runner (Furniture; *There is, there are*)
	6 **Conversation**		**SS** Unit 7 Speaking 2
	7 **Grammar Focus**	**TSS** Unit 7 Grammar Worksheet	**SB** Unit 7 Grammar plus, Focus 2 **SS** Unit 7 Grammar 2 **GAME** Sentence Stacker (*There is, there are*)
	8 **Interchange 7**		
	9 **Pronunciation**		
	10 **Listening**		
	11 **Speaking**		
	12 **Reading**	**TSS** Unit 7 Project Worksheet **VID** Unit 7 **VRB** Unit 7	**SS** Unit 7 Reading 1–2 **SS** Unit 7 Listening 1–3 **SS** Unit 7 Video 1–3 **WB** Unit 7 exercises 5–10

Key
GAME: Online Game **SB:** Student's Book **SS:** Online Self-study **TSS:** Teacher Support Site
VID: Video DVD **VRB:** Video Resource Book **WB:** Online Workbook/Workbook

My Plan for Unit 7

Use the space below to customize a plan that fits your needs.

With the following SB exercises	I am using these materials in class	My students are using these materials outside the classroom

With or instead of the following SB section	I am using these materials for assessment

7 Does it have a view?

- Describe houses and apartments
- Discuss furniture and dream homes

1 SNAPSHOT

Listen and practice.

Home Sweet Home

What rooms are in houses in your country? What rooms are in apartments?
What rooms are in your house or apartment? What is your favorite room?

2 CONVERSATION Do you live downtown?

Listen and practice.

Julia Hi Ethan. Guess what! I have a new apartment.

Ethan Hey! Cool! Do you live downtown?

Julia No, I don't. I live near the university now.

Ethan That's great! What's it like?

Julia It's really nice. It has a big living room, a bedroom, a bathroom, and a kitchen.

Ethan Awesome! Does it have an elevator?

Julia Yes, it does.

Ethan And does it have a nice view?

Julia No, it doesn't. It has a view of another apartment building!

7 Does it have a view?

Cycle 1, Exercises 1–4

In Unit 7, students describe houses and apartments, and discuss furniture and dream homes. By the end of Cycle 1, students will be able to describe houses and apartments using simple present questions and short answers. By the end of Cycle 2, students will be able to discuss furniture, appliances, and dream homes using statements with *there is/there are.*

1 SNAPSHOT

Learning Objective: describe living spaces in houses and apartments

[CD 2, Track 12]

- Focus Ss' attention on the pictures. Ask the class: "Who lives in a house? Who lives in an apartment?" Ss raise their hands.
- Set the scene. Two people are describing the house and the apartment.
- Play the audio program. Ss listen and read silently.

Audio script

House
The house has two floors, a garage, and a yard. The first floor has a living room, a dining room, a kitchen, a laundry room, and stairs to the second floor. The second floor has a hall, four bedrooms, and a bathroom.
Apartment
The apartment building has a lobby and an elevator. The apartment has a living room, a kitchen, a bedroom, a bathroom, and a closet.

- Read the words in the Snapshot aloud. Ss listen and repeat.
- Elicit or explain any new vocabulary.
- ***Option:*** Bring magazines with pictures of rooms to class. Use the pictures to explain the vocabulary.
- If needed, point out that *first floor* means "ground floor" in the U.S. Also, point out that many buildings in the U.S. don't have a 13th floor because some people think the number 13 is unlucky.
- Go over the focus questions. Ss discuss the questions in small groups. Then elicit their answers.

For more practice with house and apartment vocabulary, play the ***Chain Game*** – download it from the website. Begin with this sentence: "My house has a yard."

2 CONVERSATION

Learning Objective: use simple present short answers in a conversation about a new home

[CD 2, Track 13]

- Books closed. Set the scene. Julia is telling Ethan about her new apartment. Ask this focus question: "What rooms does the apartment have?" Encourage Ss to make guesses.
- Play the audio program and elicit the answer. (Answer: a living room, a bedroom, a bathroom, a kitchen)
- Write these focus questions on the board:
  1. *Does Julia like her apartment?*
  2. *Does it have a good view?*

  Books open. Play the audio program again. Ss listen and read silently. Elicit the answers to the focus questions. (Answers: 1. yes 2. no)

- Elicit or explain any new vocabulary.

Vocabulary
view: the scene you see from a specific place, usually a nice or interesting scene such as a lake
another: one more thing or person

- Play the audio program again. Ss listen and repeat.
- Ss practice the conversation in pairs.
- ***Option:*** Ask one or two pairs to role-play the conversation for the class.

! For a different way to practice the conversation, try ***Say It With Feeling!*** – download it from the website.

3 GRAMMAR FOCUS

Learning Objective: use simple present yes/no questions and short answers

[CD 2, Track 14]

Simple present short answers

- Focus Ss' attention on the Grammar Focus box. If needed, review the pattern for simple present yes/no questions from Unit 6, Exercise 7: *Do/Does* + subject + verb?
- Elicit or explain the pattern for short answers to simple present yes/no questions:

  Yes, + subject + *do/does.*
  No, + subject + *don't/doesn't.*
- Play the audio program. Ss listen and read silently. Point out that we usually stress *do* and *does* in short answers, but not in questions.

A

- Explain the task. Read Julia's first question and elicit Ethan's answer from the class.
- Ss complete the task individually. Then go over the answers as a class. Ask different Ss to read each line of the conversation.
- Ss practice the conversation in pairs.

Answers

Julia: **Do** you **live** in an apartment?
Ethan: No, I **don't**. I **live** in a house.
Julia: **Does** it **have** a yard?
Ethan: Yes, it **does**.
Julia: That sounds nice. **Do** you **live** alone?
Ethan: No, I **don't**. I **live** with my family.
Julia: **Do** you **have** any brothers or sisters?
Ethan: Yes, I **do**. I **have** four sisters.
Julia: Really? **Does** your house **have** many bedrooms?
Ethan: Yes, it **does**. It **has** four.
Julia: **Do** you **have** your own bedroom?
Ethan: Yes, I **do**. I'm really lucky.

B *Pair work*

- Explain the task. Ask two Ss to read the example questions aloud.
- Ss read the conversation again. Then they take turns asking and answering the questions in pairs. Go around the class and give help as needed.
- Ask different pairs of Ss to read the questions and answers. Correct any mistakes as a class.

Answers

1. No, he doesn't. (He lives in a house.)
2. Yes, it does.
3. No, he doesn't. (He lives with his family.)
4. Yes, he does.

C *Pair work*

- Ss write five questions individually. Then they take turns asking and answering the questions in pairs.

4 LISTENING

Learning Objective: listen for main ideas and details in short descriptions of homes

[CD 2, Track 15]

- Focus Ss' attention on the pictures. Elicit information about each picture.
- Explain the task. Then play the audio program. Ss listen and complete the task individually.
- Play the audio program again. Ss listen and check their answers. Then elicit the answers from the class.

Audio script

1. My family lives on the first floor of a house. Another family lives on the second floor. The people on the second floor are nice – but they're not very quiet!
2. I live in an apartment downtown. It's in a large, modern building. I have a great view of the city, and I'm close to lots of stores and restaurants.
3. My apartment is very small. It has just one room with a very small kitchen. It doesn't have a bedroom, so I sleep on the sofa.
4. My family and I live in an old house in the country. The house is a little small, but we have a nice yard and lots of trees. We like it a lot!

Answers

2, 1, 4, 3

End of Cycle 1

See the Supplementary Resources chart at the beginning of this unit for additional teaching materials and student activities related to this Cycle.

3 GRAMMAR FOCUS

Simple present short answers

Do you **live** in an apartment?
Yes, I **do**. / No, I **don't**.
Do the bedrooms **have** closets?
Yes, they **do**. / No, they **don't**.

Does Ethan **live** in a house?
Yes, he **does**. / No, he **doesn't**.
Does the house **have** a yard?
Yes, it **does**. / No, it **doesn't**.

GRAMMAR PLUS *see page 138*

A Complete the conversation. Then practice with a partner.

Julia ___Do___ you ___live___ in an apartment?
Ethan No, I ______________ . I ______________ in a house.
Julia ______________ it ______________ a yard?
Ethan Yes, it ______________ .
Julia That sounds nice. ______________ you ______________ alone?
Ethan No, I ______________ . I ______________ with my family.
Julia ______________ you ______________ any brothers or sisters?
Ethan Yes, I ______________ . I ______________ four sisters.
Julia Really? ______________ your house ______________ many bedrooms?
Ethan Yes, it ______________ . It ______________ four.
Julia ______________ you ______________ your own bedroom?
Ethan Yes, I ______________ . I'm really lucky.

B PAIR WORK Read the conversation in part A again. Ask and answer these questions about Ethan.

1. Does he live in an apartment?
2. Does his house have a yard?
3. Does he live alone?
4. Does he have his own room?

C PAIR WORK Write five questions to ask your partner about his or her home. Then ask and answer the questions.

4 LISTENING We have a nice yard.

Listen to four people describe their homes. Number the pictures from 1 to 4.

5 WORD POWER Furniture and appliances

A Listen and practice.

an armchair

a stove

curtains

pictures

a bed

a table

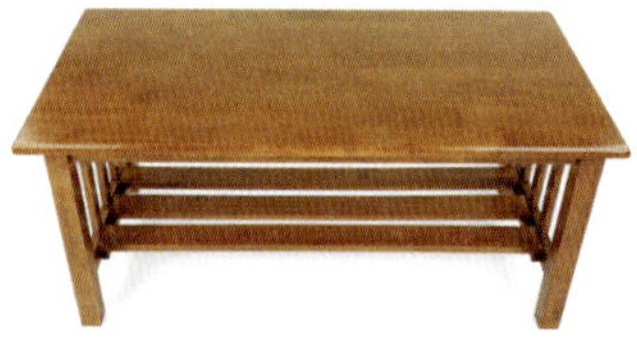
a coffee table

a microwave

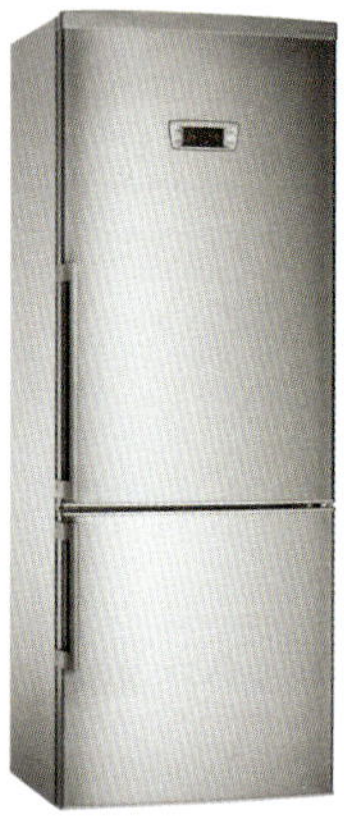
a refrigerator

lamps

a sofa

a desk

a coffee maker

a dresser

chairs

a mirror

a bookcase

a rug

cupboards

B Which rooms have the things in part A? Complete the chart.

A kitchen has . . .	*a table a stove*
A dining room has . . .	*a table*
A living room has . . .	
A bedroom has . . .	

C **GROUP WORK** What furniture is in your house or apartment? Tell your classmates.

"My living room has a sofa, a bookcase, and a rug . . ."

5 WORD POWER

Learning Objective: discuss furniture and other household items

A *[CD 2, Track 16]*

- Focus Ss' attention on the pictures. Play the audio program. Ss listen, point to the correct pictures, and repeat.
- ***Option:*** Write this model conversation on the board:

  A: What's this?
  B: It's a stove.
  A: What are these?
  B: They're lamps.

  Ss work in pairs. They use the model conversation to ask and answer questions about the items.

B

- Focus Ss' attention on the task. Ask: "Where does a table go? Where does a stove go?" Point out that some items can go in more than one room.
- Ss complete the chart individually. Then they compare answers in pairs.

Possible answers

A kitchen has: a table, a stove, chairs, curtains, a microwave, cupboards, pictures, a refrigerator, a rug, a coffee maker
A dining room has: a table, chairs, curtains, pictures, a rug, cupboards
A living room has: an armchair, a bookcase, a coffee table, curtains, a desk, lamps, a mirror, pictures, a rug, cupboards
A bedroom has: an armchair or a chair, a bed, a bookcase, curtains, a desk, a dresser, a lamp, a mirror, pictures, a rug

C *Group work*

- Explain the task and model the example sentence.
- Ss complete the task in small groups.

TIP
To help Ss connect to new vocabulary, personalize the activities whenever possible. For example, encourage Ss to talk about furniture in their homes.

- ***Option:*** Ss share information about their classmates' furniture.

For more practice with furniture vocabulary, play ***Change Chairs*** – download it from the website. Start with this instruction: "Change chairs if you have a bookcase in your living room."

6 CONVERSATION

Learning Objective: use *there is* and *there are* in a conversation about furniture

[CD 2, Track 17]

- Books closed. Set the scene. Eric is in Lara's new apartment. Lara is talking about furniture. Tell Ss to listen and write down any furniture they hear.
- Play the audio program. Elicit answers from the class. (Answers: chairs, table, sofa, armchairs, rug, lamp)
- Books open. Text covered. Focus Ss' attention on the subtitle and the picture. Write these focus questions on the board:

  1. What furniture does Lara have in the kitchen?
  2. What furniture does she need in the kitchen?
  3. What furniture does she have in the living room?
  4. What furniture does she need in the living room?

Elicit or explain the difference between *have* and *need*. Then elicit possible answers from the class. Encourage Ss to guess.

TIP

To prepare Ss for the listening task, elicit predictions by using the title and picture. Then play the audio program.

- Text uncovered. Play the audio program. Ss listen and read silently. Then elicit the answers to the focus questions. (Answers: 1. chairs 2. a table 3. a lamp 4. a sofa, armchairs, a rug)
- Play the audio program again. Ss listen and repeat.
- Ss practice the conversation in pairs.

7 GRAMMAR FOCUS

Learning Objective: use *there is/there are* and *some, no,* and *any* to describe rooms

[CD 2, Track 18]

There is, there are

- Focus Ss' attention on the Grammar Focus box. Explain that we usually use *there is/there are* to give information about the things in a place. We use *there is* with singular nouns and *there are* with plural nouns.
- Play the audio program. Ss listen and read silently.
- Remind Ss that we use *a/an* with singular nouns. Point out that we use *some* with plural nouns in positive statements, and we use *any* with plural nouns in negative statements.
- Write this on the board:

  There's no (+ singular noun).
  There isn't a (+ singular noun).
  There are no (+ plural noun).
  There aren't any (+ plural noun).

  Point out that *not any* and *no* have the same meaning.

A

- Explain the first part of the task. Focus Ss' attention on the picture of Ann's apartment. Elicit several sentences with *There* about the picture.
- Ss complete the task individually. Go around the class and give help as needed.
- Ask different Ss to write the answers on the board.

Answers

1. **There's no** dresser in the bedroom./**There isn't a** dresser in the bedroom.
2. **There are some** chairs in the kitchen.
3. **There's a** lamp in the living room.
4. **There isn't a** refrigerator./**There's no** refrigerator.
5. **There aren't any** rugs on the floor./**There are no** rugs on the floor.
6. **There aren't any** curtains on the windows./**There are no** curtains on the windows.
7. **There isn't an** armchair in the bedroom./**There's no** armchair in the bedroom.
8. **There aren't any** books in the bookcase./**There are no** books in the bookcase.

B

- Explain the task. Elicit examples from the class and write them on the board. Encourage Ss to use *some, no,* and *any* at least once in their sentences.
- Ss write sentences individually. Go around the class and give help with vocabulary and spelling as needed.
- Ss compare their sentences in pairs. Then elicit sentences from the class and ask different Ss to write them on the board.

8 INTERCHANGE 7

See page T-121 for teaching notes.

6 CONVERSATION I really need some furniture.

Listen and practice.

Eric This apartment is great, Lara.

Lara Thanks. I love it, but I really need some furniture.

Eric What do you need?

Lara Oh, lots of things. For example, there are some chairs in the kitchen, but there isn't a table.

Eric That's true. And there's no sofa in the living room.

Lara And there aren't any armchairs, there isn't a rug . . . There's only this lamp!

Eric So let's go shopping next weekend!

7 GRAMMAR FOCUS

There is, there are

There's a bed in the bedroom.	**There are some** chairs in the kitchen.	There**'s** = There is
There's no sofa in the bedroom.	**There are no** chairs in the living room.	
There isn't a table in the kitchen.	**There aren't any** chairs in the living room.	

GRAMMAR PLUS *see page 138*

A Look at the picture of Ann's apartment. Complete the sentences. Then practice with a partner.

1. *There's no* dresser in the bedroom.
2. ________ chairs in the kitchen.
3. ________ lamp in the living room.
4. ________ refrigerator.
5. ________ rugs on the floor.
6. ________ curtains on the windows.
7. ________ armchair in the bedroom.
8. ________ books in the bookcase.

B Write five sentences about things you have or don't have in your home. Then compare with a partner.

There are two sofas in my living room.

8 INTERCHANGE 7 Find the differences

Compare two apartments. Go to Interchange 7 on page 121.

9 PRONUNCIATION Words with *th*

A Listen and practice. Notice the pronunciation of /θ/ and /ð/.

/ð/ /θ/ /ð/ /ð/ /θ/ /θ/

There are **th**irteen rooms in **th**is house. **Th**e house has **th**ree ba**th**rooms.

B **PAIR WORK** List other words with /θ/ and /ð/. Then use them to write two sentences. Read them aloud.

There are thirty-three books on their bookcase.

10 LISTENING A furniture website

Listen to Jacob and Courtney talk about furniture on a website. What does Courtney like? What doesn't she like? Choose ☺ (likes) or ☹ (doesn't like).

☺ ☹ armchairs	☺ ☹ a sofa
☺ ☹ a rug	☺ ☹ lamps
☺ ☹ a bookcase	☺ ☹ a mirror
☺ ☹ a coffee table	☺ ☹ curtains

11 SPEAKING My dream home

A Write a description of your dream home.

What is your dream home?
Where is it?
What rooms does it have?
What things are in the rooms?
Does it have a view?

My dream home is a loft in a big city. There is one large living room with a lot of windows. There are two bedrooms and . . .

B **PAIR WORK** Ask your partner about his or her dream home.

A: What is your dream home?
B: My dream home is a loft in a big city.
A: What rooms does it have?
B: Well, there is a big living room, a small kitchen . . .

a beach house

a loft in a big city

a country villa

a cabin in the mountains

9 PRONUNCIATION

Learning Objective: sound more natural when using the sounds /θ/ and /ð/

A *[CD 2, Track 19]*

- Write the words *three* and *there* on the board. Point out that *th* has different sounds in these words.
- Say the words *three* and *there* aloud. Ss repeat.
- If Ss have trouble making the sounds correctly, tell them to put one hand in front of their mouths. Point out that words with /θ/ produce air. Words with /ð/ do not produce air.
- Explain the task and focus Ss' attention on the sentences. Play the audio program. Ss listen.
- Play the audio program again. Ss listen and repeat.

B *Pair Work*

- Explain the task. Then focus Ss' attention on the model sentence. Read it aloud. Ss repeat.
- Ss list words with /θ/ and /ð/ in pairs. Go around the class and give help as needed.
- Write the headings /θ/ and /ð/ on the board. Elicit words with each sound from the class. Ask different Ss to write them under the correct heading.
- Read the words aloud. Ss listen and repeat.
- Ss work in pairs. They write two sentences using words from the board. Then they read them aloud. Go around the class and give help as needed.

10 LISTENING

Learning Objective: listen for specific information in a conversation about buying furniture

[CD 2, Track 20]

- Set the scene. Courtney and Jacob are shopping for furniture for Courtney's new apartment.
- Explain the task and focus Ss' attention on the chart. Ss listen for the words in the chart and decide which things Courtney likes.
- Play the audio program two or three times. Ss listen and complete the chart. If needed, pause the audio program every few lines.

TIP
If an audio program is long, pause it where appropriate (e.g., after the speakers discuss each item). It may be helpful to mark where you plan to pause the audio program in this book.

Audio script

Jacob	What website is that?
Courtney	Oh, it's a furniture website. I'm buying a few things for the living room. Look at these blue armchairs.
Jacob	They're really cool!
Courtney	Yeah, I love them. I need two for the living room. But they're so expensive.
Jacob	What about that sofa? It's really nice.
Courtney	No. I don't like that color. And I have a sofa now – from my parents. It's blue, too!
Jacob	Hey, look at that rug. . . . It's great! And it matches the chairs.
Courtney	Um . . . it's . . . a little boring. Oh! I really like that coffee table.
Jacob	Yeah, it's really beautiful. Hey, you need a bookcase, right? Look at that bookcase.
Courtney	No, I don't like it. It's too big.
Jacob	Those yellow lamps are nice.
Courtney	I don't need any lamps. And I don't like yellow. Oh, I know! I need some curtains.
Jacob	Do you like those curtains there?
Courtney	No, not really. Hey, look at that mirror.
Jacob	It's great. But it's a little expensive.
Courtney	That's OK. It's perfect!

- Go over the answers with the class.

Answers

Likes: armchairs, a coffee table, a mirror
Doesn't like: a sofa, a rug, a bookcase, lamps, curtains

11 SPEAKING

Learning Objectives: describe a home using *there is/ there are* and the simple present

A

- Focus Ss' attention on the title and pictures. Elicit or explain the meaning of any new words.
- Explain the task and read the focus questions aloud.
- Ask a S to read the example description.
- Elicit adjectives to describe a home (e.g., *beautiful, nice, big, new, old*) and write them on the board.
- Ss complete the task individually.

B *Pair Work*

- Explain the task and ask two Ss to model the example conversation. Then Ss complete the task in pairs.

12 READING

Learning Objective: scan and read for details in an article about unusual hotels

A *[CD 2, Track 21]*

- Explain that Ss are going to read about different types of hotels. Focus Ss' attention on the first picture. Ask: "What is unusual about this room?" (Possible answers: the shape of the room; the room is *clear* [you can see through it])
- Read the task and question aloud.
- Ss scan the article to find the answer. Ask them to raise their hands when they find it. Then elicit the answer. (Answer: The Roxbury)

TIP
To encourage Ss to scan quickly, ask them to raise their hands when they find the answers.

B

- Explain the first part of the task. Focus Ss' attention on the words and phrases in the box.
- Ask Ss to scan the article and find the phrase *yellow road*. Ss raise their hands when they find it. Ask a volunteer to read the example sentence. Elicit or explain the reference to the classic movie *The Wizard of Oz*.
- Tell Ss to scan the text to find the remaining words and phrases.

TIP
To help Ss decide what reading strategy to use (here, scanning), focus their attention on the purpose of the task. For example, say: "We want to know what's in each hotel, so just look for these phrases."

- Ss scan the article again and underline any new vocabulary.
- Elicit or explain any new vocabulary. Point out that *just like* is an adverb used to describe things that are very similar.

Answers

1. In the Wizard's Emeralds room, there is a **yellow road**.
2. There is a **round bed** in Maryann's Coconut Cream Pie room.
3. In George's Spacepad, there are two **sofas**. There is a red **bathtub**, but there isn't a **shower**.
4. There is a view of the **moon/stars** and the **stars/moon**.
5. There is an **air conditioner** to keep the room cool.
6. There are sometimes **animals** playing outside.
7. There isn't a **TV**.

- Ss read the article and complete the sentences individually. Then go over their answers as a class.

Vocabulary
air conditioner: an appliance to cool the air
bathtub: the container that you sit in to wash yourself
heater: a machine that warms air or water
moon: the round object in the sky at night
nature: plants, animals, and the land outside
shower: the part of the bathroom you stand in to wash your body
stars: points of light in the sky at night
unusual: different than most

C *Group work*

- Explain the task and read the focus questions aloud.
- Ss discuss the questions in small groups. Go around the class and encourage Ss to give reasons.
- Elicit answers from each group. Encourage other Ss to ask questions.

End of Cycle 2

See the Supplementary Resources chart at the beginning of this unit for additional teaching materials and student activities related to this Cycle.

12 READING

A Scan the article. Which hotel has a room that looks like a dessert?

TRAVELNEWS Home Posts Archives

Unique Hotels

Which do you like – the world of science or the world of fiction? In this week's vacation post, we discover a hotel made for fans of nature and another hotel for fans of stories.

Bubble Hotel, Allauch, France
4 new

Just imagine sleeping in a giant, clear bubble in a forest. That's exactly what happens here. At night, hotel guests lie in bed and watch the stars and moon. Each bubble has a comfortable bed and a nice bathroom with a shower. There's also an air-conditioner to keep the room cool in summer and a heater to keep it warm when it's cold outside.

Each bubble room is different. Guests choose the "Zen" bubble if they want to feel relaxed. Or they stay in the "Love Nature" bubble for a beautiful view. Sometimes there are rabbits and squirrels playing outside. Is there anything missing? Well, yes, there isn't a TV because no one needs a TV in a bubble!

The Roxbury, New York, the United States
4 new

In the mountains near New York City, there's a very unusual hotel. Its name is the Roxbury. It has many rooms, but every single room is different. There's the Wizard's Emeralds room, for example. It has a yellow "road" in the middle – just like in *The Wizard of Oz*. There's a green shower in the bathroom with big red flowers on the walls.

Do you like sweet things? Maryann's Coconut Cream Pie room looks just like a dessert – good enough to eat! The bed is round like a pie, and the ceiling looks like whipped cream.

How about space? When you walk into George's Spacepad, you see an enormous red bathtub. It glows in the dark! There isn't a shower, but there are silver curtains, crazy lights, and two cozy sofas. It's really out of this world!

B Read the article. What's in each hotel? Complete the sentences.

sofas	animals	moon	round bed	✓ yellow road
stars	bathtub	TV	shower	air-conditioner

At The Roxbury

1. In the Wizard's Emeralds room, there is a ___yellow road___.
2. There is a ______________ in Maryann's Coconut Cream Pie room.
3. In George's Spacepad, there are two ______________. There is a red ______________, but there isn't a ______________.

At the Bubble Hotel

4. There is a view of the ______________ and the ______________.
5. There is an ______________ to keep the room cool.
6. There are sometimes ______________ playing outside.
7. There isn't a ______________.

C **GROUP WORK** Talk about these questions.

1. Which hotel do you like? Why?
2. Imagine you have a hotel. What do you do to make it interesting?

Unit 8 Supplementary Resources Overview

	After the following SB exercises	You can use these materials in class	Your students can use these materials outside the classroom
CYCLE 1	1 Word Power		**SS** Unit 8 Vocabulary 1 **GAME** Name the Picture (Jobs)
	2 Speaking		
	3 Conversation		**SS** Unit 8 Speaking 1
	4 Grammar Focus	**TSS** Unit 8 Extra Worksheet	**SB** Unit 8 Grammar plus, Focus 1 **SS** Unit 8 Grammar 1 **GAME** Speak or Swim (Simple present Wh-questions 1) **GAME** Sentence Runner (Simple present Wh-questions 2)
	5 Pronunciation		**WB** Unit 8 exercises 1–4
CYCLE 2	6 Snapshot		
	7 Conversation		**SS** Unit 8 Speaking 2
	8 Listening		
	9 Grammar Focus	**TSS** Unit 8 Vocabulary Worksheet **TSS** Unit 8 Grammar Worksheet **TSS** Unit 8 Listening Worksheet	**SB** Unit 8 Grammar plus, Focus 2 **SS** Unit 8 Vocabulary 2 **SS** Unit 8 Grammar 2 **GAME** Word Keys (Placement of adjectives)
	10 Interchange 8		
	11 Speaking		
	12 Reading	**TSS** Unit 8 Project Worksheet **VID** Unit 8 **VRB** Unit 8	**SS** Unit 8 Reading 1–2 **SS** Unit 8 Listening 1–3 **SS** Unit 8 Video 1–3 **WB** Unit 8 exercises 5–7

With or instead of the following SB section	You can also use these materials for assessment
Units 7–8 Progress Check	**ASSESSMENT PROGRAM** Units 7–8 Oral Quiz **ASSESSMENT PROGRAM** Units 7–8 Written Quiz **ASSESSMENT PROGRAM** Units 1–8 Test

Key **GAME:** Online Game **SB:** Student's Book **SS:** Online Self-study **TSS:** Teacher Support Site
VID: Video DVD **VRB:** Video Resource Book **WB:** Online Workbook/Workbook

My Plan for Unit 8

Use the space below to customize a plan that fits your needs.

With the following SB exercises	I am using these materials in class	My students are using these materials outside the classroom

With or instead of the following SB section	I am using these materials for assessment

8 Where do you work?

- Discuss jobs and workplaces using simple present Wh-questions
- Discuss opinions about jobs using *be* + adjective and adjective + noun

1 WORD POWER Jobs

A Match the jobs with the pictures. Then listen and practice.

a. accountant	e. doctor	i. office manager	m. security guard
b. bellhop	f. front desk clerk	✓ j. police officer	n. server
c. cashier	g. host	k. receptionist	o. taxi driver
d. chef	h. nurse	l. salesperson	p. vendor

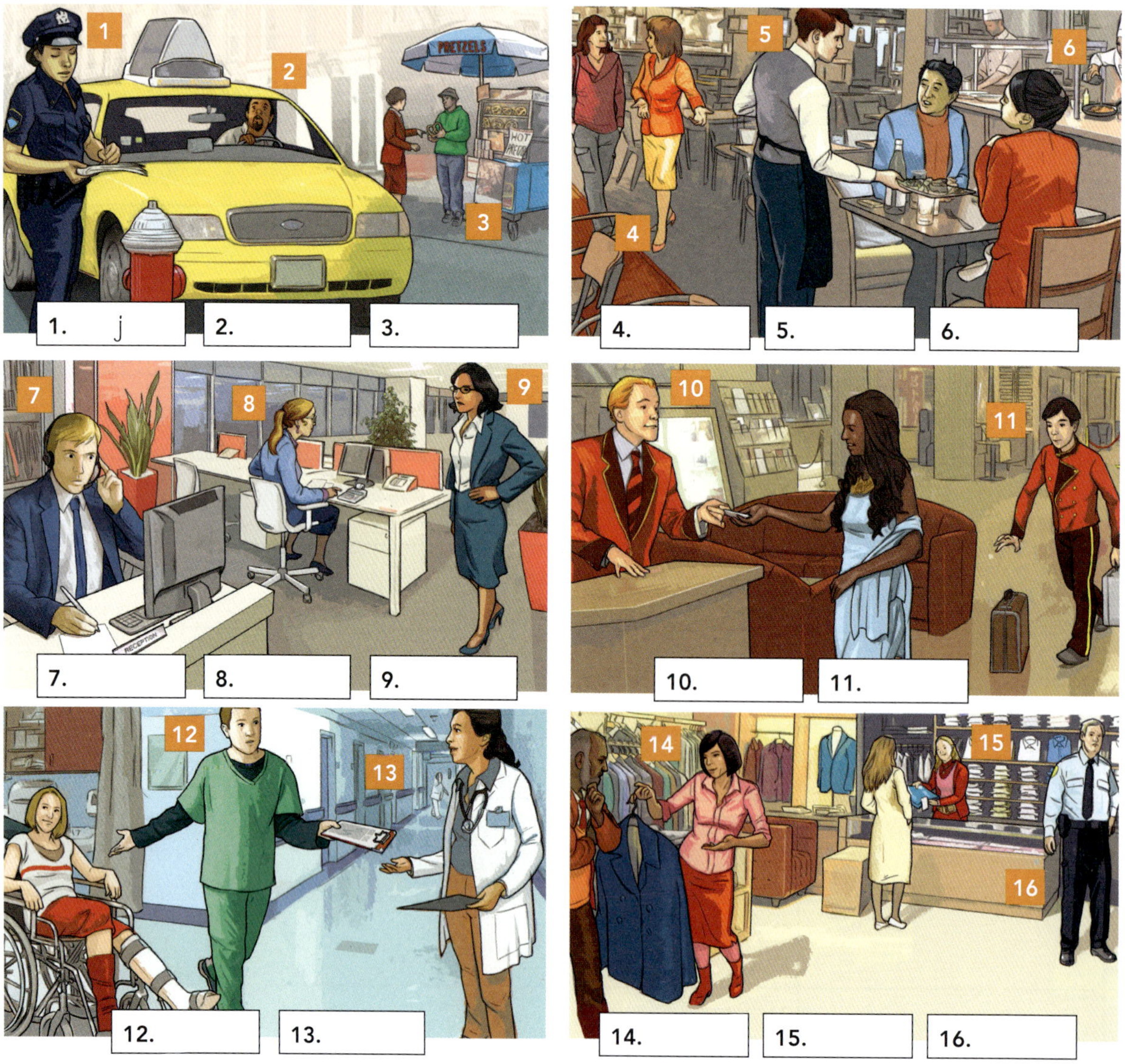

B PAIR WORK Ask questions about the people in part A. What are their jobs?

A: What does she do?

B: She's a police officer.

8 Where do you work?

Cycle 1, Exercises 1–5

In Unit 8, students discuss jobs and workplaces using simple present Wh-questions, and discuss opinions about jobs using *be* + adjective and adjective + noun. By the end of Cycle 1, students will be able to discuss jobs and workplaces using simple present Wh-questions. By the end of Cycle 2, students will be able to give opinions about jobs using *be* + adjective and adjective + noun.

1 WORD POWER

Learning Objective: discuss common jobs

A *[CD 2, Track 22]*

- Books closed. Write the word *teacher* on the board. Say: "I am a teacher. *Teacher* is a job. Name some other jobs." Elicit jobs from the class and write them on the board.

TIP
To avoid teaching words Ss already know, start by eliciting the words they know. Then teach any remaining vocabulary.

- Books open. Focus Ss' attention on the pictures. Read the jobs aloud. Ss listen and repeat.
- Explain the first part of the task. Ss match the jobs with the pictures individually. Then they compare answers in pairs.
- Play the audio program. Ss listen and check their answers. One S writes the answers on the board.

Audio script

1. j , police officer
2. o, taxi driver
3. p, vendor
4. g, host
5. n, server
6. d, chef
7. k, receptionist
8. a, accountant
9. i, office manager
10. f, front desk clerk
11. b, bellhop
12. h, nurse
13. e, doctor
14. l, salesperson
15. c, cashier
16. m, security guard

Answers

1. j	3. p	5. n	7. k	9. i	11. b	13. e	15. c
2. o	4. g	6. d	8. a	10. f	12. h	14. l	16. m

- Play the audio program again. Ss listen and repeat.

B *Pair work*

- Explain the task. Focus Ss' attention on the police officer in part A. Model the example conversation with a S.
- Focus Ss' attention on the receptionist in part A. Ask two Ss to model the task.
- Point out that Ss should ask about the people in random order.
- Ss complete the task in pairs. Go around the class and help Ss with pronunciation as needed.

For more practice with vocabulary for jobs, play ***Bingo*** – download it from the website.

TIP
Ss usually forget about 80 percent of new words after 24 hours. To help them remember new vocabulary, recycle or review the words during the next class.

2 SPEAKING

Learning Objective: discuss workplaces and other job information

A *Pair work*

- Focus Ss' attention on the pictures. Ask: "What are these places?" Elicit the answers. (Answers: a hospital, an office, a store, a hotel)
- Explain the task. Then ask two Ss to model the example conversation. Elicit other jobs in a hospital (e.g., *receptionist, security guard*).
- Ss complete the task in pairs. Go around the class and give help with vocabulary as needed.
- Copy the chart on the board. Elicit answers from the class and ask different Ss to write them on the board.

Possible answers

In a hospital: a doctor, a nurse, an accountant, a receptionist, a security guard, *a technician, a therapist, a surgeon, a custodian*
In an office: a doctor, a nurse, an office manager, a receptionist, a police officer, a salesperson, an accountant, *a manager, an architect, a dentist, a lawyer*
In a store: a cashier, a security guard, a salesperson, *a manager, a janitor, a salesclerk*
In a hotel: a front desk clerk, a bellhop, an office manager, an accountant, a receptionist, a security guard, *a housekeeper, a manager, a valet*
(Note: Additional examples are italicized.)

B *Class activity*

- Focus Ss' attention on the phrases and read them aloud. Elicit or explain the meaning of any new vocabulary. If needed, use the pictures in Exercises 1 and 2, show examples of uniforms or a team, or mime working, sitting, or standing.

TIP
To explain new words, choose appropriate techniques such as pictures, props, mime, examples, or definitions.

- Read the phrases again. Ss listen and repeat.
- Explain the task. Point out that Ss should try to ask a different S each question.
- Ask three Ss to model the example conversation.
- Ss go around the class and complete the task. Go around the class and encourage Ss to look at each other and change partners often.
- ***Option:*** Ss complete the task in small groups.
- Elicit answers from the class.

For more practice with workplace and job vocabulary, play ***Vocabulary Tennis*** – download it from the website. Call out a workplace, and each team says a different job in that workplace.

3 CONVERSATION

Learning Objective: use simple present Wh-questions in a conversation about a job

[CD 2, Track 23]

- Books closed. Set the scene. Jordan is asking Alicia about her brother's job.
- Write these focus questions on the board:
  1. *Where does Alicia's brother work?*
  2. *What's his job?*
  3. *What other person works there?*
  4. *What's his job?*
- Then play the audio program and Ss listen for the answers. Elicit the answers. (Answers: 1. a hotel 2. the manager 3. Jordan's brother 4. the/an accountant)
- Books open. Focus Ss' attention on the picture. Play the audio program again. Ss listen and read silently.
- Elicit or explain any new vocabulary.

Vocabulary
too: also; very
That's funny.: That's surprising.
Actually: In fact (used to introduce surprising information)

- Ask the class: "Does Jordan's brother like his job? Why?"

  Then elicit the answer. (Answer: No, he doesn't. He doesn't like the manager.)
- Play the audio program again. Ss listen and repeat. Then they practice the conversation in pairs.

For a new way to practice this conversation, try ***Substitution Dialog*** – download it from the website. Ss change *my brother* to *my sister* and *he* to *she*.

2 SPEAKING Workplaces

A **PAIR WORK** Who works in these places? Complete the chart with jobs from Exercise 1. Add one more job to each list.

A: A doctor works in a hospital. **B:** A nurse works in a hospital, too.

IN A HOSPITAL	IN AN OFFICE	IN A STORE	IN A HOTEL
a doctor			
a nurse			

B **CLASS ACTIVITY** Ask and answer *Who* questions about jobs. Use these words.

wears a uniform	sits all day	stands all day	works with a team
talks to people	works hard	works at night	makes a lot of money

A: Who wears a uniform?
B: A police officer wears a uniform.
C: A security guard wears a uniform, too.

3 CONVERSATION What does he do?

Listen and practice.

JORDAN Where does your brother work?
ALICIA In a hotel.
JORDAN Oh, really? My brother works in a hotel, too. He's an accountant.
ALICIA How does he like it?
JORDAN He hates it. He doesn't like the manager.
ALICIA That's too bad. What hotel does he work for?
JORDAN The Plaza.
ALICIA That's funny. My brother works there, too.
JORDAN Oh, that's interesting. What does he do?
ALICIA Actually, he's the manager!

4 GRAMMAR FOCUS

Simple present Wh-questions

Where do you **work**?	**Where does** he **work**?	**Where do** they **work**?
In a hospital.	In a hotel.	In an office.
What do you **do**?	**What does** he **do**?	**What do** they **do**?
I'm a doctor.	He's a manager.	They're accountants.
How do you **like** it?	**How does** he **like** it?	**How do** they **like** it?
I really like it.	It's OK.	They hate it.

GRAMMAR PLUS *see page 139*

A Complete these conversations. Then practice with a partner.

1. **A:** ___What___ does your sister ___do___?
   B: My sister? She's a teacher.
   A: ________ does she ________ it?
   B: It's difficult, but she loves it.

2. **A:** ________ does your brother ________?
   B: In an office. He's an accountant.
   A: Oh? ________ does he ________ it?
   B: He doesn't really like it.

3. **A:** ________ do your parents ________ their jobs?
   B: Oh, I guess they like them.
   A: I don't remember. ________ do they ________?
   B: In a big hospital. They're doctors.

4. **A:** ________ do you ________?
   B: I'm a student.
   A: I see. ________ do you ________ your classes?
   B: They're great. I like them a lot.

B **PAIR WORK** Ask questions about these people. Where do they work? What do they do? How do they like it?

Jeff

Jodie

Chad and Tracy

A: Where does Chad work?
B: He works in . . .

5 PRONUNCIATION Reduction of *do*

Listen and practice. Notice the reduction of **do**.

Where **do you** work?
What **do you** do?
Where **do they** work?
What **do they** do?

4 GRAMMAR FOCUS

Learning Objective: ask and answer simple present Wh-questions

[CD 2, Track 24]

Simple present Wh-questions

- Focus Ss' attention on the Grammar Focus box. To explain the difference between *where*, *what*, and *how*, write this on the board:

  Where do you work? = What's your workplace?
  What do you do? = What's your job?
  How do you like it? = What's your opinion about it?

- If needed, point out that we call *how* a Wh-word because we're asking for information.
- Elicit or explain the pattern for simple present Wh-questions:

  Wh-word + *do/does* + subject + verb?

- Play the audio program. Ss listen and read silently.
- ***Option:*** Play the audio program again. Ss listen and repeat.

A

- Explain the task. Then read the first two lines of the first conversation with a S.
- Ss complete the conversations individually. Go around the class and give help as needed.
- Ss practice the conversations in pairs. Tell them to correct their answers while they practice.

Answers

1. A: **What** does your sister **do**?
   B: My sister? She's a teacher.
   A: **How** does she **like** it?
   B: It's difficult, but she loves it.
2. A: **Where** does your brother **work**?
   B: In an office. He's an accountant.
   A: Oh? **How** does he **like** it?
   B: He doesn't really like it.
3. A: **How** do your parents **like** their jobs?
   B: Oh, I guess they like them.
   A: I don't remember. **Where** do they **work**?
   B: In a big hospital. They're doctors.
4. A: **What** do you **do**?
   B: I'm a student.
   A: I see. **How** do you **like** your classes?
   B: They're great. I like them a lot.

- ***Option:*** Ask four different pairs of Ss to read the conversations for the class.

B *Pair work*

- Focus Ss' attention on the pictures. Explain the task.
- Ask the class: "Where does Chad work?" Elicit the answer. (Answer: He works in a store/clothing store.)
- Ss complete the task in pairs. Go around the class and check Ss' use of grammar.

5 PRONUNCIATION

Learning Objective: sound more natural when asking simple present Wh-questions with *do*

[CD 2, Track 25]

- Focus Ss' attention on the model questions. Explain that we usually reduce *do* + pronoun in conversation.
- Play the audio program. Ss listen and read silently.
- Play the audio program again. Ss listen and repeat.
- ***Option:*** Write these questions on the board:

  Where does she work?
  What does he do?

  Point out that we also reduce *does* with pronouns. Read out the questions. Ss repeat.

- ***Option:*** Ss underline all the examples of *does* + pronoun in Exercise 3 on page 51. Then play the audio program for Exercise 3. Ss listen and pay attention to the reductions. Then they practice the conversation again in pairs.

End of Cycle 1

See the Supplementary Resources chart at the beginning of this unit for additional teaching materials and student activities related to this Cycle.

Cycle 2, Exercises 6–12

6 SNAPSHOT

Learning Objective: use adjectives to give opinions about jobs

[CD 2, Track 26]

- Focus Ss' attention on the pictures and the focus questions. Explain that they will be listening to and reading different answers to these questions.
- Play the audio program. Ss listen and read silently.
- Ask Ss to identify the jobs mentioned. (Answers: lawyer, photographer, software engineer, pilot)
- Ask Ss to identify the adjectives that the people use to describe their jobs.
- Play the audio program again. Ss listen and repeat.
- Read the focus questions aloud. Elicit the answers.
- As Ss tell you what jobs they think are interesting, write each job on the board. Elicit adjectives to describe each job and write them below the job.
- ***Option:*** Ask Ss for other jobs that these adjectives describe. Write their answers on the board.

7 CONVERSATION

Learning Objective: use adjectives + nouns in a conversation about jobs

[CD 2, Track 27]

- Books closed. Set the scene. Jack and Paula are talking about their new jobs. Ask: "What does Paula do? What does Jack do?"
- Then play the audio program and elicit the answers. (Answers: 1. She's a math teacher. 2. He's a firefighter.)
- Books open. Play the audio program again. Ss listen and read silently. Elicit or explain any new vocabulary.
- Ask the class: "What's Jack's job like? What's Paula's job like?"
- Play the audio program again. Ss listen and repeat. Then they practice the conversation in pairs.

8 LISTENING

Learning Objective: listen for specific information discussed using *be* + adjective and adjective + noun

[CD 2, Track 28]

- Focus Ss' attention on the chart. Elicit possible answers for the questions *What do they do?* and *What's it like?*
- Explain the task. Then play the audio program. Ss listen and complete the task individually. Re-play the audio if needed. Elicit the answers from the class.

Audio script

1.
Man Where do you work now, Yasmin?
Yasmin I have a new job. I work downtown.
Man What do you do, exactly?
Yasmin I'm a street vendor. I sell ice cream.
Man Really? What's it like?
Yasmin It's an exciting job. I talk to lots of cool people every day.

2.
Man What do you do, Kana?
Kana I work in an office.
Man Really? What do you do, exactly?
Kana I'm a manager.
Man What's it like? I don't think that's an easy job.
Kana No, it isn't. I have a difficult job, but I like it!

3.
Woman Where do you work, Luke?
Luke At a store.
Woman Oh, are you a salesperson? Or a cashier?
Luke No, actually, I'm a security guard.
Woman Really? How do you like it?
Luke It's pretty boring. I don't like it very much.

4.
Woman What do you do, Brandon?
Brandon I work at the city hospital.
Woman The city hospital? Are you a doctor?
Brandon No, I'm a nurse.
Woman What's that like? Is it interesting?
Brandon Oh, yes! Every day is different. I really like it!

Answers

1. street vendor/ice cream vendor, exciting
2. office manager, not easy/difficult
3. security guard, boring
4. nurse, interesting

6 SNAPSHOT

Listen and practice.

Who likes his or her job? Who doesn't? Why? Why not?
What jobs do you think are interesting? What jobs are not very interesting?

7 CONVERSATION It's a dangerous job.

Listen and practice.

JACK Hey, Paula. I hear you have a new job.

PAULA Yes. I'm teaching math at Lincoln High School.

JACK How do you like it?

PAULA It's difficult, but the students are terrific. How are things with you?

JACK Not bad. Guess what! I'm a firefighter now.

PAULA Really? Wow! How do you like it?

JACK It's a dangerous job, but it's really interesting. I love it!

PAULA OK, but please be careful!

8 LISTENING Is your job interesting?

Listen to four people talk about their jobs. Complete the chart with the correct jobs and adjectives.

	What do they do?	What's it like?
1. Yasmin		
2. Kana		
3. Luke		
4. Brandon		

9 GRAMMAR FOCUS

Placement of adjectives

***be* + adjective**	**adjective + noun**
A doctor's job **is stressful**.	A doctor has **a stressful job**.
A firefighter's job **is dangerous**.	A firefighter has **a dangerous job**.

GRAMMAR PLUS *see page 139*

A Write each sentence a different way. Then compare with a partner.

1. A photographer's job is interesting. *A photographer has an interesting job.*
2. A pilot's job is exciting. ______
3. A teacher's job is stressful. ______
4. A cashier has a boring job. ______
5. An accountant has a difficult job. ______
6. A receptionist has an easy job. ______

B **GROUP WORK** Write one job for each adjective. Do your classmates agree?

1. easy	*actor*	**4.** boring	______
2. difficult	______	**5.** exciting	______
3. dangerous	______	**6.** relaxing	______

A: A graphic designer has an easy job.
B: I don't agree. A graphic designer's job is difficult.
C: I think . . .

graphic designer

10 INTERCHANGE 8 The perfect job

What do you want in a job? Go to Interchange 8 on page 122.

11 SPEAKING Workday routines

GROUP WORK Ask three classmates about their jobs (or their friends' or family members' jobs). Then tell the class.

Ask about a classmate	Ask about a classmate's friend or family member
Do you have a job?	Tell me about your . . .
Where do you work?	Where does he/she work?
What do you do, exactly?	What does he/she do, exactly?
Is your job interesting?	Is his/her job difficult?
What time do you start work?	What time does he/she start work?
When do you finish work?	When does he/she finish work?
Do you like your job?	Does he/she like his/her job?
What do you do after work?	What does he/she do after work?

9 GRAMMAR FOCUS

Learning Objective: use *be* + adjective and adjective + noun

[CD 2, Track 29]

Placement of adjectives

- Books closed. Write this on the board:

  My job is great.
  I have a great job.

  Point out that these sentences have the same meaning.
- Ask the class: "What is the adjective in these sentences? What is the noun?" (Answers: great, job)
- Books open. Focus Ss' attention on the Grammar Focus box. Point out that the pairs of sentences in each row have the same meaning. Elicit or explain the patterns for using *be* + adjective and adjective + noun to describe a job:

  A/An + (subject)*'s* + *job* + *is* + adjective.
  A/An + (subject) + *has* + *a/an* + adjective + *job*.
- Play the audio program. Ss listen and read silently.
- ***Option:*** Ss underline the adjectives and circle the nouns in the Grammar Focus box.

A

- Explain the task. Point out that Ss should write a different sentence that has the same meaning.
- Ss complete the task individually. Go around the class and give help with grammar as needed.
- Ask different Ss to read the sentence pairs to the class.

Answers

1. A photographer has an interesting job.
2. A pilot has an exciting job.
3. A teacher has a stressful job.
4. A cashier's job is boring.
5. An accountant's job is difficult.
6. A receptionist's job is easy.

B *Group work*

- Explain the first part of the task. Focus Ss' attention on the chart. Ask: "What jobs are easy?" Elicit ideas from the class.
- Ss complete the chart individually.
- Explain the second part of the task. Elicit or explain what a graphic designer does. Ask three Ss to model the example conversation.
- Ss complete the task in small groups. Then elicit different opinions from the class.

TIP
To make Ss feel confident about sharing their opinions, give them time to write down their ideas before the discussion.

10 INTERCHANGE 8

See page T-122 for teaching notes.

11 SPEAKING

Learning Objective: discuss different people's jobs

Group work

- Explain the task. Focus Ss' attention on the two lists of questions. Ask different Ss to read out the questions. Elicit or explain any new vocabulary.
- Write this short conversation on the board:

  A: *Do you have a job?*
  B: *Yes, I do./No, I don't, but my brother has a job.*
- Ask two Ss to read out the conversation. Explain that if Student B answers "yes," Student A should ask the questions in the left column. If Student B answers "no," Student A should ask the questions in the right column.
- Tell Ss to take notes on their classmates' answers.
- Ss complete the task in small groups. All group members participate in asking Student B the questions. Go around the class and write down any errors you hear.
- Ask different Ss to tell the class about their classmates' jobs.
- ***Option:*** Write the sentences with errors you noted on the board. Then have Ss correct them in pairs or small groups.

TIP
To help Ss develop oral fluency, don't interrupt and correct their errors. Instead, take note of any errors you hear and go over them later as a class, without mentioning who made the errors.

! For a new way to teach this exercise, try the ***Onion Ring*** technique – download it from the website.

12 READING

Learning Objectives: make predictions and read for specific information in an article about jobs

A *[CD 2, Track 30]*

- Focus Ss' attention on the title. Explain that a *dream job* is someone's idea of a perfect job. It may seem difficult or impossible to achieve. Elicit Ss' dream jobs.
- Focus Ss' attention on the pictures and labels. Ask Ss to look at the photos without reading the paragraphs. Elicit or explain the meaning of any new words. Ask: "What do you think these people do?"
- Ss discuss the answers in pairs, referring to the photos. Then elicit their answers.

B

- Ss read the article individually. Point out that they should continue reading without stopping to look up new words.

TIP
To build reading fluency, encourage Ss to read the entire article without looking up new words. Point out that they will discuss any new words later.

- Ss discuss the meaning of any new words in pairs or small groups. Then elicit or explain any remaining new vocabulary.

Vocabulary
crocodile: a large reptile, with a long mouth and sharp teeth, that lives in lakes and rivers
researcher: someone who studies a subject to find out new information about it
flavor: the taste of something, such as sweet, salty, chocolate, etc.
expert: someone who has a lot of skill or knowledge about something
taste: to experience the flavor of a food in your mouth

- Explain the task and read the sentences aloud. Explain that Ss will choose *True* (correct) sentences or *False* (incorrect) sentences.
- Ss complete the task individually.
- Ss compare their answers in groups. Then go over the answers with the class and encourage Ss to correct the statements that are false.

Answers
1. F 2. T 3. F 4. T 5. F

C

- Explain the first part of the task. To help Ss, write these focus questions on the board:
  1. What is the workplace of your dream job?
  2. What days do you work?
  3. What hours do you work?
  4. What do you wear?
  5. What do you do, exactly?
  6. What do you like about your dream job?
- Ss complete the task individually. Go around the class and help with vocabulary and spelling as needed.
- ***Option:*** Ss write the description for homework.
- Once their dream job descriptions are written, each S reads the description to the class but does not tell the job. The other Ss guess the job.
- ***Option:*** In very large classes, Ss read their descriptions in groups.

! For a new way to teach this exercise, try ***Reading Race*** – download it from the website.

End of Cycle 2

See the Supplementary Resources chart at the beginning of this unit for additional teaching materials and student activities related to this Cycle and for assessment tools.

12 READING

A Do you think all jobs are boring? Think again! Look at the photos. What do these people do?

Home Posts Archives

Dream Jobs

Crocodile Researcher

I have a great job. I study crocodiles! It's an important job. Let me explain why. Here in Australia, we have a lot of crocodiles, but sometimes the crocodiles are sick. I want to know why. I study the food the crocodiles eat. I also learn how fast they grow and where they live. How do I do this? Well, in the morning, I take my camera, and I watch the crocodiles in the river. I take photos. Sometimes the crocodiles eat toads. Some toads make them sick and they die. I want to help the crocodiles.

Ice Cream Flavor Expert

Believe it or not, I taste ice cream for my job. Yes, it's a dream job, but it's also difficult! I work at a big ice cream company. Every day, I taste lots of different flavors three times each. Why is that? Well, I taste a little of the ice cream we make in the morning, afternoon, and at night. That way, I know that all the ice cream is good. I use my eyes first: Does the ice cream look nice? Then I taste the ice cream with a spoon: Does it taste fresh and sweet? Then I spit it out. Yes, I really spit it out!

Subscribe to our site

enter email **Sign up**

B Read the article. Check (✓) True or False.

	True	False
1. Both people have jobs they do outside.	☐	☐
2. The crocodile researcher studies what crocodiles eat.	☐	☐
3. The crocodile researcher watches the crocodiles at night.	☐	☐
4. The ice cream flavor expert tastes each flavor three times.	☐	☐
5. Ice cream flavor experts don't look at the ice cream.	☐	☐

C What's your dream job? Why? Write a short description. Compare with a partner.

Units 7–8 Progress check

SELF-ASSESSMENT

How well can you do these things? Check (✓) the boxes.

I can . . .	Very well	OK	A little
Ask and answer questions about living spaces (Ex. 1)	☐	☐	☐
Talk about rooms and furniture (Ex. 1)	☐	☐	☐
Ask and answer questions about work (Ex. 2)	☐	☐	☐
Understand descriptions of jobs (Ex. 3)	☐	☐	☐
Give and respond to opinions about jobs (Ex. 4)	☐	☐	☐

1 SPEAKING A new apartment

A Imagine you are moving into this apartment. What things are in the rooms? Draw pictures. Use the furniture in the box and your own ideas.

bed **chairs** **desk** **dresser** **lamp** **mirror** **sofa** **table**

B PAIR WORK Ask questions about your partner's apartment.

A: I'm moving into a new apartment!
B: That's great! Where is it?
A: . . .
B: What's it like? Does it have many rooms?
A: Well, it has . . .
B: Does the . . . have . . . ?
A: . . .
B: Do you have a lot of furniture?
A: Well, there's . . . in the . . .
There are some . . . in the . . .
B: Do you have everything you need for the apartment?
A: No, I don't. There's no . . .
There isn't any . . .
There aren't any . . .
B: OK. Let's go shopping this weekend!

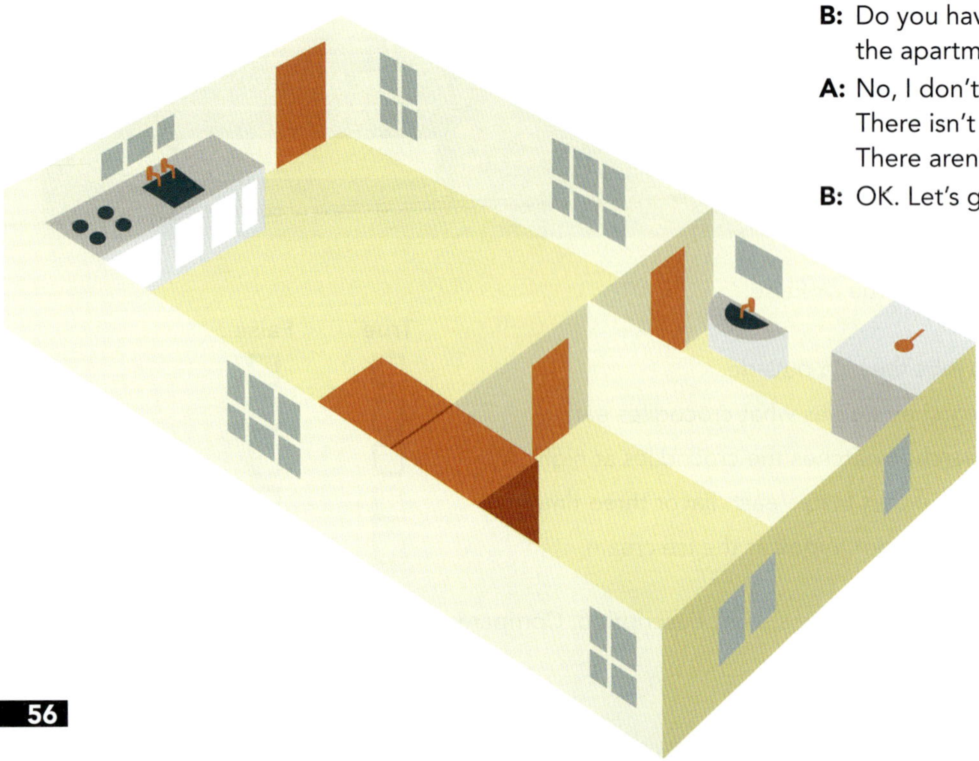

Progress check

SELF-ASSESSMENT

Learning Objectives: reflect on one's learning; identify areas that need improvement

- Ask: "What did you learn in Units 7 and 8?" Elicit Ss' answers.
- Ss complete the Self-assessment. Explain to Ss that this is not a test; it is a way for them to evaluate what they've learned and identify areas where they need additional practice. Encourage them to be honest, and point out they will not get a bad grade if they check (✓) *A little*.
- Ss move on to the Progress check exercises. You can have Ss complete them in class or for homework, using one of these techniques:
  1. Ask Ss to complete all the exercises.
  2. Ask Ss: "What do you need to practice?" Then assign exercises based on their answers.
  3. Ask Ss to choose and complete exercises based on their Self-assessment.

1 SPEAKING

Learning Objective: demonstrate one's ability to describe living spaces, rooms, and furniture

A

- Set the scene and explain the task. Point out that Ss can draw simple pictures or write the names of the furniture. Draw simple pictures on the board to demonstrate, if needed.
- ***Option:*** Ss label their pictures with the names of the furniture.
- Focus Ss' attention on the picture. Point to different rooms in the picture and ask: "What's this room?" Ss label each room in the apartment.
- Review the vocabulary in the box. Then elicit the names of other furniture and household items. Write them on the board.
- Ss complete the task individually.

B *Pair work*

- Explain the task. Then model the example conversation with a S. Take the role of Speaker A, and give the S the role of Speaker B. Ask the class to help the S if needed.
- Ss role-play the conversation in pairs. Then they change roles. Go around the class and give help as needed.
- ***Option:*** Ss change partners and role-play the conversation again.

2 SPEAKING

Learning Objective: demonstrate one's ability to ask and answer questions about work

A

- Explain the task. Ss complete the conversations individually. Then they compare answers in pairs.
- To check answers, ask different pairs of Ss to read the conversations. Correct any errors as a class.

Answers

1. A: **Where does your father work?**
   B: My father? He works in a store.
   A: **What does he do?**
   B: He's a salesperson.
   A: **How does he like it/his job?**
   B: He likes his job a lot!
2. A: **What do you do?**
   B: I'm an accountant.
   A: **Where do you work?**
   B: I work in an office.
   A: **How do you like it/your job?**
   B: It's OK. I guess I like it.

B *Pair work*

- Explain the task. Ss complete the task in pairs. Then they change roles.

3 LISTENING

Learning Objective: demonstrate one's ability to understand descriptions of jobs

[CD 2, Track 31]

- Explain the task.
- Play the audio, pausing after each conversation. Ss listen and complete the chart. Then play the audio again. Ss listen and check their answers.

Audio script

1.
Man Where do you work, Rachel?
Rachel In a doctor's office.
Man What do you do there?
Rachel I'm the receptionist. I answer the phone and welcome people.
Man How do you like your job?
Rachel I love it.
2.
Woman Hey, Daniel. I hear you're not working at the hospital now.
Daniel You're right. I have a new job in a school.
Woman Really? Are you teaching?
Daniel No. I'm still a nurse, but now I'm a school nurse.
Woman Is it stressful?
Daniel No, not really.
3.
Man Hey, Mai, where do you work?
Mai In a hotel.
Man Oh, that's interesting. What do you do there?
Mai I'm a front desk clerk. I help the guests when they arrive and leave. And I answer a lot of telephone calls from inside and outside the hotel.
Man That's a busy job! Do you like it?
Mai I do. I have a great manager.

Answers

	Workplace	Job
1. Rachel	office	receptionist
2. Daniel	school	nurse
3. Mai	hotel	front desk clerk

4 SPEAKING

Learning Objective: demonstrate one's ability to give and respond to opinions about jobs

Group work

- Explain the task. Read the names of the jobs aloud. Ss repeat. Explain the jobs as needed.
- Ask three Ss to model the example conversation. Then elicit different adjectives that can be used to describe jobs and write them on the board.
- Ss discuss the jobs in small groups.

WHAT'S NEXT?

Learning Objective: become more involved in one's learning

- Focus Ss' attention on the Self-assessment again. Ask: "How well can you do these things now?"
- Ask Ss to underline one thing they need to review. Ask: "What did you underline? How can you review it?"
- If needed, plan additional instruction, activities, or reviews based on Ss' answers.

2 SPEAKING What does he do?

A Complete the conversations with Wh-questions.

1. A: Where does your father work?
B: My father? He works in a store.
A: ______________________?
B: He's a salesperson.
A: ______________________?
B: He likes his job a lot!

2. A: ______________________?
B: I'm an accountant.
A: ______________________?
B: I work in an office.
A: ______________________?
B: It's OK. I guess I like it.

B **PAIR WORK** Your partner asks the questions in part A. Answer with your own information.

3 LISTENING How do you like your job?

Listen to Rachel, Daniel, and Mai talk about their jobs. Check (✓) the correct answers.

	Where do they work?		What do they do?	
1. Rachel	☐ office	☐ store	☐ receptionist	☐ doctor
2. Daniel	☐ hospital	☐ school	☐ nurse	☐ teacher
3. Mai	☐ hotel	☐ office	☐ manager	☐ front desk clerk

4 SPEAKING Boring or interesting?

GROUP WORK What do you think of these jobs? Give your opinions.

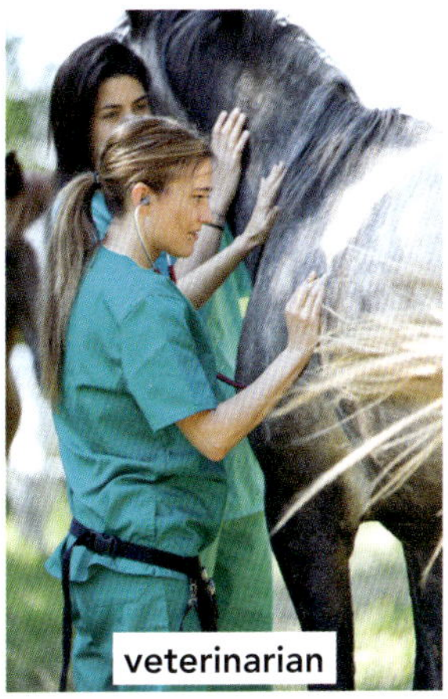
veterinarian

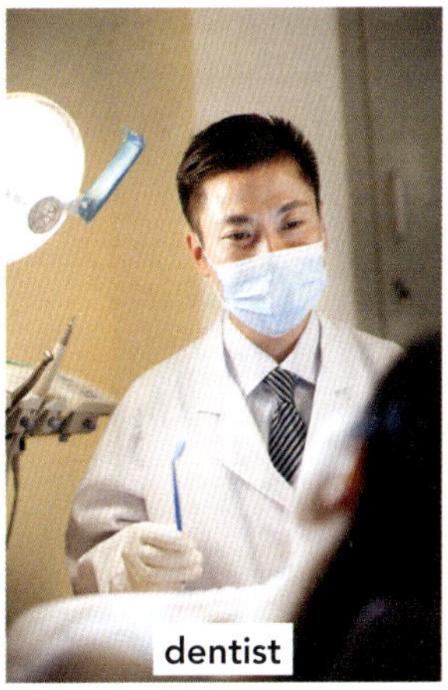
dentist

architect

hairstylist

A: I think a veterinarian has a stressful job.
B: I don't really agree. I think a veterinarian's job is relaxing.
C: Well, I think a veterinarian's job is difficult. . . .

WHAT'S NEXT?

Look at your Self-assessment again. Do you need to review anything?

Unit 9 Supplementary Resources Overview

	After the following SB exercises	You can use these materials in class	Your students can use these materials outside the classroom
CYCLE 1	1 **Word Power**		**SS** Unit 9 Vocabulary 1 **GAME** Name the Picture (Foods 1) **GAME** Sentence Runner (Foods 2)
	2 **Conversation**		**SS** Unit 9 Speaking 1
	3 **Grammar Focus**	**TSS** Unit 9 Listening Worksheet	**SB** Unit 9 Grammar plus, Focus 1 **SS** Unit 9 Grammar 1 **GAME** Sentence Stacker (Count and noncount nouns; *some* and *any*)
	4 **Pronunciation**		**WB** Unit 9 exercises 1–5
CYCLE 2	5 **Snapshot**		
	6 **Conversation**		**SS** Unit 9 Speaking 2
	7 **Grammar Focus**	**TSS** Unit 9 Vocabulary Worksheet **TSS** Unit 9 Grammar Worksheet	**SB** Unit 9 Grammar plus, Focus 2 **SS** Unit 9 Grammar 2 **GAME** Speak or Swim (Adverbs of frequency)
	8 **Listening**		
	9 **Speaking**		**SS** Unit 9 Vocabulary 2
	10 **Interchange 9**		
	11 **Reading**	**TSS** Unit 9 Extra Worksheet **TSS** Unit 9 Project Worksheet **VID** Unit 9 **VRB** Unit 9	**SS** Unit 9 Reading 1–2 **SS** Unit 9 Listening 1–3 **SS** Unit 9 Video 1–3 **WB** Unit 9 exercises 6–8

Key **GAME:** Online Game **SB:** Student's Book **SS:** Online Self-study **TSS:** Teacher Support Site
VID: Video DVD **VRB:** Video Resource Book **WB:** Online Workbook/Workbook

My Plan for Unit 9

Use the space below to customize a plan that fits your needs.

With the following SB exercises	I am using these materials in class	My students are using these materials outside the classroom

With or instead of the following SB section	I am using these materials for assessment

9 I always eat breakfast.

▸ Discuss food
▸ Describe eating habits

1 WORD POWER Foods

A Listen and practice.

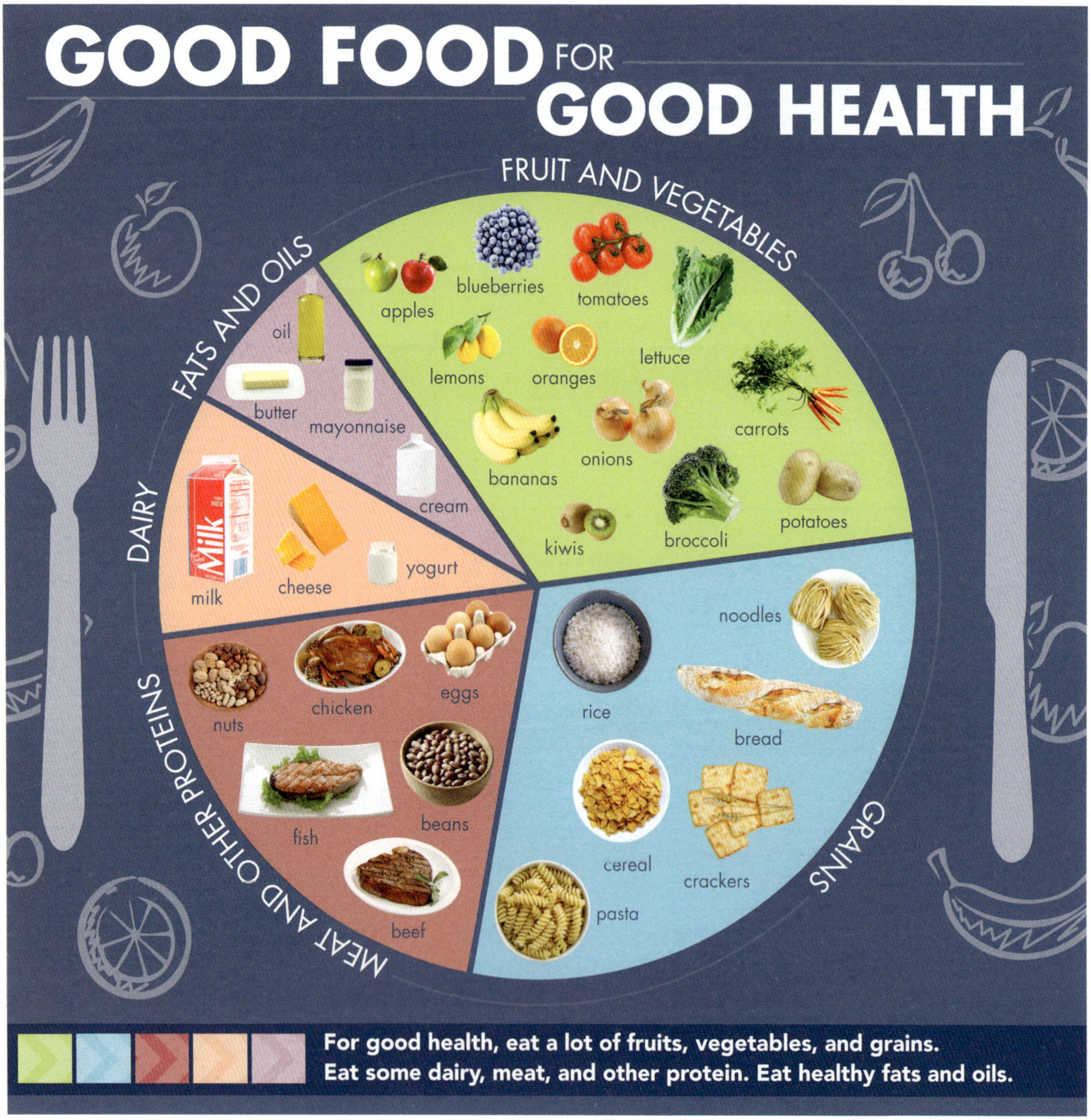

B **PAIR WORK** What foods do you like? What don't you like? Make a list. Then tell a partner.

A: I like chicken, potatoes, and apples. I don't like beef, broccoli, or onions.
B: I like . . .

I like	I don't like
chicken	beef
potatoes	broccoli
apples	onions

9 I always eat breakfast.

In Unit 9, students discuss food and describe eating habits. By the end of Cycle 1, students will be able to discuss foods they like, need, and have using *some/any* and count/noncount nouns. By the end of Cycle 2, students will be able to describe eating habits using adverbs of frequency.

Cycle 1, Exercises 1–4

1 WORD POWER

Learning Objective: discuss food likes and dislikes

A *[CD 2, Track 32]*

- Books closed. Write these headings on the board:

  Healthy foods   Unhealthy foods

- Elicit or explain that *healthy* means "good for you" and *unhealthy* means "bad for you."
- Ask: "What foods are healthy? What foods are unhealthy?"
- Elicit ideas from the class and write them under the correct headings.

TIP
To interest Ss in the topic, elicit opinions from them whenever possible.

- Books open. Focus Ss' attention on the title of the pie chart. Explain that it illustrates healthy foods. Point out that this chart doesn't show how much of these foods you should eat per day (e.g., it doesn't tell you to eat six servings of grains). It shows the portion of your foods that should come from each category, (i.e., eat mostly fruits and vegetables and only a little dairy). Also note that not everyone eats everything on the chart; for example, *vegetarians* don't eat meat, but they eat other proteins such as nuts and beans.
- Play the first paragraph of the audio program. Ss listen and read silently.
- Use hand gestures to explain *a lot of*, *some*, and *a little*.
- Play the rest of the audio program. Ss listen and read silently. Then play the audio program again. Ss listen and repeat.
- ***Option:*** Write the names of the food groups on the board. Elicit names of other foods in each group. Ask different Ss to write them on the board.

B *Pair work*

- Explain the first part of the task.
- Ss make lists individually. Go around the class and give help as needed.
- Explain the second part of the task and ask a S to read the beginning of the model conversation.
- Ss continue the conversation and compare food likes and dislikes in pairs.
- ***Option:*** Ss tell the class about their partner's food likes and dislikes.

TIP
To make your lessons more varied, change focus regularly. For example, change from pair work to a class activity or from writing to speaking.

For more practice with food vocabulary, play the ***Chain Game*** – download it from the website. Use the sentence: "I like (carrots) . . ."

2 CONVERSATION

Learning Objective: use *some/any* and count/noncount nouns in a conversation about food

[CD 2, Track 33]

- Focus Ss' attention on the picture. Ask: "What foods can you see?" (Possible answers: lettuce, vegetables)
- Play the audio program. Ss listen and read silently. Then elicit or explain any new vocabulary.

Vocabulary
all right: OK
potato salad: pieces of potato mixed with mayonnaise and seasonings
buy: to pay money to get something

- Play the audio program again. Ss listen and repeat. Then they practice the conversation in pairs

3 GRAMMAR FOCUS

Learning Objectives: differentiate between *some/any* and categorize count/noncount nouns

[CD 2, Track 34]

Count and noncount nouns

- Books closed. Put four or five count items (e.g., *lemons, oranges, books*) on your desk. Say: "I can count these (lemons). One, two, three, four, five. (Lemon) is a count noun."
- Put a noncount item (e.g., *a loaf of unsliced bread, a bowl of rice, a pitcher of water*) on your desk. Say: "I can't count this (bread). (Bread) is a noncount noun."
- Books open. Focus Ss' attention on the words at the top of each column in the Grammar Focus box. Point out that plural count nouns usually end in *-s* or *-es* and that noncount nouns don't.
- Point out that we use *a* and *an* only with singular count nouns.

Some *and* any

- Focus Ss' attention on the questions and answers in the Grammar Focus box. Explain that we use *some* and *any* with plural nouns and noncount nouns. We use *some* in positive statements. We use *any* in negative statements and questions.
- Play the audio program. Ss listen and read silently.
- Point out that we often omit the noun in answers with *some* and *any* (e.g., *Yes, let's get some.*)

A

- Explain the task. Ss complete the conversation individually. Then they compare answers in pairs. To check answers, ask Ss to read the conversation.

Answers

Keith:	Oh, they don't have **any** potato salad.
Jane:	But we have lots of potatoes at home. Let's make **some**.
Keith:	Great. Do we have **any** mayonnaise?
Jane:	No. We need to buy **some**. And we need **some** onions.
Keith:	Oh, no, I don't want **any** onions in the salad.
Jane:	OK, don't worry. Let's get **some** celery, then.
Keith:	No, I don't want **any** celery. I have an idea. Let's put **some** apples in it.
Jane:	Are you serious? Apples in potato salad? Well, OK . . .

B

- Ss complete the chart individually. Go around the class and give help as needed. If Ss have difficulty, point out that all the nouns in Exercise 1 with *-s* or *-es* endings are count nouns.
- Ss compare their charts in pairs.
- Copy the chart onto the board. Ask different Ss to write the answers in the chart.
- ***Option:*** Ss add other foods they know to the chart on the board.

For more practice reviewing food vocabulary with count and noncount nouns, play ***Picture It!*** – download it from the website. One S draws a picture of a food. The other Ss guess the word and use it in the sentence: "It's a/an . . ." or "They're . . ."

- ***Option:*** Ss discuss which foods in the chart are good (healthy) and bad (unhealthy) for you. Write this conversation on the board:

  A: *Eggs are good for you, but cream is not.*
  B: *Are you sure? I think eggs are bad for you.*

  Ss practice in pairs. Have Ss share any disagreements with the class.

TIP
Don't expect Ss to master new grammar immediately. To help them internalize the new structures, give Ss plenty of time, exposure, and practice with the new structures throughout the unit and course.

2 CONVERSATION Let's get some lettuce and some tomatoes.

Listen and practice.

Keith Do we need any lettuce for the sandwiches?

Jane Good idea. Let's get some lettuce and some tomatoes.

Keith Do we have any bread?

Jane No, we need some. And we don't have any cheese.

Keith Let's get some cheese, then. And some chicken, too.

Jane We have some chicken at home.

Keith Oh, all right. How about some potato salad?

Jane Sure. I love potato salad.

Keith Great! Let's buy some.

3 GRAMMAR FOCUS

Count and noncount nouns; *some* and *any*

Count nouns	Noncount nouns
an egg → egg**s**	bread
a potato → potato**es**	lettuce
Do we need **any** potatoes?	Do we need **any** lettuce?
Yes. Let's get **some** (potatoes).	Yes. Let's get **some** (lettuce).
No. We don't need **any** (potatoes).	No. We don't need **any** (lettuce).

GRAMMAR PLUS *see page 140*

A Complete the conversation with *some* or *any*.

Keith Oh, they don't have ___any___ potato salad.
Jane But we have lots of potatoes at home. Let's make ______.
Keith Great. Do we have ______ mayonnaise?
Jane No. We need to buy ______. And we need ______ onions.
Keith Oh, no, I don't want ______ onions in the salad.
Jane OK, don't worry. Let's get ______ celery, then.
Keith No, I don't want ______ celery. I have an idea. Let's put ______ apples in it.
Jane Are you serious? Apples in potato salad? Well, OK . . .

B Complete the chart with foods from Exercise 1. Then compare with a partner.

Count			Noncount		
crackers			bread		

4 PRONUNCIATION Sentence stress

A Listen and practice. Notice the stressed words.

A: Do we need any **beans**?
B: **Yes**. We need some **beans**.

A: Do we need any **rice**?
B: **No**. We don't need any **rice**.

B **PAIR WORK** Ask *Do we need . . . ?* questions about the food in the picture. Then look at the shopping list and answer.

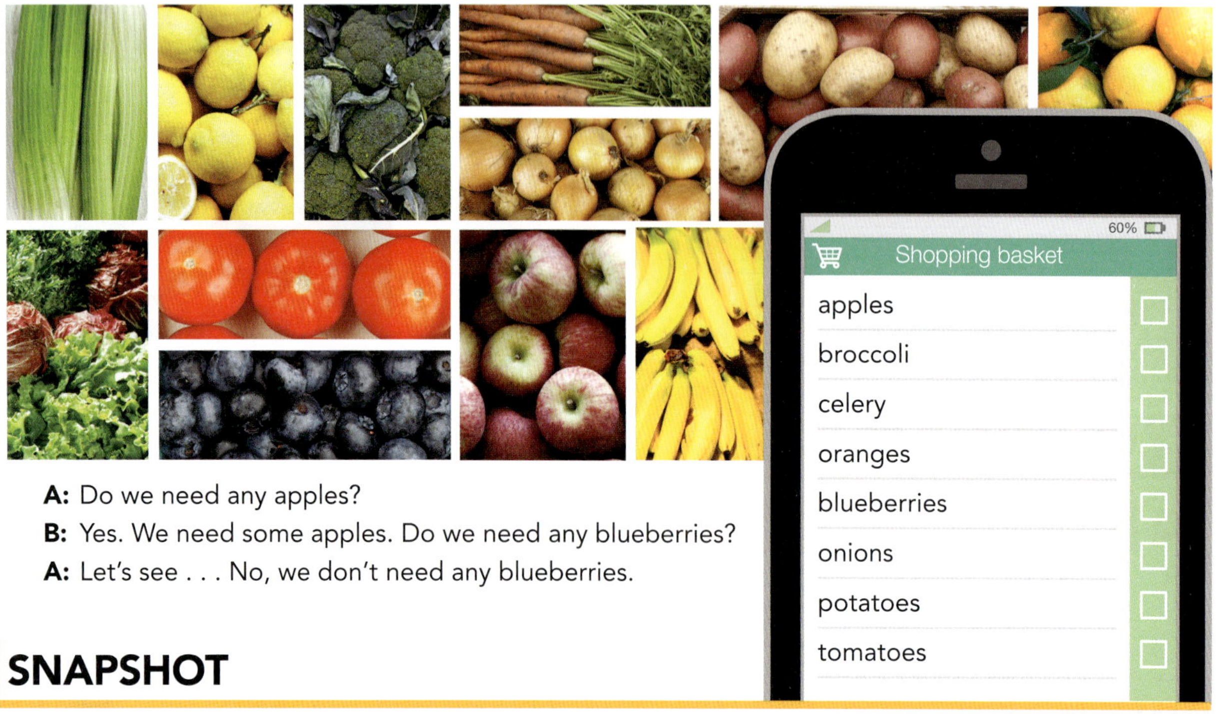

A: Do we need any apples?
B: Yes. We need some apples. Do we need any blueberries?
A: Let's see . . . No, we don't need any blueberries.

5 SNAPSHOT

Listen and practice.

BREAKFAST AROUND THE WORLD

THE UNITED STATES	JAPAN	COSTA RICA
☐ cereal with milk	☐ fish	☐ rice and beans
☐ fresh fruit	☐ rice	☐ eggs
☐ orange juice	☐ soup	☐ red peppers
☐ coffee	☐ pickles	☐ bananas
☐ pastries	☐ green tea	☐ coffee with milk

What do you have for breakfast? Check (✓) the foods and drinks.
What else do you have for breakfast?

4 PRONUNCIATION

Learning Objective: sound more natural when stressing words in sentences and questions

A *[CD 2, Track 35]*

- Books closed. Write the conversations on the board.
- Ask Ss to listen for the stressed words in each question and answer.
- Play the audio program once or twice. Elicit the stressed words from the class.
- Books open. Play the audio program. Ss listen and read silently to check their answers. Elicit or explain that we stress the important words in a sentence.
- Play the audio program again. Ss listen and repeat. Then Ss practice the conversation in pairs. Go around the class and check Ss' use of stress.

B *Pair work*

- Explain the task. Have two Ss read the example conversation. Point out that they need to ask questions about the food in the pictures and refer to the shopping list to find out what food they need.
- Have two Ss model the activity for the class.
- Ss ask and answer questions in pairs. Go around the class and check Ss' use of stress.

! For a new way to teach sentence stress, try ***Walking Stress*** – download it from the website.

End of Cycle 1

See the Supplementary Resources chart at the beginning of this unit for additional teaching materials and student activities related to this Cycle.

Cycle 2, Exercises 5–11

5 SNAPSHOT

Learning Objective: discuss common breakfast foods in different countries

[CD 2, Track 36]

- Books closed. Elicit or explain that *breakfast* is the meal that people have in the morning. Ask: "Who has a big breakfast? Who has a small breakfast? Who doesn't have breakfast?" Ss raise their hands.
- Books open. Focus Ss' attention on the pictures. Point out that these are common breakfast foods in the United States, Japan, and Costa Rica.
- Play the audio program. Ss listen and read silently. Elicit or explain any new vocabulary.
- Play the audio program again. Ss listen and repeat.
- Read out the questions and task. Ss complete the task individually.
- Ss compare answers in small groups. If possible, put Ss from different countries in each group. Then elicit answers from the class.

6 CONVERSATION

Learning Objective: use adverbs of frequency in a conversation about food

[CD 2, Track 37]

- Text covered. Focus Ss' attention on the title and picture. Set the scene. Eva and Kaito are talking about breakfast.
- Ask: "What are the people eating?" Encourage Ss to make guesses.
- Text uncovered. Play the audio program. Ss listen and read silently.
- If needed, point out that people in the United States and Canada don't usually have fish for breakfast, so Eva is surprised.
- Elicit or explain any new vocabulary. If Ss have questions about *always, usually, sometimes*, or *never*, preview the Grammar Focus box in Exercise 7.
- Play the audio program again. Ss listen and repeat.
- Ss practice the conversation in pairs.

7 GRAMMAR FOCUS

Learning Objective: use adverbs of frequency

[CD 2, Track 38]

- Books closed. Write this on the board:

  always (100%)
  usually (about 80%–99%)
  often (about 60%–80%)
  sometimes (about 20%–60%)
  hardly ever (about 1%–20%)
  never (0%)

- Elicit or explain that these words are adverbs of frequency. *Always* means "100 percent of the time," and *usually* means "almost always." *Often* means "a lot of the time," and *sometimes* means "some of the time." *Hardly ever* means "rarely," and *never* means "not ever."
- Books open. Focus Ss' attention on the Grammar Focus box. Play the audio program. Ss listen and read silently.
- Point out that adverbs usually go before the verb in a sentence, but *sometimes* can also go before the subject. Explain that *ever* means "at any time," and that questions with *ever* are usually answered with adverbs of frequency.

A

- Explain the first part of the task. Then copy the example sentence on the board. Model how to make a caret (^) between the words *you* and *have*, and write the adverb above it.
- ***Option:*** Ss underline the verb in each sentence.
- Ss put the adverbs in the correct places individually. Ask different Ss to write the complete sentences on the board.

Answers

A: Do you **usually** have a big breakfast?
B: Well, on Sunday I **always** have a big breakfast with my friends.
A: Do you **ever** eat breakfast at work on weekdays?
B: Yes, I **sometimes** have breakfast at the office restaurant./Yes, **sometimes** I have breakfast at the office restaurant.
A: Do you **often** eat breakfast at your desk?
B: No, I **hardly ever** eat breakfast at my desk.

- Explain the second part of the task. Ss practice the conversation in pairs.

B

- Books closed. Copy the words for the first item on the board. Explain the task and model how to unscramble the sentence.
- Books open. Ss complete the task individually. If needed, elicit or explain that a *snack* is food you eat between meals. Snacks include foods like apples and potato chips.
- Ss compare their sentences in pairs. Then ask different Ss to write the correct sentences on the board. If needed, correct the sentences with the class.

Answers

1. I hardly ever have beef for lunch.
2. I never eat snacks when I watch TV.
3. I sometimes eat eggs for breakfast./Sometimes I eat eggs for breakfast.
4. I usually have dinner with my family.

C

- Explain the first part of the task. Then rewrite the first sentence from part B on the board, changing the adverb of frequency if necessary to make the sentence true about you. For example:

  I never have beef for lunch.

- Ss rewrite the sentences individually.
- Explain the second part of the task. Then ask two Ss to model the example conversation.
- Ss compare information in pairs.

6 CONVERSATION We always have green tea.

Listen and practice.

Eva: What is a typical Japanese breakfast, Kaito?

Kaito: Well, we usually have fish, rice, and soup.

Eva: Fish for breakfast? That's interesting.

Kaito: Oh, it's really good. Sometimes we have a salad, too. But we never have coffee.

Eva: Really? What do you have?

Kaito: We always have green tea.

Eva: I love green tea!

Kaito: Listen, my family usually has a Japanese-style breakfast on weekends. Why don't you come to my house on Sunday?

Eva: That's very nice of you. Thanks!

7 GRAMMAR FOCUS

Adverbs of frequency

I **always** / **usually** / **often** / **sometimes** / **hardly ever** / **never** eat breakfast.	Do you **ever** have fish for breakfast?	100% **always**
Sometimes I eat breakfast.	Yes, I **always** do.	**usually**
	Sometimes I do.	**often**
	No, I **never** do.	**sometimes**
		hardly ever
		0% **never**

GRAMMAR PLUS see page 140

A Put the adverbs in the correct places. Then practice with a partner.

A: Do you ^usually have a big breakfast? (usually)
B: Well, on Sunday I have a big breakfast with my friends. (always)
A: Do you eat breakfast at work on weekdays? (ever)
B: Yes, I have breakfast at the office restaurant. (sometimes)
A: Do you eat breakfast at your desk? (often)
B: No, I eat breakfast at my desk. (hardly ever)

B Unscramble the sentences.

1. I / have / hardly ever / beef / for lunch *I hardly ever have beef for lunch.*
2. when I watch TV / I / snacks / eat / never ______
3. eat / for / eggs / breakfast / sometimes / I ______
4. have / I / dinner / with / usually / family / my ______

C Rewrite the sentences from part B with your own information. Then compare with a partner.

A: I usually have beef or chicken for lunch.
B: I never have beef. I don't like it. I often have fish and a salad for lunch.

8 LISTENING Carrots are my favorite!

A Devon and Victoria are talking about food. How often does Victoria eat these foods? Listen and check (✓) Often, Sometimes, or Never.

	OFTEN	SOMETIMES	NEVER
noodles	✓		
chicken			
fish			
eggs			
carrots			

B **GROUP WORK** Do you ever eat the foods in part A? Tell your classmates.

A: I often eat noodles.
B: Really? I never eat noodles.
C: Well, I . . .

9 SPEAKING Mealtime survey

A Add two questions about mealtime habits to the chart. Then ask two people the questions. Write their names and complete the chart.

	Name:	Name:
1. Do you always have a big breakfast?		
2. What time do you usually have lunch?		
3. What do you usually have for lunch?		
4. Do you often have snacks in the afternoon?		
5. Do you ever go to a restaurant for dinner?		
6. What's something you never eat for dinner?		
7. ______________________________?		
8. ______________________________?		

A: Pedro, do you always have a big breakfast?
B: No, I hardly ever do. I have coffee and milk. Sometimes I eat bread or crackers.

B **CLASS ACTIVITY** Tell your classmates about your partners' mealtime habits.

"Pedro hardly ever has a big breakfast. But he always eats lunch and dinner . . . "

10 INTERCHANGE 9 Planning a party

Decide what food and drinks to serve at a party. Go to Interchange 9 on page 123.

8 LISTENING

Learning Objective: identify adverbs of frequency in a spoken conversation

[CD 2, Track 39]

- Books closed. Set the scene. Devon and Victoria are in a restaurant. They are talking about food.
- Review the pronunciation of the words in the chart.

TIP
To help Ss recognize key vocabulary in an audio recording, review or pre-teach their pronunciation.

- Ask the class: "What foods do Devon and Victoria talk about?" Play the audio program and have Ss listen for the answers. Elicit the answers. (Answers: soup, noodles, chicken, meat, fish, eggs, beef, vegetables, carrots)
- Books open. Focus Ss' attention on the chart and explain the task.
- Play the audio program a few times. Pause after every few lines if needed. Ss listen and complete the chart. Then they compare answers in pairs.

Audio script

Devon So, what looks good, Victoria?
Victoria I don't know yet.
Devon Well, the soup is really good. Do you like noodles?
Victoria Oh, yeah. I often eat noodles for lunch. I just don't want them tonight.
Devon OK, well, the chicken is great here. How about that?
Victoria Oh, no. I never eat chicken. I don't like meat.
Devon Really?
Victoria Yeah. Sometimes I have fish or eggs, but never chicken or beef.
Devon So, do you eat a lot of vegetables?
Victoria Yes. Carrots are my favorite. I often have some in the afternoon for a snack.

Answers

	Often	Sometimes	Never
noodles	✓		
chicken			✓
fish		✓	
eggs		✓	
carrots	✓		

9 SPEAKING

Learning Objective: ask and answer questions about eating habits using adverbs of frequency

A

- Focus Ss' attention on the chart and explain the first part of the task. Ask different Ss to read the questions. Point out that all the questions have adverbs of frequency or the word *ever*.
- Elicit or explain any new vocabulary.

Vocabulary
habit: something you usually do
lunch: the noon meal
dinner: the evening meal

- Ss write two more questions individually. Go around the class and make sure Ss use an adverb of frequency or *ever* in each question.
- Elicit new questions from the class and write them on the board. For example, "What is something you always have for . . . ?, Do you usually make . . . ?, Do you ever make . . . for your family?"
- Explain the second part of the task. Ask two Ss to model the example conversation. Point out where the answers go on the chart.
- Ss complete the middle column in pairs, taking turns asking and answering the questions. When the pairs finish, each S finds a new partner to complete the last column with. Go around the class and make sure the Ss complete the chart.

B *Class activity*

- Explain the task and ask a S to model the example sentences. Then Ss tell the class about their partners' mealtime habits.

10 INTERCHANGE 9

See page T-123 for teaching notes.

11 READING

Learning Objective: scan and read for details in an article about food

A *[CD 2, Track 40]*

- Read the title aloud. Elicit or explain the meaning of *festival*. Ask: "What do you think a food festival is? Does your city have a food festival?"
- Focus Ss' attention on the pictures and read the question aloud. Elicit answers from the class.

B

- Explain the first part of the task. Ss read the article individually and underline any words they don't know.
- Elicit or explain any new vocabulary. Then Ss read the article again.

Vocabulary

festival: a special event or period when people celebrate something
fight: when people try to hurt each other
garlic: a vegetable like a small onion with a strong taste and smell
cooking: the activity of preparing food
monkeys: animals with long tails that live in trees
humans: people
bones: the hard pieces inside a person or animal
anise: a plant that tastes like fennel or licorice
seed: the small part of a plant from which new plants grow

- Explain the second part of the task. Use the example to model the task. Point out that Ss can find the answer quickly by scanning the article for the phrase *tomato fight*.
- Ss correct the sentences individually. Go around the class and give help as needed.
- Ss compare their answers in pairs. Ask different Ss to write the correct sentences on the board.

Answers

1. There's a big tomato fight in ~~Mexico~~ **Spain** once a year.
2. People in California ~~don't~~ **really** like garlic.
3. Some people in the U.S. use ~~tomatoes~~ **garlic** to make ice cream and popcorn.
4. The Monkey Buffet Festival happens in ~~Spain~~ **Thailand**.
5. In Thailand, people give fruit to the ~~tourists~~ **monkeys**.
6. Some Mexicans make bread in the shape of ~~houses and other buildings~~ **humans, flowers, bones, and animals**.

- ***Option:*** Play the audio program. Ss listen and read along silently.

C *Group work*

- Explain the task and read the questions. Point out that *celebration* means "a special day or event."
- Ss discuss the questions in small groups. Go around the class and encourage Ss to ask follow-up questions.
- ***Option:*** Each group shares information with the class.

End of Cycle 2

See the Supplementary Resources chart at the beginning of this unit for additional teaching materials and student activities related to this Cycle.

11 READING

A Look at the pictures. Which foods do you like?

IT'S A FOOD Festival!

LA TOMATINA

People usually eat tomatoes. But once a year, in Buñol, Spain, people just throw them! Yes, that's correct. The whole town of Buñol has a giant tomato fight! It's very messy. By the end of the day, there are squashed tomatoes all over town. In fact, there are 120 tons of squashed tomatoes!

GARLIC FESTIVAL

All over the world, people use garlic in their cooking. Some people in California, in the U.S., really like garlic. They like it so much that every year they celebrate it with a garlic festival. You can taste garlic in everything you can think of. There's even garlic ice cream and garlic popcorn.

MONKEY BUFFET FESTIVAL

There's something very interesting about this food festival. It's not for people, it's for monkeys! In Lopburi, Thailand, people bring all kinds of different fruits and leave them out for the monkeys to eat. They bring pineapples, apples, mangoes . . . and bananas, of course. It's the people's way of saying thank you to the monkeys. That's because tourists come to see the monkeys, and that helps the people's businesses. Isn't that cool?

BREAD FOR THE DAY OF THE DEAD

The Day of the Dead is a very important day in Mexico. Many people celebrate their family members and friends by baking special bread. They make bread in the shape of humans, flowers, bones, and animals. The bread is sweet, and sometimes it has anise seeds or orange in it.

B Read the article. Then correct these sentences.

1. There's a big tomato fight in ~~Mexico~~ Spain once a year.
2. People in California don't like garlic.
3. Some people in the U.S. use tomatoes to make ice cream and popcorn.
4. The Monkey Buffet Festival happens in Spain.
5. In Thailand, people give fruit to the tourists.
6. Some Mexicans make bread in the shape of houses and other buildings.

C **GROUP WORK** Do you eat any special food at celebrations in your country? What do you celebrate and which foods do you eat? Tell your classmates.

Unit 10 Supplementary Resources Overview

	After the following SB exercises	You can use these materials in class	Your students can use these materials outside the classroom
CYCLE 1	1 Snapshot		**SS** Unit 10 Vocabulary 1
	2 Conversation		**SS** Unit 10 Speaking 1
	3 Grammar Focus		**SB** Unit 10 Grammar plus, Focus 1 **SS** Unit 10 Grammar 1 **GAME** Sentence Runner (Simple present Wh-questions 1) **GAME** Word Keys (Simple present Wh-questions 2)
	4 Listening		
	5 Speaking		**WB** Unit 10 exercises 1–3
CYCLE 2	6 Conversation		**SS** Unit 10 Speaking 2
	7 Grammar Focus		**SB** Unit 10 Grammar plus, Focus 2 **SS** Unit 10 Grammar 2
	8 Pronunciation	**TSS** Unit 10 Vocabulary Worksheet **TSS** Unit 10 Grammar Worksheet **TSS** Unit 10 Extra Worksheet	
	9 Listening	**TSS** Unit 10 Listening Worksheet	**GAME** Sentence Stacker (*Can* for ability)
	10 Word Power		**SS** Unit 10 Vocabulary 2 **GAME** Speak or Swim (Abilities and talents)
	11 Interchange 10		
	12 Reading	**TSS** Unit 10 Project Worksheet **VID** Unit 10 **VRB** Unit 10	**SS** Unit 10 Reading 1–2 **SS** Unit 10 Listening 1–3 **SS** Unit 10 Video 1–3 **WB** Unit 10 exercises 4–10

With or instead of the following SB section	You can also use these materials for assessment
Units 9–10 Progress Check	**ASSESSMENT PROGRAM** Units 9–10 Oral Quiz **ASSESSMENT PROGRAM** Units 9–10 Written Quiz

Key **GAME:** Online Game **SB:** Student's Book **SS:** Online Self-study **TSS:** Teacher Support Site
VID: Video DVD **VRB:** Video Resource Book **WB:** Online Workbook/Workbook

My Plan for Unit 10

Use the space below to customize a plan that fits your needs.

With the following SB exercises	I am using these materials in class	My students are using these materials outside the classroom

With or instead of the following SB section	I am using these materials for assessment

10 What sports do you like?

- Discuss sports to watch and play
- Discuss skills, abilities, and talents

1 SNAPSHOT

Listen and practice.

SPORTS QUIZ

Brazil's favorite sport is soccer. Their second favorite is . . .

- ☐ tennis
- ☐ volleyball
- ☐ swimming

Mexico's favorite sport is soccer. Their second favorite sport is . . .

- ☐ football
- ☐ hockey
- ☐ baseball

Canada's favorite sport is ice hockey. Their second favorite sport is . . .

- ☐ basketball
- ☐ ice-skating
- ☐ snowboarding

South Korea's favorite sport is basketball. Their second favorite sport is . . .

- ☐ bike riding
- ☐ hiking
- ☐ soccer

Brazil: volleyball; Mexico: baseball; Canada: basketball; South Korea: soccer

Can you guess what sports are the second favorite in each country? Check (✓) the sports.
Do you like sports? What sports are popular in your country?

2 CONVERSATION When do you play all these sports?

Listen and practice.

TARA So, Victor, what do you do in your free time?

VICTOR Well, I really like sports.

TARA Cool! What sports do you like?

VICTOR My favorite sports are basketball, soccer, and tennis.

TARA Wow! You're a really good athlete. When do you play all these sports?

VICTOR Oh . . . I don't play them very often.

TARA What do you mean?

VICTOR I just watch them on TV!

10 What sports do you like?

Cycle 1, Exercises 1–5

In Unit 10, students discuss sports to watch and play, and discuss skills, abilities, and talents. By the end of Cycle 1, students will be able to discuss sports they watch and play using simple present Wh-questions. By the end of Cycle 2, students will be able to discuss skills, abilities, and talents using *can* and *can't*.

1 SNAPSHOT

Learning Objective: discuss popular sports

[CD 2, Track 41]

- Books closed. Elicit the names of sports and write them on the board. Ask: "Where do people play these sports?" Elicit the names of countries.
- Books open. Focus Ss' attention on the Snapshot. Point out that there is a picture for each sport listed in the quiz.
- If needed, explain that *soccer* is an American term. In other countries, people call this sport *football*. In the U.S. and Canada, *football* refers to a different sport, also called *American football*.
- ***Option:*** Write this on the board:

  play + game
  go + verb + -ing

  Explain that we use *play* with games and *go* with sports that are not games. Ask Ss to find examples in the Snapshot.
- Read the first question and the task. Ss complete the quiz.
- Play the audio program. Ss listen and read silently.
- Play the audio program again. Ss listen and check their guesses.
- Ss discuss the last two questions in small groups. If possible, put Ss from different countries in each group. Then elicit answers from the class.

For more practice with sports vocabulary, play ***Mime*** – download it from the website.

For more practice with sports vocabulary, play ***Sculptures*** – download it from the website.

2 CONVERSATION

Learning Objectives: use simple present Wh-questions in a conversation about sports

[CD 2, Track 42]

- Text covered. Set the scene. Tara and Victor are talking about sports. Ask: "What sports are they talking about?" Play the audio program and elicit the answers. (Answers: basketball, soccer, tennis)
- Text uncovered. Write these questions on the board:

  1. *Does Victor like sports?*
  2. *What sports does he like?*
  3. *Does he ever play those sports?*
- Play the audio program. Ss listen and read silently. Then elicit the answers to the focus questions. (Answers: 1. Yes, he does. 2. basketball, soccer, tennis 3. He doesn't play them very often.)
- Elicit or explain any new vocabulary.

Vocabulary
free time: time when you're not working or studying
athlete: someone who plays sports well

- Play the audio program again. Ss listen and repeat. Then they practice the conversation in pairs.
- ***Option:*** Ask a few pairs to role-play the conversation for the class.

! For a new way to practice this Conversation, try ***Look Up and Speak!*** – download it from the website.

- ***Option:*** Ss share information about free-time activities. To review adverbs of frequency, write this conversation on the board:

  A: *What do you usually do in your free time?*
  B: *I usually (go swimming), and I often (play tennis). How about you?*
  A: *Well, I never (play tennis). But sometimes I (play volleyball).*

  Model the conversation with a S. Then Ss practice it with their own information in pairs.

3 GRAMMAR FOCUS

Learning Objective: ask and answer simple present Wh-questions

[CD 2, Track 43]

Simple present Wh-questions

- Focus Ss' attention on the Grammar Focus box. Elicit or explain that Wh-questions ask for information.
- To review the meanings of Wh-question words, write this on the board:

  Who
  Where
  How often
  When
  What time

  Elicit or give examples of questions using each Wh-word.
- Elicit the pattern for simple present Wh-questions:

  Question word + *do/does* + subject + verb?

  If needed, refer Ss to Unit 8, Exercise 4.
- Play the audio program. Ss listen and read silently.

A

- Explain the first part of the task. Ask two Ss to model the first three lines of the first conversation.
- Ss complete the task individually. Then they compare answers in pairs or small groups.

TIP
In mixed-level classes, include at least one strong S in each pair or group when they complete tasks involving grammar accuracy. Encourage Ss to collaborate and help each other.

- Elicit answers from the class and write them on the board.

Answers

1. A: **How often** do you go bike riding?
   B: Oh, about once or twice a week.
   A: I love to go bike riding. I go every Sunday.
   B: Really? **What time/When** do you go?
   A: Usually at about ten in the morning.
   B: Oh, yeah? **Who** do you go with?
   A: A group of friends. Come with us next time!
2. A: I watch sports on TV every weekend.
   B: Really? **What sports/What** do you like to watch?
   A: Soccer. It's my favorite!
   B: **When** do you usually watch soccer?
   A: In the evenings or on weekends.
   B: And **where** do you usually watch it? At home?
   A: No, at my brother's house. He has a home theater!

- Ss practice the conversations in pairs.

B

- Explain the task. Then ask two Ss to model the first two lines of the conversation.
- Ss complete the task individually. Then they compare answers in pairs.
- Ask different Ss to write the questions on the board. If needed, correct the questions with the class.
- ***Option:*** Ss practice the conversation in pairs.

Answers

A: **What sports do you like**?
B: I like a lot of sports, but I really love volleyball!
A: **Who do you usually play with**?
B: I usually play with my sister and some friends.
A: **When do you practice**?
B: We practice on Saturdays.
A: **What time do you start**?
B: We start at about noon.
A: **Where do you play**?
B: We usually play at a sports club, but sometimes we play on the beach.

C *Pair work*

- Explain the task. Then ask two Ss to model the example conversation.
- Ss write questions about sports or other activities individually. Go around the class and give help as needed.
- ***Option:*** If Ss have trouble thinking of questions to ask, elicit questions from the class and write them on the board.
- Ss work in pairs. They take turns asking and answering their questions. Then ask different Ss to tell the class their partners' answers.
- ***Option:*** Ss write sentences about their partners before they tell the class.

! For a new way to practice Wh-questions, try ***Question Exchange*** – download it from the website.

3 GRAMMAR FOCUS

Simple present Wh-questions

What sports do you play?	I play **soccer and basketball**.
Who do you play basketball **with**?	I play **with some friends from work**.
Where do you play?	We play **at a gym near the office**.
How often do you practice?	We practice **twice a week**.
When do you practice?	We practice **on Tuesdays and Thursdays**.
What time do you start?	We start **at six in the evening**.

GRAMMAR PLUS *see page 141*

A Complete the conversations with the correct Wh-question words. Then practice with a partner.

1. **A:** *How often* do you go bike riding?
   B: Oh, about once or twice a week.
   A: I love to go bike riding. I go every Sunday.
   B: Really? ________ do you go?
   A: Usually at about ten in the morning.
   B: Oh, yeah? ________ do you go with?
   A: A group of friends. Come with us next time!
2. **A:** I watch sports on TV every weekend.
   B: Really? ________ do you like to watch?
   A: Soccer. It's my favorite!
   B: ________ do you usually watch soccer?
   A: In the evening or on weekends.
   B: And ________ do you usually watch it? At home?
   A: No, at my brother's house. He has a home theater!

B Complete the conversation with Wh-questions. Then compare with a partner.

A: *What sports do you like* ?
B: I like a lot of sports, but I really love volleyball!
A: ________________ ?
B: I usually play with my sister and some friends.
A: ________________ ?
B: We practice on Saturdays.
A: ________________ ?
B: We start at about noon.
A: ________________ ?
B: We usually play at a sports club, but sometimes we play on the beach.

C **PAIR WORK** Ask your partner five questions about sports or other activities. Then tell the class.

A: What sports do you like?
B: I don't like sports very much.
A: Oh? What do you like to do in your free time?

4 LISTENING What do you think of sports?

Listen to the conversations about sports. Complete the chart.

	Favorite sport	Do they play or watch it? Play	Watch
1. James	football	☑	☐
2. Brianna		☐	☐
3. Matthew		☐	☐
4. Nicole		☐	☐

5 SPEAKING Free-time activities

A Add one more question about free-time activities to the chart. Then ask two people the questions. Write their names and complete the chart.

	Name:	Name:
1. What sports do you like to watch or play?		
2. What do you do on the weekends?		
3. What do you like to do when the weather is nice?		
4. What do you like to do when it's raining?		
5. How often do you play video games?		
6. ____________________?		

A: Soo-hyun, what sports do you like?
B: I like a lot of sports. My favorites are soccer and baseball.

B CLASS ACTIVITY Tell your classmates about your partners' free-time activities.

6 CONVERSATION What can I do?

Listen and practice.

Dylan Look! There's a talent show audition on Friday. Let's enter.
Becky Oh, I can't enter a talent show. What can I do?
Dylan You can sing very well.
Becky Really? Thanks!
Dylan I can't sing at all, but I can play the piano, so . . .
Becky So maybe we can enter the contest.
Dylan Of course we can. Let's do it!
Becky OK. We can practice tomorrow!

4 LISTENING

Learning Objective: listen to a conversation about sports using simple present Wh-questions

[CD 2, Track 44]

- Explain the task. Then play the audio program three times. First, Ss listen and write the speakers' favorite sports. Then they listen and check (✓) *Play* or *Watch*. Finally, they listen and check their answers.

Audio script

1.
Woman Hey, James. What do you think of soccer?
James I like it. Actually, I like lots of sports!
Woman Oh, yeah? What sports do you like?
James Let's see. I like tennis and bike riding . . . and especially football. It's my favorite.
Woman Football's my favorite, too. So, when do you play it?
James In the fall and winter.

2.
Man What sports do you like, Brianna?
Brianna You know, I don't like sports very much.
Man So you never play sports?
Brianna No, I don't. Oh, wait – I do like tennis.
Man Oh, really? When do you play?
Brianna About once a week. I play with a friend at my gym.

3.
Woman Do you play volleyball, Matthew?
Matthew Uh, no. I think it's a little boring.
Woman I see. Do you like any sports?
Matthew Oh, sure. My favorite sport is baseball. I love baseball. Now that's an exciting sport!
Woman How often do you play?
Matthew Well, I don't really play – I'm too busy. But I watch it on TV a lot!

4.
Man Do you like tennis, Nicole?
Nicole It's OK, but it's not my favorite.
Man What's your favorite sport?
Nicole Hmm. I guess my favorite sport is basketball.
Man Really? Where do you play?
Nicole Oh, I don't play basketball. But a lot of my friends do, and I like to watch them play.

- Elicit the answers from the class.

Answers

	Favorite sport	**Play**	**Watch**
1. James	football	✓	
2. Brianna	tennis	✓	
3. Matthew	baseball		✓
4. Nicole	basketball		✓

5 SPEAKING

Learning Objective: discuss free-time activities

A

- Focus Ss' attention on the chart and explain the first part of the task. Ask different Ss to read the questions.
- Ss write one more question individually.
- Elicit new questions from the class and write them on the board. (e.g., *What's your favorite team?*)
- Explain the second part of the task. Ask two Ss to model the example conversation.
- Ss complete the task in pairs. When the pairs finish, each S finds a new partner to work with.

B *Class activity*

- Explain the task. Then Ss use their notes to tell the class about their partners' free-time activities.

End of Cycle 1

See the Supplementary Resources chart at the beginning of this unit for additional teaching materials and student activities related to this Cycle.

Cycle 2, Exercises 6–12

6 CONVERSATION

Learning Objective: use *can* for ability in a conversation about talents

[CD 2, Track 45]

- To explain *can*, say: "I can write." Then write a sentence on the board. Say: "I can't dance (or sing or draw)." Then dance (or sing or draw) badly.
- Play the audio program. Ss listen and read silently.
- Elicit or explain the meaning of any new vocabulary. (e.g., *talent show, audition*).
- Play the audio program again. Ss listen and repeat. Then they practice the conversation in pairs.

7 GRAMMAR FOCUS

Learning Objective: ask and answer questions using *can* for ability

[CD 2, Track 46]

Can *for ability*

- Focus Ss' attention on the Grammar Focus box. Point out the patterns for statements, yes/no questions, and Wh-questions:

  Subject + *can/can't* + verb.
  Can + subject + verb?
  Yes, + subject + *can.* / *No,* + subject + *can't.*
  What + *can* + subject + *do*?
  Subject + *can* + verb.
  Who + *can* + verb?
  Subject + *can.*
- Play the audio program. Ss listen and read silently.
- Point out that we pronounce *can* as /kən/ in statements and questions. However, we pronounce it as /kæn/ in short answers.
- ***Option:*** Play the audio program again. Ss listen and repeat.

A

- Focus Ss' attention on the pictures. Read the verbs aloud. Ss repeat. Then elicit or explain any new vocabulary.
- Explain the task and ask a S to model the example sentence.
- Ss complete the sentences individually. Then they compare answers in pairs. Go around the class and encourage Ss to read the sentences aloud.

TIP
To build Ss' confidence, have them compare answers in pairs or small groups. Then check answers as a class.

- Elicit the answers from the class and write them on the board.

Answers

1. Ben **can** swim.
2. Sara **can** fix cars.
3. Diane **can't** sing.
4. Jeff **can't** ice-skate.
5. Lisa **can** play the piano.
6. Megan **can't** cook.

B *Pair work*

- Explain the task. Ask two Ss to model the example conversation for the class.
- Ss practice asking and answering the questions in pairs. Then they change roles and practice again. Go around the class and check Ss' pronunciation of *can* and *can't.*

C *Group work*

- Explain the task. Ask a S: "Can you draw?"
- Ss complete the task in small groups.

TIP
To develop Ss' proficiency with grammar, it is often more effective for Ss to practice the structures in a speaking or writing activity than to complete a mechanical task.

For more practice asking and answering questions with *can* and *can't*, play ***Hot Potato*** – download it from the website.

8 PRONUNCIATION

Learning Objective: sound more natural when using *can* and *can't*

A *[CD 2, Track 47]*

- Play the audio program. Ss listen and read silently. Then play the audio program again. Ask different Ss to read the sentences aloud.

B *Pair work*

- Explain and model the task. Then Ss complete the task in pairs. Go around the class and listen to Ss' pronunciation of *can* and *can't.*
- ***Option:*** Ask Ss to get in groups. Write these patterns on the board:

  Pablo can't draw, but he can sing.
  Misaki can't sing, but she can act.

  Ss use this pattern to write five sentences about the people in their group. Then they practice reading them aloud. Go around the class and check their pronunciation of *can* and *can't.*

7 GRAMMAR FOCUS

Can for ability

I				you			I		What **can** I do?
You				I			you		You **can** sing.
She	**can**	sing very well.	**Can**	she	sing?	Yes,	she	**can**.	
He	**can't**	sing at all.		he		No,	he	**can't**.	Who **can** sing?
We				we			we		Becky **can**.
They				they			they		

GRAMMAR PLUS see page 141

A Six people are talking about things they can and can't do. Complete these sentences.

Ben

1. I ___can___ swim.

Sara

2. I ____________ fix cars.

Diane

3. I ____________ sing.

Jeff

4. I ____________ ice-skate.

Lisa

5. I ____________ play the piano.

Megan

6. I ____________ cook.

B PAIR WORK Ask and answer questions about the pictures in part A.

A: Can Ben swim?
B: Yes, he can.

C GROUP WORK Can your classmates do the things in part A? Ask and answer questions.

"Can you swim, Diego?"

8 PRONUNCIATION *Can* and *can't*

A Listen and practice. Notice the pronunciation of **can** and **can't**.

/kən/
I **can** play the piano.

/kænt/
I **can't** sing at all.

B PAIR WORK Your partner reads a sentence for each number. Check (✓) the sentence you hear.

1. ☐ I can cook.
   ☐ I can't cook.
2. ☐ I can drive.
   ☐ I can't drive.
3. ☐ I can swim.
   ☐ I can't swim.
4. ☐ I can dance.
   ☐ I can't dance.

9 LISTENING Are you good at sports?

Listen to three people talk about their abilities. Write J (Joshua), M (Monica), or A (Anthony) on the things they can do well.

10 WORD POWER Talents and abilities

A Complete the word map with talents and abilities from the list. Then listen and practice.

✓ bake cookies
build a robot
design a website
do math in your head
edit a video
fix a computer
make electronic music
play chess
ride a horse
run a marathon
skateboard
take good photos
tell good jokes

B **GROUP WORK** Who can do the things in part A? Make a list of guesses about your classmates.

A: Who can bake cookies?
B: I think Melanie can.
C: Who can design . . . ?

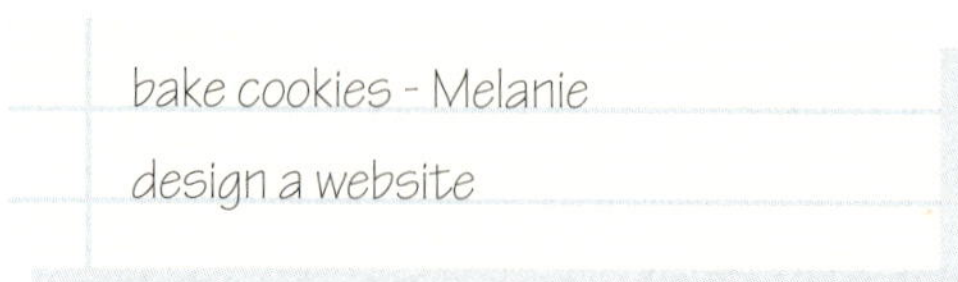

C **CLASS ACTIVITY** Go around the room and check your guesses.

A: Melanie, can you bake cookies?
B: Yes, I can.

11 INTERCHANGE 10 Hidden talents and abilities

Learn more about your classmates' hidden talents and abilities. Go to Interchange 10 on page 124.

9 LISTENING

Learning Objective: listen for details in a conversation about people's abilities using *can*

[CD 2, Track 48]

- Focus Ss' attention on the pictures. Elicit the verb for each picture and write it on the board. (Answers: draw, swim, take pictures/photos, sing, cook, use a computer, play the piano, paint)
- Explain the task. Tell Ss that they will not hear the people talk about all of the abilities in the photos. Then play the audio program two or three times. Ss listen and write their answers.

Audio script

1.
Woman Are you good at sports, Joshua?
Joshua No, not really, but I like to swim. I can swim very well. I often go swimming on the weekends. And I can play the piano well. But I can't sing.

2.
Man What do you do on weekends, Monica?
Monica I love to cook for my friends and family. I can cook well. And I love to take photos with my new camera. I think I can do that really well, too.

3.
Woman That's a beautiful picture, Anthony.
Anthony Oh, thank you very much. I'm an architect, so I can draw really well. I often do my work on a computer, so I can use computers really well, too. Oh, I can paint, too, but I don't paint for my job. It's just something I do for fun.

- Elicit the answers from the class.

Answers

1. A	3. M	5. M	7. J
2. J	4. Ø	6. A	8. A

10 WORD POWER

Learning Objective: discuss talents and abilities

A ***[CD 2, Track 49]***

- Explain the task. Then read the abilities and talents in the word map aloud. Ss repeat.
- Describe how a word map works. Then elicit or explain the meaning of any new vocabulary.

Vocabulary
talent: a natural ability to do something well
musical: related to music
artistic: related to art
athletic: related to athletes and sports
technical: related to industry or science

- Ss complete the word map individually. Then they compare answers in pairs.
- Play the audio. Ss listen and check their answers.

Answers

Musical or artistic: make electronic music, take good photos
Athletic: ride a horse, run a marathon, skateboard
Technical: build a robot, design a website, edit a video, fix a computer
Other: bake cookies, do math in your head, play chess, tell good jokes

B ***Group work***

- Explain the task and focus Ss' attention on the example list. All Ss in each group should copy of the list. Encourage groups to choose a different classmate for each talent or ability.
- Ask three Ss to model the example conversation.
- Ss complete the task in small groups.

C ***Class activity***

- Explain the task. Have two Ss model the conversation.
- Ss take their lists from part B, go around the class, and check their guesses. They check (✓) all the *yes* answers. Encourage Ss to give complete short answers.
- When Ss finish, they sit down. Elicit the number of correct guesses for each group. Then ask: "Who can bake cookies?" Elicit the answers. Continue with the remaining abilities and talents.

For more practice with abilities and talents, play ***Change Chairs*** – download it from the website. Begin: "Change chairs if you can bake cookies."

TIP
Encourage Ss to keep a vocabulary notebook to record new words, definitions, pronunciations, parts of speech, and example sentences.

11 INTERCHANGE 10

See page T-124 for teaching notes.

12 READING

Learning Objective: scan and read for details in an article about people's talents

A *[CD 2, Track 50]*

- Focus Ss' attention on the title and pictures. Explain the meaning of *world records*.
- Read the question aloud. Elicit answers from the class.
- Focus Ss' attention on the pictures. Invite Ss to talk about what they see. Ask Ss to guess what records are being set in the pictures.

B

- Explain the first part of the task. Ss read about the world records individually.
- Explain the second part of the task. Ss scan the article for specific information and check the correct answers to the questions. Point out that Ss can find the answers by scanning for the names and key words in the text.
- Ss complete the task individually.
- Elicit the answers.

Answers

1. b   2. b   3. a   4. b   5. b

- ***Option:*** Play the audio program. Ss listen and read along silently.
- Ss read the article again and underline any new words. Then elicit or explain the meanings of any new words.

Vocabulary

base jumping: the sport of jumping from a structure with a parachute
marathon: an activity that lasts a very long time; usually, a long running race
surfing: the sport of riding ocean waves on a board
squash (v): to crush something flat
muscles: parts of the body that are connected to bones and help you move

C *Group work*

- Explain the task and read the questions.
- Ss complete the task in small groups. Go around the class and give help as needed.
- Ask a S from each group to tell the class their opinions and examples.
- ***Option:*** Ss can look up world records and report on their findings to the class.

End of Cycle 2

See the Supplementary Resources chart at the beginning of this unit for additional teaching materials and student activities related to this Cycle and for assessment tools.

12 READING

A Some people like to set world records. Why do you think they like to do that?

Awesome Sports Records

base jumping

Base jumping is a dangerous sport. People jump off buildings, bridges, and other high places. The Burj Khalifa tower in Dubai, United Arab Emirates, is 824 meters (2,717 feet) tall. That's a very scary jump. But Fred Fugen and Vince Reffet of France can jump it! They also enjoy skydiving and parachuting.

Do you know what a unicycle is? It's a bicycle with just one wheel. David Weichenberger of Austria has the world record for longest jump on a unicycle. He can jump 2.95 meters (about 10 feet).

Kalamandalam Hemalatha of India has an amazing marathon record, but it's not for running. She can dance, and dance, and dance! In fact, Kalamandalam can dance for 123 hours and 15 minutes. That's the longest dance marathon on record. Kalamandalam's special dance is from India. It's called the Mohiniyattam dance.

Mohiniyattam dance

Otto the skateboarding dog

Do you know about Otto? Otto likes surfing, skateboarding, and playing soccer. Otto is a champion skateboarder, but he's a dog from Lima, Peru! Otto has the record for skateboarding through the legs of 30 people!

Can you squash an apple? Can you squash it using just the muscles in your arms? One woman can! Her name is Linsey Lindberg. Linsey is from Texas, in the U.S. In one minute, she can squash 10 apples. That's one apple every six seconds.

B Read the records. Then check (✓) the correct answers to the questions.

1. What's special about a unicycle?
   ☐ **a.** It has no wheels. ☐ **b.** It has one wheel, not two.
2. Who likes base jumping?
   ☐ **a.** David Weichenberger ☐ **b.** Fred Fugen
3. What sort of marathon can Kalamandalam do?
   ☐ **a.** a dance marathon ☐ **b.** a running marathon
4. How does Linsey Lindberg squash apples?
   ☐ **a.** with her hands ☐ **b.** with her arm muscles
5. What is one sport that Otto plays?
   ☐ **a.** basketball ☐ **b.** soccer

C **GROUP WORK** Do you think it's fun to set world records? Why or why not? What other world records do you know about? Tell your classmates.

Units 9–10 Progress check

SELF-ASSESSMENT

How well can you do these things? Check (✓) the boxes.

I can . . .	Very well	OK	A little
Make and respond to suggestions (Ex. 1)	☐	☐	☐
Talk about food and drink (Ex. 1, 2)	☐	☐	☐
Ask and answer questions about eating habits (Ex. 2)	☐	☐	☐
Understand descriptions of sporting activities (Ex. 3)	☐	☐	☐
Ask and answer questions about likes and dislikes (Ex. 4)	☐	☐	☐
Talk about job abilities (Ex. 5)	☐	☐	☐

1 SPEAKING Planning a class party

A **GROUP WORK** Plan a class party. Choose two main dishes, two salads, two drinks, and two desserts. Then tell the class.

Main dishes		
Salads		
Drinks		
Desserts		

useful expressions

Do we want any . . . ?
Let's get/make some . . .
I don't want/like . . .
Everybody likes . . .

2 SPEAKING Movie snacks

PAIR WORK Does your partner ever have these snacks at the movies? Add one more snack to the chart. Ask questions and complete the survey.

	Always	Usually	Sometimes	Hardly ever	Never
1. candy	☐	☐	☐	☐	☐
2. coffee	☐	☐	☐	☐	☐
3. pizza	☐	☐	☐	☐	☐
4. popcorn	☐	☐	☐	☐	☐
5. soda	☐	☐	☐	☐	☐
6. ______	☐	☐	☐	☐	☐

A: Do you ever have candy at the movies?
B: Yes, I sometimes have candy.

Units 9–10

Progress check

SELF-ASSESSMENT

Learning Objectives: reflect on one's learning; identify areas that need improvement

- Ask: "What did you learn in Units 9 and 10?" Elicit Ss' answers.
- Ss complete the Self-assessment. Explain to Ss that this is not a test; it is a way for them to evaluate what they've learned and identify areas where they need additional practice. Encourage them to be honest, and point out they will not get a bad grade if they check (✓) *A little*.
- Ss move on to the Progress check exercises. You can have Ss complete them in class or for homework, using one of these techniques:
  1. Ask Ss to complete all the exercises.
  2. Ask Ss: "What do you need to practice?" Then assign exercises based on their answers.
  3. Ask Ss to choose and complete exercises based on their Self-assessment.

1 SPEAKING

Learning Objective: demonstrate one's ability to make and respond to suggestions about food

Group work

- Set the scene and explain the task. Point out that Ss should complete their charts with the food they choose for the party.
- If needed, elicit examples of each type of food and write them on the board. For example:

  Main dishes: *sandwiches, hamburgers, pizza*
  Salads: *green salad, potato salad, fruit salad*
  Drinks: *lemonade, soda, coffee*
  Desserts: *cake, cookies, ice cream*
- Read out the useful expressions. Point out that Ss should use these to ask and talk about the kinds of food they want and don't want.
- Ss complete the activity in small groups. Go around the class and help as needed.
- Ask each group to tell the class about the foods for its party.
- ***Option:*** Ask each group to write the foods for its party on the board. Then the class votes for the best foods.

2 SPEAKING

Learning Objective demonstrate one's ability to discuss snacks and eating habits

Pair work

- Explain the task and read out the snacks. Then ask two Ss to model the example conversation. Point out that Student B should answer using *always, usually, sometimes, hardly ever*, or *never*. Student A should check (✓) the adverb of frequency that Student B uses.
- Ss complete the activity in pairs. They take turns asking all the questions in the survey. Go around the class and encourage Ss to listen to each other and not look at each other's charts.

TIP
If you don't have enough class time for the speaking activities, assign each S a speaking partner. Then have Ss complete the activities with their partners for homework.

3 LISTENING

Learning Objective: demonstrate one's ability to understand descriptions of sports

[CD 2, Track 51]

- Explain the task. Ss read the two choices for each answer silently.
- Play the audio program once or twice. Ss listen and complete the task. Then elicit the answers.

Audio script

1.
Stephanie Do you play any sports, Raymond?
Raymond Yes, I do.
Stephanie What do you play?
Raymond I play soccer.
2.
Stephanie So who do you play soccer with?
Raymond Some friends from work. We have a team.
3.
Stephanie When does your team practice?
Raymond We practice at 6:00 A.M.
Stephanie 6 o'clock? That's early!
4.
Stephanie So how often do you practice?
Raymond Every day. We practice before work.
Stephanie Wow!
5.
Stephanie And when do you play?
Raymond On the weekends. Please come and watch.
Stephanie OK. That sounds great!
6.
Stephanie Where do you play?
Raymond We always play at the park.

Answers

1. I play soccer.
2. Some friends from work.
3. At 6:00 A.M.
4. Every day.
5. On the weekends.
6. At the park.

4 SPEAKING

Learning Objective: demonstrate one's ability to ask and answer questions about likes and dislikes

A

- Explain the task. If needed, elicit examples of sports, activities, foods, and clothes. Point out that *I love* means you really like something a lot.
- Ss complete the chart individually.

B *Pair work*

- Explain the task. Ask two Ss to model the conversation. Then elicit follow-up questions Ss can ask with *who, where, how often*, and *when*.
- Ss complete the task in pairs.
- ***Option:*** Ask different Ss to share information about their partners.

5 SPEAKING

Learning Objective: demonstrate one's ability to talk about job-related abilities

Group work

- Focus Ss' attention on the pictures and read out the jobs. Ss listen and repeat. Then explain the task and read out the abilities in the box.
- Write *chef* on the board. Ask the class: "What can a chef do well?" Elicit Ss' answers and write them on the board. (Possible answers: plan meals, cook noodles, make salads, bake cookies, use a stove)
- Ask two Ss to model the example conversation. Encourage Student A to use an idea from the board.
- Ss make lists for the remaining three jobs in small groups. Then elicit ideas from the class and ask different Ss to write them on the board.

WHAT'S NEXT?

Learning Objective: become more involved in one's learning

- Focus Ss' attention on the Self-assessment again. Ask: "How well can you do these things now?"
- Ask Ss to underline one thing they need to review. Ask: "What did you underline? How can you review it?"
- If needed, plan additional instruction, activities, or reviews based on Ss' answers.

3 LISTENING Do you play any sports?

Listen to Stephanie ask Raymond about sports. Check (✓) Raymond's answers.

1. ☐ I play football.
   ☐ I play soccer.
2. ☐ Some friends from school.
   ☐ Some friends from work.
3. ☐ At 6:00 A.M.
   ☐ At 6:00 P.M.
4. ☐ Every day.
   ☐ Every week.
5. ☐ On the weekends.
   ☐ In the afternoons.
6. ☐ At the park.
   ☐ In the yard.

4 SPEAKING My favorite things

A Complete the chart with things you love, like, and don't like.

	I love . . .	I like . . .	I don't like . . .
Sports			
Other activities			
Foods			
Clothes			

B **PAIR WORK** Find out what your partner loves, likes, and doesn't like. Then ask more questions with *who*, *where*, *how often*, or *when*.

A: What sports do you love?
B: I love bike riding.

A: Who do you usually go bike riding with?
B: I usually go with my brother and sister.

5 SPEAKING Talents and abilities

GROUP WORK What can these people do well? Make a list. Use the abilities in the box and your own ideas. Then tell the class.

A: A chef can cook very well.
B: A chef can also bake things, like cakes and cookies.
A: Also, a chef can . . .

bake	fix a motorcycle
cook	paint
draw	play the guitar
fix a car	read music

WHAT'S NEXT?

Look at your Self-assessment again. Do you need to review anything?

Unit 11 Supplementary Resources Overview

	After the following SB exercises	You can use these materials in class	Your students can use these materials outside the classroom
CYCLE 1	1 Word Power		**SS** Unit 11 Vocabulary 1 **GAME** Sentence Runner (Months and dates)
	2 Conversation	**TSS** Unit 11 Extra Worksheet	**SS** Unit 11 Speaking
	3 Grammar Focus		**SB** Unit 11 Grammar plus, Focus 1 **SS** Unit 11 Grammar 1 **GAME** Word Keys (The future with *be going to*)
	4 Pronunciation		
	5 Listening		
	6 Interchange 11		**WB** Unit 11 exercises 1–4
CYCLE 2	7 Snapshot	**TSS** Unit 11 Vocabulary Worksheet	
	8 Conversation		**SS** Unit 11 Speaking 2
	9 Grammar Focus		**SB** Unit 11 Grammar plus, Focus 2 **SS** Unit 11 Grammar 2 **GAME** Sentence Stacker (The future and Wh-questions with *be going to*)
	10 Word Power	**TSS** Unit 11 Grammar Worksheet **TSS** Unit 11 Listening Worksheet	**SS** Unit 11 Vocabulary 2 **GAME** Say the Word (Ways to celebrate)
	11 Speaking		
	12 Reading	**TSS** Unit 11 Project Worksheet **VID** Unit 11 **VRB** Unit 11	**SS** Unit 11 Reading 1–2 **SS** Unit 11 Listening 1–3 **SS** Unit 11 Video 1–3 **WB** Unit 11 exercises 5–7

Key **GAME:** Online Game **SB:** Student's Book **SS:** Online Self-study **TSS:** Teacher Support Site
VID: Video DVD **VRB:** Video Resource Book **WB:** Online Workbook/Workbook

My Plan for Unit 11

Use the space below to customize a plan that fits your needs.

With the following SB exercises	I am using these materials in class	My students are using these materials outside the classroom

With or instead of the following SB section	I am using these materials for assessment

11 I'm going to have a party.

- Discuss evening, weekend, and birthday plans
- Discuss plans to celebrate holidays, special occasions, and festivals

1 WORD POWER Months and dates

A Listen and practice the months of the year.

Months					
January	February	March	April	May	June
July	August	September	October	November	December

B Complete the dates. Then listen and practice.

Dates					
1st	first	11th	eleventh	21st	twenty-first
2nd	second		twelfth		twenty-second
	third	13th	thirteenth	23rd	twenty-third
4th	fourth	14th	fourteenth		twenty-fourth
5th	fifth		fifteenth	25th	twenty-fifth
	sixth	16th	sixteenth		twenty-sixth
7th	seventh	17th	seventeenth	27th	twenty-seventh
8th	eighth	18th	eighteenth		twenty-eighth
9th	ninth		nineteenth	29th	twenty-ninth
	tenth	20th	twentieth		thirtieth
					thirty-first

C **CLASS ACTIVITY** Go around the room. Ask for your classmates' birthdays.

A: When's your birthday? **B:** It's November eighteenth. When's yours?

2 CONVERSATION Is she going to bake a cake?

Listen and practice.

AVA Are you going to do anything exciting this weekend?

MARTIN Well, I'm going to celebrate my birthday.

AVA Oh, happy birthday! When is it, exactly?

MARTIN It's April twenty-first – Sunday.

AVA So what are your plans?

MARTIN I'm going to go to my friend Rosa's house. She's going to cook a special dinner for me.

AVA Nice! Is Rosa going to bake a birthday cake for you, too?

MARTIN A cake for me? Mmm . . . I hope so!

11 I'm going to have a party.

Cycle 1, Exercises 1–6

In Unit 11, students discuss evening, weekend, and birthday plans, and plans to celebrate holidays, special occasions, and festivals. By the end of Cycle 1, students will be able to discuss evening, weekend, and birthday plans using statements and yes/no questions with *be going to*. By the end of Cycle 2, students will be able to discuss plans to celebrate holidays, special occasions, and festivals using Wh-questions with *be going to*.

1 WORD POWER

Learning Objective: state dates using months and ordinal numbers

A *[CD 2, Track 52]*

- Set the scene. Write today's date on the board. Say: "Today is (date)."
- Focus Ss' attention on the months.
- Play the audio program. Ss listen and read silently.
- Play the audio program again. Ss listen and repeat.

B *[CD 2, Track 53]*

- Focus Ss' attention on the dates.
- Explain the first part of the task. Ss complete the missing dates individually.
- Elicit the answers and write them on the board. Ss check their answers.
- Explain the second part of the task. Play the audio program. Ss listen and read silently.
- Play the audio program again. Ss listen and repeat.
- ***Option***: Point out that we also call these dates *ordinal numbers*. Contrast ordinal numbers with cardinal numbers (e.g., *one, two, three*).

! For a new way to practice dates, play ***Bingo*** – download it from the website.

C *Class activity*

- Books closed. Write five dates (e.g., *November 18th, May 22nd*) on the board. Point out that we write the month and then the number. Read the dates aloud and have Ss repeat.
- ***Option:*** Model other ways to write dates. For example:

  November 18th   November 18   18 November
  November eighteenth   11/18

- Write your birthday on the board. Say: "My birthday is . . ." Explain that your birthday is the date you were born.
- Books open. Explain the task. Ask two Ss to model the example conversation.
- Ss take their pencils and notebooks, go around the class, and complete the activity by making a list of their classmates' birthdays. Continue until most Ss have at least five birthdays on their list. While Ss make their lists, list the names of the Ss in the class on the board.
- Ask the class about each S in the class: "When is (Juan)'s birthday?" Ask different Ss to write the birthdays on the board. The class helps with spelling as needed.
- ***Option:*** Make a list of 10 dates (e.g., *January 21st, October 7th*). Dictate them to the class and have the Ss write them down. Then ask different Ss to write the dates on the board. Alternatively, Ss dictate dates to each other in pairs.

For more practice with months and dates, play ***Line Up!*** – download it from the website. Ss line up in the order of their birthdays.

2 CONVERSATION

Learning Objective: use the future with *be going to* in a conversation about plans

[CD 2, Track 54]

- Text covered. Focus Ss' attention on the picture and set the scene. Ava is asking Martin about his weekend plans. Elicit or explain what kind of cake is shown (a special cake/a birthday cake).
- Text uncovered. Play the audio program. Ss listen and read silently.
- Play the audio program again. Ss read, listen, and repeat.
- Ss practice the conversation in pairs.

3 GRAMMAR FOCUS

Learning Objective: use the future with *be going to* in statements and yes/no questions

[CD 2, Track 55]

***The future with* be going to**

- Focus Ss' attention on the Grammar Focus box. Elicit or explain that we use *be going to* to talk about future plans.
- Write this on the board:

  I'm going to study tonight. = I'm planning to study tonight.

  Point out that these sentences have the same meaning.
- Elicit or explain the pattern for statements and yes/no questions with *be going to*:

  Subject + *be going to* + verb.
  Be + subject + *going to* + verb?
  Yes, + subject + *be*.
  No, + subject + *be* + *not*.
- Play the audio program. Ss listen and read silently.
- ***Option:*** Play the audio program again. Ss listen and repeat.

A

- Focus Ss' attention on the pictures. Explain the task. Ask a S to model the example sentence.
- ***Option:*** Elicit the activities in the remaining pictures. Write possible phrases for each picture on the board. For example:

  1. *go biking, go bike riding*
  2. *swim, go swimming*
  3. *shop, go shopping*
  4. *watch a soccer game*
  5. *work*
  6. *dance, go dancing*
  7. *play the drums*
  8. *go to the movies, watch a movie, see a movie*
- Ss complete the task individually. Go around the class and help with spelling and punctuation as needed.
- Ss compare sentences in pairs. Then elicit sentences from the class and ask different Ss to write them on the board.

Possible answers

1. He's going to go biking.
2. He's going to swim./He's going to go swimming.
3. She's going to go shopping.
4. They are going to watch a soccer game.
5. She's going to work./She's going to go to work.
6. They're going to dance./They're going to go dancing.
7. He's going to play (the) drums.
8. They're going to go to the movies./They're going to watch/see a movie.

B *Pair work*

- Explain the task. Model the example question, and ask a S to respond.
- Ss complete the task in pairs.
- Ss share information about their partner's weekend plans with another pair.

! For a new way to practice yes/no questions with *be going to*, try ***Question Exchange*** – download it from the website.

For more practice using statements with *be going to*, play the ***Chain Game*** – download it from the website. Begin with this sentence: "This weekend, I'm going to go swimming."

4 PRONUNCIATION

Learning Objective: sound more natural by reducing *going to* when talking about future plans

A *[CD 2, Track 56]*

- Explain the task and play the audio program. Ss listen and read silently.
- Point out that we use this reduction when we talk about future plans (i.e., *be going to* + verb). We do not use it to talk about the present continuous (i.e., with *be going to* + noun).
- Write these two sentences on the board:

  I'm going to have a party.
  I'm going to a party.

  Ask: "Which sentence talks about future plans?" Ss explain their answers.
- Play the audio program again. Ss listen and repeat. Then they practice the conversations in pairs. Go around the class and check Ss' use of the reduction.

B *Pair work*

- Explain the task. Then Ss complete the task in pairs. Go around the class and check Ss' use of the reduction.

3 GRAMMAR FOCUS

The future with *be going to*

Are you **going to do** anything this weekend?	Yes, I am. **I'm going to celebrate** my birthday.
	No, I'm not. **I'm going to stay** home.
Is Rosa **going to cook** dinner for you?	Yes, she is. She**'s going to cook** a special dinner.
	No, she's not. She**'s going to order** takeout.
Are your friends **going to be** there?	Yes, they are. They**'re going to stop** by after dinner.
	No, they're not. They**'re going to be** away all weekend.

GRAMMAR PLUS *see page 142*

A What are these people going to do this weekend? Write sentences. Then compare with a partner.

1. *He's going to go biking.*

B **PAIR WORK** Is your partner going to do the things in part A this weekend? Ask and answer questions.

"Are you going to go biking this weekend?"

4 PRONUNCIATION Reduction of *going to*

A Listen and practice. Notice the reduction of **going to** to /gənə/.

A: Are you **going to** go to the game?
B: No. I'm **going to** study for a test.

A: Are you **going to** go to a restaurant?
B: Yes. We're **going to** go to Nick's Café.

B **PAIR WORK** Ask your partner about his or her evening plans. Try to reduce **going to**.

5 LISTENING Holiday plans

A What are these people's plans for a Monday holiday? Write your guesses in the chart.

B Listen to the interview. What are the people really going to do on Monday? Complete the chart.

Morgan

Isaac

Brian

Lauren

	Your guess	What they're really going to do
Morgan	*Morgan is going to go to the gym.*	
Isaac		
Brian		
Lauren		

6 INTERCHANGE 11 Take a guess

Make guesses about your classmates' plans. Go to Interchange 11 on page 125.

7 SNAPSHOT

Listen and practice.

Celebrating Holidays in the U.S.

Do you celebrate any of these holidays? Do any of your friends celebrate them? What are some holidays in your country? What's your favorite holiday?

5 LISTENING

Learning Objective: listen for specific information about future plans

A

- Focus Ss' attention on the picture and explain the task. Ss complete the left-hand column of the chart individually. Elicit guesses from the class.

B *[CD 2, Track 57]*

- Explain the task. Then play the audio program once or twice, pausing after each interview. Ss listen and complete the right-hand column of the chart.

Audio script

Jacob Hello, everyone! I'm Jacob with the Real City website. It's Friday evening, and it's going to be a long weekend, because Monday is a holiday. I'm talking with people waiting for the subway. I'm finding out how they're going to spend the Monday holiday. What's your name?
Morgan It's Morgan.
Jacob What are you going to do on Monday? Are you going to go to the gym?
Morgan No, not on Monday. I'm going to meet a friend. We're going to run together in the park.
Jacob Great! Have fun. And what's your name?
Isaac I'm Isaac. Nice to meet you.
Jacob Nice to meet you, too. Are you going home now, Isaac?
Isaac No, I'm not. I'm going to go to a concert with some friends tonight.
Jacob That's great. What are you going to do on Monday? It's a holiday, you know.
Isaac Oh, I'm going to play the drums all day. I need to practice. I really want to be in a band.
Jacob Well, good luck with that, Isaac! Hi there. I'm Jacob from Real City News. Can I ask your name?
Brian Sure. I'm Brian.
Jacob Are you going to do anything interesting on Monday, Brian?
Brian I don't think so. I'm going to work at home this weekend, and on Monday, too. I have all my work right here in my bag.
Jacob I see. So, Monday really isn't a holiday for you.
Brian No. It really isn't.
Jacob OK, I have time for one more person.
Lauren Oh, hi. I'm Lauren.
Jacob What are you going to do on Monday, Lauren?
Lauren I'm going to play computer games on my laptop.
Jacob Alone?
Lauren No, not alone. I'm going to play online. A lot of my friends are going to play online, too!
Jacob Sounds like fun.

- Elicit the answers from the class.

Answers

Morgan is going to meet a friend/run in the park.
Isaac is going to play the drums all day.
Brian is going to work at home.
Lauren is going to play computer games online.

6 INTERCHANGE 11

See page T-125 for teaching notes.

End of Cycle 1

See the Supplementary Resources chart at the beginning of this unit for additional teaching materials and student activities related to this Cycle.

Cycle 2, Exercises 7–12

7 SNAPSHOT

Learning Objective: discuss common holidays

[CD 2, Track 58]

- Focus Ss' attention on the pictures. Then play the audio program. Ss listen and read silently.
- Play the audio program again. Ss listen and repeat.
- Ss discuss the questions in small groups. Go around the class and help with vocabulary as needed. Then elicit information from each group.
- ***Option***: When Ss say their favorite holiday, have them give the date also.

8 CONVERSATION

Learning Objective: use Wh-questions with *be going to* in a conversation about a holiday

[CD 2, Track 59]

- Books closed. Write *Valentine's Day* on the board. Ask the class: "When is Valentine's Day? How do people celebrate it?" If needed, explain that Valentine's Day is on February 14th. To celebrate, people exchange cards with people they love or really like. Some people give their husband, wife, boyfriend, or girlfriend a present, such as chocolate or flowers. Sometimes they go out for dinner.
- Books open. Set the scene. Allie and Jim are talking about their plans for Valentine's Day.
- Write these questions on the board:
  1. Who is going to go out for dinner on Valentine's Day?
  2. Where are they going to go?
  3. Who is going to go dancing?
- Play the audio program. Ss listen for the answers. (Answers: 1. Jim and Marissa 2. the Red Rose/a fancy restaurant 3. Allie and Matt)
- Play the audio program again. Ss listen and repeat. Then they practice the conversation in pairs.

! For a new way to practice this Conversation, try ***Moving Dialog*** – download it from the website.

9 GRAMMAR FOCUS

Learning Objective: use *be going to* in Wh-questions

[CD 2, Track 60]

***Wh-questions with* be going to**

- Focus Ss' attention on the Grammar Focus box. Point out the pattern for the first three Wh-questions:

  Wh-question + *be* + subject + *going to* + verb?
- Point out the patterns for positive and negative statements with *be going to:*

  Positive: Subject + *be* + *going to* + verb.

  Negative: Subject + *be* + *not* + *going to* + verb.
- Play the audio program. Ss listen and read silently.
- ***Option***: Play the audio program again. Ss listen and repeat.

A

- Explain the task. Read the first line of the first conversation and elicit the second line from the class. Point out that Ss should use the words in parentheses.
- Ss complete the task individually. Go around the class and give help as needed. Then Ss compare their answers in pairs.
- Ask different Ss to read the conversations. If needed, correct any errors as a class. Then Ss practice the conversations in pairs.

Answers

1. A: Where **are** you **going to spend** Thanksgiving?
   B: My parents and I **are going to visit** my grandparents.
2. A: Who **are** you **going to invite** to your Independence Day picnic?
   B: I**'m going to ask** my family and some good friends.
3. A: What **are** you **going to do** for New Year's Day?
   B: I don't know. I**'m not going to do** anything special.
4. A: How **are** your children **going to celebrate** Halloween?
   B: They **are going to go** to their school's party.
5. A: What **is** your sister **going to do** for Valentine's Day?
   B: Her boyfriend **is going to take** her out to dinner.

B *Group work*

- Explain the task and focus Ss' attention on the time expressions in the box. Point out that these expressions are for future time.
- Read the time expressions aloud. Ss listen and read silently. Read the time expressions again. Ss listen and repeat.
- Ask three Ss to model the example conversation.
- Ss complete the activity in groups. Go around the class and encourage Ss to ask and answer questions using different time expressions and the names of holidays.
- ***Option:*** Ask different Ss to share information about their groups with the class.

8 CONVERSATION We're going to go dancing.

Listen and practice.

ALLIE So, Jim, do you have any plans for Valentine's Day?

JIM I sure do. I'm going to take Marissa out for dinner.

ALLIE Oh, really? Where are you going to eat?

JIM At the Red Rose. They have great desserts.

ALLIE Wow! That sounds really nice!

JIM Yeah! How about you? What are you and Matt going to do?

ALLIE Well, we're not going to go to a fancy restaurant. We're going to go dancing.

JIM Sounds like fun, too.

9 GRAMMAR FOCUS

Wh-questions with *be going to*

What are you **going to do** for Valentine's Day?	I**'m going to go** to a dance club.
	I**'m not going to go** to a restaurant.
How is Allie **going to get** to the dance club?	She**'s going to drive**.
	She**'s not going to take** the bus.
Where are Jim and his girlfriend **going to eat**?	They**'re going to eat** at the Red Rose.
	They**'re not going to eat** at Nick's Café.

GRAMMAR PLUS *see page 142*

A Complete these conversations with the correct form of *be going to*. Then practice with a partner.

1. **A:** Where ___*are*___ you ___*going to spend*___ (spend) Thanksgiving?
   B: My parents and I ____________ (visit) my grandparents.
2. **A:** Who ____________ you ____________ (invite) to your Independence Day picnic?
   B: I ____________ (ask) my family and some good friends.
3. **A:** What ____________ you ____________ (do) for New Year's Day?
   B: I don't know. I ____________ (not do) anything special.
4. **A:** How ____________ your children ____________ (celebrate) Halloween?
   B: They ____________ (go) to their school's party.
5. **A:** What ____________ your sister ____________ (do) for Valentine's Day?
   B: Her boyfriend ____________ (take) her out to dinner.

B **GROUP WORK** Ask your classmates about their plans. Use the names of holidays and the time expressions in the box.

A: What are you going to do tonight?
B: I'm going to go to a party.
C: Oh, really? Who's going to be there?
B: Well, Chris and Sam are going to come. . . .

time expressions	
tonight	next week
tomorrow	next month
tomorrow afternoon	next summer
tomorrow night	next year

10 WORD POWER Let's celebrate!

A Listen and practice.

wear special clothes

eat special food

decorate

give gifts

play music

go to a parade

go on a picnic

watch fireworks

B **PAIR WORK** Are you going to celebrate a special day this year? Are you (or is someone you know) going to do any of the things in part A?

A: I'm going to go to a wedding next month. I'm going to wear special clothes.
B: Is it a family member's wedding?

11 SPEAKING Holidays and festivals

A **PAIR WORK** Choose any holiday or festival. Then ask and answer these questions.

What is the holiday or festival?
When is it?
What are you going to do?
Where are you going to go?
Who's going to be there?
When are you going to go?
How are you going to get there?

A: What is the holiday or festival?
B: It's my city's Cherry Blossom Festival.
A: When is it?
B: It's on March twenty-third.
A: What are you going to do?
B: I'm going to go to the park. . . .

B **CLASS ACTIVITY** Tell the class about your partner's plans.

Carnival, Brazil

Cherry Blossom Festival, Japan

10 WORD POWER

Learning Objective: discuss ways of celebrating special occasions

A [CD 2, Track 61]

- Focus Ss' attention on the title and pictures. Elicit or explain the meaning of any new vocabulary.
- Play the audio program. Ss listen and read silently.
- Play the audio program again. Ss listen and repeat.

B *Pair work*

- Elicit special occasions from the class (e.g., a baby shower, graduation, a wedding, an anniversary, Mother's Day, Father's Day, a high school reunion). Then write them on the board.
- Explain the task. Read the questions and ask two Ss to model the example conversation. Point out that the conversation is about future plans, so Ss should use *be going to.*
- Ss discuss the questions in pairs. Go around the class and encourage Ss to ask follow-up questions and give more information.
- Ask different pairs to share their information.

11 SPEAKING

Learning Objective: discuss plans for holidays and festivals using the future with *be going to*

A *Pair work*

- Focus Ss' attention on the title. If needed, explain that a *holiday* is a special day when people don't go to work or school in order to celebrate a special occasion (e.g., *New Year's Day*). A *festival* is a special day or days that people celebrate with special activities or food. Festivals can celebrate many things, including religious events, cultural events, and times of year (e.g., *Spring Festival*).
- Focus Ss' attention on the pictures. Read the names of the holiday and festival aloud. Elicit or give information about them.

Vocabulary

Carnival: a famous street festival in Rio de Janeiro, Brazil, usually in February or March, celebrated with parades, music, and dancing

Cherry Blossom Festival: a Japanese festival that celebrates the beginning of spring and the cherry blossoms

- ***Option:*** Ask Ss to research information about these holidays before class.
- Explain the task and read the questions. Point out that Ss can choose any holiday or festival they plan to celebrate.
- Ask two Ss to model the example conversation.
- Ss work individually. They choose a holiday or festival and make notes about their plans for it. Go around the class and encourage Ss to answer all the questions. Help with vocabulary as needed.

TIP

To build Ss' confidence and make discussions more successful, give Ss time to think about what to say before they begin the discussion.

- Ss work in pairs. They take turns asking and answering questions about the holiday or festival. Have Ss take notes about their partner's plans.

B *Class activity*

- Explain the task. Then Ss use their notes to tell the class about their partner's plans.
- ***Option:*** Ss write sentences about their partner's plans before they speak.

12 READING

Learning Objective: scan and read for details in a blog post about birthday celebrations

A *[CD 2, Track 62]*

- Read the title and the heads aloud. Encourage Ss to look at the pictures. Ask the class: "Who are the people? Where are they from?" Elicit the answers. (Answers: Harry Baker, Australia; Jim Dixon, Jamaica; Victoria Smith, U.K.; Jiang Li, China)
- ***Option:*** Ss find the places on a map or in an atlas.
- Focus Ss' attention on the task. Ss complete the task individually. Tell Ss to raise their hands when they find the answer.
- To check answers, ask: "Who sends a letter when people are 100 years old?" Elicit the answer. (Answer: the Queen). Then ask a follow-up question: "In what country?" (Answer: the U.K.).

TIP
To improve Ss' reading skills, have them discuss the title, the heads, and the pictures before they read.

- Have Ss read the blog post individually and underline any words they don't know. Elicit or explain any new vocabulary.

Vocabulary
sugar: sweet granules used to flavor drinks and food
custom: something a group of people always do, especially on a special occasion
flour: a powder made from wheat or other grains that is used to make bread and cakes
Queen: the female ruler in some countries, such as the U.K.'s Queen Elizabeth II

- ***Option:*** Read the text aloud. Ss listen and read along silently.

B

- Explain the task.
- Write the first question on the board. Point out that Ss can find the information quickly by looking for key words (e.g., *eat, food*).
- Ss complete the task individually. Go around the class and give help as needed.
- Ss compare their answers in pairs. Then ask different Ss to write the correct answers on the board.

Answers

1. Australia and China celebrate birthdays with food.
2. Jim is going to the store to buy flour.
3. You need bread, butter, and sugar.
4. In China, noodles mean long life.

C *Group work*

- Read the questions and explain the task. Point out that Ss should take notes about their classmates' plans.
- Ss discuss the questions in small groups. If possible, put Ss from different countries in each group. Go around the class and help with vocabulary as needed.
- Ask Ss from each group to share information about their classmates' plans.

! For a new way to practice reading for specific information, try ***Reading Race*** – download it from the website. Include three questions about each person. For example:

1. Where does (Harry Baker) live?
2. Who is going to celebrate (his) birthday with (him)?
3. How is (he) going to celebrate (his) birthday?

End of Cycle 2

See the Supplementary Resources chart at the beginning of this unit for additional teaching materials and student activities related to this Cycle.

12 READING

A Scan the blog post. Who sends a letter when people are 100 years old?

Home Posts Archives Follow

HAPPY BIRTHDAY TO YOU!

In this week's blog, we look at some birthday customs around the world.

Harry Baker, Perth, Australia
It's my birthday next Wednesday. I'm going to be 10 years old. In my country, we always eat fairy bread on our birthdays. My mom's going to make me a huge plate of fairy bread. It's a snack. We make it with bread, butter, and colorful sugar called "hundreds and thousands."

Jim Dixon, Montego Bay, Jamaica
I love birthdays! They're a lot of fun. Here in Jamaica, we have an old custom. We like to surprise people on their birthday. Guess what we do? We throw flour at our friends! It's my best friend's birthday tomorrow. I'm going to go to the store soon. I'm going to buy a lot of flour to throw at him.

Victoria Smith, London, UK
My grandmother is going to be 100 years old in June. She's very excited because she's going to get a special letter from the Queen. The Queen sends a letter to every person who reaches 100. It's a tradition that makes people very happy.

Jiang Li, Beijing, China
In my country, we celebrate birthdays with a special type of food. Noodles are a sign of a long life for us. This year, I'm going to make some "long life noodles" for all my friends. We're going to eat them together and have a great evening!

B Read the questions. Write short answers.

1. Which two countries celebrate birthdays with food? ______
2. Why is Jim going to the store? ______
3. What three things do you need to make fairy bread? ______
4. What do noodles mean in China? ______

C GROUP WORK How do people usually celebrate birthdays in your country? Do you have plans for your next birthday? How about the birthday of a friend or a family member? What are you going to do? Tell your classmates.

Unit 12 Supplementary Resources Overview

	After the following SB exercises	You can use these materials in class	Your students can use these materials outside the classroom
CYCLE 1	1 **Word Power**	**TSS** Unit 12 Vocabulary Worksheet	**SS** Unit 12 Vocabulary 1 **GAME** Speak or Swim (Parts of the body)
	2 **Conversation**		**SS** Unit 12 Speaking 1
	3 **Grammar Focus**		**SB** Unit 12 Grammar plus, Focus 1 **SS** Unit 12 Grammar 1 **GAME** Name the Picture (Health problems) **GAME** Say the Word (Illnesses and expressions)
	4 **Listening**	**TSS** Unit 12 Extra Worksheet	**WB** Unit 12 exercises 1–3
CYCLE 2	5 **Snapshot**		**SS** Unit 12 Vocabulary 2
	6 **Conversation**		**SS** Unit 12 Speaking 2
	7 **Listening**		
	8 **Pronunciation**		
	9 **Grammar Focus**	**TSS** Unit 12 Grammar Worksheet **TSS** Unit 12 Listening Worksheet	**SB** Unit 12 Grammar plus, Focus 2 **SS** Unit 12 Grammar 2 **GAME** Speak or Swim (Advice)
	10 **Speaking**		
	11 **Interchange 12**		
	12 **Reading**	**TSS** Unit 12 Project Worksheet **VID** Unit 12 **VRB** Unit 12	**SS** Unit 12 Reading 1–2 **SS** Unit 12 Listening 1–3 **SS** Unit 12 Video 1–3 **WB** Unit 12 exercises 4–8

With or instead of the following SB section	You can also use these materials for assessment
Units 11–12 Progress Check	**ASSESSMENT PROGRAM** Units 11–12 Oral Quiz **ASSESSMENT PROGRAM** Units 11–12 Written Quiz

Key **GAME:** Online Game **SB:** Student's Book **SS:** Online Self-study **TSS:** Teacher Support Site
VID: Video DVD **VRB:** Video Resource Book **WB:** Online Workbook/Workbook

My Plan for Unit 12

Use the space below to customize a plan that fits your needs.

With the following SB exercises	I am using these materials in class	My students are using these materials outside the classroom

With or instead of the following SB section	I am using these materials for assessment

12 How do you feel?

- Discuss the body and common ailments
- Discuss common remedies and give health advice

1 WORD POWER Parts of the body

A Listen and practice.

B **GROUP WORK** Say a sentence with a body part. Take turns repeating the sentence and keep adding body parts. The group with the last student to say a correct sentence wins.

A: I have one head.

B: I have one head and two eyes.

C: I have one head, two eyes, and one nose.

D: I have one head, two eyes, one nose, and . . .

12 How do you feel?

Cycle 1, Exercises 1–4

In Unit 12, students discuss the body and common ailments, discuss common remedies, and give health advice. By the end of Cycle 1, students will be able to discuss the body and common ailments using *have* + noun and *feel* + adjective. By the end of Cycle 2, students will be able to discuss common remedies and give health advice using imperatives.

1 WORD POWER

Learning Objective: identify parts of the body

A *[CD 3, Track 1]*

- Focus Ss' attention on the pictures. Write these questions on the board:

  1. Where is the man?
  2. What's he doing?
  3. What's he wearing?
  4. What's he like?

- Ss discuss the questions in pairs. Then elicit answers from the class. (Possible answers: 1. He's on the beach. 2. He's going surfing. 3. He's wearing a T-shirt and shorts/a swimsuit. 4. He's handsome/in shape.)

TIP
To help Ss focus, start each class with a warm-up activity.

- Focus Ss' attention on the vocabulary. Play the audio program. Ss listen and read silently.
- Play the audio program again, or model the words one by one. Ss listen and repeat.
- Point out the irregular plurals *teeth* and *feet*. Note that *hair* is a noncount noun.
- Point out the silent letters: *b* in *thumb*, *k* in *knee*, and *w* in *wrist*.
- ***Option:*** Books closed. Say the parts of the body in random order. Ss repeat the words and point to their own bodies.

B *Group work*

- Explain the task and model the example conversation with four Ss.
- Books closed. Ss take turns making sentences until there are no body parts to add or someone makes a mistake.
- ***Option:*** Write these numbers and phrases on the board like column headers:

  1   2   10   32   a lot of

  Ss take turns coming to the board and writing the name of a body part in the correct column. The S says, e.g., "I have two hands."

TIP
Be sensitive to Ss' comfort levels when you talk about body parts. Some Ss are more comfortable working with classmates of the same gender. Others are more comfortable talking about pictures than themselves.

For more practice with this vocabulary, play ***Simon-Says*** – download it from the website. Give instructions such as "Simon says touch your toes."

- ***Option:*** Draw a picture of a "monster" on the board (e.g., with two heads and six arms). Ask Ss to describe the picture. For example, Ss say: "It has two heads. It has six arms." Ask Ss to draw pictures of monsters individually. Then they take turns describing each other's pictures in pairs.

2 CONVERSATION

Learning Objective: use *have* + noun and *feel* + adjective in a conversation about health problems

[CD 3, Track 2]

- Books closed. Set the scene. Craig and Nathan are talking. Nathan isn't feeling well. Ask: "What part of his body does he talk about?" Play the audio program. Ss listen for the answer. (Answer: his stomach)
- Books open. Focus Ss' attention on the title and the picture.
- Ask the class: "What is Craig going to do?" Then play the audio program. Ss listen for the answer. Elicit the answer. (Answer: He's going to have some pizza.)
- Elicit or explain the meaning of any new vocabulary. To explain the meaning of *flu*, use gestures or the picture in Exercise 3.

Vocabulary
What's wrong?: What's the problem?
That's too bad.: a phrase used to express sympathy

- Play the audio program again. Ss listen and repeat. Then Ss practice the conversation in pairs.
- ***Option:*** Ask one or two pairs to role-play the conversation for the class.

! For a new way to practice this Conversation, try ***Say It With Feeling!*** – download it from the website.

3 GRAMMAR FOCUS

Learning Objective: use *have* + noun and *feel* + adjective to discuss common health problems

[CD 3, Track 3]

- Focus Ss' attention on the Grammar Focus box. Point out that we use *How are you?* and *How do you feel?* to ask about people's health. We ask *What's the matter?* and *What's wrong?* when we think there's a problem.
- Ask the class: "What does Craig ask Nathan in Exercise 2?" Elicit the answer. (Answer: "What's wrong?") Then ask: "What does Nathan say?" Elicit the answers. (Answers: "I have a stomachache. I just feel really sick."
- Write these patterns on the board:

  have + noun
  feel + adjective

  Point out that we use *have* + noun for specific physical problems (e.g., *a headache, a backache, the flu*). We use *feel* + adjective for the way we feel in general (e.g., *better, well*).
- ***Option:*** Write these sentences on the board:

  1. Nathan __________ well.
  2. Nathan __________ a stomachache.
  3. Nathan __________ the flu.
  4. Nathan __________ really sick.

  Ss review the conversation in Exercise 2 and complete the sentences. Then elicit the answers and write them on the board. (Answers: 1. doesn't feel 2. has 3. doesn't have 4. feels)
- Play the audio program. Ss listen and read silently.
- ***Option:*** Play the audio program again. Ss listen and repeat.

A ***[CD 3, Track 4]***

- Focus Ss' attention on the pictures. Point out that all these phrases include nouns, so the pattern is *have* + noun.
- Play the audio program. Ss listen and read silently. Then play the program again. Ss listen and repeat.
- Point out that we can use *sore* with other body parts that hurt (e.g., *sore leg, sore wrist*).

B ***Class activity***

- Read out the useful expressions. Point out that Ss should use the first two expressions to respond to someone who feels healthy. They should use the second two expressions to respond to someone who doesn't feel well.
- Explain the task and model the example conversation with a S. Take the role of Speaker B and mime a backache as you answer. The S takes the role of Speaker A.
- Then ask two other Ss to role-play the conversation with a different health problem.
- Ss walk around the class to complete the activity. They take turns asking and answering questions about health and responding. Mingle with the Ss and give help as needed.

! For a new way to practice asking how people feel, try ***Question Exchange*** – download it from the website. Ss exchange pieces of paper with different adjectives (e.g., *great, awful*).

2 CONVERSATION Do you want some tea?

Listen and practice.

Craig: Hi, Nathan. How's it going?

Nathan: Oh, hi, Craig. Not so well, actually. I don't feel well.

Craig: Yeah, you don't look so good. What's wrong?

Nathan: I don't know. I have a stomachache.

Craig: That's too bad. Do you have the flu?

Nathan: No, I just feel really sick.

Craig: Well, can I get you anything? Do you want some tea?

Nathan: No, but thanks anyway.

Craig: Well, I'm going to have some pizza. Is that OK? Call me if you need me.

3 GRAMMAR FOCUS

Have + noun; *feel* + adjective

		Negative adjectives	Positive adjectives
What's the matter?	How are you?	horrible	fine
What's wrong?	How do you feel?	awful	great
I have a stomachache.	**I feel sick.**	terrible	terrific
I have a headache.	**I feel better.**	miserable	fantastic
I have the flu.	**I don't feel well.**		

GRAMMAR PLUS *see page 143*

A Listen and practice. *"He has a backache."*

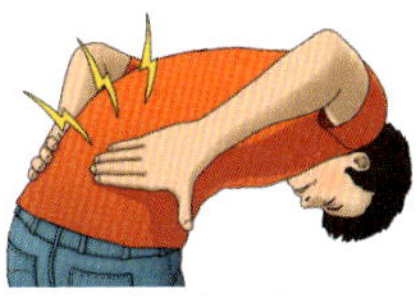
a backache

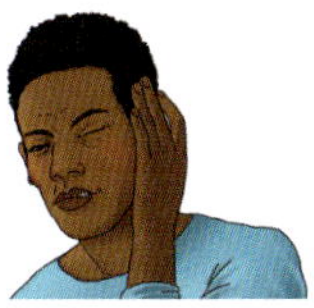
an earache

a headache

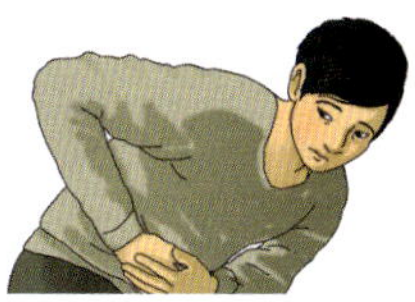
a stomachache

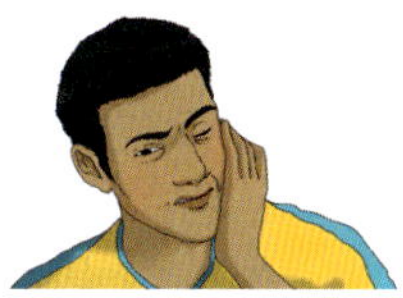
a toothache

a cold

a cough

a fever

the flu

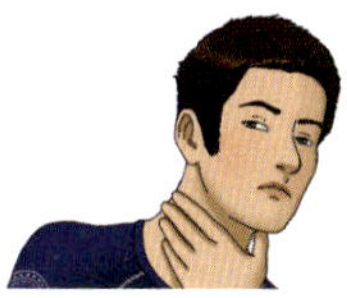
a sore throat

B CLASS ACTIVITY Imagine you don't feel well today. Go around the class. Find out what's wrong with your classmates.

A: How are you today, Paul?
B: I feel terrible. I have a backache.
A: I'm sorry to hear that.
B: How do *you* feel?

useful expressions

That's good.
I'm glad to hear that.
That's too bad.
I'm sorry to hear that.

4 LISTENING Are you OK?

A Where do these people hurt? Guess. Write down the parts of the body.

1. Amber ______________________

2. David ______________________

3. Alyssa ______________________

4. Nicholas ______________________

B Listen to the conversations. Check your guesses.

5 SNAPSHOT

Listen and practice.

Common Remedies

chamomile tea

cough syrup

chicken soup

cold medicine

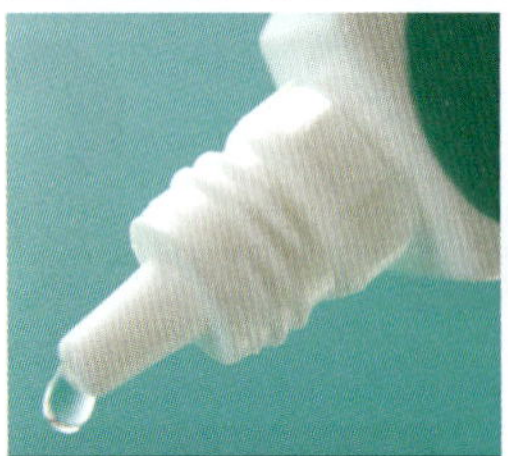

eye drops

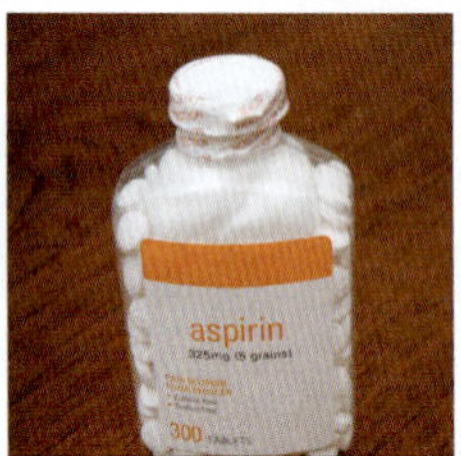

aspirin

antacid

nasal spray

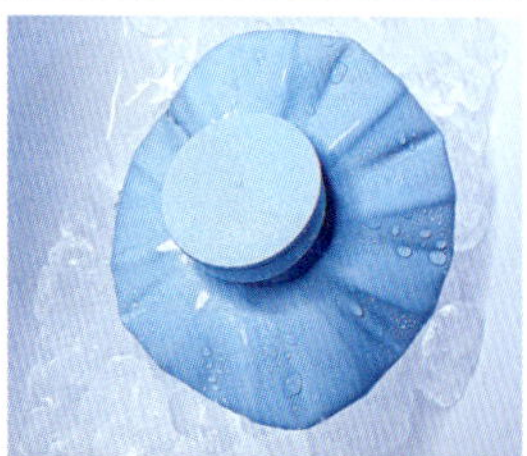

ice pack

What medications or home remedies do you use when you're sick?
What remedies are good, in your opinion? What remedies aren't good?

4 LISTENING

Learning Objective: listen for specific information in conversations about health problems

A

- Focus Ss' attention on the pictures and explain the task. Ss write their guesses under the pictures.

B *[CD 3, Track 5]*

- Play the audio program once or twice. Ss listen and check their guesses.
- Elicit the answers and write them on the board.
- ***Option:*** Ss ask and answer questions about the people in part A. Write this on the board:

  A: *What's the matter with Amber?*

  B: *Her wrist and elbow feel terrible.*

  Model the conversation with a S. Ss practice the conversation in pairs.

Audio script

1.

Amber	Ow!
Man	Are you OK, Amber?
Amber	Uh, not really. My elbow and wrist feel terrible. Ouch!
Man	Do you want to rest?
Amber	Good idea.

2.

David	I think I'm going to go home early. I don't feel well.
Woman	What's the matter, David?
David	I think I have a cold. I have a headache, and I have a sore throat.
Woman	Oh, that's too bad. Get better, OK?

3.

Alyssa	Ooh!
Man	What's wrong?
Alyssa	Oh, it's my eyes. They're really dry.
Man	Well, take a break, Alyssa. Finish your work later.
Alyssa	OK, thanks.

4.

Woman	Here. Have some ice cream, Nicholas.
Nicholas	Oh, I love ice cream, but I can't eat any cold food.
Woman	Why not?
Nicholas	I have a really bad toothache.
Woman	Oh, I'm sorry.

Answers

1. elbow, wrist
2. head, throat
3. eyes
4. tooth

End of Cycle 1

See the Supplementary Resources chart at the beginning of this unit for additional teaching materials and student activities related to this Cycle.

Cycle 2, Exercises 5–12

5 SNAPSHOT

Learning Objective: discuss common remedies for health problems

[CD 3, Track 6]

- Focus Ss' attention on the pictures. Then play the audio program. Ss listen and read silently.
- Play the audio program again. Ss listen and repeat.
- Read the questions aloud. Ss discuss them in small groups. Then elicit answers from the class.
- ***Option:*** Ask Ss to list other medications or remedies they have at home for different health problems.

6 CONVERSATION

Learning Objective: use imperatives in a conversation between a doctor and a patient

[CD 3, Track 7]

- Text covered. Set the scene and focus Ss' attention on the picture. Ms. Lake is talking to Dr. Yun. Ask the class: "How does Ms. Lake feel?" Encourage Ss to use the picture to make guesses.
- Play the audio program. Ss listen for the answers. Elicit the answers. (Answers: Ms. Lake feels exhausted. She can't sleep at night.)
- Text uncovered. Play the audio program again. Ss listen and read silently. Elicit or explain any new vocabulary.

Vocabulary

exhausted: very, very tired
Let's take a look at you.: I'm going to examine you.
take one pill: eat or swallow one pill

- Play the audio program again. Ss listen and repeat. Then they practice the conversation in pairs.

7 LISTENING

Learning Objective: listen for specific information about health advice discussed using imperatives

[CD 3, Track 8]

- Set the scene and explain the task. Dr. Yun from Exercise 6 is talking to four other patients. Ask the class: "What does she give each person?"
- Play the audio program once or twice. Ss complete the task individually. Then they compare answers in pairs or small groups.

Audio script

1.
Dr. Yun What's the matter, Roberto?
Roberto I think I have a cold. I feel awful. I have a sore throat and a headache.
Dr. Yun OK. Let's take a look. . . . Yes, you have a cold. Let me give you some cold medicine. Take one pill every four hours.
Roberto [coughs]
Dr. Yun Do you have a cough, too?
Roberto Yeah.
Dr. Yun All right. I'll give you some cough syrup, too. I hope it helps.
2.
Dr. Yun What can I do for you, Courtney?
Courtney I have really itchy eyes, and, well, it's my nose.
Dr. Yun Is it difficult to breathe?
Courtney A little. I think it's my allergies.
Dr. Yun I see. Well, try these eye drops. And I'm going to give you some nasal spray.
Courtney Thank you.
3.
Dr. Yun How are you feeling today, Ryan?
Ryan Not so great. I have a really bad earache.
Dr. Yun Let's take a look. Hmm. I'm going to give you some aspirin.
Ryan OK. Anything else?
Dr. Yun Yes. Don't go swimming for a week.
4.
Dr. Yun How do you feel today, Samantha?
Samantha A little better. But I have a sore knee. It really hurts, actually.
Dr. Yun Hmm. Let me see. Yes. Well, I'm going to give you some ice packs. Put one on your knee every evening for a few hours.
Samantha OK. Thank you, doctor.

- Play the audio program again. Ss check their answers. Elicit the answers and write them on the board.

Answers

1. Roberto: cough syrup, cold medicine
2. Courtney: eye drops, nasal spray
3. Ryan: aspirin
4. Samantha: ice packs

8 PRONUNCIATION

Learning Objective: sound more natural when using imperatives

A ***[CD 3, Track 9]***

- Explain the task and focus Ss' attention on the model sentences. Remind Ss that yes/no questions have rising intonation. Point out that statements, including the imperative, use falling intonation.
- Play the audio program. Ss listen and read silently. Play the audio program again. Ss listen and repeat.

B ***Pair work***

- Explain the task. If needed, play the audio program for Exercise 6 again.
- Ss practice the conversation in pairs.

6 CONVERSATION Try to relax.

Listen and practice.

Dr. Yun: Hello, Ms. Lake. How are you today?

Ms. Lake: Not so good.

Dr. Yun: What's wrong, exactly?

Ms. Lake: I'm exhausted!

Dr. Yun: Hmm. Why are you so tired?

Ms. Lake: I don't know. I just can't sleep at night.

Dr. Yun: OK. Let's take a look at you.

A few minutes later . . .

Dr. Yun: I'm going to give you some pills. Take one pill every evening after dinner.

Ms. Lake: OK.

Dr. Yun: And don't drink coffee, tea, or soda.

Ms. Lake: Anything else?

Dr. Yun: Yes. Try to relax.

Ms. Lake: All right. Thanks, Dr. Yun.

7 LISTENING I think I have a cold.

Listen to Dr. Yun talk to four other patients. What does she give them? Check (✓) the correct medications.

	Cough syrup	Aspirin	Cold medicine	Eye drops	Nasal spray	Ice packs
1. Roberto	☐	☐	☐	☐	☐	☐
2. Courtney	☐	☐	☐	☐	☐	☐
3. Ryan	☐	☐	☐	☐	☐	☐
4. Samantha	☐	☐	☐	☐	☐	☐

8 PRONUNCIATION Sentence intonation

A Listen and practice. Notice the intonation in these sentences.

Take these pills. Don't take cough syrup.

Drink some tea. Don't drink coffee.

Try to relax. Don't work too hard.

B PAIRWORK Practice the conversation in Exercise 6 again. Pay attention to the sentence intonation.

9 GRAMMAR FOCUS

Imperatives

Get some rest.
Drink lots of juice.
Take one pill every evening.

Don't stay up late.
Don't drink soda.
Don't work too hard.

GRAMMAR PLUS *see page 143*

Complete these sentences. Use the correct forms of the words in the box.

✓call	stay	not go	not drink
see	take	✓not worry	not eat

1. ______Call______ a dentist.
2. ___Don't worry___ too much.
3. ________________ a hot bath.
4. ________________ to school.
5. ________________ in bed.
6. ________________ a doctor.
7. ________________ coffee.
8. ________________ any candy.

10 SPEAKING Good advice?

A Write two pieces of advice for each problem.

1. ________________
2. ________________
3. ________________
4. ________________

B GROUP WORK Act out the problems from part A. Your classmates give advice.

A: I don't feel well.
B: What's the matter?

A: My feet hurt.
B: I have an idea. Take a hot bath. And don't . . .

11 INTERCHANGE 12 Problems, problems

Give advice for common problems. Go to Interchange 12 on page 126.

9 GRAMMAR FOCUS

Learning Objective: use positive and negative imperatives

[CD 3, Track 10]

Imperatives

- Focus Ss' attention on the Grammar Focus box. Elicit or explain that we use imperatives to give instructions or orders.
- Elicit or explain the pattern for making positive and negative imperatives:

  Positive: Verb.
  Negative: *Don't* + verb.

  Point out that imperatives use only the base form of the verb.
- ***Option:*** Refer Ss to the conversation in Exercise 6 on page 81. Ask the class: "What instructions does Dr. Yun give Ms. Lake?" Ss underline the instructions. Elicit the answers. (Answers: Take one pill every evening after dinner. And don't drink coffee, tea, or soda. Try to relax.)
- Play the audio program. Ss listen and read silently.
- ***Option:*** Play the audio program again. Ss repeat.
- Explain the task and go over the words in the box. Point out that four sentences are positive imperatives and four sentences are negative.
- Ask two Ss to model the example sentences.
- Ss complete the task individually. Then they compare answers in pairs.
- To check answers, ask different Ss to read the sentences aloud.

Answers

1. **Call** a dentist.
2. **Don't worry** too much.
3. **Take** a hot bath.
4. **Don't go** to school.
5. **Stay** in bed.
6. **See** a doctor.
7. **Don't drink** coffee.
8. **Don't eat** any candy.

10 SPEAKING

Learning Objective: give advice for common health problems using the imperative

A

- Explain the task. Point out that more than two answers are possible.
- Ss complete the task individually. Go around the class and help with vocabulary as needed.

Possible answers

1. Put some ice on your feet.
   Don't wear those shoes.
2. Take some aspirin.
   Don't play video games.
   Rest for a while.
3. Use some eye drops.
   See a doctor.
   Close your eyes for a few minutes.
4. Don't drink coffee.
   Listen to relaxing music.
   Drink warm milk.
   Don't exercise late at night.

- Ss compare answers in small groups. While they work, write each problem on the board.
- Elicit answers from the class and ask different Ss to write them under the correct problem on the board.

B *Group work*

- Explain the task. Model the example conversation aloud, using mime and intonation if possible. Ss repeat. Then ask two Ss to model the example conversation. Focus Ss' attention on their intonation.
- Ss complete the task in pairs. Go around the class and encourage Ss to use mime and to think about their intonation.

! For a new way to practice the conversation in part B, try ***Substitution Dialog*** – download it from the website. Tell Ss to underline *My feet hurt* and *Take a hot bath*. Then elicit substitutions and write them on the board.

11 INTERCHANGE 12

See page T-126 for teaching notes.

12 READING

Learning Objective: scan and read for main ideas in a health quiz

A ***[CD 3, Track 11]***

- Books closed. Write the title on the board and read the question.
- As a class, Ss make a list of ways their bodies keep them alive.
- Books open. Ss scan the quiz. Ask the class: "Are any of your ideas the same as these? Which ones?" Elicit answers from the class.
- Ss scan the text for new words in pairs or small groups. They ask each other about the meaning of new words. Then elicit or explain the meaning of any remaining new words. Draw on the board or mime where appropriate.
- Ss complete the quiz individually. Then they check their answers using the key at the bottom of the quiz.

TIP
To teach Ss to scan a text quickly, remind them not to read every word, but to let their eyes pass over the text quickly and look for key words.

Vocabulary
heart: the part of the body in the chest that moves blood around the body
skin: the outer layer that covers a person
brain: the part inside the head that thinks and feels
billion: 1,000,000,000
million: 1,000,000
cell: the smallest part of a plant or animal

B

- Focus Ss' attention on the questions. Have different Ss read the questions aloud.
- Point out that Ss can find the answers easily by scanning the article for key words in each question. Ask: "What are the key words in the questions?" Elicit the answers. (Answers: 1. lose, hour 2. signals, electricity 3. changes, age 4. cells, stomach 5. small living things)
- Ss complete the task individually. Go around the class and give help as needed.
- Ss compare their answers in pairs. Then ask different Ss to share their answers with the class.
- ***Option***: After answers have been checked, have Ss come to the board and write the answers as complete sentences. (See Answers.)

Answers

1. Your body loses **small pieces of skin** every hour.
2. **Your brain** sends signals and makes electricity.
3. **Your natural smell** changes as you age.
4. **Brain cells** live in the stomach.
5. **Bacteria** is another name for small living things.

C ***Group work***

- Read the questions and explain the task.
- Ss discuss the questions in small groups.
- Elicit groups' answers.

For more practice with this vocabulary, play ***Tic-Tac-Toe*** – download it from the website. Play using nine words from the reading, such as *heart, brain, skin, asleep, cells, stomach, electricity, smell, bacteria.*

End of Cycle 2

See the Supplementary Resources chart at the beginning of this unit for additional teaching materials and student activities related to this Cycle and for assessment tools.

12 READING

A What does your body do to keep you alive? Take the quiz to find out!

DO YOU KNOW YOUR BODY?

1. The human heart beats about 200 times a minute.
☐ True ☐ False

2. Your body loses about 40,000 tiny pieces of skin an hour.
☐ True ☐ False

3. Your brain sends billions of signals every minute.
☐ True ☐ False

4. Your brain stops working when you're asleep.
☐ True ☐ False

5. 140 million cells in your eyes help to tell you what you can see.
☐ True ☐ False

6. Brain cells do not live in the stomach.
☐ True ☐ False

7. Women's hearts beat faster than men's hearts.
☐ True ☐ False

8. Your brain makes electricity.
☐ True ☐ False

9. Your natural smell changes as you age.
☐ True ☐ False

10. Some bacteria (small living things) in your body help you live.
☐ True ☐ False

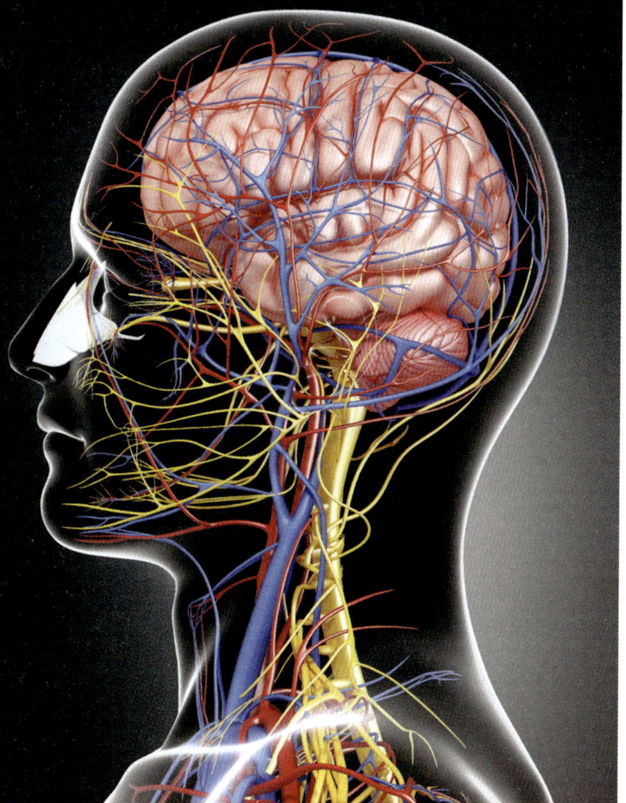

1. False 2. True 3. True 4. False 5. True 6. False 7. True 8. True 9. True 10. True

B Read and answer the quiz. Check your answers. Then answer the questions.

1. What does your body lose every hour? ____________
2. What part of the body sends signals and makes electricity? ____________
3. What is one thing that changes as you age? ____________
4. What cells live in the stomach? ____________
5. What's another name for small living things? ____________

C **GROUP WORK** What information in the quiz is most surprising? What else do you know about the human body? Tell your classmates.

Units 11–12 Progress check

SELF-ASSESSMENT

How well can you do these things? Check (✓) the boxes.

I can . . .	Very well	OK	A little
Talk about ways to celebrate holidays (Ex. 1)	☐	☐	☐
Use future time expressions (Ex. 1, 2)	☐	☐	☐
Understand conversations about problems (Ex. 3)	☐	☐	☐
Talk about problems (Ex. 4)	☐	☐	☐
Ask how people are and give advice (Ex. 4)	☐	☐	☐

1 SPEAKING Holiday customs

A Complete the questions with names of different holidays.

Are you going to . . . ?	Name
eat special food on	
give gifts on	
have a party on	
play music on	
wear special clothes on	

B CLASS ACTIVITY Are your classmates going to do the things in part A? Go around the class and find out. Try to write a different person's name on each line.

2 SPEAKING Future plans

Complete these questions with different time expressions. Add one more question. Then ask a partner the questions.

1. How are you going to get home *tonight* ?
2. What time are you going to go to bed ______________?
3. Where are you going to go ______________?
4. What are you going to do ______________?
5. Who are you going to eat dinner with ______________?
6. ____?

Units 11–12

Progress check

SELF-ASSESSMENT

Learning Objectives: reflect on one's learning; identify areas that need improvement

- Ask: "What did you learn in Units 11 and 12?" Elicit Ss' answers.
- Ss complete the Self-assessment. Explain to Ss that this is not a test; it is a way for them to evaluate what they've learned and identify areas where they need additional practice. Encourage them to be honest, and point out they will not get a bad grade if they check (✓) *A little*.
- Ss move on to the Progress check exercises. You can have Ss complete them in class or for homework, using one of these techniques:
  1. Ask Ss to complete all the exercises.
  2. Ask Ss: "What do you need to practice?" Then assign exercises based on their answers.
  3. Ask Ss to choose and complete exercises based on their Self-assessment.

1 SPEAKING

Learning Objective: demonstrate one's ability to ask and answer questions about holiday plans

A

- Focus Ss' attention on the chart and explain the task. Point out that Ss should choose popular holidays. If needed, elicit names of holidays from the class and write them on the board.
- Ss complete the questions in the first column individually. Go around the class and help with spelling if needed.

B *Class activity*

- Explain the task. To model the task, choose a holiday and ask different Ss the first question: "Are you going to eat special food on (holiday)?" When a S answers "Yes, I am," pretend to write the S's name in the second column of the chart.
- Ss go around the class and ask their questions. Go around the class and encourage Ss to change partners often.
- ***Option:*** Elicit results from the class. Ask: "What did you find out about your classmates' holiday plans?"

2 SPEAKING

Learning Objective: demonstrate one's ability to ask and answer questions about future plans using future time expressions

- Explain the task. If needed, elicit future time expressions (e.g., *tonight, tomorrow, next week*) and write them on the board.
- Ss complete the questions individually and add one more question. Then they ask and answer their questions in pairs. Go around the class and check Ss' grammar, intonation, and reduction of *going to*.
- ***Option:*** Ss change partners and ask the questions again.

3 LISTENING

Learning Objective: demonstrate one's ability to understand conversations about problems

[CD 3, Track 12]

- Explain the task and focus Ss' attention on the pictures. Have Ss read the sentences silently.
- Play the audio program once or twice. Ss complete the task individually.

Audio script

1.
Man Hi. How are you?
Woman Oh, not so good.
Man What's the matter? Are you sick?
Woman No, I'm not sick. I just don't feel very happy.
2.
Man This hamburger isn't very good.
Woman Really? What's wrong with it?
Man I don't know. It needs . . . something.
Woman Well, it has lettuce and onions on it.
Man Yeah, but something is wrong. Oh, I know.
3.
Man How do you feel?
Woman Terrible. I have a headache, and my whole body feels sore.
Man I think you have the flu. Go home and get some rest.
Woman: Good idea.
4.
Woman Are you going to go to Angela's party?
Man No, I don't think so.
Woman Why not? It's going to be fun.
Man Well, it's a dance party, and everyone's going to dance. But I can't dance at all.
5.
Man How do you feel today?
Woman Oh, about the same.
Man Maybe you need a new chair.
Woman Maybe I need a new job!
6.
Woman So, how is it today?
Man It's OK. It doesn't hurt much.
Woman John! You have a toothache. You need to go today.
Man I'll just take some more aspirin.
Woman Dr. Vance is really nice. And I'll go with you.
Man I don't know. Maybe this afternoon.

- To check answers, elicit the problem with the person in each conversation.

Answers

1. This person feels sad.
2. This person needs some ketchup.
3. This person has the flu.
4. This person can't dance very well.
5. This person has a backache.
6. This person doesn't want to go to the dentist.

4 SPEAKING

Learning Objectives: demonstrate one's ability to discuss problems, ask how people are, and give advice

A

- Explain the task. Then ask two Ss to model the example sentences. Point out that the problems can be real or imaginary.
- Ss complete the task individually. Go around the class and give help as needed.

B *Class activity*

- Explain the first part of the task. Collect problems and advice from each S. Put the problems in one box and the advice in another box.
- Explain the second part of the task. Each S takes a paper from each box. Make sure Ss don't take their own papers.
- Ask two pairs of Ss to model the example conversations. Point out that when Ss find good advice for their problems, they keep both papers. After they find good advice for their problem and give their advice to another S, they sit down.
- Ss go around the class and complete the activity. When most Ss are sitting down, ask the Ss to read out their problems and the advice they got.

WHAT'S NEXT?

Learning Objective: become more involved in one's learning

- Focus Ss' attention on the Self-assessment again. Ask: "How well can you do these things now?"
- Ask Ss to underline one thing they need to review. Ask: "What did you underline? How can you review it?"
- If needed, plan additional instruction, activities, or reviews based on Ss' answers.

3 LISTENING Everyone has problems.

Listen to six conversations. Number the pictures from 1 to 6.

☐ This person can't dance very well.

☐ This person has the flu.

☐ This person needs some ketchup.

☐ This person has a backache.

☐ This person doesn't want to go to the dentist.

[1] This person feels sad.

4 SPEAKING Thanks for the advice!

A Write a problem on a piece of paper. Then write advice for the problem on a different piece of paper.

I have a toothache.

Call your dentist.

B CLASS ACTIVITY Put the papers with problems and the papers with advice in two different boxes. Then take a new paper from each box. Go around the class and find the right advice for your problem.

A: I feel terrible.
B: What's the matter?
A: I have a toothache.
B: I can help. Drink some tea.
A: Er . . . I don't know. But thanks, anyway.

A: I feel awful.
C: Why? What's wrong?
A: I have a toothache.
C: I know! Call your dentist.
A: That's great advice. Thanks!

WHAT'S NEXT?

Look at your Self-assessment again. Do you need to review anything?

Unit 13 Supplementary Resources Overview

	After the following SB exercises	You can use these materials in class	Your students can use these materials outside the classroom
CYCLE 1	**1 Word Power**	**TSS** Unit 13 Vocabulary Worksheet	**SS** Unit 13 Vocabulary 1 **GAME** Speak or Swim (Places and things 1) **GAME** Spell or slime (Places and things 2)
	2 Listening		
	3 Conversation		**SS** Unit 13 Speaking 1
	4 Pronunciation		
	5 Grammar Focus		**SB** Unit 13 Grammar plus, Focus 1 **SS** Unit 13 Grammar 1
	6 Listening	**TSS** Unit 13 Listening Worksheet	**WB** Unit 13 exercises 1–4
CYCLE 2	**7 Snapshot**		**SS** Unit 13 Vocabulary 2
	8 Conversation	**TSS** Unit 13 Extra Worksheet	**SS** Unit 13 Speaking 2
	9 Grammar Focus	**TSS** Unit 13 Grammar Worksheet	**SB** Unit 13 Grammar plus, Focus 2 **SS** Unit 13 Grammar 2 **GAME** Speak or Swim (Prepositions of place; Directions 1) **GAME** Sentence Runner (Prepositions of place; Directions 2)
	10 Interchange 13		
	11 Reading	**TSS** Unit 13 Project Worksheet **VID** Unit 13 **VRB** Unit 13	**SS** Unit 13 Reading 1–2 **SS** Unit 13 Listening 1–3 **SS** Unit 13 Video 1–3 **WB** Unit 13 exercises 5–7

Key **GAME:** Online Game **SB:** Student's Book **SS:** Online Self-study **TSS:** Teacher Support Site
VID: Video DVD **VRB:** Video Resource Book **WB:** Online Workbook/Workbook

My Plan for Unit 13

Use the space below to customize a plan that fits your needs.

With the following SB exercises	I am using these materials in class	My students are using these materials outside the classroom

With or instead of the following SB section	I am using these materials for assessment

13 How do I get there?

- Discuss stores, their locations, and things to buy there
- Ask for and give directions to various locations

1 WORD POWER Places to go, things to buy

A Where can you get these things? Match the things with the places. Then listen and practice.

"You can buy a backpack at a department store."

a. a post office

b. a drugstore

c. a gas station

1. a backpack ___d___
2. cold medicine ______
3. a debit card ______
4. eggs ______
5. an espresso ______
6. gasoline ______
7. a magazine ______
8. stamps ______

d. a department store

e. a bank

f. a bookstore

g. a coffee shop

h. a supermarket

B **PAIR WORK** What else can you get or do in the places in part A?

A: You can send packages at a post office.
B: And you get cereal and milk at a supermarket.

13 How do I get there?

Cycle 1, Exercises 1–6

In Unit 13, students discuss stores, their locations, and things to buy there, and ask for and give directions to various locations. By the end of Cycle 1, students will be able to discuss stores, items to buy in stores, and store locations using prepositions of place. By the end of Cycle 2, students will be able to ask for and give directions to various locations.

1 WORD POWER

Learning Objective: describe places and where to buy certain items or do certain things

A *[CD 3, Track 13]*

- Focus Ss' attention on the list of things. Read out the things. Ss repeat. Elicit or explain any new vocabulary.

Vocabulary
debit card: a card used to pay for things from your bank account
gasoline: gas; a liquid that makes cars go

- Focus Ss' attention on the pictures. Read out the places. Ss repeat. Elicit or explain any new vocabulary.
- Explain the first part of the task. Ss match the items individually. Then they compare their answers in pairs.
- Play the audio program. Ss listen and check their answers. Then elicit the answers from the class.

Audio script

1. You can buy a backpack at a department store.
2. You can buy cold medicine at a drugstore.
3. You can get a debit card at a bank.
4. You can buy eggs at a supermarket.
5. You can get an espresso at a coffee shop.
6. You can buy gasoline at a gas station.
7. You can buy a magazine at a bookstore.
8. You can get stamps at a post office.

Answers

1. d 2. b 3. e 4. h 5. g 6. c 7. f 8. a

- Play the audio program again. Ss listen and repeat.
- ***Option:*** Ask the class: "Where can you get (stamps)?" Elicit the answer. Repeat with the other items, in random order.

B *Pair work*

- Explain the task. Elicit other things you can get or do in a bank (e.g., *get money, change money, deposit a check*) and write them on the board. Help with vocabulary if needed. Then ask two Ss to model the example conversation.
- Ss complete the task in pairs. Go around the class and help with vocabulary as needed.
- Write the places in part A as headings on the board. Then elicit ideas from the class and ask different Ss to write them under each heading. If some ideas are true only in some countries, ask Ss to write the appropriate countries next to the ideas.

Possible answers

a post office: mail a letter, send a package, rent/check a post office box
a drugstore: buy/get newspapers, candy, medications, or cards
a gas station: buy/get drinks, candy, snacks, or maps
a department store: buy/get furniture, clothes, or personal items; have a snack
a bank: get/change/deposit money, deposit a check, pay a bill
a bookstore: buy/get magazines, books, newspapers, or maps
a coffee shop: eat breakfast, lunch, or dinner; have coffee/tea and a dessert
a supermarket: buy/get food, medications, or magazines

For more practice with vocabulary for places, play ***Sculptures*** – download it from the website. Teams form sculptures that illustrate different activities in different places.

For more practice with vocabulary for places and things, play ***Vocabulary Tennis*** – download it from the website. Write nine places on the board, and have each team say something you can get or do there.

TIP
Review vocabulary regularly by making it part of your teaching routine. For example, ask each S to say a word from a previously taught category (e.g., *places, things you buy*) when you take attendance. Alternatively, you can start each class with a vocabulary warm-up activity.

2 LISTENING

Learning Objective: listen to a conversation about looking for a missing item and shopping

A *[CD 3, Track 14]*

- Set the scene. Vanessa can't find her phone and is talking about places where she may have left it. Tom is talking about things he needs to buy at those places.
- Tell Ss to listen only for the things Tom needs. Then play the audio program. Ss listen and complete the *What does Tom need?* column in the chart.
- Tell Ss to listen only for the places to buy the things Tom needs. Then play the audio program again. Ss listen and complete the *Where is he going to get it?* column in the chart.
- Play the audio again. Ss check their answers.

Audio script

1.
Tom Hi, Vanessa. What's the matter?
Vanessa I can't find my cell phone!
Tom That's too bad. What are you going to do?
Vanessa Well, first I'm going to go back to the bookstore. Maybe it's there.
Tom Great! I'll go with you.
Vanessa Why? Do you need a book?
Tom No. But I'm going to buy some magazines.
2.
Vanessa They don't have my phone. This is terrible.
Tom Where are you going to look next? The post office?
Vanessa No, I'm going to go to the drugstore. I hope it's there.
Tom Oh, cool. I'll go with you again. I need some ice packs for my elbow.
Vanessa OK. Let's go.
3.
Tom So, do you have it?
Vanessa No, it's not here! I'm really worried now.
Tom Let's see. What about the supermarket? Do you think it's there?
Vanessa No, I never go shopping there. But maybe it's at the department store. I'm going to go there next.
Tom Can I come, too?
Vanessa You're really nice, Tom, but I can go alone.
Tom No, really, I want to go. I need a new coat.
4.
Tom So, do you have your phone?
Vanessa No, I don't. I'm going to ask at the coffee shop and then go home, because . . .
Tom What's that?
Vanessa Oh! It's my cell phone! It's in one of my shopping bags, under a sweater.
Tom That's wonderful. So, umm, you're not going to the coffee shop, then?
Vanessa Well, no. I have my phone now, so I can go home.
Tom OK. I think I'll go to the coffee shop anyway. I really need a cup of coffee.
Vanessa You know what? I'll go with you!

- Ss compare their answers in pairs. Elicit answers from the class and write them on the board.

Answers

1. magazines; the bookstore
2. ice packs; the drugstore
3. a coat; the department store
4. (a cup of) coffee; the coffee shop

B *Pair work*

- Read the questions and explain the task. Then model the example sentence. Ss complete the task in pairs.

3 CONVERSATION

Learning Objective: use prepositions of place in a conversation about looking for a specific location

[CD 3, Track 15]

- Focus Ss' attention on the picture and set the scene. Ask: "What is the woman looking for? Where is it?"
- Play the audio program. Ss listen for the answer. Then elicit the answers. (Answers: 1. a restroom 2. in the department store on Third Avenue/on the corner of Third and Market). Elicit any new vocabulary.
- Play the audio program again. Ss listen and repeat. Then they practice the conversation in pairs.

4 PRONUNCIATION

Learning Objective: sound more natural when using compound nouns

A *[CD 3, Track 16]*

- Focus Ss' attention on the compound nouns. Explain that *compound nouns* are two words that join together to make a new noun. Point out that we usually stress the first word in a compound noun.
- Play the audio program. Ss listen and read silently. Then play the audio program again. Ss listen and repeat.

B *Pair work*

- Explain the task. Model the first sentence for Ss.
- Ss complete the task in pairs.

2 LISTENING I can't find my cell phone.

A Vanessa is looking for her cell phone with her friend Tom. What does Tom need? Where is he going to get the things? Complete the chart.

	What does Tom need?	Where is he going to get it?
1.		
2.		
3.		
4.		

B **PAIR WORK** What do you need? Where are you going to get it? Tell your partner.

"I need some gas, so I'm going to go to the gas station. . . ."

3 CONVERSATION Excuse me. Can you help me?

Listen and practice.

Mother: Excuse me. Can you help me? Is there a public restroom around here?

Passer-by: A public restroom? Hmm. I'm sorry. I don't think so.

Mother: Oh, no. My son needs a restroom – now. It's an emergency!

Passer-by: Hmm . . . Let's see . . . Oh, there's a restroom in the department store on Third Avenue.

Mother: Where on Third Avenue?

Passer-by: It's on the corner of Third Avenue and Market Street.

Mother: On the corner of Third and Market?

Passer-by: Yes, it's across from the park. You can't miss it.

Mother: Thanks a lot.

4 PRONUNCIATION Compound nouns

A Listen and practice. Notice the stress in these compound nouns.

bookstore	department store	gas station	post office
coffee shop	drugstore	restroom	supermarket

B **PAIR WORK** Practice these sentences. Pay attention to the stress in the compound nouns.

There's a bookstore in the gas station.
There's a coffee shop in the supermarket.
There isn't a post office in the supermarket.
There aren't restrooms in the drugstore.

5 GRAMMAR FOCUS

Prepositions of place

on

on the corner of

across from

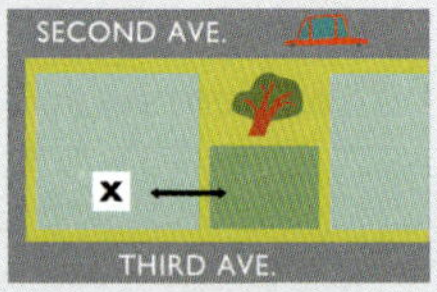

next to

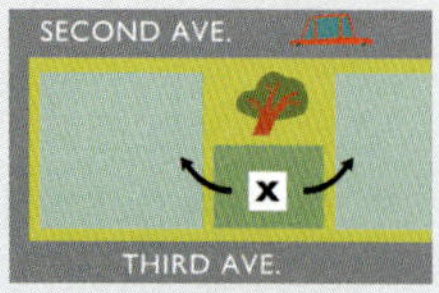

between

The department store is **on** Third Avenue.
It's **on the corner of** Third and Market.
It's **across from** the park.

It's **next to** the bank.
The bank is **between** the department store **and** the restaurant.

GRAMMAR PLUS *see page 144*

A Look at the map and complete the sentences. Then compare with a partner.

1. The coffee shop is ____on____ Main Street. It's ______________ the shoe store.
2. The movie theater is ______________ Park and Third. It's ______________ the park.
3. The gas station is ______________ the parking lot. It's ______________ Second and Market.
4. The post office is ______________ Main and Second. It's ______________ the hospital.
5. The bank is ______________ the restaurant and the department store.
   It's ______________ Third Avenue.

B **PAIR WORK** Where are these places on the map? Ask and answer questions.

the park **the drugstore** **the bookstore** **the hospital** **the shoe store**

A: Where is the park?
B: It's between Park and Market, across from the department store.

5 GRAMMAR FOCUS

Learning Objective: use prepositions of place to describe locations

TIP
To show Ss the purpose of your lesson, explain the connection between exercises. For example, say: "You just learned the names of different places and how to pronounce them. In this Grammar Focus, you're going to learn to describe their location."

[CD 3, Track 17]

Prepositions of place

- Focus Ss' attention on the Grammar Focus box. If desired, remind Ss that we use the prepositions *next to* and *on* to talk about the location of things. (See Unit 2, Exercise 9.) Explain that when we talk about the location of places, the meaning of *next to* is the same, but the meaning of *on* is a little different.
- Focus Ss' attention on the pictures. Elicit or explain the rules for using each preposition:
  1. Use *on* with a street or avenue.
  2. Use *on the corner of* with two streets or avenues.
  3. Use *across from* with a place.
  4. Use *next to* with a place.
  5. Use *between* with two places.
- Play the audio program. Ss listen and read silently.
- ***Option:*** Play the audio program again. Ss listen and repeat.

A

- Focus Ss' attention on the map. Read the names of the streets and places aloud. Ss repeat. Elicit or explain any new vocabulary.
- Explain the task and model the example sentence.
- Ss complete the task individually. Then they compare answers in pairs.
- Ask Ss to raise their hands when they finish comparing answers in pairs. Go around the class and mark an *X* next to any wrong answers. Then Ss correct the wrong answers in pairs.
- Elicit the answers from the class.

Answers

1. The coffee shop is **on** Main Street. It's **next to** the shoe store.
2. The movie theater is **on the corner of** Park and Third. It's **next to/across from** the park.
3. The gas station is **across from** the parking lot. It's **on the corner of** Second and Market.
4. The post office is **on the corner of** Main and Second. It's **next to** the hospital.
5. The bank is **between** the restaurant and the department store. It's **on** Third Avenue.

- ***Option:*** For more practice, write these sentences on the board:
  1. The drugstore is ________ the supermarket.
  2. The supermarket is ________ Main and Third.
  3. Maria's Restaurant is ________ Third Ave.
  4. The bank is ________ Market and Main.
  5. The bookstore is ________ the post office.

  Ss write the sentences and complete them with the correct prepositions. Then elicit the answers from the class. (Answers: 1. next to 2. on the corner of 3. on 4. between 5. across from)

B *Pair work*

- Explain the task and ask a S to read the places. Model the example conversation with a S.
- Ss complete the task in pairs. They take turns asking about the places. Go around the class and give help as needed.
- ***Option:*** Ss ask their partners about additional places on the map.
- Elicit locations for each place from the class. Ask: "Where is . . . ?"
- ***Option:*** Bring in maps of the area around the school. Ss ask and answer questions about places near the school.

6 LISTENING

Learning Objectives: listen for details and make inferences about locations

[CD 3, Track 18]

- Explain the task. Then play the audio program two or three times, pausing after each conversation. Ss listen, look at the map, and number the places.

Audio script

1.
Man Hmm. I think it's on Third Avenue.
Woman Is it near the Globe Movie Theater?
Man Yes, it is. It's right across from the movie theater.
Woman Oh, yeah, yeah. There's a restaurant there.
Man Right. It's between the restaurant and Harrow's Department Store.

2.
Woman Is it near Harrow's Department Store?
Man Not really. It's on Main Street, next to the shoe store.
Woman Is there a shoe store on Main Street? I don't know it.
Man OK, well, it's also across from the Globe Movie Theater.
Woman OK. I know the Globe. Thank you very much.

3.
Man Where is it?
Woman Well, it's not far from the Second Avenue Bookstore.
Man So it's on Second Avenue?
Woman Yes, it is. And it's next to the post office.
Man Is it near the corner of Second Avenue and Market Street?
Woman Actually, it's on that corner. It's across from the gas station.
Man Thanks.

4.
Woman Is it near the movie theater?
Man No, it isn't. It's on Second Avenue, across from the parking lot.
Woman On the corner of Second Avenue and Market Street?
Man Yes, that's right. It's across from the hospital, too.
Woman OK. Thanks!

- Ss compare their answers in pairs. Elicit the answers and write them on the board.

Answers

3, 1, 4, 2

End of Cycle 1

See the Supplementary Resources chart at the beginning of this unit for additional teaching materials and student activities related to this Cycle.

Cycle 2, Exercises 7–11

7 SNAPSHOT

Learning Objective: discuss popular tourist attractions

[CD 3, Track 19]

- Focus Ss' attention on the pictures. Play the audio program. Ss listen and repeat.
- Ss discuss the questions in small groups. Then elicit answers from the class.
- ***Option:*** Display a large map of New York City and talk about the location of each tourist attraction.

8 CONVERSATION

Learning Objectives: ask for and give directions in a conversation about finding a popular tourist destination

[CD 3, Track 20]

- Focus Ss' attention on the picture and set the scene. A tourist in New York City is asking a man for directions.
- Write these questions on the board:

  1. What buildings does the woman ask about?
  2. Where are they?

- Play the audio program. Ss listen for the answers. Then elicit the answers. (Answers: 1. Rockefeller Center, Radio City Music Hall, the Empire State Building 2. Sixth Avenue and 49th Street, across from Rockefeller Center, right behind her)
- Point out that in the phrase *on the right*, *right* is a direction. In the phrases *right across from* and *right behind you*, however, *right* means "exactly" or "directly."
- Play the audio program again. Ss listen and repeat. Then they practice the conversation in pairs.

6 LISTENING I think it's on Main Street.

Look at the map in Exercise 5. Listen to four conversations. Where are the people going? Number the places from 1 to 4.

☐ the hospital ☐ the bank ☐ the gas station ☐ the coffee shop

7 SNAPSHOT

Listen and practice.

NEW YORK CITY'S Tourist Attractions

The Empire State Building

Brooklyn Bridge

Central Park

Times Square

Rockefeller Center

The Statue of Liberty

What do you know about these places? What makes them popular?
What are some popular tourist attractions in your country? What are your top five attractions?

8 CONVERSATION How do I get to Rockefeller Center?

Listen and practice.

Tourist: Excuse me, sir. Can you help me? How do I get to Rockefeller Center?

Man: Just walk up Sixth Avenue to 49th Street. Rockefeller Center is on the right.

Tourist: Is it near Radio City Music Hall?

Man: Yes, it's right across from Radio City Music Hall.

Tourist: Thank you. And where is the Empire State Building? Is it far from here?

Man: It's right behind you. Just turn around and look up!

9 GRAMMAR FOCUS

Directions

How do I get to Rockefeller Center?
Walk up/Go up Fifth Avenue.
Turn left on 49th Street.
It's **on the right**.

How can I get to the New York Public Library?
Walk down/Go down Fifth Avenue.
Turn right on 42nd Street.
It's **on the left**.

GRAMMAR PLUS see page 144

A PAIR WORK Imagine you are tourists at Grand Central Terminal. Ask for directions. Follow the arrows.

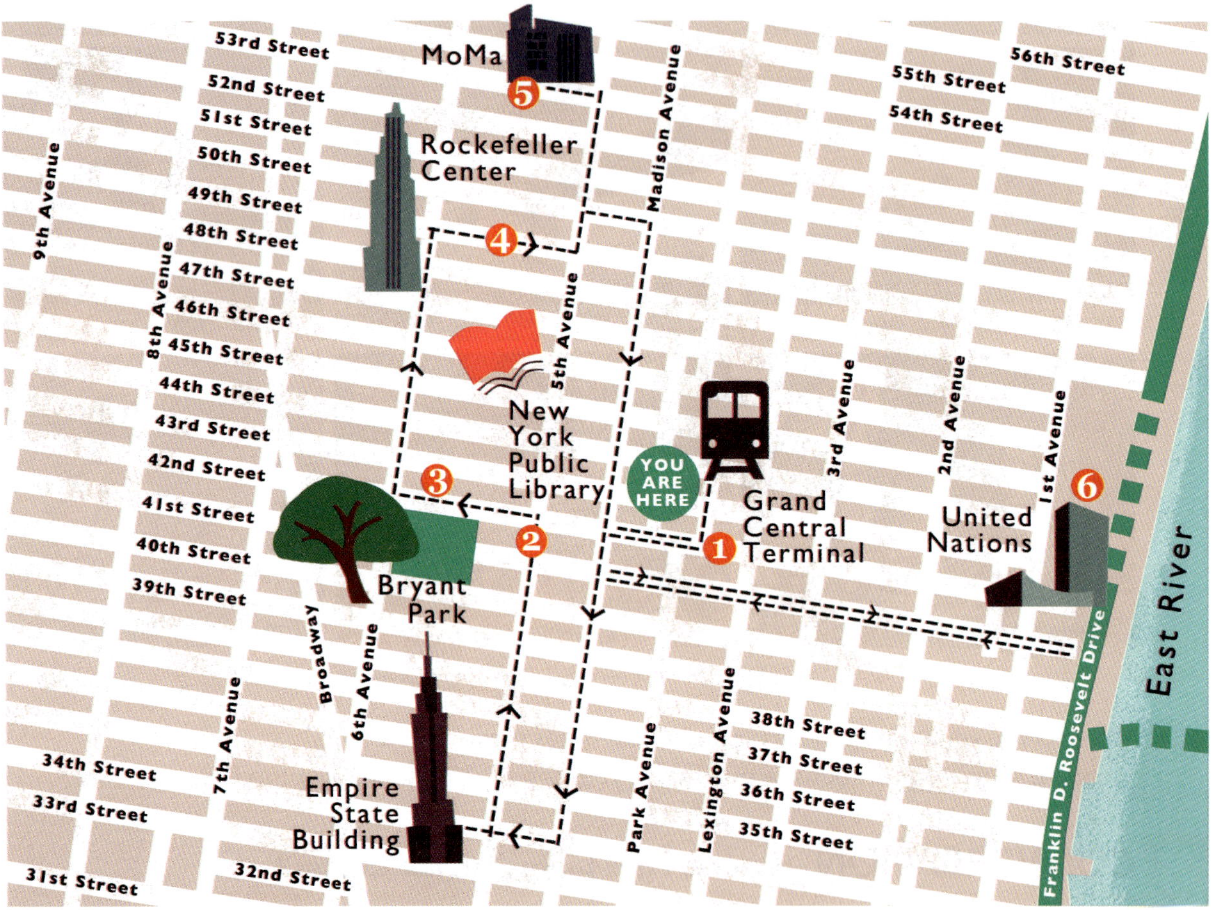

A: Excuse me. How do I get to the Empire State Building?
B: Walk up 42nd Street. Turn left on . . .

B PAIR WORK Ask for directions to places near your school.

A: How do I get to the bus stop?
B: Walk . . .

10 INTERCHANGE 13 Giving directions

Student A, go to Interchange 13A on page 127; Student B, go to Interchange 13B on page 128.

9 GRAMMAR FOCUS

Learning Objective: ask for and give directions

[CD 3, Track 21]

Directions

- Focus Ss' attention on the Grammar Focus box. Point out that *How do I get to . . . ?* and *How can I get to . . . ?* have the same meaning. Also, point out that *Walk up* and *Go up* mean about the same thing.
- ***Option:*** Point out that the avenues on this map go north and south. When people go north, they often say "go/walk up." When they go south, they often say "go/walk down." Use gestures to explain the meanings of *turn right*, *turn left*, *on the right*, and *on the left*.
- Play the audio program. Ss listen and read silently.

A

- Set the scene. Ss imagine they are tourists in New York City. They are at Grand Central Terminal, and they want to go to six places:

  1. The Empire State Building
  2. The New York Public Library
  3. Bryant Park
  4. Rockefeller Center
  5. The Museum of Modern Art (MoMA)
  6. The United Nations

  Read out the names of the places. Ss repeat.
- Elicit the locations of the places on the map:

  1. The Empire State Building: on Fifth Avenue between 33rd and 34th streets
  2. The New York Public Library: on Fifth Avenue between 40th Street and 42nd Street
  3. Bryant Park: on Sixth Avenue between 40th Street and 42nd Street
  4. Rockefeller Center: between Fifth Avenue and Sixth Avenue and between 48th Street and 51st Street
  5. MoMA: on 53rd Street, between Fifth Avenue and Sixth Avenue
  6. The United Nations: on First Avenue, between 42nd Street and 49th Street
- Explain the task. Ss take turns role-playing the tourist and the New Yorker. The tourist asks for directions and the New Yorker gives directions. Point out that they should follow the arrows to each place.
- Model the example conversation with a S, and ask the class to follow the arrows with their finger.

  S: Excuse me. How do I get to the Empire State Building?

  T: Walk up 42nd Street. Turn left on Madison Avenue, and go down Madison Avenue. Then turn right on 34th Street. Walk up 34th Street and turn left on Fifth Avenue. It's between 33rd and 34th Streets.
- Ss complete the activity in pairs. S1 plays the tourist and S2 plays the New Yorker. Then they change roles and complete the activity again.
- Elicit directions to each place from the class. Encourage Ss to give alternate directions if possible.

Possible answers

1. *The Empire State Building:* Walk up 42nd Street. Turn left on Madison Avenue, and go down Madison Avenue. Then turn right on 34th Street. Walk up 34th Street and turn left on Fifth Avenue. It's between 33rd Street and 34th Street.
2. *The New York Public Library:* Walk up Fifth Avenue. It's on the left, between 40th Street and 42nd Street.
3. *Bryant Park:* Walk up Fifth Avenue. Turn left on 42nd Street. It's behind the library, between Fifth Avenue and Sixth Avenue.
4. *Rockefeller Center:* Go up Sixth Avenue. It's between 48th Street and 51st Street.
5. *The Museum of Modern Art (MoMA):* Walk up Fifth Avenue to 53rd Street. Turn left. It's on 53rd between Fifth and Sixth Avenues.
6. *The United Nations:* Walk down Madison Avenue to 42nd Street. Turn left. Go down 42nd Street to First Avenue. Turn left on First Avenue. It's right in front of you.

B *Pair work*

- Explain the task. Elicit names of local places that Ss might ask about and write them on the board.
- Model the task with a S. The S reads part A and you read part B. Starting from the school, give directions to the nearest bus stop. (Use one of the examples from the board if there is no bus stop nearby.)
- Ss work in pairs. They take turns asking for and giving directions to places near the school.
- Ask a couple of pairs of Ss to repeat one of their conversations for the class. Have the class listen for whether the directions are correct.

10 INTERCHANGE 13

See pages T-127 and T-128 for teaching notes.

11 READING

Learning Objective: read for details and make inferences in an article about a popular destination

A *[CD 3, Track 22]*

- Set the scene and explain the task. The guide has information for tourists in Palermo, Buenos Aires. If possible, point out the location on a world map.
- Ss skim the guide individually to find where they can have some tea. Elicit the answer. (Answer: the Japanese Gardens)
- ***Option:*** Ss listen to the audio program and read the information silently.

B

- Explain that Ss should follow the map as they read.
- Ss read the tourist information individually and underline any new words.
- Explain the second part of the task. Point out that Ss can find most of the answers easily by scanning the article for the key words and phrases.
- Ss complete the task individually. Then they compare answers in pairs. Elicit the answers from the class and write them on the board.

Answers

1. You can see horses at the Campo Argentino del Polo.
2. You can look at the sky at the Galileo Galilei planetarium.
3. You can see many types of plants in the Japanese Gardens.
4. You can find a statue of a writer at the Statue of Domingo Faustino Sarmiento.
5. You can see some art at MALBA/the art museum.

- Elicit or explain the meaning of any new vocabulary.

Vocabulary

sculpture: a piece of art made from stone, wood, or clay
planetarium: a building with a machine showing the stars and planets
telescope: a tube-shaped piece of equipment used to see things far away
monument: a building or structure to remember a historical event or famous person
statue: a sculpture of a person or animal
polo: a game played on horseback, with long wooden hammers and a ball

- ***Option:*** Ss write three more *Where can you . . . ?* questions about the article in pairs. Then they exchange questions with another pair and answer the questions.

C *Pair work*

- Explain the task. Elicit some ideas for places and things to see or do from the class.
- Ss complete the task in pairs.
- ***Option:*** Put Ss who like different places in pairs. They ask for information about each other's places.
- ***Option:*** Write these question-starters on the board to help Ss with their conversations:

  Where can you see . . . ?
  Where can you eat . . . ?
  Where can you play . . . ?
  Where can you . . . ?
- Elicit information from several pairs.

End of Cycle 2

See the Supplementary Resources chart at the beginning of this unit for additional teaching materials and student activities related to this Cycle.

11 READING

A Skim the guide. Where can you have some tea?

A Tour of Palermo, Buenos Aires

The art museum

Why not start at MALBA, the art museum on Avenida Figuero Alcorta? There are some fantastic sculptures and paintings there.

Japanese Gardens

Next, walk up to the park, turn left, and get a taste of Japan in Argentina. You can visit the Japanese Gardens and see about 150 different types of plants from Japan. Don't forget to taste some Japanese tea before you leave.

Galileo Galilei planetarium

Then turn right on Avenida Sarmiento and head over to the Galileo Galilei planetarium. There, you can see a piece of rock from the moon. There's a telescope you can look at the sky through, too.

The Spanish Monument

Across the park from the planetarium, you can see the Spanish Monument. It's a huge statue. It's a gift from the Spanish people to the Argentinian people.

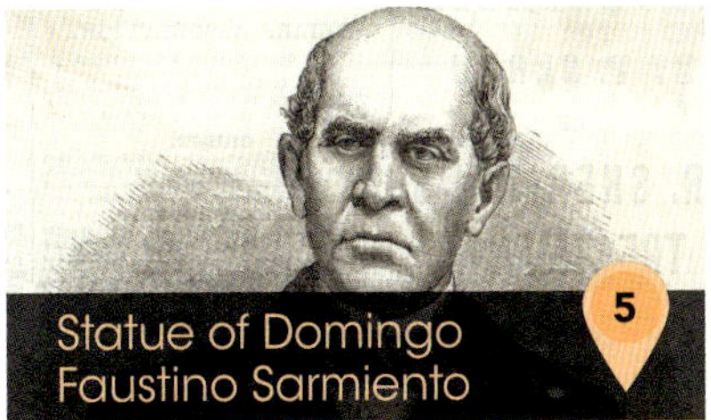

Statue of Domingo Faustino Sarmiento

Turn right to see another big statue. That's the statue of Domingo Faustino Sarmiento. He was a writer and a president of Argentina. Auguste Rodin, a famous French artist, made the statue.

Campo Argentino del Polo

End your tour at the Campo Argentino del Polo. That's where people play a sport named polo, on horseback. The biggest polo competition in the world takes place there!

B Read the information in the guide. Where can you . . . ?

1. see horses ______
2. look at the sky ______
3. see many types of plants ______
4. find a statue of a writer ______
5. see some art ______

C **PAIR WORK** Think of a place you both know and like. Plan a guide to tell visitors where things are.

Unit 14 Supplementary Resources Overview

	After the following SB exercises	You can use these materials in class	Your students can use these materials outside the classroom
CYCLE 1	**1 Snapshot**		**SS** Unit 14 Vocabulary 1 **GAME** Name the Picture (Things people hate to do)
	2 Conversation		**SS** Unit 14 Speaking 1
	3 Grammar Focus		**SB** Unit 14 Grammar plus, Focus 1 **SS** Unit 14 Grammar 1
	4 Pronunciation		
	5 Grammar Focus	**TSS** Unit 14 Vocabulary Worksheet	**GAME** Key Words (Simple past statements)
	6 Speaking		**WB** Unit 14 exercises 1–4
CYCLE 2	**7 Conversation**		**SS** Unit 14 Speaking 2
	8 Grammar Focus	**TSS** Unit 14 Grammar Worksheet	**SB** Unit 14 Grammar plus, Focus 2 **SS** Unit 14 Grammar 2 **GAME** Say the Word (Simple past yes/no questions) **GAME** Sentence Runner (Simple past)
	9 Listening	**TSS** Unit 14 Listening Worksheet	
	10 Word Power	**TSS** Unit 14 Extra Worksheet	**SS** Unit 14 Vocabulary 2
	11 Interchange 14		
	12 Reading	**TSS** Unit 14 Project Worksheet **VID** Unit 14 **VRB** Unit 14	**SS** Unit 14 Reading 1–2 **SS** Unit 14 Listening 1–3 **SS** Unit 14 Video 1–3 **WB** Unit 14 exercises 5–7

With or instead of the following SB section	You can also use these materials for assessment
Units 13–14 Progress Check	**ASSESSMENT PROGRAM** Units 13–14 Oral Quiz **ASSESSMENT PROGRAM** Units 13–14 Written Quiz

Key **GAME:** Online Game **SB:** Student's Book **SS:** Online Self-study **TSS:** Teacher Support Site
VID: Video DVD **VRB:** Video Resource Book **WB:** Online Workbook/Workbook

My Plan for Unit 14

Use the space below to customize a plan that fits your needs.

With the following SB exercises	I am using these materials in class	My students are using these materials outside the classroom

With or instead of the following SB section	I am using these materials for assessment

14 I had a good time.

- Discuss past weekend activities
- Discuss past vacation activities

1 SNAPSHOT

Listen and practice.

THINGS TO DO ON THE WEEKEND

Check (✓) the activities you usually do on weekends. Do you like doing them? Why or why not? What other activities do you do on the weekends?

2 CONVERSATION Did you have a good weekend?

Listen and practice.

Shaun: Hi, Yuna. Did you have a good weekend?

Yuna: Well, I had a busy weekend, so I'm a little tired.

Shaun: Really? Why?

Yuna: Well, on Saturday, I exercised in the morning. Then I cleaned the apartment, did the laundry, and went shopping. And in the evening, I visited my parents.

Shaun: And what did you do on Sunday?

Yuna: I studied for our test all day.

Shaun: Oh, no! I didn't study for the test! I just watched TV shows all weekend!

14 I had a good time.

Cycle 1, Exercises 1–6

In Unit 14, students discuss past weekend activities and past vacation activities. By the end of Cycle 1, students will be able to discuss weekend activities using simple past statements with regular and irregular verbs. By the end of Cycle 2, students will be able to discuss vacation activities using simple past yes/no questions and short answers.

1 SNAPSHOT

Learning Objective: talk about weekend activities and chores

[CD 3, Track 23]

- Books closed. Elicit activities that Ss do on the weekends (e.g., *watch television, play sports*) and write them on the board. Encourage Ss to say both things they like to do and things they don't like to do.
- Ss make lists of things they do on the weekends individually. Then they compare answers in small groups.
- Books open. Focus Ss' attention on the title and pictures. Then play the audio program. Ss listen and read silently.
- Encourage Ss to use the pictures to guess the meaning of any new vocabulary. Explain the meaning of any remaining vocabulary.
- Play the audio program again. Ss listen and repeat.
- Read the focus questions aloud. Ss check (✓) the activities they do on weekends. Then Ss discuss the questions in small groups. Go around the class and help with vocabulary as needed.
- Write each activity in the Snapshot on the board. Then ask the class: "Who answers email?" Ss raise their hands. Write the number of Ss who raise their hands next to the activity. Continue with the remaining activities.
- Ask the class: "What other things do you do on the weekends?" Elicit answers from the class and write them on the board. For each activity, ask: "Who likes to do this?" Write the number of Ss who raise their hands next to the activity and elicit Ss' reasons.

! For a new way to practice the vocabulary in this Snapshot, try ***Vocabulary Steps*** – download it from the website. Ss rank the activities from most favorite to least favorite.

For more practice with this vocabulary, play ***Simon Says*** – download it from the website. Give instructions such as "Simon says exercise." Include the activities you elicited from the class. Ss mime the activities.

2 CONVERSATION

Learning Objective: use simple past statements with regular verbs in a conversation about last weekend

[CD 3, Track 24]

- Text covered. Set the scene. Shaun and Yuna are in class on Monday morning. They are talking about their weekends.
- Focus Ss' attention on the title and picture. Ask the class: "Who studied? Who didn't study?" Encourage Ss to guess. Then play the audio program. Ss listen for the answers. Elicit the answers. (Answers: Yuna studied. Shaun didn't study.)
- Write these activities on the board:

  1. exercise
  2. clean
  3. visit parents
  4. study for our test
  5. watch TV shows

  Ask the class: "Who did each activity – Shaun or Yuna?" Play the audio program once or twice. Ss listen for the answers. Then elicit the answers. (Answers: 1. Yuna 2. Yuna 3. Yuna 4. Yuna 5. Shaun)

TIP
To give Ss a reason for listening, ask focus questions before playing the audio program.

- Text uncovered. Play the audio program again. Ss listen and read silently. Then elicit or explain any new vocabulary.
- ***Option:*** Point out that Shaun and Yuna are talking about activities in the past. Ask Ss to find and underline the simple past tense forms of the activities on the board. Then elicit the answers. (Answers: 1. exercised 2. cleaned 3. visited (parents) 4. studied (for our test) 5. watched (TV shows)
- Play the audio program again. Ss listen and repeat. Then they practice the conversation in pairs.
- ***Option:*** Ask one or two pairs to role-play the conversation for the class.

! For a new way to practice this conversation, try the ***Onion Ring*** technique – download it from the website.

3 GRAMMAR FOCUS

Learning Objective: use positive and negative simple past statements with regular verbs to talk about activities

[CD 3, Track 25]

Simple past statements

- Focus Ss' attention on the Grammar Focus box. Point out that we use the simple past to talk about actions that happened in the past.
- Elicit or explain the pattern for positive and negative simple past statements:

  Positive: Subject + simple past form of verb.

  Negative: Subject + *didn't* + base form of verb.
- Elicit or explain that *did* is the past form of *do*, and *didn't* is the contraction of *did not*. Point out that we use *didn't* for all subjects.
- Play the audio program for the first two columns. Ss listen and read silently.

Regular simple past verbs

- Elicit or explain that regular simple past verbs end in *-ed*.
- Focus Ss' attention on the Spelling column of the Grammar Focus box. Explain these rules for spelling regular simple past verbs:
  1. For most verbs, add *-ed* (e.g., *stayed, watched*).
  2. For verbs ending with *e*, add *-d* (e.g., *exercised*).
  3. For verbs ending with a consonant + *y*, change the *y* to *i* and add *-ed* (e.g., *studied*).
  4. For some verbs ending with a vowel + a consonant, double the consonant and add *-ed* (e.g., *shopped*).
- Play the audio program. Ss listen and read silently.
- ***Option:*** Play the audio program again. Ss listen and repeat.

A

- Explain the task and model the first sentence. Point out that Ss should use the verbs in parentheses.
- Ss complete the task individually. Then they compare their answers in pairs.
- Ask different Ss to write the answers on the board. Go over any grammar or spelling errors with the class.

Answers

On Friday night, I **wanted** to go out, but my friends **didn't call**. I **decided** to stay home, and I **played** video games. On Saturday, I **visited** my friend Pablo. We **talked** and **listened** to music. In the evening, he **invited** some friends over, and we **cooked** a great meal. I **didn't work** very hard on Sunday. I **didn't study** at all. I just **walked** to the mall and **shopped.**

B

- Explain the task.
- Ss complete the sentences individually. Go around the class and help with grammar and spelling. Then Ss compare answers in pairs.

Answers

1. Yesterday, I **watched/didn't watch** a basketball game.
2. Last night, I **stayed/didn't stay** home.
3. Last week, I **cleaned/didn't clean** the house.
4. Last month, I **shopped/didn't shop** for clothes.
5. Last year, I **visited/didn't visit** a different country.

4 PRONUNCIATION

Learning Objectives: differentiate between the three pronunciations of simple past *-ed* endings and sound more natural when using them

A [CD 3, Track 26]

- Explain the task and focus Ss' attention on the chart.
- Play the audio program. Ss listen and read silently.
- ***Option:*** Explain these pronunciation rules:
  1. *-ed* sounds like /t/ when the verb ends with a voiceless consonant sound such as /k/ or /tʃ/ (e.g., *worked, watched*).
  2. *-ed* sounds like /d/ when the verb ends with a vowel sound or a voiced consonant sound such as /n/ (e.g., *cleaned, stayed*).
  3. *-ed* sounds like /ɪd/ when the verb ends with the sound /t/ or /d/ (e.g., *wanted, visited*).
- Play the audio program again. Ss listen and repeat.

B [CD 3, Track 27]

- Explain the task and play the audio program. Ss listen and complete the task.
- Play the audio program again. Ss listen and check their answers. Then they compare their answers in pairs.
- Copy the chart onto the board. Elicit the correct answers and write them in the chart.

Answers

/t/	/d/	/ɪd/
worked	cleaned	wanted
watched	stayed	visited
cooked	exercised	decided
shopped	listened	invited

- ***Option:*** Ss work in pairs. They practice the conversation in Exercise 2 on page 92 again and concentrate on pronouncing the *-ed* endings.

3 GRAMMAR FOCUS

Simple past statements; regular verbs

I	**stayed**	home.	I	**didn't stay**	home.
You	**watched**	a TV show.	You	**didn't watch**	a game.
She	**exercised**	on Saturday.	She	**didn't exercise**	on Sunday.
We	**studied**	English.	We	**didn't study**	math.
They	**shopped**	for groceries.	They	**didn't shop**	for clothes.
				didn**'t** = did **not**	

Spelling

stay	→	stay**ed**
watch	→	watch**ed**
exercise	→	exercise**d**
study	→	stud**ied**
shop	→	shop**ped**

GRAMMAR PLUS see page 145

A Ray is talking about his weekend. Complete the sentences. Then compare with a partner.

On Friday night, I __wanted__ (want) to go out, but my friends ________ (not call). I ________ (decide) to stay home, and I ________ (play) video games. On Saturday, I ________ (visit) my friend Pablo. We ________ (talk) and ________ (listen) to music. In the evening, he ________ (invite) some friends over, and we ________ (cook) a great meal. I ________ (not work) very hard on Sunday. I ________ (not study) at all. I just ________ (walk) to the mall and ________ (shop).

B Complete the sentences. Use your own information. Then compare with a partner.

1. Yesterday, I ________ (watch) a basketball game.
2. Last night, I ________ (stay) home.
3. Last week, I ________ (clean) the house.
4. Last month, I ________ (shop) for clothes.
5. Last year, I ________ (visit) a different country.

4 PRONUNCIATION Simple past *–ed* endings.

A Listen and practice. Notice the pronunciation of –**ed**.

/t/	/d/	/ɪd/
worked	cleaned	wanted
watched	stayed	visited

B Listen and write these verbs under the correct sounds.

cooked **decided** **exercised** **invited** **listened** **shopped**

5 GRAMMAR FOCUS

Simple past statements: irregular verbs

I **did** my homework.
I **didn't do** the laundry.

You **got up** at noon.
You **didn't get up** at 8:00.

She **went** to the bookstore.
She **didn't go** to the library.

We **met** our classmates.
We **didn't meet** our teacher.

You **came** home late.
You **didn't come** home early.

They **had** a barbecue.
They **didn't have** a picnic.

GRAMMAR PLUS *see page 145*

A Complete the chart. Then listen and check.

Present	Past	Present	Past	Present	Past
________	bought	________	made	________	saw
________	ate	________	read /rɛd/	________	sat
________	felt	________	rode	________	took

B **PAIR WORK** Did you do the things in the pictures yesterday? Tell your partner.

"Yesterday, I didn't do my homework. But I did the laundry. . . ."

6 SPEAKING Last weekend

A Write five things you did and five things you didn't do last weekend.

Things I did	Things I didn't do
I went to a party.	I didn't clean the house.
I danced a lot.	I didn't see a movie.
I . . .	I didn't . . .

B **GROUP WORK** Tell your classmates about your weekend.

A: I went to a party last weekend.
B: I didn't go to a party. But I met my friends.
C: I met my friends, too! We went . . .

5 GRAMMAR FOCUS

Learning Objective: use positive and negative simple past statements with irregular verbs to talk about activities

[CD 3, Track 28]

Simple past statements: irregular verbs

- Remind Ss of the pattern for positive and negative simple past statements:

  Subject + simple past form of verb. (positive)

  Subject + *didn't* + base form of verb. (negative)
- Focus Ss' attention on the sentences below the pictures. Point out that the verbs *do*, *get*, *go*, *come*, *meet*, and *have* are irregular. We do not make the simple past form of these verbs by adding *-ed*.
- Play the audio program. Ss listen and read silently. Elicit the irregular past tense forms of *do*, *get*, *go*, *come*, *meet*, and *have*.
- ***Option:*** Play the audio program again. Ss listen and repeat.

A *[CD 3, Track 29]*

- Focus Ss' attention on the chart and explain the task. Point out that the verbs in the *Past* columns are irregular simple past forms. Ss complete the *Present* columns with the simple present forms. Encourage Ss to guess.
- Ss complete the chart individually. Then they compare their answers in small groups. While they work, copy the chart onto the board.
- Play the audio program once or twice. Ss listen and check their answers. Then elicit answers from the class and ask different Ss to write them in the chart on the board. Point out that the past form of *read* is spelled the same as the present form but is pronounced /rɛd/.

Answers

buy	make	see
eat	read	sit
feel	ride	take

B *Pair work*

- Explain the task and focus Ss' attention on the pictures in the Grammar Focus box. Then model the example sentences.
- Ss complete the task in pairs. Then they change partners and complete the task again.
- ***Option:*** Ss complete the task in pairs. Then each pair joins another pair to talk about their partner's activities.
- ***Option:*** To make the task more challenging, Ss also use the verbs in part A.

6 SPEAKING

Learning Objective: discuss activities and chores from last weekend

A

- Explain the task and focus Ss' attention on the example list. Point out that Ss can use regular and irregular simple past verbs from pages 92–94. They can also use irregular verbs from the appendix in the back of the book.
- Ss complete the task individually. Go around the class and help with vocabulary and spelling as needed.

B *Group work*

- Explain the task and ask three Ss to model the conversation.
- Ss discuss their weekends in small groups. Go around the class and note any grammar or pronunciation errors.
- Ask Ss to share information about their classmates' weekends.
- ***Option:*** Correct any grammar or pronunciation errors with the class.

For more practice with regular and irregular simple past verbs, play the ***Chain Game*** – download it from the website. Start with this sentence: "Last (weekend/week/month/year), I saw a movie."

End of Cycle 1

See the Supplementary Resources chart at the beginning of this unit for additional teaching materials and student activities related to this Cycle.

7 CONVERSATION

Learning Objective: use simple past yes/no questions in a conversation about a vacation

[CD 3, Track 30]

- Focus Ss' attention on the picture and set the scene. Kim is asking Martin about his vacation last summer. Write these focus questions on the board:
  1. Did Martin go to Sydney?
  2. Did he go with his brother?
  3. Did they climb a bridge?
  4. Did Martin have fun?
  5. Did his sister like climbing?
- Play the audio program. Ss listen and read silently. Then elicit the answers to the focus questions. (Answers: 1. yes 2. no 3. yes 4. yes 5. no)
- Elicit or explain the meaning of any new vocabulary. Use pictures or mime where appropriate.
- Play the audio program again. Ss listen and repeat. Then they practice the conversation in pairs.
- ***Option:*** Ask one or two pairs to role-play the conversation for the class.

! For a new way to practice this conversation, try ***Musical Dialog*** – download it from the website.

8 GRAMMAR FOCUS

Learning Objective: ask and answer simple past yes/no questions

[CD 3, Track 31]

Simple past yes/no questions

- Focus Ss' attention on the Grammar Focus box. Point out the pattern for simple past yes/no questions and short answers:

  Did + subject + (simple present verb)?
  Yes, + (subject) + *did.*
  No, + (subject) + *didn't.*
- Point out that we use *did* and *didn't* for all subjects.
- Play the audio program. Ss listen and read silently.

A

- Explain the first part of the task. Then model the example question in the first conversation.
- Ss complete the task individually. Then they compare answers in pairs.
- Tell Ss to raise their hands when they finish the exercise. Go around, circle any wrong answers, and have Ss correct them in pairs.
- To check the answers, ask different pairs to read each conversation. If needed, correct the answers with the class.

Answers

1. A: **Did** you **have** a good summer?
   B: Yes, I **did**. I **had** a great summer. I **went** out with my friends a lot.
2. A: **Did** you **go** anywhere last summer?
   B: No, I **didn't**. I **stayed** here. I **got** a part-time job, so I **made** some extra money.
3. A: **Did** you **take** any classes last summer?
   B: Yes, I **did**. I **took** tennis lessons, and I **played** tennis every day!
4. A: **Did** you **speak** English last summer?
   B: No, I **didn't**. But I **read** blogs in English, and I **watched** English movies.

- Explain the second part of the task. Ss practice the conversations in pairs. Go around the class and help Ss with pronunciation and intonation.

B *Pair work*

- Write the four questions from part A on the board. Then explain the task and ask two Ss to model the example conversation.
- Books closed. Ss ask you the questions on the board one by one. Answer with your own information.
- Ss ask and answer the questions in pairs. Go around the class and encourage Ss to ask follow-up questions and give more information.

TIP
To decide if your Ss need more grammar explanation or controlled practice, pay attention to how they use the grammar in speaking activities. If they make a lot of errors, review or further explain the grammar in a later class.

For more practice with simple past yes/no questions, play ***Hot Potato*** – download it from the website.

7 CONVERSATION Did you have fun?

Listen and practice.

KIM Hi, Martin! Welcome back! So, did you go to Montreal?

MARTIN No, I didn't. I went to Sydney with my sister.

KIM Really? Did you like it?

MARTIN Yeah, we loved it! We visited the Opera House and went to Bondi Beach.

KIM Did you go surfing?

MARTIN No, we didn't. Actually, we went swimming in the Ocean Pool. And one day we climbed Sydney Harbor Bridge.

KIM Wow! Did you have fun?

MARTIN Yes, I did. But my sister didn't like climbing very much. She got really tired.

8 GRAMMAR FOCUS

Simple past yes/no questions

Did you **have** a good summer?
Yes, I **did**. I **had** a great summer.
Did you **go** surfing?
No, I **didn't**. I **went** swimming.

Did Martin **like** his vacation?
Yes, he **did**. He **liked** it a lot.
Did Martin and his sister **go** to Montreal?
No, they **didn't**. They **went** to Sydney.

GRAMMAR PLUS *see page 145*

A Complete the conversations. Then practice with a partner.

1. **A:** ___Did___ you ___have___ (have) a good summer?
   B: Yes, I ________. I ________ (have) a great summer.
   I ________ (go) out with my friends a lot.
2. **A:** ________ you ________ (go) anywhere last summer?
   B: No, I ________. I ________ (stay) here.
   I ________ (get) a part-time job, so I ________ (make) some extra money.
3. **A:** ________ you ________ (take) any classes last summer?
   B: Yes, I ________. I ________ (take) tennis lessons, and I ________ (play) tennis every day!
4. **A:** ________ you ________ (speak) English last summer?
   B: No, I ________. But I ________ (read) blogs in English, and I ________ (watch) English movies.

B PAIR WORK Ask the questions from part A. Answer with your own information.

A: Did you have a good summer?
B: Yes, I did. I went to the beach every day.

9 LISTENING Did you have a good summer?

Listen to Fernando, Olivia, Cameron, and Abigail. What did they do last summer? Check (✓) the correct answers.

Fernando	Olivia	Cameron	Abigail
☐ stayed home	☐ watched videos	☐ went bike riding	☐ worked in the yard
☐ visited his brother	☐ read books	☐ went swimming	☐ got a job
☐ went to the beach	☐ watched TV	☐ played baseball	☐ painted the house

10 WORD POWER Summer activities

A Find two words from the list that go with each verb in the chart. Then listen and check.

a barbecue
beach volleyball
camping
✓ a new bike
new people
old friends
a picnic
soccer
a summer class
swimming
a trip
✓ up late

get	a new bike	up late
go		
have		
meet		
play		
take		

B PAIR WORK Add two activities to the list. Check (✓) six things to ask your partner. Then ask and answer questions.

Did you . . . last summer?

☐ do anything interesting
☐ eat any new foods
☐ see any museum exhibits
☐ meet any interesting people
☐ play any sports
☐ ____________
☐ play any games
☐ read any books
☐ see any movies
☐ take any classes
☐ take any trips
☐ ____________

A: Did you do anything interesting last summer?
B: Yes, I did. I went white-water rafting.

C CLASS ACTIVITY Tell the class about your partner's summer.

"Last summer, Alma went white-water rafting with some friends. They had a lot of fun."

11 INTERCHANGE 14 Past activities

Did you and your partner do similar things when you were children? Go to Interchange 14 on page 129.

9 LISTENING

Learning Objective: listen for specific information about activities discussed using simple past yes/no questions

[CD 3, Track 32]

- Set the scene. Different people are asking Fernando, Olivia, Cameron, and Abigail about their summers.
- Explain the task. Then play the first conversation in the audio program. Ss listen.
- Play the rest of the audio program two or three times, pausing after each conversation. Ss listen and complete the chart individually.

Audio script

1.

Woman	Hello, Fernando. Did you have a good summer?
Fernando	Oh, I had an OK summer, I guess. I visited my brother in Veracruz.
Woman	That's nice! Did you go to the beach?
Fernando	No, I didn't. It rained all summer, so we usually did things indoors.

2.

Man	Hi, Olivia. How are you? Did you have a good summer?
Olivia	Yes, I did, thanks. I just relaxed.
Man	Did you read any good books?
Olivia	Books? Well, no . . . but I watched a lot of interesting videos online!

3.

Woman	So, Cameron, did you do anything interesting last summer?
Cameron	Oh, yeah! You know how I love to be outdoors. I played baseball and rode my bike every day!
Woman	Baseball and bike riding! You're a really good athlete!
Cameron	Yeah, . . . well, I try.

4.

Man	Did you have a job last summer, Abigail?
Abigail	Well, no, . . . but I did a lot of work.
Man	What do you mean? Did you get a job?
Abigail	No. But my parents and I painted our house. And I worked in the yard a lot.

- To check answers, ask the class: "What did Fernando do last summer?" Elicit the answer. Then ask about the remaining three people.

Answers

1. Fernando: visited his brother
2. Olivia: watched videos
3. Cameron: went bike riding, played baseball
4. Abigail: worked in the yard, painted the house

10 WORD POWER

Learning Objective: discuss free-time activities

A ***[CD 3, Track 33]***

- Explain the first part of the task and read out the words in the list. Then focus Ss' attention on the chart and read out the verbs. Point out that each verb goes with two words or phrases in the list.
- Ss complete the chart individually. Then they compare answers in pairs.
- Play the audio program. Ss check answers.

Answers

get: a new bike, up late
go: camping, swimming
have: a barbecue, a picnic
meet: new people, old friends
play: beach volleyball, soccer
take: a summer class, a trip

B ***Pair work***

- Focus Ss' attention on the list. Ask different Ss to read each phrase in the list. Elicit or explain any new vocabulary. *Exhibits* are special shows of paintings or artifacts at museums. Explain the first part of the task. Ss add two activities to the list. Then each S chooses six questions.
- Explain the second part of the task and ask two Ss to model the example conversation. Point out that the Ss answering the questions should give more information about their summer activities. The Ss asking the questions should take notes.
- Ss take turns asking and answering questions in pairs. Go around the class and encourage Ss to add information to their answers.

C ***Class activity***

- Explain the task and model the example. Elicit other things Alma did. Encourage Ss to make guesses.
- Ask different Ss to tell the class about their partner's summer. Encourage them to use their notes.

11 INTERCHANGE 14

See page T-129 for teaching notes.

12 READING

Learning Objectives: scan and read for main ideas and details in texts about people's activities

A *[CD 3, Track 34]*

- Focus Ss' attention on the pictures. Read out the questions.
- Point out that main ideas are usually found at the beginning or end of a paragraph. Tell Ss to read only the beginning and end of each paragraph.
- Ss complete the task individually.
- Elicit the answers from the class. (Possible answers: Armando had a busy weekend. Juliette saw an old friend. Jessie had fun learning something new. Nick had a terrible weekend.)

B

- Explain the first part of the task. Ss read the social media posts individually and underline any new words.
- Ss discuss the meanings of any new words they don't understand in small groups. Then elicit or explain any remaining new vocabulary. Use pictures or mime where appropriate.

Vocabulary
broke down: stopped working
bang: a sudden loud noise
parasailing: a sport in which you wear a parachute and sail through the air being pulled by a boat
instructor: someone who teaches
chores: boring jobs you must do

- ***Option:*** Play the audio program. Ss listen and read silently.
- Explain the second part of the task. Tell Ss that there is one mistake in each sentence. Ask a S to model the example sentence and identify the error. Then ask different Ss to read the remaining sentences. Explain any new vocabulary, if needed.
- Ss correct the sentences individually. Then they compare answers in pairs.
- Ask different Ss to write the correct sentences on the board. Go over the sentences with the class and correct any errors.

Possible answers

1. Nick's best friend got married.
2. On the way to the wedding, Nick's car broke down.
3. Jessie's parasailing class was amazing.
4. It was Jessie's first parasailing class.
5. Armando did chores on Saturday morning.
6. Armando fixed his bike and walked his dog.
7. Juliette went running on Saturday evening.
8. Marie is married and has a baby.

C *Pair work*

- Explain the task. Model the answers to the questions with your own information.
- Ss tell about their weekend in pairs. Go around the class and help with vocabulary and pronunciation.
- ***Option:*** Ss write about their weekend for homework.
- Ss tell the class about their weekend. Encourage Ss to ask follow-up questions.
- ***Option:*** In large classes, Ss share their weekend activities in small groups.

TIP
If you don't have enough class time, do only Part A in class. Then have Ss read the article in detail and complete the remaining activities for homework.

End of Cycle 2

See the Supplementary Resources chart at the beginning of this unit for additional teaching materials and student activities related to this Cycle and for assessment tools.

12 READING

A Scan the social media posts. Who had a busy weekend? Who saw old friends on the weekend? Who had fun learning something new? Who had a terrible weekend?

SOCIAL | Find friends

DID YOU HAVE A GOOD WEEKEND?

Nick Bond

I just had the worst weekend ever! It was my best friend Pete's wedding and my car broke down on the drive. I was on a quiet road and suddenly there was a bang. Then the car just didn't move! I missed the wedding and came home on the back of a truck. ☹

like comment Share post

Jessie Taylor

Hey guys! Guess what? I just got back from my first ever parasailing class! It was amazing! I traveled to a town by the ocean and met my instructor. We went high up above the ocean where people jump off the rocks. It was kind of scary but so exciting. Here's a picture of me. See? That's me!

like comment Share post

Armando Torres

So . . . on Saturday morning I did chores at home. You know, laundry and stuff. Then I went grocery shopping because . . . well, because there was no food in the house! Sunday morning, I fixed my bike, walked the dog, called my mom, and made lunch. Then I wrote a report for work, cleaned the house, and went to bed.

like comment Share post

Juliette Blum

Wow. What an awesome weekend. I went running in the park on Saturday evening, and I met someone I knew from school 10 years ago. It was so cool. Her name is Marie and we always hung out together when we were kids. She's married now and has a baby!

like comment Share post

B Read the social media posts. Then correct these sentences.

1. Nick got married. *Nick's best friend got married.*
2. On the way to the wedding, Nick's truck broke down. ______
3. Jessie's parasailing class was terrible. ______
4. It was Jessie's second parasailing class. ______
5. Armando watched TV on Saturday morning. ______
6. Armando fixed his car and walked his dog. ______
7. Juliette went running on Sunday morning. ______
8. Juliette is married and has a baby. ______

C **PAIR WORK** How was your weekend? Did you have fun? Why? Why not? Tell your partner.

Units 13–14 Progress check

SELF-ASSESSMENT

How well can you do these things? Check (✓) the boxes.

I can . . .	Very well	OK	A little
Understand conversations about where to get things in a town (Ex. 1)	☐	☐	☐
Ask and answer questions about where places are (Ex. 2)	☐	☐	☐
Ask for and give directions (Ex. 2)	☐	☐	☐
Talk about past activities (Ex. 3, 4)	☐	☐	☐
Ask and answer questions about past activities (Ex. 4)	☐	☐	☐

1 LISTENING What are you looking for?

Listen to the conversations. What do the people need? Where can they get or find it? Complete the chart.

What?	Where?
1.	
2.	
3.	
4.	

2 SPEAKING Is there a . . . near here?

A **PAIR WORK** Are these places near your school? Where are they? Ask and answer questions.

bank	coffee shop	hospital	post office
bookstore	department store	park	supermarket

A: Is there a bank near here?
B: Yes, there's a bank on Second Avenue. It's across from the Korean restaurant.

B **PAIR WORK** Give directions from your school to the places in part A. Your partner guesses the place.

A: Go out of the school and turn left. Walk for about three minutes. It's on the right, next to the drugstore.
B: It's the coffee shop.
A: That's right!

Units 13–14

Progress check

SELF-ASSESSMENT

Learning Objectives: reflect on one's learning; identify areas that need improvement

- Ask: "What did you learn in Units 13 and 14?" Elicit Ss' answers.
- Ss complete the Self-assessment. Explain to Ss that this is not a test; it is a way for them to evaluate what they've learned and identify areas where they need additional practice. Encourage them to be honest, and point out they will not get a bad grade if they check (✓) *A little*.
- Ss move on to the Progress check exercises. You can have Ss complete them in class or for homework, using one of these techniques:
  1. Ask Ss to complete all the exercises.
  2. Ask Ss: "What do you need to practice?" Then assign exercises based on their answers.
  3. Ask Ss to choose and complete exercises based on their Self-assessment.

1 LISTENING

Learning Objective: demonstrate one's ability to understand conversations about where to get things

[CD 3, Track 35]

- Explain the task and read out the focus questions. Then play the audio program once or twice. Ss listen and complete the chart individually.

Audio script

1.
Man What are you looking for?
Woman I'm mailing some postcards, and I need some stamps.
Man Well, you can get some at the drugstore. It's across from the park.
Woman Oh. Great! Thanks!
2.
Woman So what do we need?
Man I think we have everything – sandwiches, fruit salad, cookies. Oh, wait. We don't have any drinks. We need some juice.
Woman Let's stop at the supermarket on the way. We can get some juice there.
Man Good idea.
3.
Man Excuse me. Is there a gas station around here?
Woman Um, I think there's a gas station on the corner of Main and First. Just drive down Main Street for four blocks. It's on the left. You can't miss it.
Man I'm glad it's not far. I really need more gas!
4.
Woman Can you help me? Is there a restroom around here?
Man Oh, sure. There's a library not far from here. They have a restroom. Go up this street for two blocks and turn left.
Woman Thanks a lot.

- To check answers, ask: "What does the woman in the first conversation need? Where can she find it?" Elicit the answers from the class. Continue with the remaining people.

Answers

	What?	Where?
1.	stamps	drugstore
2.	juice	supermarket
3.	gasoline	gas station
4.	restroom	library

2 SPEAKING

Learning Objectives: demonstrate one's ability to discuss where places are and to ask for and give directions

A *Pair work*

- Explain the task and read out each place. Then ask two Ss to model the example conversation.
- Ss work in pairs. They take turns asking and answering questions about the places.
- To check answers, ask the class about each place: "Is there a . . . near here?" Then elicit the answers.

B *Pair work*

- Explain the task. Ask Ss to model the conversation.
- Ss work in pairs. They take turns giving directions and making guesses.
- ***Option:*** Ss change partners and repeat the activity.

3 SPEAKING

Learning Objective: demonstrate one's ability to discuss past activities

A

- Focus Ss' attention on the picture and explain the task. Then model the task. Write on the board two sentences about your last vacation that are true, and two that are false. Point out which sentences are true and which are false, but do not label them.
- Ss write four statements individually. Go around the class and help with vocabulary and spelling as needed.

B *Pair work*

- Explain the task and ask two Ss to model the example conversation. Tell Ss to check (✓) each correct guess.
- Ss complete the task in pairs.
- Elicit who got the most correct guesses. Ask the class: "Who has four correct guesses? three correct guesses? two correct guesses?" Ss raise their hands.

4 SPEAKING

Learning Objective: demonstrate one's ability to ask and answer questions about past activities

A

- Explain the task and focus Ss' attention on the list of activities. If needed, read out each phrase. Explain that *to download* is to copy files, such as computer programs, music, or movies off the Internet.
- Ss complete the task individually. Go around the class and help Ss with vocabulary and spelling as needed.

B *Pair work*

- Explain the task and ask two Ss to model the example conversation. Point out that Ss should ask about each activity and answer with follow-up information. Also point out that Ss can ask: "What else did you do last weekend?" to find out about the additional activities.
- ***Option:*** For lower-level classes, elicit a *Did you . . . ?* question for each phrase.
- Ss complete the activity in pairs. Go around the class and give help as needed. Encourage Ss to change the order of the questions and take notes on their partner's answers.

C *Group work*

- Explain the task. Ask a S to model the example sentence.
- Each pair joins another pair. Ss talk about their partner's weekend.

WHAT'S NEXT?

Learning Objective: become more involved in one's learning

- Focus Ss' attention on the Self-assessment again. Ask: "How well can you do these things now?"
- Ask Ss to underline one thing they need to review. Ask: "What did you underline? How can you review it?"
- If needed, plan additional instruction, activities, or reviews based on Ss' answers.

3 SPEAKING On my last vacation . . .

A Write four statements about your last vacation. Two are true and two are false.

B PAIR WORK Read your statements. Your partner says, "I think it's true," OR "I think it's false." Who has more correct guesses?

I went to New Zealand.
It rained all day, every day.
I didn't go to the beach.
I read two books.

A: On my last vacation, I went to New Zealand.
B: I think it's false.
A: That's right. It's false. OR Sorry. It's true.

4 SPEAKING Did you . . . last weekend?

A Check (✓) the things you did last weekend. Then add two more things you did.

Last weekend, I . . .

- ☐ ate at a restaurant
- ☐ cleaned the house
- ☐ did homework
- ☐ did the laundry
- ☐ downloaded movies
- ☐ exercised
- ☐ played video games
- ☐ rode my bicycle
- ☐ visited relatives
- ☐ washed the car
- ☐ watched a game on TV
- ☐ uploaded photos
- ☐ went shopping
- ☐ went out with friends
- ☐ ______________
- ☐ ______________

B PAIR WORK Ask your partner about his or her weekend.

A: Did you eat at a restaurant last weekend, Narumi?
B: Yes, I did. I ate at a very good Italian restaurant. What about you? Did you eat at a restaurant?
A: No, I didn't. . . .

C GROUP WORK Join another pair. Tell them about your partner's weekend.

"Narumi ate at a very good Italian restaurant."

WHAT'S NEXT?

Look at your Self-assessment again. Do you need to review anything?

Unit 15 Supplementary Resources Overview

	After the following SB exercises	You can use these materials in class	Your students can use these materials outside the classroom
CYCLE 1	**1 Snapshot**		
	2 Conversation		**SS** Unit 15 Speaking 1
	3 Grammar Focus		**SB** Unit 15 Grammar plus, Focus 1 **SS** Unit 15 Grammar 1 **GAME** Speak or Slime (Past of *be*)
	4 Pronunciation		
CYCLE 2	**5 Conversation**		**SS** Unit 15 Speaking 2
	6 Grammar Focus	**TSS** Unit 15 Grammar Worksheet **TSS** Unit 15 Extra Worksheet	**SB** Unit 15 Grammar plus, Focus 2 **SS** Unit 15 Vocabulary 1 **SS** Unit 15 Grammar 2 **GAME** Sentence Stacker (Wh-questions *with did, was,* and *were*) **GAME** Sentence Runner (Past of *be* and Wh-questions)
	7 Listening	**TSS** Unit 15 Listening Worksheet	
	8 Word Power	**TSS** Unit 15 Vocabulary Worksheet	**SS** Unit 15 Vocabulary 2 **GAME** Spell or Slime (School days)
	9 Speaking		
	10 Interchange 15		
	11 Reading	**TSS** Unit 15 Project Worksheet **VID** Unit 15 **VRB** Unit 15	**SS** Unit 15 Reading 1–2 **SS** Unit 15 Listening 1–3 **SS** Unit 15 Video 1–3 **WB** Unit 15 exercises 1–7

Key **GAME:** Online Game **SB:** Student's Book **SS:** Online Self-study **TSS:** Teacher Support Site
VID: Video DVD **VRB:** Video Resource Book **WB:** Online Workbook/Workbook

My Plan for Unit 15

Use the space below to customize a plan that fits your needs.

With the following SB exercises	I am using these materials in class	My students are using these materials outside the classroom

With or instead of the following SB section	I am using these materials for assessment

15 Where were you born?

- ▸ Discuss family and personal history
- ▸ Discuss school experiences and memories

1 SNAPSHOT

Listen and practice.

Where Were They Born?

Esperanza Spalding
musician

John Oliver
comedian

Lupita Nyong'o
actress

Shin-Soo Choo
baseball player

Shigeru Miyamoto
game designer

1. ____________ 2. ____________ 3. ____________ 4. ____________ 5. ____________

a. Japan
b. Mexico
c. South Korea
d. the U.K.
e. the U.S.

Answers: 1. e 2. d 3. b 4. c 5. a

Match the people with the countries where they were born. Then check your answers.
What famous people were born in your country? What do they do?

2 CONVERSATION I was born in Brazil.

Listen and practice.

Mario: Bianca. That's a nice name. Where were you born?
Bianca: I was born in Brazil.
Mario: Oh! So you weren't born in the U.S. Your English is really good.
Bianca: Thanks. I studied English for many years.
Mario: Did you study English in Brazil?
Bianca: Yeah, I started when I was seven.
Mario: You were pretty young.
Bianca: Yes, I went to a bilingual school. I had classes in English and in Portuguese.
Mario: You were lucky to learn another language so well.
Bianca: Do you speak a second language, too?
Mario: Well, I speak a little Italian. My parents were born in Milan.

15 Where were you born?

Cycle 1, Exercises 1–4

In Unit 15, students discuss family and personal history, school experiences, and memories. By the end of Cycle 1, students will be able to discuss family and personal history using the past of *be*. By the end of Cycle 2, students will be able to discuss school experiences and memories using Wh-questions with *did*, *was*, and *were*.

1 SNAPSHOT

Learning Objective: talk about where famous people were born

[CD 3, Track 36]

- Focus Ss' attention on the title and pictures. Ask: "What do you know about these people?" Elicit information from the class.
- Play the audio program. Ss listen and read silently.
- Elicit or explain any new vocabulary.

Vocabulary
comedian: someone who tells jokes, often as a job
actress: a woman who performs in plays, in movies, or on TV [Note: *Actor* is often used for both males and females.]
game designer: someone who creates video games

- Play the audio program again. Ss listen and practice.
- Read the first task. Ss match the people with the countries individually. Then they check their answers at the bottom of the Snapshot. Ask: "Who has five correct answers? four? three?" Ss raise their hands.
- Read the last two questions: "What famous people were born in your country? What do they do?" Ss discuss the questions in small groups. Then elicit information from the class.

2 CONVERSATION

Learning Objective: use the past of *be* in a conversation about someone's personal history

[CD 3, Track 37]

- Books closed. Set the scene. Bianca is a customer in a beauty salon. The hairstylist, Mario, is asking her about her life. Write these questions on the board:

  1. Where is Bianca from?
  2. Where are Mario's parents from?

- Play the audio program. Ss listen for the answers. Then elicit the answers. (Answers: 1. Brazil 2. Milan)
- Play the audio program again. Ss listen and read along silently. Elicit or explain the meaning of any new vocabulary.

Vocabulary
pretty: quite; very
bilingual: able to use or speak two languages

TIP
If Ss ask about new structures in the Conversation, explain that they'll learn about them in the Grammar Focus on the next page.

- Play the audio program again. Ss listen and repeat. Then they practice the conversation in pairs.
- ***Option:*** Ask one or two pairs to role-play the conversation for the class.

! For a new way to practice this conversation, try ***Moving Dialog*** – download it from the website.

3 GRAMMAR FOCUS

Learning Objectives: use the past of *be* in short statements and to ask and answer questions

[CD 3, Track 38]

Statements with the past of be

- Write this on the board:

  I/He/She/It + was + complement.
  You/We/They + were + complement.

  If needed, explain that a *complement* follows the verb at the end of a sentence.
- Elicit or explain that *was* and *were* are the past forms of *be*. We use *was* with the pronouns *I*, *he*, *she*, and *it*. We use *were* with the pronouns *you*, *we*, and *they*.
- Focus Ss' attention on the first two columns of the Grammar Focus box. Play the audio program. Ss listen and read silently.
- Point out that *wasn't* is the contraction for *was not* and *weren't* is the contraction for *were not*.

Yes/No questions with the past of be

- Focus Ss' attention on the right-hand column of the grammar chart. Point out that this column has yes/no questions.
- Elicit or explain the pattern for yes/no questions and short answers with the past of *be*:

  Was/Were + subject + complement?
  Yes, + subject + *was/were*.
  No, + subject + *wasn't/weren't*.
- Ask individual Ss the questions in the chart.

TIP
To demonstrate contractions, use your hands. For example, say "This thumb is *was*. This finger is *not*. When you push them together, you get *wasn't*."

- ***Option:*** Play the audio program again. Ss listen and repeat.

A

- Set the scene and explain the task. Then model the example sentence.
- Ss complete the task individually. Then they compare answers in pairs.
- To check answers, ask different Ss to read the sentences.

Answers

My family and I **were** all born in Brazil – we **weren't** born in the U.S. I **was** born in the city of Recife, and my brother **was** born there, too. My parents **weren't** born in Recife. They **were** born in Rio de Janeiro. In Rio, my father **was** a teacher and my mother **was** an engineer. They have their own business in Recife now.

B *Pair work*

- Direct Ss' attention to the picture. Have Ss identify the teacher. (Mr. Walker) Ask what subject the students are studying. (chemistry/science)
- Explain the task and model the first question with a S.
- Ss ask and answer the questions in pairs.

Answers

1. No, she wasn't. She was late.
2. No, it wasn't. It was chemistry/science class.
3. No, it wasn't. It was raining.
4. No, it wasn't. It was 10:05.
5. No, he wasn't.
6. No, they weren't.
7. No, they weren't. They were at their desks.
8. No, they weren't. They were closed.

For more practice with the past tense of *be*, play ***Run For It!*** – download it from the website. Read out sentences with *was*, *were*, *wasn't*, and *weren't*.

3 GRAMMAR FOCUS

Past of *be*

I **was** born here.	I **wasn't** born in Italy.	**Were** you in class yesterday?
You **were** pretty young.	You **weren't** very old.	Yes, I **was**. / No, I **wasn't**.
She **was** seven.	She **wasn't** in college.	**Was** your first teacher American?
We **were** at the hair salon.	We **weren't** at the café.	Yes, she **was**. / No, she **wasn't**.
They **were** born in Milan.	They **weren't** born in Rome.	**Were** your parents born in the U.S.?
		Yes, they **were**. / No, they **weren't**.
were**n't** = were **not**	was**n't** = was **not**	

GRAMMAR PLUS *see page 146*

A Bianca is talking about her family. Choose the correct verb forms. Then compare with a partner.

My family and I ___*were*___ (was / were) all born in Brazil – we __________ (wasn't / weren't) born in the U.S. I __________ (was / were) born in the city of Recife, and my brother __________ (was / were) born there, too. My parents __________ (wasn't / weren't) born in Recife. They __________ (was / were) born in Rio de Janeiro. In Rio, my father __________ (was / were) a teacher and my mother __________ (was / were) an engineer. They have their own business in Recife now.

B **PAIR WORK** Look at the picture below. Ask and answer these questions.

1. Was Tessa on time for class yesterday?
2. Was it English class?
3. Was it a sunny day?
4. Was it 10:00?
5. Was Mr. Walker very angry?
6. Were Alyssa and Jacob late to class?
7. Were they at the board?
8. Were the windows open?

A: Was Tessa on time for class yesterday?

B: No, she wasn't. She was late. Was it English class?

4 PRONUNCIATION Negative contractions

A Listen and practice.

one syllable		two syllables	
aren't	don't	isn't	doesn't
weren't	can't	wasn't	didn't

B Listen and practice.

They **didn't** like the comedy because it **wasn't** funny.
I **don't** like coffee, and she **doesn't** like tea.
This **isn't** my book. I **can't** read French.
They **weren't** in class yesterday, and they **aren't** in class today.

C Write four sentences with negative contractions.
Then read them to a partner.

I didn't go to the party because
my friends weren't there.

5 CONVERSATION I grew up in New York.

Listen and practice.

Bianca So, Mario, where did you grow up?
Mario I grew up in New York.
Bianca Were you born there?
Mario Yeah. I was born in Brooklyn.
Bianca And when did you come to Los Angeles?
Mario In 2008.
Bianca How old were you then?
Mario I was eighteen. I went to college here.
Bianca Oh. What was your major?
Mario Photography. I was a photographer for five years after college.
Bianca Really? Why did you become a hairstylist?
Mario Because I needed the money. And I love it. So, what do you think?
Bianca Well, uh . . .

4 PRONUNCIATION

Learning Objective: sound more natural when using negative contractions

A *[CD 3, Track 39]*

- Focus Ss' attention on the chart. Point out that some contractions have one syllable and others have two syllables. Play the audio program. Ss listen and repeat.

B *[CD 3, Track 40]*

- Play the audio program. Ss listen and read silently. Then play the audio program again. Ss listen and repeat.
- Ask different Ss to read the sentences aloud. Check their pronunciation of negative contractions.

! For a different way to teach this Pronunciation, try ***Stand Up, Sit Down*** – download it from the website.

TIP
To hear if Ss are using correct pronunciation or intonation, ask them to repeat the word, sentence, or question individually.

C

- Explain the task. Then model the example sentence. Ss listen and repeat.
- Ss write four sentences individually. Go around the class and give help as needed.
- Ss read their sentences in pairs. Go around the class and listen for correct pronunciation.
- ***Option:*** Ask different Ss to write their sentences on the board. Read each sentence aloud. Ss listen and repeat.

End of Cycle 1

See the Supplementary Resources chart at the beginning of this unit for additional teaching materials and student activities related to this Cycle.

Cycle 2, Exercises 5–11

5 CONVERSATION

Learning Objective: use Wh-questions with *did*, *was*, and *were* in a conversation about someone's personal history

[CD 3, Track 41]

- Text covered. Focus Ss' attention on the picture and set the scene. Remind Ss that Mario and Bianca were in Exercise 2 on page 100. In that conversation, Mario asked Bianca about her life. Explain that now Bianca is asking Mario about his life.
- Write this on the board:

  1. What was Mario's major in college?
     a) hair design
     b) English
     c) photography
  2. Why did he become a hairstylist?
     a) He needed the money.
     b) He liked hair design.
     c) He liked people.

  Play the audio program. Ss listen for the answers. Then elicit the answers. (Answers: 1. c 2. a)
- Text uncovered. Play the audio program again. Ss listen and read silently.
- Elicit or explain the meaning of any new vocabulary.

Vocabulary
grow up: grow from a child into an adult
college: university
major: the main subject someone studies in college

- Play the audio program again. Ss listen and practice. Then they practice the conversation in pairs.
- ***Option:*** Ask one or two pairs to role-play the conversation for the class.
- ***Option:*** Ss underline all the Wh-questions. Then elicit the Wh-questions from the class. (Answers: . . . where did you grow up? And when did you come to Los Angeles? How old were you then? What was your major? Why did you become a hairstylist? So, what do you think?)

6 GRAMMAR FOCUS

Learning Objective: ask and answer Wh-questions with *did*, *was*, and *were*

[CD 3, Track 42]

- Books closed. Write this on the board:

  1. Wh-word + *did* + subject + verb (+ complement)?
  2. Wh-word + *was/were* + subject (+ complement)?

  Point out that the first pattern is for simple past Wh-questions. The second pattern is for Wh-questions with the past of *be*.
- Books open. Focus Ss' attention on the Grammar Focus box. Then play the audio program. Ss listen and read silently.
- ***Option:*** Play the audio program again. Ss listen and repeat.

A

- Explain the task. Then ask two Ss to model the first question and answer.
- Ss complete the task individually. Then they compare answers in pairs.
- Ask different pairs of Ss to read out the questions and matching answers. Then write the answers on the board. (Answers: 1. e, 2. d, 3. f, 4. a, 5. b, 6. c)

B *Pair work*

- Explain the task. To model the task, have the class ask you a few of the questions from part A. Answer with your own information.
- Ss complete the task in pairs. They take turns asking and answering the questions.
- ***Option:*** Each pair joins another pair. Ss take turns sharing information about their partners.

C *Group work*

- Focus Ss' attention on the *saying years* box. Say the years and have Ss repeat. Ask several Ss when they were born. Encourage them to answer with a complete sentence.
- Ss ask and answer the questions in small groups.
- ***Option:*** Ask Ss about their classmates (e.g., *When was [S's name]'s mother born?*).

For more practice with Wh-questions and answers, play ***Concentration*** – download it from the website. Ss match Wh-questions with answers.

7 LISTENING

Learning Objective: listen for specific information about peoples' lives discussed using Wh-questions with *did*, *was*, and *were*

A *[CD 3, Track 43]*

- Focus Ss' attention on the sentences and explain the task. Play the audio program. Ss listen and write the year of birth. Then play the audio program again. Ss listen and check their answers.

Audio script

1. **Melissa**
My name is Melissa, and I was born in 1984 in Canada, but I didn't grow up there. My family moved to the United States in 1986, so I really grew up here in America. I went to school and college here, and I became a tour guide in 2004. I give tours to Canada.
2. **Colin**
I'm Colin. I grew up in the U.K., and I still live here now, but I wasn't born here. I was born in South Africa in 2000. My parents moved to the U.K. in 2002, so I went with them, of course. I'm a student, and I'm going to be a doctor someday.
3. **Kumiko**
My name is Kumiko and I live here in Japan, but I wasn't born here. I was born in Hawaii, in 1965. My parents, two sisters, and I moved to Japan in 1967, and I grew up here. I'm a reporter for a local Japanese-language TV station.
4. **Omar**
I'm Omar. I'm an architect. I was born in 1974, in Egypt. I grew up in Egypt – I went to school and college there, and I became an architect in Egypt. I moved here to France last year. I really like it here, but I'm planning to return to Egypt next year. I want to start my own business there.

- To check answers as a class, ask different Ss to read out the sentences. (Answers: 1. 1984, 2. 2000, 3. 1965, 4. 1974)

B *[CD 3, Track 44]*

- Play the audio program again. Ss listen and write the place (country) where the people grew up in the sentences. Then play the audio program again. Ss listen and check their answers.
- To check answers as a class, ask different Ss to read out the sentences. (Answers: 1. the United States/ America, 2. the U.K., 3. Japan, 4. Egypt)

6 GRAMMAR FOCUS

Wh-questions with *did, was,* and *were*

Where **did** you **grow up**?	I **grew up** in New York.
What **did** your father **do** there?	He **worked** in a department store.
When **did** you **come** to Los Angeles?	I **came** to Los Angeles in 2008.
Why **did** you **become** a hairstylist?	Because I **needed** the money.
Where **were** you **born**?	I **was born** in Brooklyn.
When **were** you **born**?	I **was born** in 1990.
How old **were** you in 2008?	I **was** eighteen.
What **was** your major in college?	Photography. I **was** a photographer for five years.

GRAMMAR PLUS *see page 146*

A Match the questions with the answers. Then compare with a partner.

1. Where were you born? _e_
2. Where did you grow up? ____
3. How was your first day of school? ____
4. Who was your best friend in school? ____
5. What was he like? ____
6. Why did you take this class? ____

a. His name was Akio.
b. He was really friendly.
c. I wanted to improve my English.
d. I grew up in Tokyo.
e. In Kyoto, Japan.
f. It was a little scary.

B PAIR WORK Ask and answer the questions in part A. Use your own information and make the necessary changes.

C GROUP WORK Ask the questions. Use a year in your answers.

1. When were you born?
2. When was your father born?
3. When was your mother born?
4. When did you turn 13?
5. When did you start high school?
6. When did you begin to study English?

saying years

1900 = nineteen hundred
1906 = nineteen oh six
1995 = nineteen ninety-five
2000 = two thousand
2007 = two thousand (and) seven
2015 = two thousand (and) fifteen
OR twenty-fifteen

7 LISTENING I wasn't born here.

A Listen. What year were these people born? Complete the sentences.

1. Melissa was born in ____________.
2. Colin was born in ____________.
3. Kumiko was born in ____________.
4. Omar was born in ____________.

B Listen again. Where did these people grow up? Complete the sentences.

1. Melissa grew up in ____________.
2. Colin grew up in ____________.
3. Kumiko grew up in ____________.
4. Omar grew up in ____________.

8 WORD POWER School days

A Complete the word map with words from the list. Then listen and check.

✓ auditorium
cafeteria
college
computer lab
elementary school
geography
high school
history
library
middle school
physical education
science

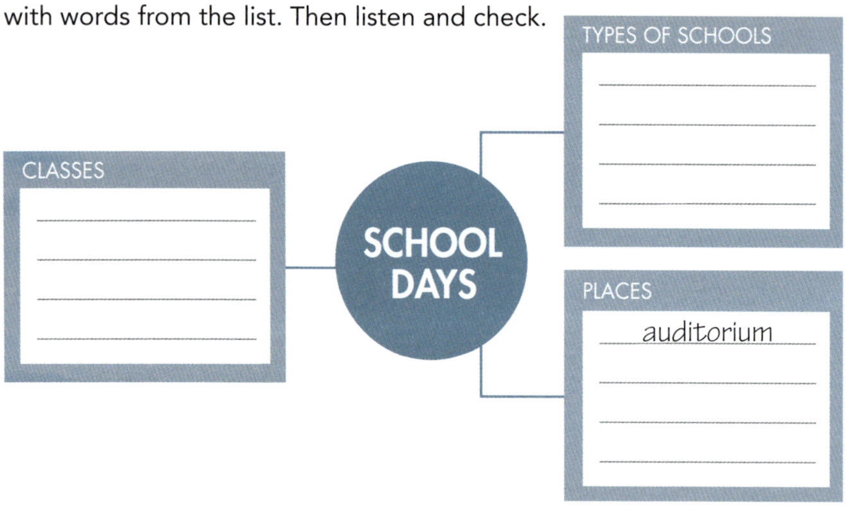

B **PAIR WORK** Find out about your partner's elementary, middle, or high school days. Ask these questions. Then tell the class.

What classes did you take?	Who was your favorite teacher? Why?
What was your favorite class? Why?	Where did you spend your free time? Why?
What classes didn't you like? Why not?	What was a typical day of school like?
Who was your best friend?	What didn't you like about school?

"In high school, Julian's favorite class was physical education because he liked to play sports . . ."

9 SPEAKING Can you remember . . . ?

A **GROUP WORK** How often do you have English class? What do you remember from your last class? Ask and answer these questions.

1. Who was in class? Who wasn't there?
2. Who was late that day?
3. Who was very tired?
4. What color were your teacher's shoes?
5. What were your teacher's first words?
6. Did all the students bring their books?
7. What did you learn?
8. What did you do after class?

B **CLASS ACTIVITY** What does your group remember? Tell the class.

10 INTERCHANGE 15 This is your life.

Did you and your partner do similar things when you were children? Go to Interchange 15 on page 130.

8 WORD POWER

Learning Objective: discuss school memories

A ***[CD 3, Track 45]***

- Explain the task and focus Ss' attention on the word map. Read the categories and the words in the list.
- Ss complete the word map individually. Then they compare their answers in small groups.
- Play the audio program. Ss listen and check their answers.

Answers

Classes	Types of Schools	Places
geography	college	auditorium
history	elementary school	cafeteria
P.E.	high school	computer lab
science	middle school	library

- ***Option:*** Play the audio program. Ss listen and repeat.
- Elicit or explain any new vocabulary.

Vocabulary

auditorium: a large room where people sit to watch a performance
cafeteria: a large room in a school or office where people eat
elementary school: school for children from about 5 to 11 years old
geography: the study of countries of the world and the earth's surface
high school: school for teenagers from about 14 to 18 years old
history: the study of important past events
middle school: school between elementary school and high school for young teenagers from about 11 to 14 years old
physical education: exercise and sports classes in school
science: the study of biology, chemistry, physics, etc.

- ***Option:*** Ss work in small groups. They add other words to the categories. Elicit new words from each group and write them on the board.
- ***Option:*** Because the names and grades of schools differ from place to place, you may want to discuss variations with the class. For example, other names for *elementary school* include *primary school*, *grade school*, and *grammar school*. In addition, some places don't have separate middle schools or junior high schools.

B ***Pair work***

- Explain the first part of the task and focus Ss' attention on the questions. Ask different Ss to read the questions aloud. Point out that Ss should take notes on their partner's answers.
- Ss complete the task in pairs. They take turns asking and answering the questions. Go around the class and give help as needed.
- Explain the second part of the task and ask a S to read the example sentence.
- Ss tell the class about their partner's school days.
- ***Option:*** For large classes, Ss share information in groups.

For more practice with words about school, play ***Vocabulary Tennis*** – download it from the website. Call out different categories, such as *subjects*, *schools*, and *places*.

9 SPEAKING

Learning Objective: discuss and compare memories with others

A ***Group work***

- Explain the task and read out the questions. Elicit or explain any new vocabulary. Point out that one S in each group should take notes.
- Ss complete the activity in small groups.
- ***Option:*** Each group votes for the S with the best memory.

B ***Class activity***

- Explain the task. Then one S in each group shares their information with the class.

10 INTERCHANGE 15

See page T-130 for teaching notes.

11 READING

Learning Objectives: scan and read for specific information; sequence events in an article about events in someone's life

A *[CD 3, Track 46]*

- Focus Ss' attention on the map. Explain that Sri Lanka is a country near India. Have Ss look at the map and identify the largest city in Sri Lanka. (Answer: Colombo).
- Read out the task. Ask Ss to raise their hands when they find what a "third culture kid" is.

TIP
To help Ss develop their scanning skills, focus their attention on the purpose of the task. For example, say: "We're looking for the meaning of *third culture kid*, so scan the article for sentences that explain this phrase."

- Ss complete the first part of the task individually. Elicit the answer. (Answer: A third culture kid is a person who grew up in a different country from his or her parents. Third culture kids know and understand more than one culture.)
- Ss discuss the second part of the task as a group. Ask Ss to talk about any third culture kids they know.

B

- Ss read the article individually and underline any new words.
- Ss discuss the meanings of any new words in pairs or small groups. Then elicit or explain any remaining new vocabulary.

Vocabulary
culture: the habits, traditions, and beliefs of a group of people
communicate: to share or exchange information with someone else
raise: to take care of a child until he or she becomes an adult
charity: an organization that gives money, food, or help to people who need it
way of life: the typical habits and behavior of a person or a culture

- Explain the second part of the task. Explain that Ss choose *True* (correct) or *False* (incorrect) sentences. Then elicit the first answer from the class.
- Ss complete the task individually. Then they compare their answers in small groups.
- Ask different Ss to state the answers. With the class, restate the false statements to make them true.

Answers

1. False
2. True
3. True
4. False
5. False
6. True

C

- Explain the task. Ask a different S to read each event.
- Ss complete the task individually. Then they compare their answers in pairs.
- To check answers, ask: "What was the first event? the second event?" Continue until Ss read out the eighth event.

Answers

a. 5	c. 4	e. 6	g. 3
b. 7	d. 2	f. 1	h. 8

D *Group work*

- Explain the task and read the questions aloud. Point out that one S in each group should take notes.
- Ss complete the activity in small groups.
- Have groups share their answers with the class. Do most Ss think living in another culture is a good thing? Who gave the best reasons for their answer?

End of Cycle 2

See the Supplementary Resources chart at the beginning of this unit for additional teaching materials and student activities related to this Cycle.

11 READING

A Scan the article. What is a "third culture kid?" Do you know anyone who moved to another country?

THE STORY OF A THIRD CULTURE KID

Tommy was born in Colombo, the largest city in the island country of Sri Lanka. The streets of Colombo were busy, and Tommy loved the colors, sights, and smells. He played on sandy beaches with his friends. He spoke Sinhalese with his friends and family and learned English at school. He loved visiting the neighborhood markets with his family to buy fresh fruits and vegetables. Typical Sri Lankan dishes made with coconuts and rice were some of his favorite foods.

When he was six, Tommy moved with his parents to a small town near New York City. His parents both had new jobs there. For Tommy, life in his new town was a big surprise. Everything was different! The streets were quieter and less colorful. The grocery stores sold so many different types of fruits, vegetables, cheeses, and cereals. There were so many restaurants in his new town – he tried Italian food, Chinese food, Greek food, and Mexican food. The weather was different, too. Tommy saw snow for the very first time!

Looking back, Tommy remembers learning that the culture in the United States was different from the culture in Sri Lanka. Not better, not worse, just different. Tommy learned new things every day. He learned Spanish in school. He also learned ways that people in the U.S. communicate with each other. Tommy remembers everyone saying "How are you doing?" but it wasn't a question. It was like saying "Hi!"

Tommy was a "third culture kid." That means he was raised in a different country than his parents. Many third culture kids believe that they are lucky. They know and understand more than one culture, and they often speak more than one language. Tommy went to college in Los Angeles and studied languages. Now he works for a big charity that helps children around the world get a good education.

Sometimes it's hard to learn a whole new way of life, but Tommy says it's the best thing that ever happened. He calls Sri Lanka "home" and the U.S. "home," too!

B Read the article. Check (✓) True or False.

	True	False
1. Tommy lived in Sri Lanka most of his life.	☐	☐
2. He was born in Sri Lanka.	☐	☐
3. Tommy liked traditional Sri Lankan food.	☐	☐
4. He didn't learn any new languages in the U.S.	☐	☐
5. In the U.S., Tommy ate mostly at Sri Lankan restaurants.	☐	☐
6. Tommy is happy to be a third culture kid.	☐	☐

C Number these events in Tommy's life from 1 (first) to 8 (last).

_____ **a.** Tommy saw snow for the first time.
_____ **b.** Tommy went to college.
_____ **c.** Tommy moved to the U.S.
_____ **d.** As a small boy, Tommy played on the beach.
_____ **e.** He learned a new language in the U.S.
__1__ **f.** Tommy was born on an island.
_____ **g.** In Sri Lanka, Tommy studied English in school.
_____ **h.** He works for a charity in the U.S.

D GROUP WORK Tommy thinks living in another culture is a good thing. Why do you think he says that? Do you agree? Tell your classmates.

Unit 16 Supplementary Resources Overview

	After the following SB exercises	You can use these materials in class	Your students can use these materials outside the classroom
CYCLE 1	1 **Conversation**		**SS** Unit 16 Speaking 1
	2 **Word Power**	**TSS** Unit 16 Vocabulary Worksheet **TSS** Unit 16 Extra Worksheet	**SS** Unit 16 Vocabulary 1 **GAME** Sentence Stacker (Prepositional phrases)
	3 **Listening**		
	4 **Grammar Focus**		**SB** Unit 16 Grammar plus, Focus 1 **SS** Unit 16 Grammar 1 **GAME** Speak or Swim (Subject and object pronouns) **WB** Unit 16 exercises 1–5
CYCLE 2	5 **Snapshot**		**SS** Unit 16 Vocabulary 2
	6 **Conversation**		**SS** Unit 16 Speaking 2
	7 **Pronunciation**		
	8 **Grammar Focus**	**TSS** Unit 16 Listening Worksheet	**SB** Unit 16 Grammar plus, Focus 2 **SS** Unit 16 Grammar 2 **GAME** Word Keys (Invitations; verb + *to*) **GAME** Speak or Swim (Verb + *to*)
	9 **Speaking**	**TSS** Unit 16 Grammar Worksheet	
	10 **Listening**		
	11 **Interchange 16**		
	12 **Reading**	**TSS** Unit 16 Project Worksheet **VID** Unit 16 **VRB** Unit 16	**SS** Unit 16 Reading 1–2 **SS** Unit 16 Listening 1–3 **SS** Unit 16 Video 1–3 **WB** Unit 16 exercises 6–9

With or instead of the following SB section	You can also use these materials for assessment
Units 15–16 Progress Check	**ASSESSMENT PROGRAM** Units 15–16 Oral Quiz **ASSESSMENT PROGRAM** Units 15–16 Written Quiz **ASSESSMENT PROGRAM** Units 9–16 Test

Key **GAME:** Online Game **SB:** Student's Book **SS:** Online Self-study **TSS:** Teacher Support Site
VID: Video DVD **VRB:** Video Resource Book **WB:** Online Workbook/Workbook

My Plan for Unit 16

Use the space below to customize a plan that fits your needs.

With the following SB exercises	I am using these materials in class	My students are using these materials outside the classroom

With or instead of the following SB section	I am using these materials for assessment

16 Can I take a message?

- Make phone calls and leave messages
- Make, accept, and decline invitations

1 CONVERSATION Please ask her to call me.

Listen and practice.

Receptionist: Good morning – Creative Tours.
Nathan: Hello. Can I speak to Julie Wilson, please?
Receptionist: I'm sorry, but she's in a meeting right now.
Nathan: Oh, OK.
Receptionist: Can I take a message?
Nathan: Yes, thanks. This is her friend Nathan. Please ask her to call me tonight.
Receptionist: Does she have your number?
Nathan: Yes, she does.
Receptionist: OK. I'll give her your message.
Nathan: Thank you so much.

2 WORD POWER Prepositional phrases

A Listen and practice.

at home	**at** the mall	**in** bed	**in** the shower	**on** vacation
at work	**at** the library	**in** class	**in** the hospital	**on** a trip
at school	**at** the beach	**in** Mexico	**in** a meeting	**on** his/her break

at work

on vacation

in a meeting

B PAIR WORK Make a list of five friends and family members. Give it to your partner. Where are these people right now? Ask and answer questions.

A: Where's your brother right now?
B: He's on vacation. He's in India.

16 Can I take a message?

Cycle 1, Exercises 1–4

In Unit 16, students make phone calls and leave messages, and make, accept, and decline invitations. By the end of Cycle 1, students will be able to make phone calls and leave messages using subject and object pronouns. By the end of Cycle 2, students will be able to make, accept, and decline invitations using *Do you want to . . . ?*, *Would you like to . . . ?*, and verb + *to*.

1 CONVERSATION

Learning Objective: use subject and object pronouns in a conversation about phone messages

[CD 3, Track 47]

- Set the scene. Nathan is calling a friend at work. Write these focus questions on the board:
  1. *Who is Nathan calling?*
  2. *Where is Julie?*
  3. *Does Julie have Nathan's phone number?*
- Play the audio program. Ss read and listen for the answers. Elicit the answers. (Answers: 1. his friend Julie Wilson 2. in a meeting 3. yes)
- Elicit or explain any new vocabulary. Use pictures where appropriate.

Vocabulary
meeting: a group of people that get together for a specific reason
message: information from one person to another
take a message: write a message

- Play the audio program again. Ss listen and repeat.
- Ss take turns practicing the conversation in pairs.
- ***Option:*** Ask one or two pairs to role-play the conversation for the class.

! For a new way to practice this Conversation, try ***Disappearing Dialog*** – download it from the website.

2 WORD POWER

Learning Objective: describe locations using the prepositional phrases with *at*, *in*, and *on*

A *[CD 3, Track 48]*

- Books open. Focus Ss' attention on the phrases in the box. Play the audio program. Ss listen and read silently.
- Elicit or explain any new vocabulary.

Vocabulary
break: a short pause from work

- ***Option:*** Explain when to use these prepositions:
  1. Use *at* with *home*, *work*, and *school*.
  2. Use *at the* with places in cities or towns (e.g., *mall*, *library*, *beach*).
  3. Use *in* with *bed*, *class*, and the names of countries, cities, or towns (e.g., *Mexico*, *Toronto*).
  4. Use *in the* with *hospital* and places in houses or apartments (e.g., *shower*, *yard*).
  5. Use *on* with *vacation*, *a trip*, and *his/her break*.
- Play the audio program again. Ss listen and repeat.

B *Pair work*

- Explain the first part of the task. Elicit some names of Ss' friends or family members and write them on the board.
- Ss make lists of people they know individually.
- Explain the second part of the task and ask two Ss to model the example conversation.
- Ss exchange lists in pairs. Then they ask and answer *Where* questions about the people on the lists.

For more practice with prepositional phrases, play ***Run For It!*** – download it from the website.

3 LISTENING

Learning Objective: listen for specific information about locations discussed using prepositions of place

A *[CD 3, Track 49]*

- Explain the task. Point out that Ss should check the reason he missed each of the three calls. Then play the audio program once or twice, pausing after each conversation. Ss listen and complete the task.

Audio script

1.
Hannah Hello?
Nathan Hi, Hannah. It's Nathan.
Hannah Oh, hi, Nathan. Thanks for calling me back.
Nathan Sure. Sorry I missed your call.
Hannah Were you out shopping?
Nathan No. I was in the shower.
Hannah Well, I called you because I'm having a party on Saturday. It starts at about 8:00. Can you come?
Nathan Sure.

2.
Andrea Hello?
Nathan Hello, Andrea? It's Nathan.
Andrea Hey, Nathan.
Nathan Sorry I missed your call.
Andrea That's OK. You were busy studying, right?
Nathan No. I was at the mall. I didn't hear my phone.
Andrea That's OK. Listen. Can I see your notes from history class yesterday? I was sick, so I missed class.
Nathan No problem.

3.
Alexis Hello?
Nathan Alexis?
Alexis Yes. Is this Nathan?
Nathan Yes. I'm returning your call. Sorry I missed you. I was in class.
Alexis Really? Are you sure you weren't sleeping?
Nathan No, no. I wasn't sleeping.
Alexis I know. Hey, can you work on Saturday night? I know you usually work on Sunday, but Sam can't come in on Saturday, and the coffee shop gets so busy then.
Nathan I'm so sorry, Alexis, but I have plans on Saturday. Maybe Elizabeth can do it?

- Ss compare their answers in pairs. Then elicit the answers from the class. (Answers: 1. He was in the shower. 2. He was at the mall. 3. He was in class.)

B *[CD 3, Track 50]*

- Explain the task. Replay the audio. Ss complete the task. Elicit the answers. (Answers: 1. Hannah called Nathan because she is having a party. 2. Andrea called Nathan because she needs to see Nathan's notes. 3. Alexis called Nathan because Sam can't come in to work on Saturday.)

4 GRAMMAR FOCUS

Learning Objective: use subject and object pronouns in a short phone conversation

[CD 3, Track 51]

- Focus Ss' attention on the Grammar Focus box. Play the audio program. Ss listen and read silently.

A

- Ss complete the conversations individually. Elicit the answers. Then Ss practice the conversations in pairs.

Answers

1. A: Can **I** speak with Ms. Murphy, please?
   B: **She**'s not here. But maybe **I** can help you.
   A: Please give **her** my new cell number. It's 555-2981.
2. A: Hi, this is Colin Shaw. Is Mr. Kerr there?
   B: **I**'m sorry, but **he**'s not here right now. Do you want to leave a message?
   A: Yes. Please tell **him** to call me at work.
3. A: Hello, this is Carol's Café. Are Lauren and Matt in?
   B: No, **they**'re not. I'm their son. Can I help **you**?
   A: **I** found their keys. **They** left **them** on the table.
   B: Just bring **me** the keys. I can give **them** to my parents.
   A: I'm sorry, but **I** can't. Can your mom or dad call **me**?
   B: OK.

B *Pair work*

- Explain the task. Direct Ss' attention to number 1 in part A for reference. Ss role-play the conversation in pairs. Elicit or explain the meaning of *assistant* (someone who helps another person do work).
- ***Option:*** Model the role play with a S for the class. Then invite pairs to role-play their conversations.

C *Pair work*

- Explain the task. Ss practice the conversation in pairs.

End of Cycle 1

See the Supplementary Resources chart at the beginning of this unit for additional teaching materials and student activities related to this Cycle.

3 LISTENING Sorry I missed your call.

A Listen to Nathan return three phone calls. Why did he miss each call? Check (✓) the correct answers.

1. He was . . .	☐ shopping.	☐ in the shower.	☐ at a party.
2. He was . . .	☐ studying.	☐ at the mall.	☐ sick.
3. He was . . .	☐ in class.	☐ sleeping.	☐ at work.

B Listen again. Why did they call Nathan? Correct the sentences.

1. Hannah called Nathan because he is having a party.
2. Andrea called Nathan because she needs to see Nathan's textbook.
3. Alexis called Nathan because Sam can come in to work on Saturday.

4 GRAMMAR FOCUS

Subject and object pronouns

Subjects		Objects	
I		**me**	
You		**you**	
He		**him**	
She got Nathan's message.	Nathan left	**her**	a message.
We		**us**	
They		**them**	

GRAMMAR PLUS *see page 147*

A Complete the phone conversations with the correct pronouns. Then practice with a partner.

1. **A:** Can ___I___ speak with Ms. Murphy, please?
   B: ________'s not here. But maybe ________ can help you.
   A: Please give ________ my new cell number. It's 555-2981.
2. **A:** Hi, this is Colin Shaw. Is Mr. Kerr there?
   B: ________'m sorry, but ________'s not here right now. Do you want to leave a message?
   A: Yes. Please tell ________ to call me at work.
3. **A:** Hello, this is Carol's Café. Are Lauren and Matt in?
   B: No, ________'re not. I'm their son. Can I help ________?
   A: ________ found their keys. ________ left ________ on the table.
   B: Just bring ________ the keys. I can give ________ to my parents.
   A: I'm sorry, but ________ can't. Can your mom or dad call ________?
   B: OK.

B PAIR WORK Role-play this phone conversation.

Student A: "Call" your business partner Robert White's office. You want a meeting on Monday at 4:00 P.M.

Student B: You are Robert White's assistant. Answer the phone. Mr. White is not in. Take a message.

C PAIR WORK Change roles. This time you want a meeting on Tuesday at 2:00 P.M.

5 SNAPSHOT

Listen and practice.

Popular Activities in the U.S.

Check (✓) the activities that are popular in your country.
What other activities are popular in your country?
What are your favorite activities? Are there any activities you don't like? Why?

6 CONVERSATION Do you want to see a movie?

Listen and practice.

NATHAN Hello?

JULIE Hi, Nathan. I got your message.

NATHAN Hi. Thanks for calling me back. Sorry I called you at work.

JULIE Oh, that's OK. I was in a meeting, so I turned my cell phone off. What's up?

NATHAN Well, do you want to see a movie with me tonight?

JULIE Tonight? I'm sorry, but I can't. I have to work late tonight.

NATHAN Oh, that's too bad. How about tomorrow night?

JULIE Sure, I'd love to. What time do you want to meet?

NATHAN How about around seven o'clock at the Astoria on Pratt Avenue?

JULIE Terrific! Text me when you leave your office, OK?

5 SNAPSHOT

Learning Objective: talk about free-time activities

[CD 3, Track 52]

- Books closed. Ask the class: "What activities do you do in your free time?" Elicit Ss' answers and write them on the board. Then ask: "What activities are popular in the U.S.?" Encourage Ss to make guesses.
- Books open. Ss look at the Snapshot and discuss whether any of their guesses are pictured.

TIP
To generate interest in a topic, tell Ss to close their books and share what they already know about the topic. Then have them open their books and check the answers.

- Play the audio program. Ss listen and read silently. Then play the audio program again. Ss listen and repeat.
- Elicit or explain the meaning of any new vocabulary.

Vocabulary
popular: liked or enjoyed by many people
concert: a music performance
amusement park: a fun park with rides, games, and other entertainment
street fair: a neighborhood festival held on the street, usually with food, art, and things to buy
play: a live theatrical performance
musical: a play with songs and music

- Read out the task and questions. Ss check (✓) the activities individually.
- Ss discuss the questions in small groups. If possible, put Ss from different countries in each group.
- Elicit answers from each group.

! For a different way to practice this Snapshot, try ***Vocabulary Steps*** – download it from the website. Ss rank the activities using criteria such as most popular, most fun, most expensive, and most dangerous.

6 CONVERSATION

Learning Objectives: make, accept, and decline invitations in a conversation about making plans; use verb + *to* to make plans

[CD 3, Track 53]

- Books closed. Set the scene. Julie is calling Nathan. Remind Ss that Nathan left a message for Julie in Exercise 1.
- Write these focus questions on the board:
  1. *What does Nathan invite Julie to do?*
  2. *What is Julie going to do tonight?*
  3. *Does Julie accept Nathan's invitation?*
- Play the audio program. Ss listen for the answers. Elicit the answers. (Answers: 1. He invites her to see a movie. 2. She's going to work late. 3. Yes, she does.)
- Books open. Focus Ss' attention on the picture and conversation. Ss read the conversation silently.
- Elicit or explain any new vocabulary.

Vocabulary
What's up?: What's new?

- Play the audio program. Ss listen and read silently.
- Play the audio program again. Ss listen and repeat.
- Ss practice the conversation in pairs.

TIP
To encourage Ss to listen to each other when they work in pairs, tell them to practice conversations from a distance. They can also sit back-to-back.

- ***Option:*** Ask one or two pairs to role-play the conversation for the class.

! For a new way to practice this Conversation, try ***Say It With Feeling!*** – download it from the website.

7 PRONUNCIATION

Learning Objective: sound more natural by using reductions of *want to* and *have to*

A *[CD 3, Track 54]*

- Focus Ss' attention on the picture and set the scene. Speaker A is inviting Speaker B to dinner.
- Play the audio program. Ss listen and read silently.
- Play the audio program again. Ss listen and repeat.
- Elicit other things people invite each other to do and write them on the board. If needed, refer Ss to Exercise 5 on page 108.
- Ss practice the short conversation in pairs. Encourage them to substitute other activities. Go around the class and listen to Ss' pronunciation of *want to* and *have to*.

TIP
To help Ss use reductions in a fun way, ask them to practice conversations faster and faster. This reduces anxiety and makes pronunciation sound more natural.

B *Pair work*

- Focus Ss' attention on the Conversation on page 108. Play the audio program for Exercise 6. Ss pay attention to the pronunciation of *want to* and *have to*.
- Ss practice the conversation in pairs. Go around the class and help with pronunciation as needed.

8 GRAMMAR FOCUS

Learning Objectives: make, accept, and decline invitations using verb + *to*

[CD 3, Track 55]

- Focus Ss' attention on the Grammar Focus box. Elicit or explain that we use *Do you want to . . . ?* and *Would you like to . . . ?* to make invitations. Point out that *Would you like to . . . ?* is more formal than *Do you want to . . . ?*
- Ask: "What phrases have the pattern verb + *to*?" Elicit the answer. (Possible answers: *want to, have to, need to, would like to, would love to*) Point out that *I'd* is the contraction for *I would*. Also, point out that another verb usually follows the verb + *to* pattern (e.g., *I need to work.*).
- Play the audio program. Ss listen and read silently.

A

- Explain the first part of the task and model the example invitation.
- ***Option:*** For lower-level classes, point out that all the answers are either *want to* or *like to*.
- Ss complete the invitations individually. Then they compare answers in pairs.
- Ask different Ss to read out the invitations. Encourage Ss to use reductions when they read the questions with *want to*.

Answers

1. Would you **like to** go to an art festival this weekend?
2. Do you **want to** go to a volleyball game tomorrow night?
3. Would you **like to** see a comedy tonight?
4. Do you **want to** go swimming on Saturday?
5. Do you **want to** play soccer after school today?
6. Would you **like to** go to a hip-hop concert on Saturday night?

- Explain the second part of the task. Ask a S to model the example invitation and a different S to read the response.
- Ss match the invitations with the responses in pairs.
- To check answers, ask different pairs to read each invitation and response.

Answers

1. d. I'd like to, but I can't. I'm going to go on a trip this weekend.
2. c. I don't really like volleyball. Do you want to do something else?
3. f. Tonight? I can't. I need to help my parents.
4. a. I'd like to, but I don't have a swimsuit!
5. b. I'm sorry, but I have to talk to the teacher after school.
6. e. Yes, I'd love to. It's my favorite type of music.

- Ss practice the conversations in pairs. Go around the class and check Ss' pronunciation and intonation.

B *Pair work*

- Write these time expressions on the board:

  tomorrow night   *after school today*
  tonight   *this weekend*
  on Saturday   *on Sunday afternoon*

  Tell Ss to copy the time expressions and write their plans next to each one.
- Explain the task and ask two Ss to model the example conversation.
- Ss complete the task in pairs. Go around the class and encourage Ss to use their own information.

7 PRONUNCIATION Reduction of *want to* and *have to*

A Listen and practice. Notice the reduction of **want to** and **have to**.

/wanə/
A: Do you **want to** go to dinner with me tonight?

/hæftə/
B: I'm sorry, but I can't. I **have to** study for a test.

B PAIR WORK Practice the conversation in Exercise 6 again. Try to reduce **want to** and **have to**.

8 GRAMMAR FOCUS

Invitations; verb + *to*

Do you want to see a play with me tonight?	**Would you like to go** to an amusement park?
Sure. **I'd** really **like to** see a good play.	Yes, **I'd love to** (go to an amusement park)!
I'd like to (see a play), but I **have to** work late.	**I'd like to** (go), but I **need to** study.
I'd = I would	

GRAMMAR PLUS *see page 147*

A Complete the invitations. Then match them with the responses.

Invitations

1. Would you ___like to___ go to an art festival this weekend? ___d___
2. Do you ____________ go to a volleyball game tomorrow night? _____
3. Would you ____________ see a comedy tonight? _____
4. Do you ____________ go swimming on Saturday? _____
5. Do you ____________ play soccer after school today? _____
6. Would you ____________ go to a hip-hop concert on Saturday night? _____

Responses

a. I'd like to, but I don't have a swimsuit!
b. I'm sorry, but I have to talk to the teacher after school.
c. I don't really like volleyball. Do you want to do something else?
d. I'd like to, but I can't. I'm going to go on a trip this weekend.
e. Yes, I'd love to. It's my favorite type of music.
f. Tonight? I can't. I need to help my parents.

B PAIR WORK Practice the invitations from part A. Respond with your own information.

A: Would you like to go to an art festival this weekend?
B: I'd like to, but I can't. I have to . . .

9 SPEAKING What is your excuse?

A Do you ever use these excuses? Check (✓) Often, Sometimes, or Never. Add your own excuse, and then compare with a partner.

	Often	Sometimes	Never
I have to work late.	☐	☐	☐
I have a headache.	☐	☐	☐
I have to babysit.	☐	☐	☐
I have a class.	☐	☐	☐
I need to do the laundry.	☐	☐	☐
I need to go to bed early.	☐	☐	☐
I need to study for a test.	☐	☐	☐
I want to visit my family.	☐	☐	☐
I'm not feeling well.	☐	☐	☐
I already have plans.	☐	☐	☐
______________	☐	☐	☐

B Write down three things you want to do this weekend.

I want to go to the street fair on Saturday.

C CLASS ACTIVITY Go around the class and invite your classmates to do the things from part B. Your classmates respond with excuses.

A: Would you like to go to a concert tonight?

B: I'm sorry, but I can't. I have to work late tonight.

10 LISTENING I'll see you then!

A These four people need to change their plans. Listen to their phone calls. Who will be late? Who can't come? Check (✓) the correct answers.

	Will be late	Can't come
1. Jason	☐	☐
2. Jessica	☐	☐
3. Christian	☐	☐
4. Danielle	☐	☐

B Listen again. Which two people can't come? Write their first names and their excuses.

First name	Excuse
______________	______________________________
______________	______________________________

11 INTERCHANGE 16 The perfect weekend

Make plans with your classmates. Go to Interchange 16 on page 131.

9 SPEAKING

Learning Objective: make invitations and give excuses with *have to*, *need to*, and *want to*

A

- Focus Ss' attention on the title. Elicit or explain that an *excuse* is a reason for not doing something. Point out that an excuse can be the truth or a lie.
- Explain the task and ask different Ss to read out the excuses. Elicit or explain any new vocabulary. (e.g., *babysit, already*).
- Ss check (✓) *Often*, *Sometimes*, or *Never* individually. Then they compare answers in pairs.
- ***Option:*** Elicit other excuses and write them on the board.

B

- Explain the task and model the example sentence. Then Ss write three sentences individually. Go around the class and help as needed.

C *Class activity*

- Explain the task. Then ask two Ss to model the example conversation. Student B completes the response with an excuse (e.g., *I have to babysit.*).
- Ask two Ss to model the conversation using a different invitation and excuse. For example:

  S1: Do you want to go to a musical on Friday night?

  S2: I'm sorry, but I can't. I have to study.
- Ss go around the class, making invitations and responding with excuses.

10 LISTENING

Learning Objective: listen for main ideas and details as people change plans

A *[CD 3, Track 56]*

- Set the scene and explain the task. Then play the audio program. Ss listen and check (✓) *Will be late* or *Can't come*. Then play the audio program again. Ss listen and check their answers.

Audio script

1.
Woman Hello. Doctor Roy's office.
Jason Hello. This is Jason Miller. I'm sorry, but I can't come at 11:00 today.
Woman I see. Well, how about 3:00?
Jason No, sorry, I can't come in today. I have to work. Is 11:00 tomorrow OK?
Woman Let me see. . . . Yes. That's fine. See you tomorrow.

2.
Man Hello. Zachary Kendall's office.
Jessica Hi. This is Jessica Pascal. I have a meeting with Mr. Kendall at 10:00, but I'm not going to be on time. My bus was late this morning.
Man OK. What time can you be here?
Jessica At 10:30.
Man OK. I'll tell him. Thanks for calling.

3.
Woman Hello. Easton Art Museum.
Christian Hi. My name's Christian Everly. I bought a ticket to the art festival on Saturday, but I can't come. My parents are visiting from out of town. Can I get my money back?
Woman I'm sorry; we can't do that. But I can sell you two more tickets for your parents.
Christian No, I don't think so. They don't really like festivals.

4.
Grandpa Hello?
Danielle Hi, Grandpa!
Grandpa Hi, Danielle! Are you coming to help me with my computer tonight?
Danielle Well . . . I'm calling about that. I can't come tonight because I need to study for a test.
Grandpa OK. I understand. School comes first. You can help me another time.
Danielle Thanks for being so nice, Grandpa.

- Ss compare their answers in pairs. Then go over the answers with the class. (Answers: 1. Jason can't come. 2. Jessica will be late. 3. Christian can't come. 4. Danielle can't come.)

B *[CD 3, Track 57]*

- Play the audio program again. Ss listen and write the names of the people who can't come and their excuses. Play the audio program again if needed.
- Elicit the answers from the class.

Answers

First name	Excuse
Jason	He has to work.
Christian	His parents are visiting.
Danielle	She needs to study for a test.

TIP
To help Ss focus on a complex listening task, have them listen two or three times. Each time they should listen for a different thing.

11 INTERCHANGE 16

See page T-131 for teaching notes.

12 READING

Learning Objective: skim and scan a text for information about special events

A *[CD 3, Track 58]*

- Focus Ss' attention on the guide. Point out that the article is intended to interest readers in a festival in Austin, Texas.
- Explain the task. Ss skim the guide and complete the task individually. Then they compare their answers in small groups. (Answer: Austin City Limits is a music festival.)

B

- Explain the first part of the task. Ss read the guide individually and underline any new words.
- Ss discuss the meanings of any new words in small groups. Elicit or explain any remaining new vocabulary.

Vocabulary

stage: a platform that people perform on
autograph: a famous person's signature
food court: an area where different types of food are sold
art market: an area where different arts and crafts are sold

- Explain the second part of the task.
- Point out that Ss can find the answers quickly by scanning the guide for the key words in each statement.
- Ss complete the task individually. Then they compare the answers in small groups.
- Elicit answers from the class. Ask different Ss to read the statements and say *true* or *false*. For false statements, elicit a correction from the class.

Answers

1. False (195,000 people)
2. True
3. False (You can buy clothes.)
4. False (ACL Eats is the name of the food court.)
5. True

C *Group work*

- Explain the task. Ss their favorite kinds of events, and any special events where they live, in small groups.
- Ask groups to share information about their favorite events with the class.

! For a new way to teach this reading, try ***Reading Race*** – download it from the website.

End of Cycle 2

See the Supplementary Resources chart at the beginning of this unit for additional teaching materials and student activities related to this Cycle and for assessment tools.

12 READING

A Look at the guide. What type of festival is Austin City Limits?

AUSTIN CITY LIMITS!

Where to start

Some people call Austin the "Live Music Capital of the World." Every year, it hosts Austin City Limits. About 195,000 people go to this amazing festival. Most years, there are around 130 different bands that play. That's a lot of cool music to listen to!

Where's the music?

Check out the AMD stage and the Austin Ventures stage. These stages are where many musicians perform, but there are eight stages in total, so continue exploring. If you're lucky, you might hear Kendrick Lamar or Florence and the Machine! Sometimes musicians even play on a bridge.

Autograph hunters: this way!

Do you want a famous person's autograph? Look for the autograph booth. Maybe your favorite band member is there. Don't forget to take a poster or a T-shirt for the band to sign.

Snack attack

When you get hungry or thirsty, walk over to ACL Eats. It's a big food court. Local restaurants serve up delicious local food from the state of Texas. You can get salads, tacos, pizza, hot dogs, hamburgers, and drinks there. There's something for everyone.

Where to shop

Do you like to shop? Go straight to the art market – right next to the shopping center. There's a lot there – from cell phone cases to handmade African clothes. You can buy hats, photographs, books, paintings, and . . . guess what? You can even buy a guitar!

B Read the website. Check (✓) True or False.

	True	False
1. About 130,000 people go to enjoy the festival.	☐	☐
2. There are eight stages for musicians.	☐	☐
3. You can buy food at the festival, but you can't buy clothes.	☐	☐
4. ACL Eats is the name of a stage.	☐	☐
5. The art market is near the shopping center.	☐	☐
6. It's possible to get an autograph at the festival.	☐	☐

C **GROUP WORK** What events do you like to go to? Is there a special event in your city or town? Tell your classmates.

Units 15–16 Progress check

SELF-ASSESSMENT

How well can you do these things? Check (✓) the boxes.

I can . . .	Very well	OK	A little
Talk about my past (Ex. 1)	☐	☐	☐
Ask about famous people using simple past yes/no questions (Ex. 2)	☐	☐	☐
Ask and answer questions about someone's past (Ex. 2)	☐	☐	☐
Understand phone calls and leave or pass on messages (Ex. 3)	☐	☐	☐
Ask and answer questions about things I want, need, and have to do (Ex. 4)	☐	☐	☐
Make and respond to invitations (Ex. 5)	☐	☐	☐

1 SPEAKING Interview

A **PAIR WORK** Write three years in the first line of the chart and add your question. Ask your partner four questions about his or her life in these years and complete the chart.

	20 ____	20 ____	20 ____
How old were you in . . .?			
Who was your best friend in . . .?			
What were you like in . . .?			
________ were / was ________ in . . .?			

B **CLASS ACTIVITY** Tell the class about your partner's life.

"In 2001, Leo was two. He . . ."

2 SPEAKING Who were they?

GROUP WORK Think of a famous person from the past. Your classmates ask yes/no questions to guess the person.

Was he/she born in . . . ?
Was he/she a singer? an actor? a politician?
Was he/she tall? heavy? good-looking?

A: I'm thinking of a famous man from the past.
B: Was he born in the U.S.?
A: No, he wasn't.
C: Was he . . . ?

Audrey Hepburn

Nelson Mandela

Paul Walker

Units 15–16

Progress check

SELF-ASSESSMENT

Learning Objectives: reflect on one's learning; identify areas that need improvement

- Ask: "What did you learn in Units 15 and 16?" Elicit Ss' answers.
- Ss complete the Self-assessment. Explain to Ss that this is not a test; it is a way for them to evaluate what they've learned and identify areas where they need additional practice. Encourage them to be honest, and point out they will not get a bad grade if they check (✓) *A little*.
- Ss move on to the Progress check exercises. You can have Ss complete them in class or for homework, using one of these techniques:
  1. Ask Ss to complete all the exercises.
  2. Ask Ss: "What do you need to practice?" Then assign exercises based on their answers.
  3. Ask Ss to choose and complete exercises based on their Self-assessment.

1 SPEAKING

Learning Objective: demonstrate one's ability to discuss one's past

A *Pair work*

- Explain the task and focus Ss' attention on the chart. Point out that Ss should choose three years and add a new question. Then Ss complete the chart with information about their partners.
- To model how to complete the chart, write a year on the board. Then have different Ss ask you each question about that year. Answer the questions with information about your life.
- Working individually, Ss choose three years and write them down. Then they complete the last question with their own idea.
- Ss work in pairs. They take turns asking and answering questions to complete the chart.

B *Class activity*

- Explain the task and ask a S to model the example sentence.
- Elicit information from different Ss in the class.
- ***Option***: For large classes, Ss can tell about just one year. Alternatively, Ss can share information in groups.

2 SPEAKING

Learning Objective: demonstrate one's ability to ask and answer questions about someone from the past

Group work

- Focus Ss' attention on the pictures. Ask: "Who are these people?" (Answers: Audrey Hepburn, Nelson Mandela, Paul Walker) Then ask: "What do you know about them?"
- Explain the first part of the task. Point out that Ss should not choose people who are still alive today.
- Model the example questions. Elicit other possible questions and write them on the board. Then ask three Ss to model the example conversation.
- To model the task, think of a famous person from the past, someone no longer living. The class asks you yes/no questions with *was/were* to guess the person.
- Ss play the game in small groups. The S who guesses the person correctly thinks of the next person.
- ***Option:*** Tell Ss they can ask only ten questions to guess the person.
- ***Option:*** Ss research information about famous people from the past before class.

3 LISTENING

Learning Objective: demonstrate one's ability to understand phone calls and leave or take a messages

[CD 3, Track 59]

- Explain the task. Ss listen to statements and questions from six phone conversations. They choose the best response to each statement or question.
- Ss read the answer choices silently. Then play the audio program once or twice. Ss listen and complete the task.

Audio script

1. Can I give her a message?
2. Can you ask him to call me?
3. Do you have my number?
4. We had a great barbecue on Sunday. Why didn't you come?
5. There's an interesting new movie at Cinema City. Do you want to go tonight?
6. Hi. This is Amanda. Is Benjamin there, please?

- Elicit the answers from the class.

Answers

1. Yes. Please tell her to call me.
2. Sure. Does he have your number?
3. No, I don't.
4. I had a terrible headache.
5. I'd love to, but I can't.
6. I'm sorry. He's not here right now.

4 SPEAKING

Learning Objective: demonstrate one's ability to ask and answer questions about things one wants, needs, and has to do

A *Class activity*

- Explain the task and focus Ss' attention on the chart. Then elicit yes/no questions for each phrase from the class.
- Ask two Ss to model the example conversation. Point out that when Student B answers "Yes, I do," Student A should write Student B's name in the chart.
- Ss go around the class and complete the chart. Encourage Ss to change partners often and to try to write a different name on each line.

B *Pair work*

- Explain the task and write this model conversation on the board:

  A: *Emiko needs to do laundry tomorrow.*
  B: *Vlad needs to do laundry, too.*

  Ss use the model conversation to compare their answers in pairs.
- Elicit answers from the class. Ask: "Who needs to do laundry tomorrow? Who wants to go home early?" Continue with the remaining questions.

5 SPEAKING

Learning Objective: demonstrate one's ability to make, accept, and refuse invitations

A

- Elicit weekend activities from the class (e.g., *go to the beach, have a picnic, study*). Write them on the board.
- Explain the task. Then Ss complete the task individually. Go around the class and give help as needed.

B *Class activity*

- Explain the task. Ask two different pairs of Ss to model the example conversations.
- Ss go around the class and complete the task, using their lists from part A.

WHAT'S NEXT?

Learning Objective: become more involved in one's learning

- Focus Ss' attention on the Self-assessment again. Ask: "How well can you do these things now?"
- Ask Ss to underline one thing they need to review. Ask: "What did you underline? How can you review it?"
- If needed, plan additional instruction, activities, or reviews based on Ss' answers.

3 LISTENING Give me a call!

Listen and check (✓) the best response.

1. ☐ Yes. Please tell her to call me.
   ☐ Yes. Please tell him to call me.
2. ☐ Sure. Does he have your number?
   ☐ No, sorry. He's not here right now.
3. ☐ Yes, you do.
   ☐ No, I don't.
4. ☐ I have to babysit.
   ☐ I had a terrible headache.
5. ☐ I'd love to, but I can't.
   ☐ No, I didn't go. I was at work.
6. ☐ I'm sorry. He's not here right now.
   ☐ No, Amanda is at work right now.

4 SPEAKING Find someone who . . .

A CLASS ACTIVITY Go around the class. Ask questions to complete the chart. Try to write a different name on each line.

Find someone who . . .	Name
has to babysit this weekend	
needs to do the laundry tomorrow	
wants to go home early	
wants to go shopping on Saturday	
wants to see a movie tonight	
has to go to the doctor this week	
needs to work this weekend	
doesn't want to do homework tonight	

A: Ayumi, do you have to babysit this weekend?
B: Yes, I do. I have to babysit my little sister.

B PAIR WORK Share your answers with a partner.

5 SPEAKING Would you like to . . . ?

A Make a list of five things you want to do this weekend.

B CLASS ACTIVITY Go around the class. Invite your classmates to do the things from part A. Your classmates accept or refuse the invitations.

A: Would you like to go to the Natural History Museum this weekend?
B: I'm sorry, but I can't. I have to . . .
C: Do you want to go to a soccer match on Sunday?
D: Sure, I'd love to! When would you like to . . . ?

WHAT'S NEXT?

Look at your Self-assessment again. Do you need to review anything?

INTERCHANGE 1

Learning Objective: speak more fluently when exchanging names, phone numbers, and email addresses

A

- Explain the task. If needed, explain who Emma Watson and Usain Bolt are. Elicit examples of celebrities.
- Focus Ss' attention on the example screen. Ask Ss to spell the name and say the phone number. Then read aloud the email address: "U-S-A-I-N-B-O-L-T underscore eight-seven at C-U-P dot O-R-G." Point out that this is not Bolt's real phone number or email address.
- Ss complete the task individually. Go around the class and give help as needed.

B *Class activity*

- Explain the activity and model the conversation with a strong S. Take the role of Student B and give the S the role of Student A.
- Focus Ss' attention on the useful expressions in the box. Write them on the board and read them aloud. Ss repeat.
- Ss practice the conversation in pairs. Then they change roles.
- Ss complete the activity. They take their books, go around the class, introduce themselves to three "celebrities," and complete the cards.

TIP
To modify this activity for small classroom or one-on-one situations, the T and S/Ss can fill out several cards and leave them at stations around the room. Then pairs move around and pretend to be different celebrities at each spot.

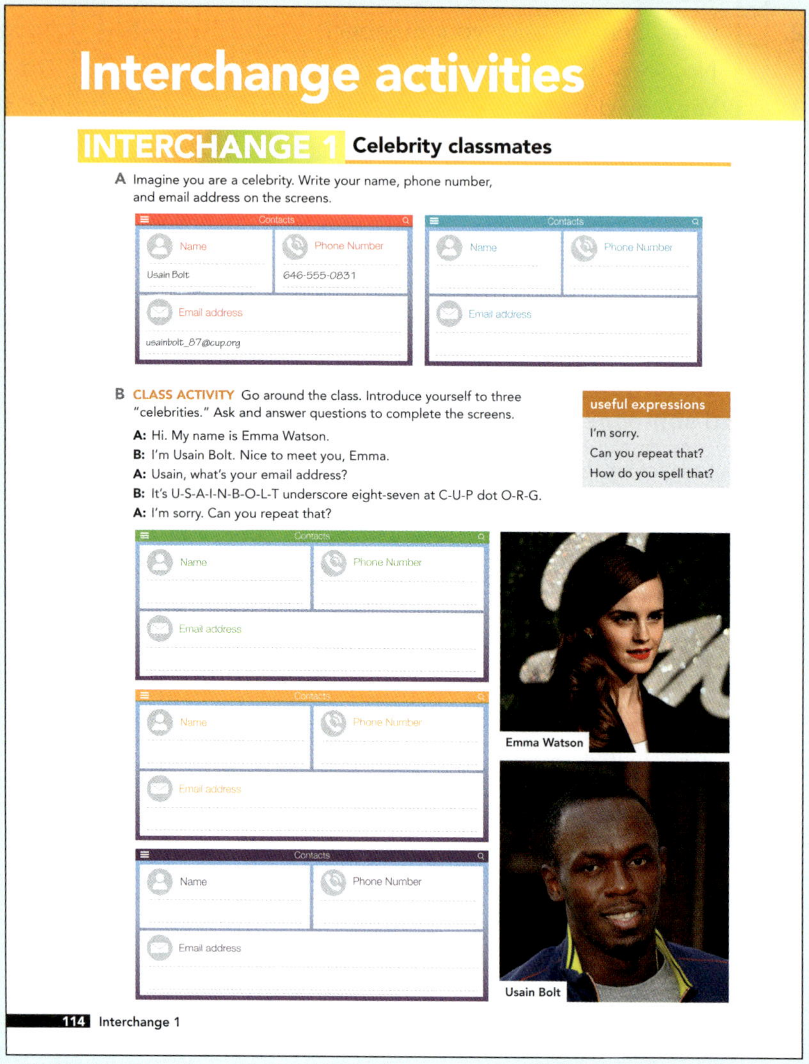

Interchange activities

INTERCHANGE 1 Celebrity classmates

A Imagine you are a celebrity. Write your name, phone number, and email address on the screens.

Contacts
Name: Usain Bolt
Phone Number: 646-555-0831
Email address: usainbolt_87@cup.org

Contacts
Name
Phone Number
Email address

B CLASS ACTIVITY Go around the class. Introduce yourself to three "celebrities." Ask and answer questions to complete the screens.

A: Hi. My name is Emma Watson.
B: I'm Usain Bolt. Nice to meet you, Emma.
A: Usain, what's your email address?
B: It's U-S-A-I-N-B-O-L-T underscore eight-seven at C-U-P dot O-R-G.
A: I'm sorry. Can you repeat that?

useful expressions
I'm sorry.
Can you repeat that?
How do you spell that?

Contacts
Name
Phone Number
Email address

Contacts
Name
Phone Number
Email address

Contacts
Name
Phone Number
Email address

Emma Watson

Usain Bolt

114 Interchange 1

INTERCHANGE 2 Find the differences

PAIR WORK How are the two pictures different? Ask questions to find the differences.

A: Where are the sunglasses?
B: In picture 1, they're on the bicycle.
A: In picture 2, they're on the table.

INTERCHANGE 2

Learning Objective: speak more fluently when comparing the locations of items in a room

Pair work

- Focus Ss' attention on the pictures. Elicit the names of the things in the pictures and write them on the board (e.g., *bag, bed, bicycle, book, cell phone, chair, desk, laptop, pizza box, slice of pizza, sunglasses, table, tablet, umbrella, wastebasket*).
- Explain that there are six differences between the pictures. All of the things on the board are in both pictures, but some are in different locations.
- Explain the activity and model the conversation with a S. Then Ss complete the activity in pairs.
- Ss complete the activity. Then review the answers as a class. Write the headings Picture 1 and Picture 2 on the board. Ask a S to read the model sentences and write the items and their locations under the correct headings:

	Picture 1	Picture 2
sunglasses	on the bicycle	on the table

- Elicit other differences from the class. Encourage Ss to use complete sentences, and correct them if needed. Ask different Ss to go to the board and write the locations under each heading.

Possible answers

	Picture 1	**Picture 2**
cell phone	in front of the tablet	next to the tablet
bag	under the table	under the bed
book	on the chair	on the bed
sunglasses	on the bicycle	on the table
laptop	on the bed	on the desk
umbrella	in the wastebasket	next to the wastebasket

INTERCHANGE 4

Learning Objective: speak more fluently when describing what people are wearing

Group work

- Focus Ss' attention on the pictures. Ask: "Who are these people?" Elicit answer from the class. (Answer: celebrities)
- Read the names of the celebrities aloud. Ss listen and repeat.
- ***Option:*** Ask Ss to share information about the celebrities.
- Explain the task. Ask two Ss to model the example conversation.
- Point out that the conversation uses present continuous statements, yes/no questions, and short answers. Explain that we usually ask: "Is it . . . ?" in guessing games about people.
- Ss complete the activity in small groups.
- ***Option:*** To make the game more challenging, Ss give very little information. The other Ss ask more questions about the clothes. Write this example conversation on the board:

  A: He's wearing a jacket.
  B: Is he wearing a tie?
  A: No, he isn't.
  C: Is the jacket gray?
  A: Yes, it is.
  C: Is it Bradley Cooper?
  A: Yes, it is.

TIP
To increase Ss' talking time, introduce challenging rules. For example, Ss must ask at least two questions about a person's clothes before they guess the person's identity.

INTERCHANGE 4 Celebrity fashions

GROUP WORK Describe the people in the pictures. Don't say the person's name. Your classmates guess the person.

A: He's wearing blue jeans, a beige shirt, and a black jacket. Who is it?
B: Is it John Cho?
A: No, it isn't.
B: Is it Liam Hemsworth?
A: That's right.

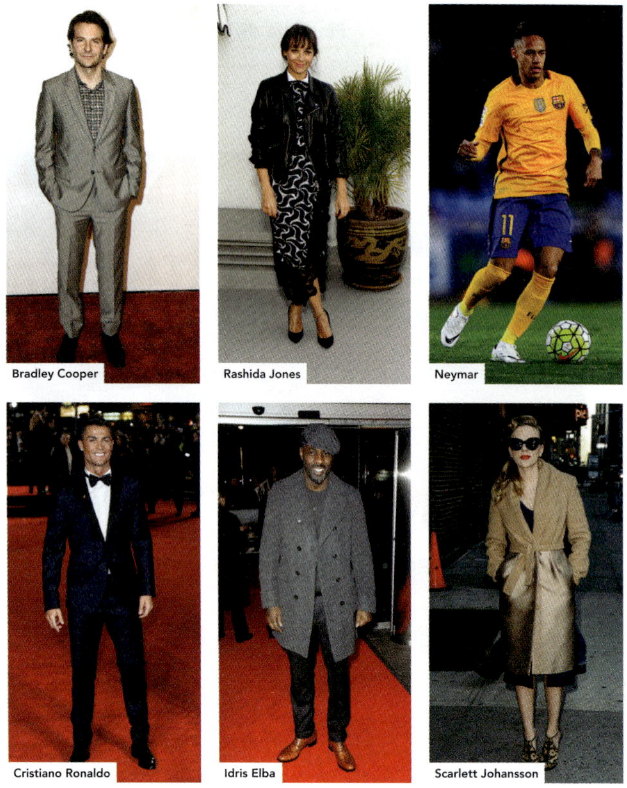

Bradley Cooper — Rashida Jones — Neymar
Cristiano Ronaldo — Idris Elba — Scarlett Johansson

Ariana Grande

John Cho

Ang Lee

Kate Middleton

Zoe Saldana

Liam Hemsworth

INTERCHANGE 3

Learning Objective: speak more fluently when asking and answering personal questions

A *Class activity*

- Write the first two rows of the chart on the board: the headings (*Question*, *Name*, *Name*) and the first question (*What's your last name?*).
- Focus Ss' attention on the chart in their books. Explain that they will ask one classmate all the questions and record the answers in the first column of the chart. Then they will repeat with a second classmate.
- Model the activity by asking a S the first question and writing the answer on the chart on the board.
- Ss go around the classroom taking turns asking and answering the questions. Encourage Ss to talk to someone new or that they don't talk to usually. Go around the class and give help as needed.
- ***Option:*** If Ss finish early, they can do the activity again with new partners.

TIP
When teaching one-on-one, have the S answer a second time, pretending to be a friend or celebrity.

B *Class activity*

- Explain the task. Ask a S to read the example aloud. Model an example using information about two Ss.
- Ss tell the class two things about their partners.
- ***Option:*** For very large classes, Ss can share information in large groups.

INTERCHANGE 3 Let's talk!

A CLASS ACTIVITY Talk to your classmates. Ask two different classmates each question. Write their names and answers.

Question	Name:	Name:
What's your last name?		
Where are you from?		
What is your parents' first language?		
How do you spell your best friend's name?		
What's your best friend like?		
What is your email address?		
What is your phone number?		

B CLASS ACTIVITY Tell the class two things about your partners.
"Yumi's last name is Suzuki. Francisco is from Guatemala."

118 Interchange 3

- ***Option:*** While Ss do the activity, write down any errors you hear. Pay particular attention to use of the pronouns *he* and *she*. After Ss finish, write the errors on the board. Ss correct them as a class.

INTERCHANGE 5 What's wrong with this picture?

GROUP WORK What's wrong with this picture? Tell your classmates.

"Mia and Karen are playing basketball, but they're wearing dresses!"

INTERCHANGE 5

Learning Objective: speak more fluently when discussing people's actions

Group work

- Focus Ss' attention on the picture. Elicit or explain any new vocabulary (e.g., *park, tree, lake, pizza, carry, giraffe, washing machine*).
- Explain the task and read the model statement.
- Set a 10-minute time limit. Ss complete the task in small groups.

TIP

To challenge Ss to work more quickly on any exercise, set a time limit. Write the time limit on the board. Every few minutes, revise the number and tell the class how much time they have left.

- Elicit answers from different groups.

Possible answers

Mrs. Chen is wearing a coat, a scarf, and boots. It's snowing under her umbrella.
Mia and Karen are playing basketball, but they're wearing dresses, Mia is wearing boots, and Karen is wearing high heels.
Ethan is under the tree. He's wearing headphones, but music is coming from the tree.
Robert and Erica are dancing near the tree, but they're wearing suits.
Mr. Jones is watching a soccer game on TV, but he's sitting on top of the car. A giraffe is driving the car.
Sarah is making spaghetti, but she's making it on the washing machine.
Mr. Torres, Mrs. Torres, Camila Torres, and **Samuel Torres** are eating pizza, but they're wearing pajamas, robes, and slippers.
Zach is riding his bike, but he's riding it in the lake.
Chris is carrying (shopping) bags, but she's walking in the lake.
Liz is swimming in the lake, but she's wearing a dress, boots, and a hat.

- ***Option:*** Groups of Ss write sentences about the picture for five minutes. Encourage them to use the conjunctions *and* and *but*. The group with the most grammatically and factually correct sentences wins.

INTERCHANGE 6

Learning Objective: speak more fluently about daily and weekly routines

A *Class activity*

- Explain the task and focus Ss' attention on the chart. Ask different Ss to read the phrases. Use the illustrations to explain new vocabulary. Then ask three Ss to model the example conversation.
- Point out that Ss must change the phrases to yes/no questions. For example, they change *Find someone who . . . gets up at 5:00 A.M. on weekdays* to *Do you get up at 5:00 A.M. on weekdays?*
- If needed, elicit how to change two or three more phrases in the chart to yes/no questions. Point out that Ss must use positive questions for phrases with *doesn't*. For example, *Find someone who . . . doesn't eat breakfast* changes to *Do you eat breakfast?*
- ***Option:*** For lower-level classes, tell the Ss to write Wh-questions for all the phrases.
- Ss go around the class and complete the chart. Go around the class and encourage them to look at each other, change partners often, and write different names on each line.

TIP
To control large classes during *Find someone who . . .* activities, divide the class in half. Ask each half to stay on one side of the classroom.

- Continue until most Ss complete the chart.

INTERCHANGE 6 Class survey

A CLASS ACTIVITY Go around the class and find this information. Try to write a different name on each line.

Find someone who ...	Name
gets up at 5:00 A.M. on weekdays	
gets up at noon on Saturdays	
does homework on Sunday night	
works at night	
works on weekends	
has a pet	
dances on Friday night	
lives alone	
takes a bus to class	
rides a motorcycle to class	
cooks on weekends	
plays the drums	
has two brothers	
writes emails every day	
speaks three languages	
doesn't eat breakfast	

work at night

cook on the weekends

play the drums

A: Do you get up at 5:00 A.M. on weekdays, Kun-woo?
B: No, I get up at six-thirty.
A: Do you get up at 5:00 A.M. on weekdays, Yasmin?
C: Yes, I get up at 5:00 A.M. every day.

B GROUP WORK Compare your answers.

A: Kun-woo gets up at six-thirty on weekdays.
B: Yasmin gets up at 5:00 on weekdays.
C: Lucas gets up at . . .

B *Group work*

- Explain the task. Then ask three Ss to model the example conversation. Point out that they can also ask *Who* questions to compare information (e.g., *Who gets up at 5:00 A.M. on weekdays?*).
- Ss complete the task in small groups. Go around the class and encourage Ss to use complete sentences.
- ***Option:*** Ss take notes on the answers. Then ask *Who* questions to elicit answers from the class for each phrase.

INTERCHANGE 7 Find the differences

A **PAIR WORK** Find the differences between Tony's apartment and Nicole's apartment.

A: There are four chairs in Tony's kitchen, but there are three chairs in Nicole's kitchen.
B: There is a sofa in Tony's living room, but there is no sofa in Nicole's living room.

B **GROUP WORK** Compare your answers.

INTERCHANGE 7

Learning Objective: speak more fluently when comparing rooms and furniture

A *Pair work*

- Focus Ss' attention on the pictures. Explain the task and ask two Ss to model the example conversation. Then Ss complete the task in pairs.

B *Group work*

- Each pair joins another pair, and Ss compare their answers.

Possible answers

Kitchen

1. There are four chairs in Tony's kitchen, but there are three chairs in Nicole's kitchen.
2. There are some curtains in Nicole's kitchen, but there aren't any curtains in Tony's kitchen.
3. There's a microwave in Tony's kitchen, but there's no microwave in Nicole's kitchen.
4. There's a clock in Nicole's kitchen, but there's no clock in Tony's kitchen.
5. There's a coffee maker in Nicole's kitchen, but there's no coffee maker in Tony's kitchen.

Bathroom

6. There are some curtains in Nicole's bathroom, but there are no curtains in Tony's bathroom.
7. There's a rug in Nicole's bathroom, but there's no rug in Tony's bathroom.

Bedroom

8. There's a dresser in Nicole's bedroom, but there's no dresser in Tony's bedroom.
9. There's a mirror in Nicole's bedroom, but there isn't a mirror in Tony's bedroom.
10. There's a desk in Tony's bedroom, but there isn't a desk in Nicole's bedroom.
11. There's a chair in Tony's bedroom, but there isn't a chair in Nicole's bedroom.
12. There are some pictures in Nicole's bedroom, but there are no pictures in Tony's bedroom.

Living room

13. There's a sofa in Tony's living room, but there's no sofa in Nicole's living room.
14. There's one lamp in Tony's living room, but there are two lamps in Nicole's living room.
15. There's a coffee table in Nicole's living room, but there isn't a coffee table in Tony's living room.
16. There's a bookcase in Nicole's living room, but there's no bookcase in Tony's living room.
17. There's a TV in Tony's living room, but there isn't a TV in Nicole's living room.

INTERCHANGE 8

Learning Objective: speak more fluently when discussing the perfect job

A Pair work

- Explain the first part of the task.
- If needed, explain the patterns for simple present statements and yes/no questions with *want to*:

  Subject + *want to* + verb.

  Do/Does + subject + *want to* + verb?
- Ask different Ss to read the survey questions aloud. Elicit or explain any new vocabulary. Use the pictures as needed.

Vocabulary
outdoors: outside
perform: act, sing, or dance in front of people

- Ss check *Yes* or *No* in the *Me* column individually.
- Explain the second part of the task. Ss take turns asking a partner the questions. As they listen to the answers, they check *Yes* or *No* in the *My partner* column. Model the task with a S.
- Ss complete the task in pairs.
- ***Option:*** Ask: "Do you want to talk to people? Who says yes? Who says no?" Elicit responses from the class and write the totals on the board. Continue with other questions from the survey.

B Pair work

- Explain the task. Focus Ss' attention on the positive and negative sentences in the box. Have Ss read them aloud. Elicit or explain any new vocabulary. Tell Ss to use sentences like these in their conversations.
- Then ask two Ss to model the example conversation.

INTERCHANGE 8 The perfect job

A PAIR WORK Imagine you're looking for a job. What do you want to do? First, check (✓) your answers to the questions. Then ask your partner the same questions.

	Me		My partner	
Do you want to . . . ?	Yes	No	Yes	No
work from 9 to 5	☐	☐	☐	☐
work in an office	☐	☐	☐	☐
work outdoors	☐	☐	☐	☐
work at home	☐	☐	☐	☐
work with a team	☐	☐	☐	☐
use a computer	☐	☐	☐	☐
use English	☐	☐	☐	☐
travel	☐	☐	☐	☐
talk to people	☐	☐	☐	☐
help people	☐	☐	☐	☐
wear a suit	☐	☐	☐	☐
perform in front of people	☐	☐	☐	☐

work from 9 to 5

perform in front of people

work outdoors

work with a team

Positive	Negative
It's easy. / It's an easy job.	It's difficult. / It's a difficult job.
It's exciting. / It's an exciting job.	It's boring. / It's a boring job.
It's terrific. / It's a terrific job.	It's very stressful. / It's a very stressful job.
It's pretty relaxing. / It's a pretty relaxing job.	It's really dangerous. / It's a really dangerous job.

B PAIR WORK Think of a good job for your partner. Go to pages 50 and 53 for ideas.

A: You want to travel and use English. Do you want to be a pilot?
B: No, a pilot's job is very stressful.
A: OK, do you want to be . . . ?

- Ss complete the task in pairs. Then they share the information with the class.
- ***Option:*** Ss write about a good job for themselves or their partners.

INTERCHANGE 9 Planning a party

A You're planning a small party. Choose two sweet and two salty snacks you want to serve.

B PAIR WORK Get together with a partner. Compare your choices and decide on only two sweet and two salty snacks for your party.

A: Let's have pizza, popcorn, chocolates, and candy.
B: Oh, I never eat pizza and popcorn together. And I hardly ever eat chocolates or candy. Let's have pizza, hot dogs, grapes, and watermelon.
A: Well, I like grapes, but I don't like watermelon. Let's have . . .

C GROUP WORK Present your choices to the other pairs. Can you decide on only four snacks for the class?

Interchange 9 123

INTERCHANGE 9

Learning Objective: speak more fluently about eating habits and preferences

A

- Focus Ss' attention on the pictures. Read the name of each food aloud. Ss repeat.
- Explain the task.
- Elicit or explain *sweet* and *salty* using examples from the pictures.
- Ss complete the activity individually. Go around the class and give help as needed.

B *Pair work*

- Explain the task and ask two Ss to model the example conversation.
- Point out that Ss should talk about each type of food and use adverbs of frequency.
- Ss compare their answers in pairs. Go around the class and give help as needed while each pair tries to agree on two sweet and two salty snacks for the party.

C *Group work*

- Ask pairs to share the two sweet and two salty snacks they chose with another pair. While pairs talk, copy these headings onto the board:

  Sweet *Salty*

- Explain the second part of the task. Elicit answers from the small groups and write them on the board. Get the class to agree on four snacks for the party.

INTERCHANGE 10

Learning Objective: speak more fluently about talents and abilities

A *Class activity*

- Focus Ss' attention on the chart. Ask different Ss to read the questions. Use the pictures to explain or elicit the meaning of a *hidden talent* and any other new vocabulary.
- Explain the first part of the task. Ss work individually to write two more questions.
- Explain the second part of the task. Ask two Ss to model the example conversation.
- ***Option:*** Elicit possible follow-up questions for each answer. For example, to follow the first question:

  B: Yes, I can.

  A: Is it fun to do handstands?

  OR

  B: No, I can't.

  A: Can you stand on one leg?
- Point out that Ss should write the names of classmates who answer yes in the *Can* column. They should write the names of classmates who answer no in the *Can't* column.
- Ss complete the activity. Go around the class and encourage Ss to change partners often and ask follow-up questions.
- Continue until most Ss have completed their charts.

B *Class activity*

- Explain the task and ask a S to model the example sentences. Point out that Ss should change the pronoun *your* in *make your own clothes* to *his* or *her*.
- Ask different Ss to share answers about their classmates.
- ***Option:*** In large classes, Ss can share their answers in groups.

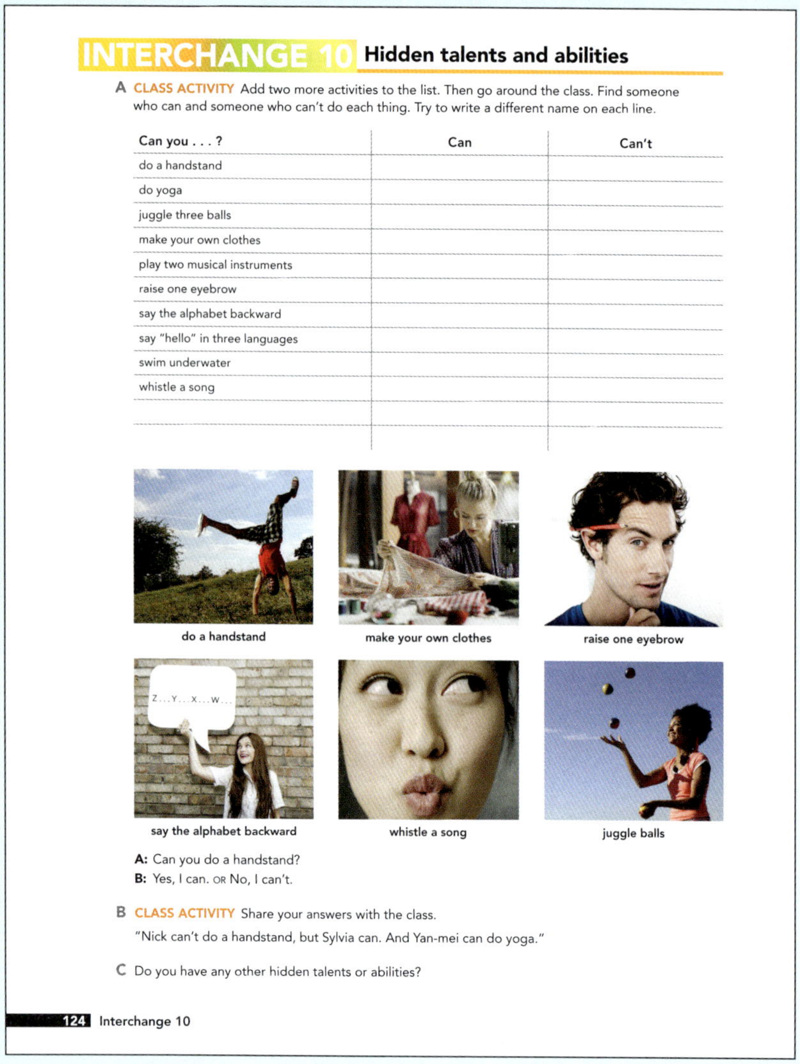

INTERCHANGE 10 **Hidden talents and abilities**

A CLASS ACTIVITY Add two more activities to the list. Then go around the class. Find someone who can and someone who can't do each thing. Try to write a different name on each line.

Can you . . . ?	Can	Can't
do a handstand		
do yoga		
juggle three balls		
make your own clothes		
play two musical instruments		
raise one eyebrow		
say the alphabet backward		
say "hello" in three languages		
swim underwater		
whistle a song		

do a handstand

make your own clothes

raise one eyebrow

say the alphabet backward

whistle a song

juggle balls

A: Can you do a handstand?
B: Yes, I can. OR No, I can't.

B CLASS ACTIVITY Share your answers with the class.
"Nick can't do a handstand, but Sylvia can. And Yan-mei can do yoga."

C Do you have any other hidden talents or abilities?

C

- Ask: "Do you have any other hidden talents?" Ss raise their hands.
- Ask different Ss to share their answers.

INTERCHANGE 11 Take a guess

A PAIR WORK Add one more activity to the list. Is your partner going to do any of these things? Check (✓) your guesses.

Is your partner going to . . . ?	My guesses: Yes	My guesses: No	My partner's answers: Yes	My partner's answers: No
1. play video games tonight	☐	☐	☐	☐
2. eat special food this month	☐	☐	☐	☐
3. buy some cheese this week	☐	☐	☐	☐
4. wear a suit this month	☐	☐	☐	☐
5. wake up early tomorrow	☐	☐	☐	☐
6. have a big breakfast on Saturday	☐	☐	☐	☐
7. study for a test tomorrow night	☐	☐	☐	☐
8. drive a car over the weekend	☐	☐	☐	☐
9. get a new apartment next year	☐	☐	☐	☐
10. watch a soccer game on Sunday	☐	☐	☐	☐
11. ______________	☐	☐	☐	☐

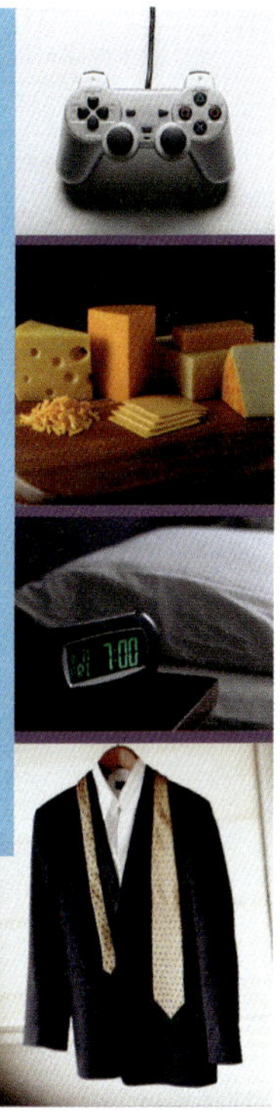

B PAIR WORK Ask and answer questions to check your guesses.

A: Are you going to play video games tonight?
B: Yes, I am. I'm going to play my favorite video game.

C CLASS ACTIVITY How many of your guesses are correct? Who has the most correct guesses?

INTERCHANGE 11

Learning Objective: speak more fluently when discussing plans

A *Pair work*

- Explain the task and focus Ss' attention on the chart. Ask different Ss to read the activities aloud. Have Ss add their own question to the chart. Point out that Ss check (✓) their answers in the *My guesses* column.
- Ss complete the task in pairs. Go around the class and make sure Ss complete the task without asking their partner the questions.

TIP
To check Ss' understanding of your instructions, ask questions regularly. For example: "So who are you working with?" or "In which column do you check the answers?"

B *Pair work*

- Explain the task and ask two Ss to model the example conversation. Point out that Ss should check the answers in the *My partner's answers* column.
- ***Option:*** For lower-level Ss, elicit how to change the remaining activities into yes/no questions.
- Ss complete the task in pairs.

C *Class activity*

- Explain the task. Ss count the number of answers in each column that match.
- Ask: "Who has eleven correct guesses? How about ten? Nine?" Ss raise their hands.

INTERCHANGE 12

Learning Objective: speak more fluently when giving advice

A *Pair work*

- Explain the task and ask different Ss to read the problems.
- Ask two Ss to model the example conversation. Elicit other advice from the class.
- Ss complete the activity in pairs. Go around the class and give help as needed. Then elicit possible advice from the class.

Possible answers

buy a car: Save some money every month. / Get a bike instead.
late for school: Get a louder alarm clock. / Go to bed early.
don't know any people: Join a club. / Talk to people at work or school.
big test tomorrow: Ask your family to be quiet. / Study at a friend's house.
job is stressful: Get a new job. / Don't work on weekends.
best friend's birthday: Bake a cake for her. / Buy something online. Tell her the gift is coming.

- ***Option:*** Write the advice for each problem on the board. Then have Ss vote for the best advice.

B *Class activity*

- Explain the first part of the task. Point out that the problem can be real or imaginary.
- Ss write down a problem individually. Go around the class and help with vocabulary. If Ss have trouble thinking of ideas, elicit ideas from the class.
- Explain the second part of the task and ask three Ss to model the example conversation.
- Elicit problems from different Ss. The class gives advice.

INTERCHANGE 12 **Problems, problems**

A PAIR WORK Imagine you have these problems. Your partner gives advice.

A: I really want to buy a car, but . . .
B: Save some money every month. Don't . . .

B CLASS ACTIVITY Think of a problem you have. Then tell the class. Your classmates give advice.

A: I don't understand some vocabulary in this unit.
B: Review the unit and do your homework.
C: Don't worry. Ask the teacher.

126 Interchange 12

- ***Option:*** Ss sit in a circle, write a problem at the top of a piece of paper, and pass it to the left. Then they write advice for the problem on their new paper and pass it to the left. Ss continue the activity for 10 minutes, and then find the papers with their original problems. Elicit problems and advice from the class.

INTERCHANGE 13A Giving directions

Student A

A **PAIR WORK** Look at the map. You are outside the Windsor Hotel on Oak Street between Second and Third Avenues. Ask your partner for directions to the three places below. Your map does not have names on these buildings, but your partner's map does. Listen to your partner, find the places on the map, and write their names.

garage   supermarket   flower shop

A: Excuse me. How do I get to the garage?
B: Walk down Maple Street to First Avenue. Turn . . .

B **PAIR WORK** Your partner asks you for directions to three places. Your partner's map does not have names on these buildings, but your map does. Use the expressions in the box to give directions.

Go up/Go down . . .	It's on the corner of . . . Street	It's next to . . .
Walk up/Walk down . . .	and . . . Avenue.	It's behind . . .
Turn right/Turn left . . .	It's between . . . and . . .	It's in front of . . .
It's across from . . .		

INTERCHANGE 13A/B

Learning Objectives: speak more fluently when giving directions

A *Pair work*

- Ss work in pairs. Student A in each pair looks at Interchange 13A. Student B in each pair looks at Interchange 13B. Point out that Ss should not look at each other's pages.

TIP
For information gap activities, tell Ss to sit across from each other and place a divider, such as a large book, between them. That way, they can hear each other but not see each other's pages.

- Set the scene and explain the task. Student A asks Student B for directions to the garage, the supermarket, and the flower shop. Student B gives directions, and Student A labels the buildings.
- Ask two Ss to model the example conversation. Then go over the meanings and pronunciation of any new words.
- Ss complete the activity in pairs.

B *Pair work*

- Explain the task. Student B asks Student A for directions to the coffee shop, the shoe store, and the bookstore. Student A gives directions, and Student B labels the buildings.
- Ss complete the activity in pairs.
- To check answers, each pair compares maps and labels.

TIP
To check answers at the end of an information gap activity, ask each pair to compare information. It's not necessary to go over the answers as a class.

INTERCHANGE 13B Giving directions

Student B

A **PAIR WORK** Look at the map. You are outside the Windsor Hotel on Oak Street between Second and Third Avenues. Your partner asks you for directions to three places. Your partner's map does not have names on these buildings, but your map does. Use the expressions in the box to give directions.

A: Excuse me. How do I get to the garage?
B: Walk down Oak Street to First Avenue. Turn . . .

Go up/Go down . . .	It's on the corner of . . . Street and . . . Avenue.	It's next to . . .
Walk up/Walk down . . .	It's between . . . and . . .	It's behind . . .
Turn right/Turn left . . .		It's in front of . . .
It's across from . . .		

B **PAIR WORK** Ask your partner for directions to the three places below. Your map does not have names on these buildings, but your partner's map does. Listen to your partner, find the places on the map and write their names.

coffee shop **shoe store** **bookstore**

INTERCHANGE 14 Past activities

A **PAIR WORK** What did you do when you were a child? First, check (✓) your answers to the questions. Then ask your partner the same questions. Check (✓) your partner's answers.

A: Did you argue with your friends as a child?
B: Yes, I did. OR No, I didn't.

A: Did you clean your room?
B: Yes, I did. OR No, I didn't.

argue with your friends

wear braces

	Me		My partner	
Did you . . . as a child?	**Yes**	**No**	**Yes**	**No**
argue with your friends	☐	☐	☐	☐
clean your room	☐	☐	☐	☐
make your bed	☐	☐	☐	☐
get up early on weekdays	☐	☐	☐	☐
sleep late on weekends	☐	☐	☐	☐
have a tablet	☐	☐	☐	☐
play video games	☐	☐	☐	☐
listen to rock music	☐	☐	☐	☐
play a musical instrument	☐	☐	☐	☐
play a sport	☐	☐	☐	☐
ride a bicycle	☐	☐	☐	☐
wear braces	☐	☐	☐	☐

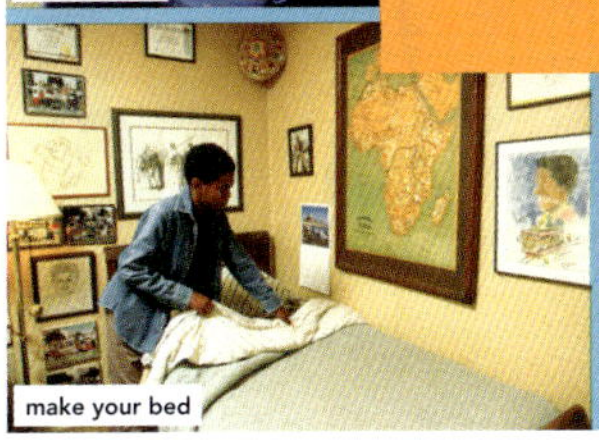
make your bed

play a musical instrument

B **PAIR WORK** Join another pair. Tell them what your partner did and didn't do as a child.
"Yu-jin didn't argue with her friends as a child. She cleaned her room."

INTERCHANGE 14

Learning Objective: speak more fluently when asking about past activities

A *Pair work*

- Explain the first part of the task and and focus Ss' attention on the chart. Elicit or explain the meaning of any new vocabulary. Use the pictures or mime where appropriate. Ss complete the first part of the task by checking their answers to the questions.
- Then ask two Ss to model the example conversations. Ask different Ss to read each question. For example:

  S1: Did you argue with your friends as a child?

  S2: Did you clean your room as a child?
- Ss complete the second part of the task in pairs. Go around the class and make sure both Ss check (✓) the answers in their charts.

B *Group work*

- Explain the task and ask a S to model the examples.
- Each pair joins another pair. Ss complete the activity in groups of four.
- ***Option:*** Each group of four joins another group of four. They share information as a group.

INTERCHANGE 15

Learning Objective: speak more fluently about important life events

A

- Focus Ss' attention on the pictures. Ask different Ss to read the sentence starters under the pictures.
- Elicit other important life events from the class and write them on the board (e.g., *started a job, visited Australia*). Explain that Ss choose four events and write the years they happened in the box. Tell Ss to add another event from their lives and the year it happened.
- Ss complete the task individually. Go around the class and give help as needed.

B *Pair work*

- Explain the task and ask two Ss to model the example conversation.
- Point out that Ss should ask follow-up questions and take notes on their partner's answers. Elicit possible follow-up questions for each picture in part A and write them on the board (e.g., *How old were you? Where was your elementary school?*).
- Ss complete the task in pairs. Go around the class and encourage Ss to ask follow-up questions.
- Ask different Ss to share information about one or two important events in their partner's life.
- ***Option:*** In large classes, Ss can share information about their partner's life in small groups.

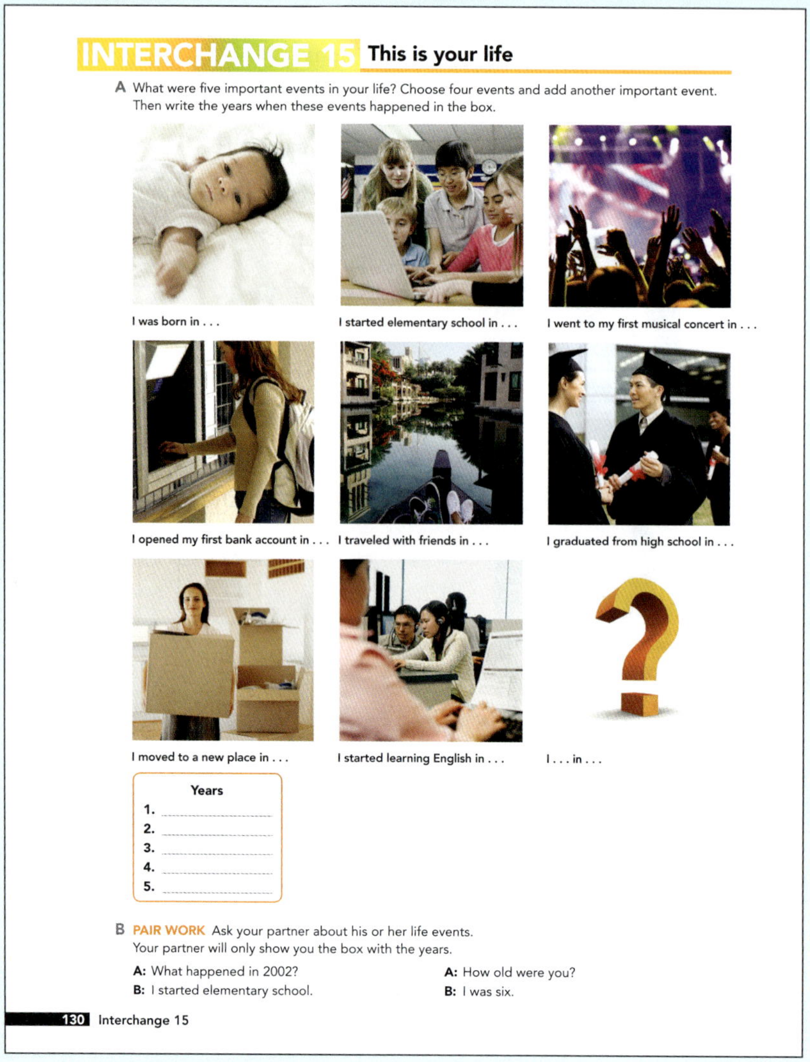

INTERCHANGE 15 This is your life

A What were five important events in your life? Choose four events and add another important event. Then write the years when these events happened in the box.

I was born in . . .

I started elementary school in . . .

I went to my first musical concert in . . .

I opened my first bank account in . . .

I traveled with friends in . . .

I graduated from high school in . . .

I moved to a new place in . . .

I started learning English in . . .

I . . . in . . .

Years

1. ....
2. ....
3. ....
4. ....
5. ....

B **PAIR WORK** Ask your partner about his or her life events. Your partner will only show you the box with the years.

A: What happened in 2002?
B: I started elementary school.

A: How old were you?
B: I was six.

130 Interchange 15

INTERCHANGE 16 The perfect weekend

A You are planning your dream weekend. Write your plans for Saturday and Sunday in the charts. Use these expressions and your own ideas.

go to (the movies/a party)	play (basketball/video games)
go (dancing/shopping)	meet (my friend/teacher)
go (on a trip/picnic)	have dinner with (my brother/parents)
study for (a test/an exam)	visit (my parents/grandparents)
go out with (my girlfriend/boyfriend)	see (the dentist/doctor)

WEEKEND PLANS

Saturday	Me	My partner
morning		
lunch		
afternoon		
evening		
dinner		
after dinner		

WEEKEND PLANS

Sunday	Me	My partner
morning		
lunch		
afternoon		
evening		
dinner		
after dinner		

B PAIR WORK Compare your plans with your partner. Choose activities to do together.

A: What do you want to do on Saturday morning?
B: Let's go swimming. They opened a new pool at the gym.
A: Oh, I can't swim. Sorry. Maybe we can go bike riding . . .

C GROUP WORK Join another pair. Can you decide what to do over the weekend together?

A: So, would you like to go bike riding on Saturday morning?
C: Good idea. And how about a barbecue for lunch?
B: Oh, we don't have time for a barbecue. We want to go to an art festival in the afternoon . . .

INTERCHANGE 16

Learning Objective: speak more fluently when making, accepting, and declining invitations

A

- Set the scene and explain the task. Read out the expressions in the box. If needed, explain that an *exam* is usually longer and more formal than a *test*.
- Ss complete the first column of each chart individually. Go around the class and give help as needed. If Ss have difficulty thinking of ideas, suggest different activities they can write down.

B *Pair work*

- Explain the task. Ask two Ss to model the conversation. Point out that Student A should answer with a plan from one of his or her own charts. Point out that Ss write their partner's activities in the *My partner* column on the charts.
- Explain that Ss are to find some activities to do together on both days, and to make adjustments to their charts to reflect this. Model how to do this with a S and show the class how they can write the shared activity over both the *Me* and *My partner* columns.

TIP

To help Ss finish at about the same time, assign an additional task to Ss who finish early. Then go around the class and help slower Ss.

- Ss complete the task in pairs. Go around the class and make sure pairs decide on some shared activities for both days.

C *Group work*

- Explain the task. Ask three Ss to model the example conversation. Create groups by combining two pairs of Ss from part B. Tell the groups to make one new chart with weekend plans for the whole group.
- Ss complete the task in their small groups (two pairs).
- ***Option***: If some groups finish early, have them create a new weekend plan with different activities.
- Elicit plans from each group.

Grammar plus

UNIT 1

1 *My, your, his, her* page 3

- Use *his* with males and *her* with females: **His** name is Travis. (NOT: ~~Her name is Travis.~~) **Her** name is Nicole. (NOT: ~~His name is Nicole.~~)

Complete the conversations with *my*, *your*, *his*, or *her*.

1. **A:** Hello. ___My___ name is Carlos.
   B: Hi, Carlos. What's ________ last name?
   A: It's Gonzales.
   B: How do you spell ________ last name? Is it G-O-N-Z-A-L-E-Z?
   A: No, it's G-O-N-Z-A-L-E-S. And what's ________ name?
   B: ________ name is Bill Powers. Nice to meet you.

2. **A:** What's Ms. Robinson's first name?
   B: ________ first name is Elizabeth. ________ nickname is Liz.
   A: I'm sorry. What's ________ first name again?
   B: It's Elizabeth. And what's Mr. Weber's first name?
   A: ________ first name is Peter.
   B: That's right. And ________ nickname is Pete.
   A: That's right, too!

2 The verb *be* page 5

- In questions, the verb *be* comes before the noun or pronoun: **Are you** Joshua Brown? **Is he** in our English class? **Is she** the teacher?
- Don't use contractions in short answers with *Yes*: Are you in my class? Yes, **I am**. (NOT: ~~Yes, I'm.~~)

Complete the conversations with the words in the box.

am	I'm	it's	she's	you're
✓ are	I am	I'm not	you	

1. **A:** Excuse me. ___Are___ you Layla Moore?
   B: No, ________. ________ over there.
   A: OK. Thanks.

2. **A:** Hi. Are ________ Layla Moore?
   B: Yes, ________.
   A: Nice to meet you. ________ Sergio Oliveira.
   ________ in my English class.
   B: Yes, I ________. ________ nice to meet you too, Sergio.

UNIT 2

1 *This/these; it/they*; plurals page 10

- Don't use a contraction with *What* + *are*: **What** are these? (NOT: ~~What're these?~~)
- Use *this* with singular nouns: **This** is a laptop. Use *these* with plural nouns: **These** are flash drives.

Choose the correct words.

1. A: **What's** / **What are** these?
   B: **It's** / **They're** my **flash drive** / **flash drives**.
2. A: **What's** / **What are** this?
   B: **It's** / **They're a** / **an** cell phone.
3. A: What's **this** / **these**?
   B: **It's** / **They're a** / **an** English book.

2 Yes/No and *where* questions with *be* page 11

- In questions with *where*, the verb comes after *Where*: **Where** is my credit card? (NOT: ~~Where my credit card is?~~) **Where** are my sunglasses? (NOT: ~~Where my sunglasses are?~~)

A Match the questions with the answers.

1. Is that your wallet? ___c___
2. Are these your glasses? _____
3. Where are my keys? _____
4. Is this your bicycle? _____
5. Where's your tablet? _____

a. They're in your backpack.
b. No, it's not.
c. Oh, yes, it is!
d. It's on my desk.
e. No, they're not.

B Complete the conversation. Use the words in the box.

are they	it is	they are	where
it	it's	this	✓ where's

A: ___Where's___ my dictionary?
B: I don't know. Is __________ in your backpack?
A: No, __________ not.
B: Is __________ your dictionary?
A: Yes, __________ Thanks! Now, __________ are my glasses?
B: __________ on your desk?
A: Yes, __________. Thank you!

UNIT 3

1 Negative statements and yes/no questions with *be* page 17

- Use *be* + *not* to form negative statements: Ana **isn't** a student. (NOT: ~~Ana no is a student.~~)
- *You* is a singular and a plural pronoun: Are **you** from Rio? Yes, **I** am./Yes, **we** are.

A Unscramble the words to write negative statements.

1. is / of Canada / Toronto / the capital / not
   Toronto is not the capital of Canada.
2. Buenos Aires / not / from / we're
   ____
3. not / you and Ashley / in my class / are
   ____
4. is / my first language / Korean / not
   ____
5. from / my mother / not / is / Italy
   ____
6. my parents / not / are / they
   ____

B Complete the conversations.

1. **A:** ___Are___ you and your friend from Costa Rica?
   B: No, ____________ not. ____________ from the Dominican Republic.
2. **A:** ____________ your first language Spanish?
   B: Yes, it ____________. My parents ____________ from Ecuador.
3. **A:** ____________ Nadia and Rayan Lebanese?
   B: Yes, ____________ are. But ____________ in France now.
4. **A:** ____________ my friends and I late?
   B: No, ____________ not. ____________ early!

2 Wh-questions with *be* page 20

- Use *what* to ask about things. Use *where* to ask about places. Use *who* to ask about people. Use *What is/are . . . like?* to ask for a description.
- Use *how* to ask for a description: **How are** you today? Use how old to ask about age: **How old** is he?
- In answers about age, you can use only the number or the number + years old: He's **18**. OR He's **18 years old.** (NOT: ~~He has 18 years.~~)

Complete the questions with *how*, *what*, *where*, or *who*. Then match the questions with the answers.

1. __Who__ is that? __d__
2. ______ is her name? ______
3. ______ is she like? ______
4. ______ old is she? ______
5. ______ your family from? ______
6. ______ is Kyoto like? ______

a. We're from Japan – from Kyoto.
b. She's 18.
c. Her name is Hina.
d. She's my sister.
e. Oh, it's really beautiful.
f. She's very nice and friendly.

UNIT 4

1 Possessives page 24

- The noun comes after a possessive adjective: This is **my** T-shirt.
- Don't include the noun after a possessive pronoun: This T-shirt is **mine**.
- *Whose* can be used with singular and plural nouns: **Whose** scarf is this? **Whose** sneakers are these?

Complete the conversations. Use the words in the boxes. There are two extra words in each box.

his	mine	my	your	yours	✓ whose

1. **A:** ___Whose___ jacket is this? Is it ______________, Ethan?
   B: No, it's not ______________. Ask Matt. I think it's ______________.

her	my	mine	your	yours

2. **A:** These aren't ______________ gloves. Are they ______________?
   B: No, they're not ______________. Maybe they are Young-min's.

her	hers	their	theirs	whose

3. **A:** ______________ sweaters are these? Are they Rachel's?
   B: No, they're not ______________ sweaters. But these shorts are ______________.

2 Present continuous statements; conjunctions page 26

- The present continuous is the present of *be* + verb + *-ing*: It**'s raining**. She**'s wearing** a raincoat.
- The two negative contractions mean the same: **He's not/He isn't** wearing a coat.
  We're not/We aren't wearing gloves.

Change the affirmative sentences to negative sentences. Change the negative sentences to affirmative sentences.

1. Mr. and Mrs. Liu are wearing green caps. ___Mr. and Mrs. Liu aren't wearing green caps.___
2. It isn't snowing. ______________________________
3. I'm wearing a winter coat. ______________________________
4. You're wearing David's sunglasses. ______________________________
5. Ayumi isn't wearing a scarf. ______________________________

3 Present continuous yes/no questions; adjective + noun page 26

- In questions, the present continuous is *be* + subject + verb + *–ing*: **Is** it **raining**? **Are** you **wearing** a raincoat?
- Adjectives can come before nouns or after the verb *be*: He's wearing **a blue hat**. His hat **is blue**.
- Adjectives don't have a plural form: a **green hat**; two **green hats**.

Write questions using the words in parentheses. Then complete the responses.

1. **A.** ___Is Mr. Thomas wearing a dark blue coat?___ (wear, dark blue coat)
   B: No, he ______________.
2. **A:** ______________________________ (wear, high heels)
   B: No, we ______________.
3. **A:** ______________________________ (wear, a sweater)
   B: Yes, I ______________.
4. **A:** ______________________________ (rain)
   B: Yes, it ______________.

UNIT 5

1 What time is it? / Is it A.M. or P.M.? page 31

■ Remember: You can say times different ways: 1:15 = *one-fifteen* OR *a quarter after one.*

Write each sentence in a different way.

1. It's a quarter to four. It's three forty-five.
2. It's 7:00 P.M. It's seven in the evening.
3. It's six-fifteen. ______
4. It's 10 o'clock at night. ______
5. It's three-oh-five. ______
6. It's twenty-five to eleven. ______
7. It's one o'clock in the morning. ______
8. It's midnight. ______

2 Present continuous Wh-questions page 33

■ Use the present continuous to talk about actions that are happening right now: What **are** you **doing**? **I'm talking** to you!

■ In questions, the *be* verb comes after the question word: What **are you** doing?

■ To form the continuous of verbs ending in –e, drop the e and add *–ing*: have → having.

■ For verbs ending in vowel + consonant, double the consonant and add *–ing*: get → getting.

What are the people doing? Write conversations. Use the words in parentheses.

1. A: What's Matt doing? (Matt)
   B: He's swimming. (swim)
2. A: ______ (Jon and Megan)
   B: ______ (shop)
3. A: ______ (you)
   B: ______ (write a message)
4. A: ______ (Chris)
   B: ______ (cook dinner)
5. A: ______ (you and Tyler)
   B: ______ (watch a movie)
6. A: ______ (Sara)
   B: ______ (have pizza)
7. A: ______ (you and Joseph)
   B: ______ (study for the test)
8. A: ______ (Laura and Paulo)
   B: ______ (chat online)

1 Simple present statements page 37 and Simple present statements with irregular verbs page 38

- In affirmative statements, verbs with *he/she/it* end in *–s*: He/She **walks** to school. BUT I/You/We/They **walk** to school.
- In negative statements, use doesn't with *he/she/it* and don't with all the others: He/She/It **doesn't** live here. I/You/We/They **don't** live here.
- Don't add *–s* to the verb: She **doesn't live** here. (NOT: ~~She doesn't lives here.~~)

Elena is talking about her family. Complete the sentences with the correct form of the verbs in parentheses.

My family and I ___live___ (live) in the city. We ________ (have) an apartment on First Avenue. My sister ________ (go) to school near our apartment, so she ________ (walk) to school. My father ________ (work) in the suburbs, so he ________ (drive) to his job. My mother ________ (use) public transportation – she ________ (take) the bus to her office downtown. She ________ (have) a new job, but she ________ (not like) it very much. And me? Well, I ________ (not work) far from our apartment, so I ________ (not need) a car or public transportation. I ________ (ride) my bike to work!

2 Simple present questions page 39

- In questions, use *does* with *he/she/it* and *do* with all the others: **Does** he/she/it get up early? **Do** I/you/we/they get up early?
- Don't add *–s* to the verb: Does she **live** alone? (NOT: ~~Does she lives alone?~~)

A Write questions to complete the conversations.

1. **A:** _Do you use public transportation?_
   B: Yes, I use public transportation.
2. **A:** ________________________
   B: No, my family doesn't eat dinner at 5:00.
3. **A:** ________________________
   B: No, my brother doesn't take the bus to work.
4. **A:** ________________________
   B: No, I don't get up late on weekends.

- Use *in* with *the morning/the afternoon/the evening*. Use *at* with *night*: I go to school **in** the afternoon and work **at** night.
- Use *at* with clock times: She gets up **at** 8:00.
- Use *on* with days: He sleeps late **on** weekends. She has class **on** Mondays.

B Complete the conversation with *at*, *in*, or *on*.

A: Does your family have breakfast together ___in___ the morning?
B: Well, we eat together ________ weekends, but ________ weekdays we're all busy. My parents go to work early – ________ 6:30. But we eat dinner together ________ the evening, and we have a big lunch together ________ Sundays. We eat ________ noon. Then ________ the afternoon, we take a walk or go to the movies.

UNIT 7

1 Simple present short answers page 45

- Remember: I/You/We/They **do/don't**. He/She/It **does/doesn't**.

Choose the correct words.

A: **Do / Does** your family **live / lives** in an apartment?
B: No, we **don't / doesn't**. We **have / has** a house.
A: That's nice. **Do / Does** your house have two floors?
B: Yes, it **do / does**. It **have / has** four rooms on the first floor. And we **have / has** three bedrooms and a bathroom on the second floor.
A: And **do / does** you and your family **have / has** a yard?
B: Yes, we **do / does**. And how about you, Tim? **Do / Does** you **live / lives** in a house, too?
A: No, I **don't / doesn't**. My wife and I **have / has** a small apartment in the city.
B: Oh. **Do / Does** you **like / likes** the city?
A: Yes, I **do / does**. But my wife **don't / doesn't**.

2 *There is, there are* page 47

- Use *there is* with singular nouns: **There's** a bed. Use *there are* with plural nouns: **There are** two chairs.
- Use *some* in affirmative statements: There are **some** chairs in the kitchen. Use *any* in negative statements: There aren't **any** chairs in the bedroom.

Read the information about the Perez family's new house. Write sentences with the phrases in the box.

there's a	there are some
there's no	there are no
there isn't a	there aren't any

1. A living room?	Yes.
2. A dining room?	No.
3. A microwave in the kitchen?	No.
4. A table in the kitchen?	Yes.
5. Curtains on the windows?	Yes.
6. Rugs on the floors?	No.
7. Closets in the bedrooms?	Yes.
8. Bookcases in the bedrooms?	No.

1. *There's a living room.*
2. ______
3. ______
4. ______
5. ______
6. ______
7. ______
8. ______

UNIT 8

1 Simple present Wh-questions page 52

- Use *What* to ask about things: **What do** you do? Use *Where* to ask about places: **Where do** you work? Use *How do/does . . . like . . . ?* to ask for an opinion: **How does** he **like** his job?

Complete the conversations.

1. **A:** *What does your husband do* ?
   B: My husband? Oh, he's a nurse.
   A: Really? Where ________________ ?
   B: He works at Mercy Hospital.
2. **A:** Where ________________ ?
   B: I work in a restaurant.
   A: Nice! What ________________ ?
   B: I'm a chef.
3. **A:** How ________________ ?
   B: My job? I don't really like it very much.
   A: That's too bad. What ________________ ?
   B: I'm a cashier. I work at a clothing store.
4. **A:** What ________________ ?
   B: My brother is a doctor, and my sister is a lawyer.
   A: How ________________ ?
   B: They work very hard, but they love their jobs.

2 Placement of adjectives page 54

- Adjectives come after the verb *be*: A doctor's job **is stressful**. Adjectives come before nouns: A police officer has a **dangerous job**. (NOT: ~~A police officer has a job dangerous.~~)
- Adjectives have the same form with singular or plural nouns: Firefighters and police officers have stressful jobs. (NOT: . . . have ~~stressfuls~~ jobs.)

Use the information to write two sentences.

1. accountant / job / boring
   An accountant's job is boring.
   An accountant has a boring job.
2. salesperson / job / stressful
   ____
   ____
3. security guard / job / dangerous
   ____
   ____
4. actor / job / exciting
   ____
   ____
5. host / job / interesting
   ____
   ____
6. nurse / job / difficult
   ____
   ____

UNIT 9

1 Count and noncount nouns; *some* and *any* page 59

- Count nouns name things you can count: *bananas, crackers, carrots.* Count nouns have a singular and plural form: ***1 orange, 2 oranges***. Noncount nouns name things you can't count: *milk, oil, rice.*
- Use *some* in affirmative sentences: We have **some** butter. Use *any* in negative sentences and questions: We don't have **any** lettuce. Do we have **any** tomatoes?

Complete the conversations with *some* or *any.*

1. **A:** What do you want for lunch?
   B: Let's make ___some___ sandwiches.
   A: Good idea! We have ________ bread. Do we have ________ cheese?
   B: Yes, I think there's ________ in the refrigerator. Let me see. . . .
   No, I don't see ________.
   A: Well, let's go to the store. We need ________ milk, too.
   And do we have ________ cheese?
   B: Yes, we do. There's ________ lettuce here, and there are
   ________ tomatoes, too.
   A: Do we have ________ mayonnaise? I love ________ mayonnaise
   on my sandwiches.
   B: Me, too. But there isn't ________ here. Let's buy ________.
2. **A:** Let's make a big breakfast tomorrow morning.
   B: Good idea! What do we need? Are there ________ eggs?
   A: There are ________ but I think we need to buy ________ more.
   B: OK. And let's get ________ cereal, too. We don't have ________,
   and I love cereal for breakfast.
   A: Me, too. Do we have ________ blueberry yogurt?
   B: Yes, there's ________ in the refrigerator.
   A: Great! So we don't need to buy ________ at the store.
   B: That's right. Just eggs and cereal!

2 Adverbs of frequency page 61

- Adverbs of frequency usually go before the main verb: *always, almost always, usually, often, sometimes, hardly ever, almost never, never*: She **never eats** breakfast. I **almost always have** tea in the morning.
  Sometimes can also begin a sentence: **Sometimes** I **eat** broccoli.

Rewrite the conversation. Add the adverbs in the correct places.

A: Where do you have lunch? (usually) ___Where do you usually have lunch?___
B: I go to a restaurant near work. (often) ________________
A: Do you eat at your desk? (ever) ________________
B: No, I stay in for lunch. (hardly ever) ________________
A: And what do you have? (usually) ________________
B: I have soup or a salad. (always) ________________
A: Me, too. I have a big lunch. (never) ________________

UNIT 10

1 Simple present Wh-questions page 65

- Remember: *Who* = what person; *where* = what place; *how often* = what frequency; *when* = what days; *what time* = what time of day
- Remember: Use *do* or *does* after the question word.

Complete the questions with the correct question word and *do* or *does*. Then match the questions with the answers.

1. ___What___ sport ___do___ you like? ___c___
2. ________ you go to games with? _____
3. ________ often ________ your team play? _____
4. ________ they play? _____
5. ________ they play? _____
6. ________ time ________ the games start? _____

a. My father and my two brothers.
b. Usually at four o'clock.
c. Soccer. I love to watch my team.
d. Once or twice a month.
e. On Sunday afternoons.
f. At the Olympic Stadium.

2 *Can* for ability page 67

- Use the base form of the verb with *can*. With third-person singular, don't add an –*s* to *can* or to the base form: She **can play** the piano. (NOT: ~~She can plays the piano.~~)

A Write sentences about the things people can and can't do. Use *can* or *can't* with *and*, *but*, or *or*. (✓ = can, ✗ = can't)

1. Olivia: ride a bike ✓ drive a car ✗
   Olivia can ride a bike, but she can't drive a car.
2. Juan: play the piano ✓ play the violin ✓
   ____
3. Matt and Drew: act ✓ sing ✗
   ____
4. Alicia: snowboard ✓ ice-skate ✗
   ____
5. Ben: take good photos ✓ edit videos ✓
   ____
6. Corinne: write poems ✗ tell good jokes ✓
   ____

B Look at part A. Answer the questions. Write short sentences.

1. Can Matt and Drew sing? No, they can't.
2. Who can tell good jokes? ________________
3. Can Olivia drive a car? ________________
4. Can Juan play the piano? ________________
5. Who can snowboard? ________________
6. What can Matt do? ________________

UNIT 11

1 The future with *be going to* page 73

- Use *am/is/are* + *going to* + base form for the future: We**'re going to have** dinner with my parents tonight.
- In questions with *be going to*, the *be* verb comes before the subject: **Is he going to buy** me a gift?

A Complete Matthew's story. Use the correct form of *be going to* and the verbs in parentheses.

Tomorrow is ___going to be___ (be) a very exciting day. It's my birthday, and my friends and I ________________ (celebrate). In the morning, Stephen and I ________________ (drive) to the beach. Our friend Rosa ________________ (meet) us there. We ________________ (stay) at the beach for a few hours. Then we ________________ (have) lunch at my favorite restaurant. After lunch, Stephen ________________ (go) to work, and Rosa and I ________________ (see) a movie. After the movie, we ________________ (go) to our friend Philip's house. He ________________ (make) his special homemade pizza for Rosa and me.

B Write questions. Then look at part A and answer the questions.

1. Matthew / celebrate / with his family?
   Q: Is Matthew going to celebrate with his family?
   A: No, he's going to celebrate with his friends.
2. Stephen and Matthew / ride their bikes / to the beach?
   Q: ________________
   A: ________________
3. the friends / have lunch / at a restaurant?
   Q: ________________
   A: ________________
4. Rosa and Matthew / go to a museum?
   Q: ________________
   A: ________________
5. Rosa and Matthew / have pizza / at a restaurant?
   Q: ________________
   A: ________________

2 Wh-questions with *be going to* page 75

- Use *is* in questions with *Who* as the subject: **Who's** going to be there? (NOT: ~~Who are going to be there?~~)

Complete the conversation with the correct form of *be going to*.

A: What ___are___ you ___going to do___ (do) this weekend?

B: I ________________ (have) a very busy weekend. My friend Amir ________________ (visit) me, and we ________________ (spend) the weekend in the city.

A: That's nice. ____________ you ________________ (stay) in a hotel?

B: No, we ________________ (stay) with our friend Lara. And Lara ________________ (have) a big party on Saturday night.

A: Really? And who ________________ (be) at the party? Do you know any of Lara's friends?

B: No, I don't. But Amir and I ________________ (meet) everyone on Saturday night.

UNIT 12

1 *Have* + noun; *feel* + adjective page 79

- For most health problems, use *a/an*: I have **a** cold. I have **an** earache. With *flu*, use *the*: I have **the** flu. (NOT: ~~I have a flu.~~)

Complete the conversation. Use the sentences in the box.

I think I have a fever.
Thanks.
I feel awful, actually.
Yes. I'm going to call my doctor in a few minutes.
Yes, I do. And I have a stomachache, too.
✓ Hi, Vanessa. How are you?

A: *Hi, Vanessa. How are you?*
B: I'm terrific, thanks. How about you?
A: ______
B: Oh, no! What's the matter?
A: ______
B: That's too bad. Do you have a headache?
A: ______
B: Are you going to see a doctor?
A: ______
B: Well, feel better soon.
A: ______

2 Imperatives page 82

- Use the base form of the verb in affirmative imperatives: **Go** home and **rest**, Ms. Lake.
- Use *don't* + base form of the verb in negative imperatives. The form doesn't change: **Don't go** to work today, Ms. Lake.

Read the situations. Give the people advice. Use the phrases in the box.

✓ drink coffee in the evening
eat any cold food
exercise today or tomorrow
take an antacid
take two aspirins
work too hard

1. Dave: "I can't sleep at night." *Don't drink coffee in the evening.*
2. Corey: "I have a headache." ______
3. Lucia: "I work 12 hours a day." ______
4. William: "My legs hurt." ______
5. Min-ho: "I have a toothache." ______
6. Fatima: "I have an awful stomachache." ______

UNIT 13

1 Prepositions of place page 88

- Use *on* with the names of streets and avenues: The bookstore is **on** Center Street. The theater is **on** Park Avenue.
- *Across from* is another way of saying *opposite*: The library is **across from** the theater. = The library is **opposite** the theater.

Choose the correct words.

A: Excuse me. Is there a post office around here?
B: Yes, there is. It's **in / on** Maple Street.
A: Where on Maple?
B: It's **in / on** the corner of Maple Street and Second Avenue.
A: Next **from / to** Charlie's Restaurant?
B: Yes, that's right. It's across the street **from / to** the Windsor Hotel.
A: Thanks. Oh, and where is the bank?
B: It's on Oak Street – **between / next to** the hospital and police station.
A: Great. Thanks very much.
B: You're welcome.

2 Directions page 90

- *Walk up/Go up* mean the same thing. *Walk down/Go down* also mean the same thing.

Jenna doesn't know Manhattan at all. Correct Jenna's directions.
Write the opposite of what she says.

1. Cal How do I get to Washington Square Park?
Jenna Walk up Fifth Avenue.
You *No, don't walk up Fifth Avenue. Walk down Fifth Avenue.*

2. Cal How can I get to the Empire State Building?
Jenna Turn right on 32nd Street.
You ______________________________

3. Cal How do I get to Bryant Park from Rockefeller Center?
Jenna Go down Sixth Avenue.
You ______________________________
Jenna It's on the left.
You ______________________________

4. Cal How do I get to Central Park?
Jenna Walk down Eighth Avenue.
You ______________________________

UNIT 14

1 Simple past statements: regular verbs and irregular verbs page 93–94

- Use simple past verbs to talk about the past. Regular verbs end in *–ed*: I **watched** TV last night. For verbs ending in *–e*, add *–d*: *live* ⟶ *lived*. For verbs ending in vowel + consonant, double the consonant and add *–ed*: *shop* ⟶ *shopped*.
- Use *didn't* + base form in negative statements. The form doesn't change: He **didn't shop** for groceries yesterday. (NOT: ~~He didn't shopped for groceries yesterday.~~)

Maya wrote an email to a friend. Complete the sentences with the simple past form of the verbs in parentheses.

Hi!

I ___didn't do___ (not do) anything special this weekend, but I ________ (have) a lot of fun. I ________ (not go) out on Friday night. I ________ (stay) home. I ________ (clean) my room and ________ (do) the laundry. I ________ (help) my sister with her homework, and then we ________ (watch) our favorite series. On Saturday, my friend Lori ________ (come) over. She ________ (need) some new shoes, so we ________ (take) the bus downtown to Todd's Shoe Store. We ________ (shop) for a long time, but Lori ________ (not like) any of the shoes at Todd's. She ________ (buy) some purple socks, but she ________ (not buy) any shoes. On our way back to my house, we ________ (stop) at the gym and ________ (exercise). We ________ (not exercise) very hard. I ________ (invite) Lori for dinner, and my dad ________ (cook) hamburgers in the yard. After dinner, Lori and I ________ (talk) and ________ (play) video games. She ________ (not stay) very late – my mother ________ (drive) her home at around ten. On Sunday, my whole family ________ (visit) my mother's best friend and her family. They have a swimming pool, so my sister and I ________ (go) swimming all afternoon.

Tell me about your weekend!

Maya

2 Simple past yes/no questions page 95

- Use *did* + base form in questions. The form doesn't change: **Did** you **have** fun yesterday? (NOT: ~~Did you had fun yesterday?~~)

Complete the conversation. Use the simple past form of the verbs in parentheses.

A: ___Did___ you ___enjoy___ (enjoy) your vacation?

B: Yes, I ________. My brother and I ________ (have) a great time.

A: ________ you ________ (make) any videos?

B: No, we ________. But we ________ (take) a lot of pictures.

A: That's good. ________ you ________ (see) a lot of interesting things?

B: Yes, we ________. And we ________ (eat) a lot of new foods. How about you? ________ you (have) a good summer?

A: Well, I ________ (not go) anywhere, but I ________ (read) a lot of good books and ________ (see) some great movies.

UNIT 15

1 Past of *be* page 101

Present		Past
am/is	→	**was**
are	→	**were**

Complete the conversations with *was*, *wasn't*, *were*, or *weren't*.

1. **A:** ___Were___ you here yesterday?
   B: No, I ________. I ________ home in bed.
   A: Oh, ________ you sick?
   B: No. I ________ just really tired.
2. **A:** Where ________ you born?
   B: I ________ born in Mexico City.
   A: Really? What about your parents? ________ they born here, too?
   B: No, they ________. They ________ born in Guadalajara.
3. **A:** Where ________ Jamil last week? ________ he on vacation?
   B: Yes, he ________. He and his best friend ________ in Portugal.
   They ________ in Oporto.
   A: ________ it a good trip?
   B: Yes, it was. Jamil said it ________ a terrific trip!

2 Wh-questions with *did*, *was*, and *were* page 101

- Don't use *did* with the past of *be*: Where **were** you last Tuesday? (NOT: ~~Where did you were last Tuesday?~~) Use *did* in simple past questions with other verbs: Where **did** you **go** last Tuesday?
- *Because* answers the question *Why?*

Complete the questions. Use the words in the box.

✓ how	what	where	why
how old	when	who	

1. **A:** ___How___ was your childhood?
   B: I had a fantastic childhood!
2. **A:** ________ did you grow up?
   B: I grew up in Incheon, a small city in South Korea.
3. **A:** ________ were you when you started school?
   B: I think I was five or six.
4. **A:** ________ was your best friend in high school?
   B: My best friend was a boy named Joon-ho.
5. **A:** ________ did you leave home?
   B: In 2012.
6. **A:** ________ did you leave Incheon?
   B: Because I wanted to live in a big city.
7: **A:** ________ was your first job in Seoul?
   B: I worked as a server in a restaurant.

UNIT 16

1 Subject and object pronouns page 107

- Subject pronouns usually come before verbs, and object pronouns go after verbs: **I** saw **him**, but **he** didn't see **me**.

Complete the conversations.

1. **A:** Hello. Is Mr. Chang there?
   B: No, ___he's___ not here right now. Can take a message?
   A: Yes. Please tell ________ to call Todd Harris.
   B: Does ________ have your number?
   A: No, but please give it to ________. It's 555-0987.
2. **A:** Oh, hello, Kimberly!
   A: Hello, Mrs. Sanchez. Is Veronica home?
   B: No, ________ at the mall with her brother. Their dad drove ________ there this morning. Would ________ like to come in?
   A: Thank you, Mrs. Sanchez, but I need to go home. Anyway, my sister and ________ are going to an amusement park tomorrow and maybe Veronica can go with ________. Is that all right?
   B: Sure. I can give ________ your message, or ________ can text her.
   A: Oh, don't worry, Mrs. Sanchez. I'll text ________. Thanks a lot. Bye!

2 Invitations; verb + *to* page 109

- You can use both *Do you want to . . . ?* and *Would you like to . . . ?* to invite a person to do something.
- Don't confuse *would like to* with *like to*. *Would like to* means the same as *want to*.
- *I'd (really) like to* and *I'd love to* both mean the same as *I want to*.

Rewrite the conversations. Write the sentences in a different way.

1. **A:** Do you want to see a movie tonight?	**A:** ___Would you like to see a movie tonight?___
B: Oh, I can't. I need to work.	**B:** ________
2. **A:** Do you want to play tennis on Saturday?	**A:** ________
B: I'd love to, but I have to help my parents.	**B:** ________
3. **A:** I want a job at Carol's café.	**A:** ________
B: You need to speak to her.	**B:** ________
4. **A:** Would you like to go to a party with me?	**A:** ________
B: I want to, but I can't. I have to study.	**B:** ________

Grammar plus answer key

Unit 1

1 *My, your, his, her*

1. A: Hello. **My** name is Carlos.
   B: Hi, Carlos. What's **your** last name?
   A: It's Gonzales.
   B: How do you spell **your** last name? Is it G-O-N-Z-A-L-E-Z?
   A: No, it's G-O-N-Z-A-L-E-S. And what's **your** name?
   B: **My** name is Bill Powers. Nice to meet you.
2. A: What's Ms. Robinson's first name?
   B: **Her** first name is Elizabeth. **Her** nickname is Liz.
   A: I'm sorry. What's **her** first name again?
   B: It's Elizabeth. And what's Mr. Weber's first name?
   A: **His** first name is Peter.
   B: That's right. And **his** nickname is Pete.
   A: That's right, too!

2 The verb *be*

1. A: Excuse me. **Are** you Layla Moore?
   B: No, **I'm not**. **She's** over there.
   A: OK. Thanks.
2. A: Hi. Are **you** Layla Moore?
   B: Yes, **I am**.
   A: Nice to meet you. **I'm** Sergio Oliveira. **You're** in my English class.
   B: Yes, I **am**. **It's** nice to meet you too, Sergio.

Unit 2

1 *This/These; it/they;* plurals

1. A: **What are** these?
   B: **They're** my flash drives.
2. A: **What's** this?
   B: **It's** a cell phone.
3. A: What's **this**?
   B: **It's an** English book.

2 Yes/No and *where* questions with *be*

A

1. c 2. e 3. a 4. b 5. d

B

A: **Where's** my dictionary?
B: I don't know. Is **it** in your backpack?
A: No, **it's** not.
B: Is **this** your dictionary?
A: Yes, **it** is. Thanks! Now, where **are** my glasses?
B: **Are** they on your desk?
A: Yes, **they are**. Thank you!

Unit 3

1 Negative statements and yes/no questions with *be*

A

2. We're not from Buenos Aires.
3. You and Ashley are not in my class.
4. My first language is not Korean. / Korean is not my first language.
5. My mother is not from Italy.
6. They are not my parents.

B

1. B: No, **are** not. **We're/We are** from the Dominican Republic.
2. A: **Is** your first language Spanish?
   B: Yes, it **is**. My parents **are** from Ecuador.
3. A: **Are** Nadia and Rayan Lebanese?
   B: Yes, **they** are. But **they're/they are** in France now.
4. A: **Are** my friends and I late?
   B: No, **you're/you are** not. **You're/You are** early!

2 Wh-questions with *be*

2. **What** is her name? c
3. **What** is she like? f
4. **How** old is she? b
5. **Where** is your family from? a
6. **What** is Kyoto like? e

Unit 4

1 Possessives

1. A: **Whose** jacket is this? Is it **yours**, Ethan?
   B: No, it's not **mine**. Ask Matt. I think it's **his**.
2. A: These aren't **my** gloves. Are they **yours**?
   B: No, they're not **mine.** Maybe they are Young-min's.
3. A: **Whose** sweaters are these? Are they Rachel's?
   B: No, they're not **her** sweaters. But these shorts are **hers**.

2 Present continuous statements; conjunctions

2. It's snowing.
3. I'm not wearing a winter coat.
4. You're not/You aren't wearing David's sunglasses.
5. Ayumi is wearing a scarf.

3 Present continuous yes/no questions

1. B: No, **he's not/he isn't.**
2. A: **Are you wearing** high heels?
   B: No, **we're not/we aren't.**
3. A: **Are you wearing** a sweater?
   B: Yes, **I am**.
4. A: **Is it** raining?
   B: Yes, **it is.**

Unit 5

1 What time is it? / Is it A.M. or P.M.?

3. It's a quarter after six.
4. It's 10:00 P.M.
5. It's five (minutes) after three.
6. It's ten thirty-five.
7. It's one A.M.
8. It's 12:00 A.M./It's twelve (o'clock) at night.

2 Present continuous Wh-questions

2. A: What are Jon and Megan doing?
   B: They're shopping.
3. A: What are you doing?
   B: I'm writing a message.
4. A: What's Chris doing?
   B: He's cooking dinner.
5. A: What are you and Tyler doing?
   B: We're watching a movie.
6. A: What's Sara doing?
   B: She's having pizza.
7. A: What are you and Joseph doing?
   B: We're studying for a test.
8. A: What are Laura and Paulo doing?
   B: They're chatting online.

Unit 6

1 Simple present statements and Simple present statements with irregular verbs

My family and I **live** in the city. We **have** an apartment on First Avenue. My sister **goes** to school near our apartment, so she **walks** to school. My father **works** in the suburbs, so he **drives** to his job. My mother **uses** public transportation – she **takes** the bus to her office downtown. She **has** a new job, but she **doesn't like** it very much. And me? Well, I **don't work** far from our apartment, so I **don't need** a car or public transportation. I **ride** my bike to work!

2 Simple present questions

A

2. A: Does your family eat dinner at 5:00?
3. A: Does your brother take the bus to work?
4. A: Do you get up late on weekends?

B

B: Well, we eat together **on** weekends, but **on** weekdays we're all busy. My parents go to work early – **at** 6:30. But we eat dinner together **in** the evening, and we have a big lunch together **on** Sundays. We eat **at** noon. Then **in** the afternoon, we take a walk or go to the movies.

Unit 7

1 Simple present short answers

A: **Does** your family **live** in an apartment?
B: No, we **don't**. We **have** a house.
A: That's nice. **Does** your house have two floors?
B: Yes, it **does**. It **has** four rooms on the first floor. And we **have** three bedrooms and a bathroom on the second floor.
A: And **do** you and your family **have** a yard?
B: Yes, we **do**. And how about you, Tim? **Do** you **live** in a house, too?
A: No, I **don't**. My wife and I **have** a small apartment in the city.
B: Oh. **Do** you **like** the city?
A: Yes, I **do**. But my wife **doesn't**.

2 *There is, there are*

2. There's no / There isn't a dining room.
3. There's no / There isn't a microwave in the kitchen.
4. There's a table in the kitchen.
5. There are some curtains on the windows.
6. There are no / There aren't any rugs on the floors.
7. There are closets in the bedrooms.
8. There are no / There aren't any bookcases in the bedroom.

Unit 8

1 Simple present Wh-questions

1. A: Really? Where **does he work**?
2. A: Where **do you work**?
   B: I work in a restaurant.
   A: Nice! What **do you do**?
   B: I'm a chef.
3. A: How **do you like your job**?
   B: My job? I don't really like it very much.
   A: That's too bad. What **do you do**?
   B: I'm a cashier. I work at a clothing store.
4. A: What **do your brother and sister do**?
   B: My brother is a doctor, and my sister is a lawyer.
   A: How **do they like their jobs**?
   B: They work very hard, but they love their jobs.

2 Placement of adjectives

2. A salesperson's job is stressful.
   A salesperson has a stressful job.
3. A security guard's job is dangerous.
   A security guard has a dangerous job.
4. An actor's job is exciting.
   An actor has an exciting job.
5. A host's job is interesting.
   A host has an interesting job.
6. A nurse's job is difficult.
   A nurse has a difficult job.

Unit 9

1 Count and noncount nouns; *some* and *any*

1. A: What do you want for lunch?
   B: Let's make **some** sandwiches.
   A: Good idea! We have **some** bread. Do we have **any** cheese?
   B: Yes, I think there's **some** in the refrigerator. Let me see. . . . No, I don't see **any**.
   A: Well, let's go to the store. We need **some** milk, too. And do we have **any** cheese?
   B: Yes, we do. There's **some** lettuce here, and there are **some** tomatoes, too.
   A: Do we have **any** mayonnaise? I love **some** mayonnaise on my sandwiches.
   B: Me, too. But there isn't **any** here. Let's buy **some**.
2. A: Let's make a big breakfast tomorrow morning.
   B: Good idea! What do we need? Are there **any** eggs?
   A: There are **some** but I think we need to buy **some** more.
   B: OK. And let's get **some** cereal, too. We don't have **any**, and I love cereal for breakfast.
   A: Me, too. Do we have **any** blueberry yogurt?
   B: Yes, there's **some** in the refrigerator.
   A: Great! So we don't need to buy **any** at the store.
   B: That's right. Just eggs and cereal!

2 Adverbs of frequency (page 61)

B: I often go to a restaurant near work.
A: Do you ever eat at your desk?
B: No, I hardly ever stay in for lunch.
A: A: And what do you usually have?
B: I always have soup or a salad.
A: Me, too. I never have a big lunch.

Unit 10

1 Simple present Wh-questions

2. Who do you go to games with? a
3. How often does your team play? d
4. When do they play? e or Where do they play? f
5. Where do they play? f or When do they play? e
6. What time do the games start? b

2 *Can* for ability

A

2. Juan can play the piano, and he can play the violin.
3. Matt and Drew can act, but they can't sing.
4. Alicia can snowboard, but she can't ice-skate.
5. Ben can take good photos, and he can edit videos.
6. Corinne can't write poems but she can tell good jokes.

B

2. Corinne can.
4. Yes, he can.
6. He can act.
3. No, she can't.
5. Alicia can.

Unit 11

1 The future with *be going to*

A Tomorrow **is going to be** a very exciting day. It's my birthday, and my friends and I **are going to celebrate**. In the morning, Stephen and I **are going to drive** to the beach. Our friend Rosa **is going to meet** us there. We**'re going to stay** at the beach for a few hours. Then we**'re going to have** lunch at my favorite restaurant. After lunch, Stephen **is going to go** to work, and Rosa and I **are going to see** a movie. After the movie, we**'re going to go** to our friend Philip's house. He **is going to cook** dinner for Rosa and me.

B Q: Are Stephen and Matthew going to ride their bikes to the beach?
A: No, they're going to drive to the beach.

4. Q: Are the friends going to have lunch at a restaurant?
   A: Yes, they are.
5. Q: Are Rosa and Matthew going to go to a museum?
   A: No, they're not. (They're going to see a movie.)
6. Q: Are Rosa and Matthew going to have dinner at a restaurant?
   A: No, they're not. (They're going to have dinner at Philip's house.)

2 Wh-questions with *be going to*

A: What **are** you **going to do** this weekend?
B: I**'m going to have** a very busy weekend. My friend Amir **is going to visit** me, and we**'re going to spend** the weekend in the city.
A: That's nice. **Are** you **going to stay** in a hotel?
B: No, we**'re going to stay** with our friend Lara. And Lara **is going to have** a big party on Saturday night.
A: Really? And who**'s going to be** at the party? Do you know any of Lara's friends?
B: No, I don't. But Amir and I **are going to meet** everyone on Saturday night.

Unit 12

1 *Have* + noun; *feel* + adjective

A: **Hi, Vanessa. How are you?**
B: I'm terrific, thanks. How about you?
A: **I feel awful, actually.**
B: Oh, no! What's the matter?
A: **I think I have a fever.**
B: That's too bad. Do you have a headache?
A: **Yes, I do. And I have a stomachache, too.**
B: Are you going to see a doctor?
A: **Yes. I'm going to call my doctor in a few minutes.**
B: Well, feel better soon.
A: **Thanks.**

2 Imperatives

2. Take two aspirins.
3. Don't work too hard.
4. Don't exercise today or tomorrow.
5. Don't eat any cold food.
6. Take an antacid.

Unit 13

1 Prepositions of place

A: Excuse me. Is there a post office around here?
B: Yes, there is. It's **on** Maple Street.
A: Where on Maple?
B: It's **on** the corner of Maple Street and Second Avenue.
A: Next **to** Charlie's Restaurant?
B: Yes, that's right. It's across the street **from** the Windsor Hotel.
A: Thanks. Oh, and where is the bank?
B: It's on Oak Street – **between** the hospital and police station.
A: Great. Thanks very much.
B: You're welcome.

2 Directions

2. You: No, don't turn right on 32nd Street. Turn left on 32nd Street.
3. You: No, don't go down Sixth Avenue. Go up First Avenue.
   You: No, it's not on the left. It's on the right.
4. You: No, don't walk down Eight Avenue. Walk up Eighth Avenue.

Unit 14

1 Simple past statements: regular verbs and irregular verbs

Hi!
I **didn't do** anything special this weekend, but I **had** a lot of fun. I **didn't go** out on Friday night. I **stayed** home. I **cleaned** my room and **did** laundry. I **helped** my sister with her homework, and then we **watched** our favorite series. On Saturday, my friend Lori **came** over. She **needed** some new shoes, so we **took** the bus downtown to Todd's Shoe Store. We **shopped** for a long time, but Lori **didn't like** any of the shoes at Todd's. She **bought** some purple socks, but she **didn't buy** any shoes. On our way back to my house, we **stopped** at the gym and **exercised**. We **didn't exercise** very hard. I **invited** Lori for dinner, and my dad **cooked** hamburgers in the yard. After dinner, Lori and I **talked** and **played** video games. She **didn't stay** too late – Mom **drove** her home at around ten. On Sunday, my whole family **visited** my mother's best friend and her family. They have a swimming pool, so my sister and I **went** swimming all afternoon.

2 Simple past yes/no questions

A: **Did** you **enjoy** your vacation?
B: Yes, I **did**. My brother and I **had** a great time.
A: **Did** you **make** a lot any videos?
B: No, we **didn't**. But we **took** a lot of pictures.
A: That's good. **Did** you **see** a lot of interesting things?
B: Yes, we **did**. And we **ate** a lot of new foods.
How about you? **Did** you **have** a good summer?
A: Well, I **didn't go** anywhere, but I **read** a lot of good books and **saw** some great movies.

Unit 15

1 Past of *be*

1. A: **Were** you here yesterday?
   B: No, I **wasn't**. I **was** home in bed.
   A: Oh, **were** you sick?
   B: No. I **was** just really tired.
2. A: Where **were** you born?
   B: I **was** born in Mexico City.
   A: Really? What about your parents? **Were** they born here, too?
   B: No, they **weren't**. They **were** born in Guadalajara.
3. A: Where **was** Jamil last week? **Was** he on vacation?
   B: Yes, he **was**. He and his best friend **were** in Portugal. They **were** in Oporto.
   A: **Was** it a good trip?
   B: Yes, it was. Jamil said it **was** a terrific trip!

2 Wh-questions with *did*, *was*, and *were*

1. A: **How** was your childhood?
   B: I had a fantastic childhood!
2. A: **Where** did you grow up?
   B: I grew up in Incheon, a small city in South Korea.
3. A: **How old** were you when you started school?
   B: I think I was five or six.
4. A: **Who** was your best friend in high school?
   B: My best friend was a boy named Joon-ho.
5. A: **When** did you leave home?
   B: In 2012.
6. A: **Why** did you leave Incheon?
   B: Because I wanted to live in a big city.
7: A: **What** was your first job in Seoul?
   B: I worked as a server in a restaurant.

Unit 16

1 Subject and object pronouns

1. A: Hello. Is Mr. Chang there?
   B: No, **he's** not here right now. Can take a message?
   A: Yes. Please tell **him** to call Todd Harris.
   B: Does **he** have your number?
   A: No, but please give it to **him**. It's 555-0987.
2. A: Oh, hello, Kimberly!
   A: Hello, Mrs. Sanchez. Is Veronica home?
   B: No, **she's** at the mall with her brother. Their dad drove **them** there this morning. Would **you** like to come in?
   A: Thank you, Mrs. Sanchez, but I need to go home. Anyway, my sister and **I** are going to an amusement park tomorrow and maybe Veronica can go with **us**. Is that all right?
   B: Sure. I can give **her** your message, or **you** can text her.
   A: Oh, don't worry, Mrs. Sanchez. I'll text **her.** Thanks a lot. Bye!

2 Invitations; verb + *to*

1. B: Oh, I can't. I **have** to work.
2. A: **Would you like** to play tennis on Saturday?
   B: **I'd like to,** but I need to help my parents.
3. A: **I'd like** a job at Carol's café.
   B: You **have** to speak to her.
4. A: **Do you want** to go to a party with me?
   B: **I'd like to**, but I can't. I **need** to study.

Appendix

Countries, nationalities, and languages

This is a partial list of countries, nationalities, and languages, many of which are presented in this book.

Countries	Nationalities	Countries	Nationalities	Countries	Nationalities
Argentina	Argentine	Haiti	Haitian	the Philippines	Filipino
Australia	Australian	Honduras	Honduran	Poland	Polish
Austria	Austrian	India	Indian	Portugal	Portuguese
Bolivia	Bolivian	Indonesia	Indonesian	Puerto Rico	Puerto Rican
Brazil	Brazilian	Ireland	Irish	Russia	Russian
Cambodia	Cambodian	Israel	Israeli	Saudi Arabia	Saudi Arabian
Canada	Canadian	Italy	Italian	Singapore	Singaporean
Chile	Chilean	Japan	Japanese	Somalia	Somalian
China	Chinese	Jordan	Jordanian	South Africa	South African
Colombia	Colombian	Laos	Laotian	South Korea	Korean
Costa Rica	Costa Rican	Lebanon	Lebanese	Spain	Spanish
Cuba	Cuban	Malaysia	Malaysian	Sudan	Sudanese
the Dominican Republic	Dominican	Mexico	Mexican	Sweden	Swedish
Ecuador	Ecuadorian	Morocco	Moroccan	Switzerland	Swiss
Egypt	Egyptian	Nepal	Nepalese	Tanzania	Tanzanian
El Salvador	El Salvadoran	the Netherlands	Dutch	Thailand	Thai
England	English	New Zealand	New Zealander	Turkey	Turkish
France	French	Nicaragua	Nicaraguan	the United Kingdom (the U.K.)	British
Germany	German	Nigeria	Nigerian	the United States (the U.S.)	American
Ghana	Ghanian	Panama	Panamanian	Uruguay	Uruguayan
Greece	Greek	Paraguay	Paraguayan	Venezuela	Venezuelan
Guatemala	Guatemalan	Peru	Peruvian	Vietnam	Vietnamese

Languages

Afrikaans	English	Hebrew	Japanese	Portuguese	Swedish
Arabic	French	Hindi	Korean	Russian	Thai
Chinese	German	Indonesian	Malay	Spanish	Turkish
Dutch	Greek	Italian	Polish	Swahili	Vietnamese

Irregular verbs

Present	Past	Present	Past	Present	Past
(be) am/is, are	was, were	have	had	sell	sold
become	became	know	knew	sing	sang
buy	bought	leave	left	sit	sat
come	came	make	made	sleep	slept
do	did	meet	met	speak	spoke
drink	drank	pay	paid	swim	swam
drive	drove	read	read /rɛd/	take	took
eat	ate	ride	rode	teach	taught
feel	felt	run	ran	think	thought
get	got	say	said /sɛd/	wear	wore
give	gave	see	saw	write	wrote
go	went				

1 Language summary

VOCABULARY

Nouns
The alphabet
See Exercise 4 on page 3.

Numbers
(0–10)
See Exercise 11 on page 6.

Titles
Miss
Mr.
Mrs.
Ms.

Other
book
celebrity
cell phone (number)
class
classmate
email address
female
history
home phone (number)
male
name
nickname
phone number
teacher
work phone (number)

Pronouns
Subjects
I
you
he
she
it

Other
this
what

Adjectives
Possessives
my
your
his
her
our

Other
celebrity
first
last
married
popular
single

Article
the

Verbs
am
are
is

Adverbs
Responses
no
yes

Other
not
(over) there
too (= also)

Preposition
in (my class)

Conjunctions
and
or

EXPRESSIONS

Saying hello
Hello.
Hi.
Good morning.
Good afternoon.
Good evening.
How are you?
How's it going?
How are you doing?
  Great. How about you?
  I'm (just) fine.
  I'm OK.
  Pretty good.

Saying good-bye
Bye.
Bye-bye.
Good-bye.
See you later.
See you tomorrow.
Have a great weekend.
Have a good evening.
  Thank you. You, too.
Good night.

Introducing yourself and others
Hi. My name is . . .
  I'm . . .
It's nice to meet you.
  Nice to meet you, too.
This is . . .

Checking and confirming information
What's your (last) name (again)?
  It's . . .
Is that . . . ?
  Yes, that's right.
  No, it's . . .
Are you . . . ?
  Yes, I am.
  No, I'm not.
How do you spell . . . ?
Can you repeat that?

Getting someone's attention
Excuse me.
Hey, . . .

Thanking someone
Thank you./Thanks.

Expressing surprise
Oh!

Apologizing
I'm sorry.

Giving an opinion
I think . . .

2 Language summary

VOCABULARY

Nouns

Classroom objects
backpack
board
(English) book
chair
clock
desk
dictionary
door
eraser
notebook
outlet
paper clip
pen
pencil
poster
table
wall
wastebasket
window

Personal items
bag
bicycle
cell phone
credit card
energy bar
flash drive
glasses
hairbrush
headphones
(student) ID
(car) keys
laptop
newspaper
phone case
purse
sunglasses
tablet
tablet case
television
ticket
umbrella
wallet

Other
box
car
class(es)
pocket
restaurant
quiz
sentence

Pronouns
it
this
that
these
they

Adjectives
cool
different
great
interesting

Articles
a
an

Adverbs
maybe
now
where

Prepositions
behind
in
in front of
next to
on
under

EXPRESSIONS

Identifying things
What's this (called in English)?
  I don't know.
  It's a . . .
What are these (called in English)?
  They're . . .
  I think they're (called) . . .

Identifying the owner of something
Is this your . . . ?
  Yes, it is.
  No, it's not.
Are these your . . . ?
  Yes, they are.
  No, they're not.

Thanking someone
Thank you!
You're welcome.

Expressing pleasure
Wow!
Oh, cool!
It's great!

Expressing disbelief
Really?

Expressing disappointment
Oh, no!

Thinking before responding
Let me see.
Huh . . .
Hmm . . .

Agreeing
You're right.

Realizing something
Wait (a minute)!

3 Language summary

VOCABULARY

Nouns
Countries, nationalities, and languages
See the appendix on page T-151.

People
brother
daughter
family
father
(best) friend
mother
parent(s)
partner
sister
student

Places
capital
city (*plural*: cities)
country (*plural*: countries)
world

Pronouns
Subjects
they
we

Other
that
who

Determiner
a little

Adjectives
Appearance
beautiful
cute
good-looking
handsome
heavy
pretty
short
tall
thin

Personality
friendly
funny
kind
nice
quiet
serious
shy
smart
talkative

Numbers and ages
(11–30; 40, 50, etc.)
See Exercise 7 on page 19.

Other
early
false
first (language)
large (largest)
late
new
old
true

Adverbs
originally
really (+ adjective)
this week
very (+ adjective)

Prepositions
from (Brazil)
in (Florida)

Conjunctions
but
so

EXPRESSIONS

Asking about countries, nationalities, and languages
Where are you from?
  I'm from (Canada).
What's (San Francisco) like?
  It's . . .
Are you from (Florida)?
  Yes, I am.
  No, I'm not.
Are you (Japanese)?
  Yes, I am.
  No, I'm not.
Is your first language (Portuguese)?
  Yes, it is.
  No, it's not.

Asking about people
Who's that?
  She's . . .
What's her name?
  Her name is . . .
How old is she?
  She's (28) years old.
What's she like?
  She's . . .
Is she (talkative)?
  Yes, she is.
  No, she's not.

Getting someone's attention
Look!

Introducing a different topic
By the way, . . .

Introducing an explanation or idea
Well, . . .

Expressing surprise
Really?
Wow!

4 Language summary

VOCABULARY

Nouns
Clothes
belt
blouse
boot(s)
cap
coat
dress
glove(s)
hat
(high) heels
jacket
jeans
pajamas
pants
raincoat
scarf
shirt
shoe(s)
shorts
skirt
sneakers
socks
suit
sweater
swimsuit
tie
T-shirt

Seasons
spring
summer
fall
winter

Other
disaster
free time
home
problem
taxi
work

Adjectives
Colors
beige
black
(dark/light) blue
(dark/light) brown
(dark/light) gray
(dark/light) green
orange
pink
purple
red
white
yellow

Weather
cloudy
cold
cool
hot
humid
sunny
warm
windy

Possessives
my
your
his
her
our
their

Other
all
dry
favorite
new

Pronouns
Possessives
mine
yours
his
hers
ours
theirs
whose

Verbs
ask
rain
snow
wear

Adverb
today

Prepositions
around (the world)
at (home)

Conjunction
and
but
so

EXPRESSIONS

Talking about preferences
What are your favorite colors?
My favorite colors are . . .

Asking about and describing clothing
What color is/are . . . ?
It's/They're . . .
Are you wearing . . . ?
Yes, I am.
No, I'm not. I'm wearing . . .

Talking about the weather
It's snowing/raining/. . .
It's cloudy/cold/hot/sunny/. . .

Making a contrast
. . . , but . . .

Getting someone's attention
Hey!
Look.

Asking about a problem
What's the matter?

Expressing distress
Oh, no!

Making a suggestion
Let's . . .

Agreeing with a suggestion
Good idea!

Expressing pleasure
Great!

5 Language summary

VOCABULARY

Nouns

Meals
breakfast
lunch
dinner

Other
basketball
bike
boss
cheese
coffee
job
messages
movie
report
soccer
social media
spaghetti
time zone
tomato sauce
vacation

Adjectives

hungry
same

Verbs

call
check (messages)
cook
dance
do
drive
eat
get (hungry/married)
get up
go (to work)
have (breakfast/lunch)
help
listen to music
make (coffee)
message
play (soccer/basketball)
read
remember
ride (a bike)
ring
run
shop
sleep
study
swim
take (a walk)
visit
watch (a movie)
work
write (a report)

Adverbs

Times
at night
in the afternoon
in the evening
in the morning

Clock times
6:00 A.M./6:00 P.M.
midnight
noon
a quarter after (six)
a quarter to (six)

Other
(right) now
there
why

Conjunction

so

EXPRESSIONS

Talking about the time
What time is it?
It's . . . A.M./P.M.
It's . . . o'clock (in the morning/. . .).
It's . . . after . . .
It's a quarter after . . .
It's . . . -thirty.
It's a quarter to . . .
It's . . . to . . .

Talking about current activities
What are you doing?
I'm . . .
Are you . . . -ing?
Sure.
Yes, I am.
No, I'm not. I'm . . . -ing.

Pausing while messaging
Oh, wait.
Be right back.

Talking on the phone
Hello?
Hi, ... This is . . .

Checking information
Right?
That's right.
Oh, really?

Apologizing
I'm really sorry.
That's OK.

Giving a reason
. . . , so . . .

Expressing a positive opinion
I love . . .
Oh, that's good.
Lucky you.

Wishing someone well
Congratulations
Good luck

6 Language summary

VOCABULARY

Nouns

Transportation
bike
bus
car
motorcycle
subway
train
taxi/cab

Family
brother
child (*plural*: children)
daughter
father/dad
husband
kid(s)
mother/mom
parents
sister
son
wife

Places
apartment
hotel
house
park
restaurant
room
school
suburbs

Days of the week
Monday
Tuesday
Wednesday
Thursday
Friday
Saturday
Sunday
weekday
weekend

Other
bed
blog
businesspeople
drums
homework
job
lights
noise
pet
routine
schedule
survey
tourist
travel agency

Pronouns

Object pronouns
me
us

Determiner

a lot of

Adjectives

alone
busy
professional
public
retired
strange

Verbs

exercise
live
meet
need
pay
see (family/friends)
serve
start
stop
take (a taxi/cab; the train/subway)
use

Adverbs

Times
all day
at night
early
every day
late
weekly

Places
downtown
far (from here)
here
near (our house)

Other
also
sometimes
then
together
when

Prepositions

at (9:00/noon/midnight/night)
by (bus/car)
in (the morning/the afternoon/the evening)
on (Sundays/weekdays/weekends)
with (our parents)

EXPRESSIONS

Talking about routines
What time do you . . . ?
At . . .
When do they . . . ?
On . . .
Does he . . . ?
Yes, he . . . every morning.
What do you do on . . . ?
On . . . , I . . .

Idioms
early bird
night owl

Responses
Sure.
Yeah.

Asking for more information
What else . . . ?

7 Language summary

VOCABULARY

Nouns

Parts of houses and apartment buildings
bathroom
bathtub
bedroom
closet
dining room
elevator
(first/second) floor
garage
hall
kitchen
laundry room
living room
lobby
room
shower
stairs
window
yard

Kinds of homes
cabin
beach house
loft
villa

Furniture
armchair(s)
bed
bookcase
chair(s)
coffee table
cupboard(s)
curtain(s)
dresser
lamp
mirror
picture(s)
rug
sofa

Appliances
air conditioner
coffee maker
heater
microwave
refrigerator
stove

Other
bubble
difference
fan (person)
fiction
forest
moon
mountains
outside
rabbit
science
squirrel
stars
story
TV
view

Determiners
any
lots of
no
some

Adjectives
another
big
clear
dream (home)
expensive
giant
lucky
outside
small
unusual

Verb
love

Adverbs
just (like)
next (weekend)

EXPRESSIONS

Asking about and describing a home
What's the house/apartment like?
  It's (really) nice.
  It has . . .
Does it have . . . ?
  Yes, it does.
  No, it doesn't.
There's a/an . . .
There's no . . .
There isn't a/an . . .
There are some . . .
There aren't any . . .
There are no . . .

Expressing agreement
That's true.

Expressing approval
Awesome!
That's great.
This . . . is great.
That sounds nice.

Expressing luck
I'm lucky.

Giving an example
For example . . .

8 Language summary

VOCABULARY

Nouns

Jobs

accountant
bellhop
cashier
chef
doctor
firefighter
front desk clerk
graphic designer
host
ice cream flavor expert
lawyer
manager
nurse
office manager
photographer
pilot
police officer
receptionist
researcher
salesperson
security guard
server
software engineer
taxi driver
vendor

Workplaces

(high) school
hospital
hotel
office
store

Other

camera
computer
crocodile
ice cream
money
people (*singular*: person)
photo
uniform

Adjectives

boring
dangerous
difficult
easy
exciting
fun
important
interesting
perfect
professional
relaxing
stressful
sweet
terrific

Verbs

agree
guess
hate
perform
sit
stand
talk
taste
teach
travel

Adverbs

after (work)
exactly
hard
outdoors
pretty (+ adjective)

EXPRESSIONS

Exchanging information about work

Where do you work?
  I work in a/an . . .
What do you do?
  I'm a/an . . .
What time/When do you start/finish work?
  I start/finish work at . . .
What do you do after work?
  I . . .
Where does your brother work?
  He works . . .
What does he do?
  He . . .

Talking about likes and dislikes

She loves it.
How do you like it?
  I really like it.
  It's OK.
  They hate it.
  I like it a lot.

Exchanging personal information

How are things (with you)?
  Not bad.
I hear . . .

Giving surprising information

Actually, . . .
Guess what!

Expressing interest

That's funny.
That's interesting.

Expressing uncertainty

I guess . . .

Expressing concern

Please be careful!

9 Language summary

VOCABULARY

Nouns

Meals
breakfast
lunch
dinner
snack

Dairy (food)
cheese
milk
yogurt

Desserts
cake
candy
chocolate(s)
cookies
ice cream

Drinks
coffee
milk
(orange) juice
(green) tea

Fats and oils
butter
cream
mayonnaise
oil

Grains
bread
cereal
cracker(s)
noodles
pasta
rice

Fruit
apple(s)
banana(s)
blueberries (*singular*: blueberry)
grape(s)
kiwi(s)
lemon(s)
mango(es)
orange(s)
pineapple
watermelon

Meat and other proteins
almond(s)
bean(s)
beef
chicken
egg(s)
fish
hamburger(s)
hot dog(s)
nuts
peanuts

Vegetables
broccoli
carrot(s)
celery
garlic
lettuce
onion(s)
(red) peppers
potato(es)
tomato(es)

Other food
corn chips
dip
pickle(s)
popcorn
potato chips
(potato) salad
pizza
sandwich(es)
soup

Other
animal(s)
bone(s)
celebration
festival
fight
flower
habit
health
human(s)
monkey(s)
ton(s)

Adjectives
good
mealtime
messy
other
squash(ed)
sweet
typical

Verbs
buy
come
put
throw
try
want

Adverbs

Adverbs of frequency
always
hardly ever
never
often
sometimes
usually

Other
(Japanese-) style

Prepositions
at (my desk)
for (breakfast)

EXPRESSIONS

Talking about likes and dislikes
I like . . .
I don't like . . .
I don't want . . .
I hate . . .
I love . . .

Talking about things you need
Do we have any . . . ?
No. We need some.
Yes, we do.
Do we need any . . . ?
Yes, we need some . . .
No, we don't need any . . .

Making a suggestion
How about . . . ?

Agreeing to do something
All right.
OK.
Sure.

Accepting an invitation
That's very nice of you. Thanks!

Expressing surprise
Are you serious?
Really?

10 Language summary

VOCABULARY

Nouns

Sports

base jumping
baseball
basketball
bike riding
football
golf
hiking
hockey
ice-skating
parachuting
skateboarding
skydiving
snowboarding
soccer
surfing
swimming
tennis
volleyball

Other

ability
athlete
audition
beach
chess
(sports) club
contest
eyebrow
free time
gym
handstand
head
horse
joke
marathon
muscles
music
record
robot
piano
poem
song
talent
talent show
team
theater
tower
TV
unicycle
video
video games
violin
website

Determiner

all

Adjectives

artistic
athletic
electronic
hidden
musical
technical

Verbs

act
bake
build
cook
dance
design
do (yoga/math)
draw
drive
edit
enter
fix
juggle
make (clothes)
paint
play (chess/the piano/
the violin)
practice
raise
ride
sing
squash
swim
take (photos)
tell
whistle

Adverbs

about
backward
well

Time expressions

once/twice a week
tomorrow

EXPRESSIONS

Talking about sports

What sports do you like/play/watch?
I love/play/watch (soccer).
I don't like/play (golf).
I (really) love (tennis).
Who do you play/watch soccer with?
With some friends from work.
How often do you practice?
We practice twice a week.
When do you practice?
We practice on Tuesdays and Thursdays.
What time do you start?
We start at six in the evening.
Where do you play?
We play on the beach/at a gym/
at a sports club.

Expressing an opinion

I think . . .

Talking about abilities and talents

What can I do?
Can you sing?
Yes, I can.
No, I can't.
Can they sing?
Yes, they can sing very well.
No, they can't sing at all.

Giving a compliment

You can . . . very well.
Thanks.

Asking for clarification

What do you mean?

Expressing interest

Really?
Oh, yeah?

Agreeing to do something

Of course we can.

11 Language summary

VOCABULARY

Nouns

Months
January
February
March
April
May
June
July
August
September
October
November
December

Holidays, festivals, and special occasions
birthday
Christmas
Halloween
Independence Day
New Year's Day/Eve
Thanksgiving
Valentine's Day
wedding

Other
birthday cake
boyfriend
dance
fireworks
flour
gift
girlfriend
letter
parade
party
picnic
present
Queen
restaurant
sugar
surprise

Pronoun
anything

Adjectives

Dates
(1st–31st)
See Exercise 1 on page 72.

Other
fancy
special
traditional

Verbs
ask
bake
celebrate
cook
decorate
give
go on a picnic
invite
order
take (someone) out

Adverbs

Time expressions
next month
next summer
next week
next year
this weekend
tomorrow
tomorrow afternoon
tomorrow night
tonight

EXPRESSIONS

Talking about future plans
Are you going to do anything exciting this weekend?
  Yes, I am. I'm going to . . .
  No, I'm not. I'm going to . . .
What are your plans?
What are you going to do?
  I'm going to . . .
Where are you going to go?
  I'm going to go to . . .
How are you going to get there?
  We're going to . . .
Who's going to be there?
  . . . is/are going to be there.
When are you going to . . . ?
  We're going to . . . at . . .

Talking about dates
When is your birthday?
  It's August 9th.

Wishing someone a good birthday
Happy birthday!

Expressing anticipation
I hope so!

Exchanging information
How about you?

Expressing approval
(That) sounds like fun.
Nice!
That's nice.
How fancy!
Wow!

12 Language summary

VOCABULARY

Nouns

Parts of the body
ankle
arm
back
brain
chest
chin
ear
elbow
eye
eyebrow
finger(s)
foot (*plural*: feet)
hair
hand
head
heart
hip
knee
leg
mouth
neck
nose
shoulder
skin
stomach
throat
thumb
toe(s)
tooth (*plural*: teeth)
wrist

Health problems
backache
cold
cough
dry eyes
earache
fever
the flu
headache
sore throat
stomachache
toothache

Medications/ remedies
antacid
aspirin
chamomile tea
chicken soup
cold medicine
cough syrup
eye drops
ice pack
nasal spray

Other
bacteria
cells
dentist
electricity
hour
part
patient
rest
signals
soda

Adjectives

Positive feelings
better
fantastic
fine
great
terrific

Negative feelings
awful
exhausted
horrible
miserable
sick
sore
terrible
tired

Other
noisy
wrong

Verbs
beat
feel
have
hurt
lose
relax
stay up
take a look

Adverbs
much
so (= very)
well

EXPRESSIONS

Talking about health problems
How are you?
How do you feel (today)?
  I feel better.
  Not so good/well.
What's the matter?
What's wrong?
  I feel sick/terrible.
  I don't feel well.

Expressing sympathy
That's too bad.
I'm sorry to hear that.
That's good.
I'm glad to hear that.

Refusing something politely
Do you want . . . ?
  No, but thanks anyway.

Asking for permission
Is that OK?

Giving a suggestion
I have an idea.
Take/Don't take . . .
Eat/Don't eat . . .

Asking for more information
Anything else?

13 Language summary

VOCABULARY

Nouns

Places

avenue
bank
bookstore
center
coffee shop
department store
drugstore
flower shop
garage
gas station
library
movie theater
museum
parking lot
planetarium
post office
restaurant
restroom
shoe store
square
street
supermarket

Form of address

sir

Other

attraction
competition
debit card
espresso
garden
gasoline
magazine
map
monument
package
painting
plant(s)
polo
sculpture
stamps
statue
telescope
tourist

Verbs

go down/up
turn around
turn left/right
walk down/up

Adverb

right

Prepositions

across from
behind
between
next to
on
on the corner of
on the left/right

EXPRESSIONS

Asking for and giving locations

Is there a . . . around here?
   Yes, there is. It's next to/across from/. . .
   (No.) I don't think so.
Where is the . . . ? Is it far from here?
   It's right behind you.

Asking for and giving directions

How do/can I get to . . . ?
   Walk/Go up . . .
   Walk/Go down . . .
   Turn left/right on . . .
   It's on the left/right.
   You can't miss it.

Getting someone's attention

Excuse me.

Asking for help

Can you help me?

Expressing urgency

It's an emergency!

Pausing before responding

Hmm.

14 Language summary

VOCABULARY

Nouns
bang
barbecue
beach volleyball
braces
chores
exhibit
instructor
lesson
library
mall
music
parasailing
relatives
shopping
tablet
test
vacation
white-water rafting

Adjective
different

Verbs
argue
break down
clean
climb
come home
decide
do laundry
get married
go camping
go out
hang out
have fun
invite (someone) over
listen
make (your) bed
paint
play
see (a movie)
speak
stay
take (classes/lessons)
travel
visit
watch

Adverbs
Time expressions
last month
last night
last summer
last week
last weekend
last year
yesterday

Other
anywhere

EXPRESSIONS

Talking about past activities
Did you . . . last summer?
  Yes, I did. I . . .
  No, I didn't. I . . .
What did you do?
  I . . .
  I didn't . . .
Did you do anything else?

Giving opinions about past experiences
Did you like . . . ?
  Yes, I did. I liked it a lot.
  We loved it!
Did you have a good summer?
  Yes, I did. I had a great summer.
  No, I didn't.

Greeting someone who's been away
Welcome back.

15 Language summary

VOCABULARY

Nouns

Classes at school
chemistry
geography
history
photography
physical education
science

Places at school
auditorium
cafeteria
classroom
computer lab
library

Types of Schools
elementary school
middle school
high school
college

Jobs
actress
comedian
engineer
game designer
hairstylist
musician
photographer
singer
teacher

Other
charity
communicate
culture
raise
major
way of life

Adjectives
angry
bilingual
on time
sunny
young

Verbs
be born
begin
believe
graduate
grow up
need
open a bank account
spend (time)
start (school)
turn (an age)
work

Adverb
on time

Preposition
for (. . . years)

Conjunction
because

EXPRESSIONS

Exchanging personal information
When were you born?
  I was born in 1990.
Where were you born?
  I was born in Brazil.
Were you born in the United States?
  Yes, I was.
  No, I wasn't. I was born in . . .
Where did you grow up?
  I grew up in New York.
How old were you in . . . ?
  I was . . .
What was your favorite . . . ?
  It was . . .

Asking about someone
Who was . . . ?
  He was . . .
What was he like?
  He was . . .
  He wasn't . . .

Asking for an opinion
What do you think?

16 Language summary

VOCABULARY

Nouns
amusement park
art market
autograph
barbecue
camping
comedy
concert
excuse
(street) fair
(art) festival
food court
invitation
message
musical
musician
play
show
shower
stage
trip

Verbs
babysit
call (you) back
go out with (my girlfriend/boyfriend)
have to
help
need to
want to
would like/love to

Adjective
amazing

Adverbs
already
around (seven o'clock)

Prepositions
at (home/school/work)
at the (beach/library/mall)
in (bed/class/Mexico)
in a (meeting)
in the (hospital/shower)
on (her break/a trip/vacation)

EXPRESSIONS

Making a phone call
Hello. Is . . . there/in?
Hi. Can I speak to/with . . . ?
  I'm sorry, but she's in a meeting right now.
Sorry I called you at work.

Taking a phone message
Do you want to leave a message?
Can I take a message?
  Sure. Please give her my number.
  Yes. Please ask/tell her to call me.
I'll give her your message.

Making and accepting an invitation
Do you want to . . . (with me)?
Would you like to . . . (with me)?
  Sure. I'd really like to . . . (with you).
  Yes, I'd love to.

Declining an invitation and making an excuse
I'm sorry, but I can't. I have to . . ./I need to . . .
I'd like to, but . . .

Suggesting a different activity
I don't really like . . .
  Do you want to do something else?

Asking what is happening
What's up?

Asking for a favor
Can you . . . ? Please . . .

Offering to help
Can I help you?

Expressing happy surprise
Terrific!

Workbook answer key

1 What's your name?

Exercise 1

Hi, *Nancy*.
Hello, Mr. Garcia.
It's nice to meet you, Ms. Baker.
Nice to meet you, too, John.

Exercise 2

1. A: Hi. What's *your* name?
B: My name is Lisa. And what's your name?
A: My name is James.
2. A: What's his name?
B: His name is Michael.
A: And what's her name?
B: Her name is Susan.

Exercise 3

1. A: Hello, *Mr.* Wilson.
B: Good morning, David. How are you?
A: I'm OK, thank you.
2. A: Hi. How are you, Mrs. Turner?
B: I'm just fine, thank you. How about you, Mr. Smith?
A: Pretty good, thanks.
3. A: How's it going, Ken?
B: Great. How are you doing?
A: Pretty good.

Exercise 4

2. A: My name is Ellen Miller.
B: I'm Rob Williams.
3. A: Hello, Carol. How's it going?
B: Fine, thanks.
4. A: How do you spell your last name?
B: R-O-G-E-R-S
5. A: I'm Rich Martinez.
B: It's nice to meet you

Exercise 5

3: three
8: eight
1: one
7: seven
10: ten
5: five
6: six
0: zero
9: nine
4: four

Exercise 6

3. 604-555-4731
4. 949-555-3802
5. brian.johnson039@cup.org
6. 773-555-1779
7. mariabrady_7@cup.org
8. tina-fox_952@cup.org

Exercise 7

1. A: What's your name?
B: I'm Momoko Sato.
A: It's nice to meet you, Momoko.
2. A: Hello. I'm Josh Brown. I'm in your English class.
B: Yes, and you're in my math class, too.
3. A: What's his name?
B: It's Chris Allen.
A: He's in our English class.
B: You're right!

Exercise 8

1. *Amy:* Excuse *me*. Are you Alex Walker?
Carlos: No, I'm not. He's over there.
Amy: Oh, I'm sorry.
2. *Amy:* Excuse me. Are you Alex Walker?
Alex: Yes, I am.
Amy: Hi, Alex. My name is Amy Clark.
Alex: Oh, you're in my English class.
Amy: That's right. It's nice to meet you.
Alex: Nice to meet you, too.

Exercise 9

A: Hi. *Are you Andrea Nelson?*
B: No, I'm not.
A: Oh, I'm sorry. What's your name?
B: Kerry Moore.
A: How do you spell your first name?
B: K-E-R-R-Y.
A: And how do you spell your last name?
B: M-O-O-R-E.
A: What's your phone number?
B: It's 618-555-7120.
A: And what's your email address?
B: It's kmoore19@cup.org.

Exercise 10

A

2. A: Good-bye.
B: See you tomorrow.
3. A: Excuse me. Are you Min-ji Park?
B: Yes, I am. It's nice to meet you.
4. A: Good evening.
B: Hello.

B

b. 3
c. 4
d. 2

2 Where are my keys?

Exercise 1

A

2. a laptop
3. an umbrella
4. a wallet
5. a wastebasket
6. a tablet
7. a notebook
8. a hairbrush

B

2. This is a laptop.
3. This is an umbrella.
4. This is a wallet.
5. This is a wastebasket.
6. This is a tablet.
7. This is a notebook.
8. This is a hairbrush.

Exercise 2

/z/ = *doors*, umbrellas, keys, energy bars
/s/ = *books*, laptops, desks, tablets
/ɪz/ = *quizzes*, boxes, purses, hairbrushes

Exercise 3

2. A: What's this?
B: It's a flash drive.
3. A: What are these?
B: They're pencils.
4. A: What are these?
B: They're paper clips.
5. A: What are these?
B: They're sunglasses.
6. A: What's this?
B: It's a purse.

Exercise 4

Clara: Wow! What's this?
Kevin: It's a purse.
Clara: Oh, cool. Thank you, Kevin.
Kevin: You're welcome.
Eva: Now open this box.
Clara: OK. What's this?
Eva: It's a tablet case.
Clara: Oh, thank you, Eva. And what are these?
Eva: They're sunglasses.
Clara: Thanks! They're great!
Laura: Open this, too!
Clara: Oh, it's an umbrella. Thanks, Laura!

Exercise 5

2. A: Excuse me. Is this the math class?
B: Yes, it is. And I'm your teacher.
3. A: Is my purse on the chair?
B: No, it's not. It's under the table.
4. A: Where's my laptop?
B: It's in your backpack.
5. A: Where are your glasses?
B: They're in my purse.
6. A: Hi. Are you in my math class?
B: Yes, I am. And I'm in your English class, too!
7. A: Are these your keys?
B: Yes, they are. Thank you.
8. A: Excuse me. Are you Min-soo Cho?
B: No, I'm not. My name is Jin-ho Han. Min-soo isn't in this class.

Exercise 6

1. A: Oh, no! Where *is* my tablet?
B: Is it in your backpack?
A: No, it's not.
B: Hmm. Is it under your math book?
A: Yes, it is! Thank you!
2. A: Is this my cell phone?
B: No, it's not. It's my cell phone.
A: Sorry. Where is my cell phone?
B: Is it in your purse?
A: Oh, yes, it is. Thanks.
3. A: Where are my keys?
B: Are they in your pocket?
A: No, they're not.
B: Are they on the table?
A: Hmm. Yes, they are. Thanks.
4. A: Is my notebook in your backpack?
B: No, it's not. Sorry.
A: Hmm. Where is my notebook?
B: Is it behind your laptop?
A: Let me see. Yes, it is. Thank you!

Exercise 7

Answers will vary.
2. No, it's not. It's . . .
3. No, it's not. It's . . . / Yes, it is.
4. No, it's not. It's . . .
5. No, I'm not. I'm in an English class.

Exercise 8

2. The umbrella is under the table.
3. The keys are next to the wallet.
4. The pen is in front of the purse.
5. The laptop is on the desk.
6. The wastebasket is behind the chair.

Exercise 9

A

2. A: Where are the books?
B: They're under the table.
3. A: Where is the cell phone?
B: It's in the purse.
4. A: Where are the pens?
B: They're on the table.
5. A: Where is the purse?
B: It's in front of the TV.
6. A: Where are the sunglasses?
B: They're behind the chair.

B

Answers will vary.

3 Where are you from?

Exercise 1

A

Countries	*Nationalities*	*Languages*
Brazil	*Brazilian*	*Portuguese*
Colombia	Colombian	Spanish
South Korea	South Korean	Korean
Canada	Canadian	English and French
Turkey	Turkish	Turkish
Argentina	Argentine	Spanish
Japan	Japanese	Japanese
Egypt	Egyptian	Arabic

B

2. Bogotá is in Colombia.
3. Tokyo is in Japan.
4. São Paulo and Rio de Janeiro are in Brazil.
5. Seoul and Daejeon are in South Korea.
6. Buenos Aires is in Argentina.
7. Vancouver and Ottawa are in Canada.
8. Cairo is in Egypt.

Exercise 2

1. A: *Are* you and your family from New Zealand?
B: No, we're not. We're from Australia.
A: Oh, so you're Australian.
B: Yes, I am. I'm from Melbourne.
2. A: Is Brazil in Central America?
B: No, it's not. It's in South America.
A: Oh. Are we from Brazil, Dad?
B: Yes, we are. We're from Brazil originally, but we're here in the U.S. now.
3. A: Is this your wallet?
B: Yes, it is. Thanks.
A: And are these your sunglasses?
B: Yes, they are.
A: Well, they're very nice sunglasses.
B: Thank you!
4. A: Is your English teacher from the U.S.?
B: No, she's not. She's from Canada. Montreal, Canada.
A: Is English her first language?
B: No, it's not. Her first language is French.

Exercise 3

2. A: Is she from India?
B: Yes, she is.
3. A: Is she from Canada?
B: No, she's not. She's from the U.S.
4. A: Are they in Mexico?
B: No, they're not. They're in Japan.
5. A: Is he in Bangkok?
B: No, he's not. He's in New York.
6. A: Are they in Egypt?
B: Yes, they are.

Exercise 4

1. fourteen
2. forty
3. sixty
4. thirteen
5. twenty-seven
6. one hundred (and) two
7. eleven
8. thirty
9. eighteen
10. eighty

Exercise 5

2. A: Is your first language English?
B: No, it's Japanese.
3. A: What are they like?
B: They're very serious.
4. A: Who's that?
B: He's the new math teacher.
5. A: Where are Rahul and his family?
B: They're in the U.S. now.
6. A: How old is he now?
B: He's twenty-eight.
7. A: What's Marrakech like?
B: It's very interesting.

Exercise 6

A

2. Mark and Carlos are talkative
3. Brian is thin and Owen is heavy.
4. Daniel is serious.
5. Mariko is short and Ben is tall.
6. Ginny is funny.
7. Dr. Lopez is kind.

B

2. No, she's not.
3. No, he's not.
4. Yes, she is.
5. Yes, they are.
6. No, she's not.
7. Yes, I am. / No, I'm not.
8. Yes, I am. / No, I'm not.

Exercise 7

1. A: Annette, *what's* your best friend like?
B: She's very nice. Her name is Valentina. I call her Tina.
A: Where is she from? Is she from Spain?
B: No, she's not. She's from Italy.
2. A: Toshi, are you and Naomi from Japan?
B: Yes, we are. We're from Osaka.
A: What's your first language?
B: My first language is Japanese, but Naomi's first language is English. Her parents are from New York originally.

Exercise 8

Answers will vary.
1. I'm from . . .
2. It's . . .
3. I'm . . .
4. She's from . . . / He's from . . .
5. She's . . . / He's . . .
6. I'm . . .

4 Is this coat yours?

Exercise 1

1. *jacket*
2. blouse
3. belt
4. skirt
5. high heels
6. cap
7. T-shirt
8. shorts
9. socks
10. sneakers

Exercise 2

Check these items:

For work	***For home***	***For cold weather***	***For warm weather***
shorts	suit	shorts	boots
swimsuit	coat	T-shirt	sweater

Exercise 3

Answers will vary.

Exercise 4

A

2. A: Whose tie is this?
B: It's Max's.
3. A: Whose boots are these?
B: They're Maya's.
4. A: Whose shoes are these?
B: They're Max's.
5. A: Whose cap is this?
B: It's Lisa's.
6. A: Whose pants are these?
B: They're Max's.

B

1. A: *Whose* T-shirt is this? Is it Ayumi's?
B: No, it's not hers. It's mine.
2. A: Are these your jeans?
B: No, they aren't my jeans. Let's ask Mohammed. I think they're his.
3. A: Are these Stephanie's and Jennifer's socks?
B: No, they aren't theirs. They're yours.
A: I don't think so. These socks are white, and mine are blue.

Exercise 5

Answers will vary. Possible answers:

2. It's spring. It's raining.
3. It's winter. It's snowing. It's very cold.
4. It's summer. It's very hot. It's humid. It's sunny.
5. It's fall. It's sunny. It's cool.
6. It's winter. It's sunny. It's very cold.

Exercise 6

A

3. Sung-min is wearing a T-shirt.
4. Liz is wearing a skirt.
5. Allison is wearing a dress.
6. Liz and Sung-min are wearing sneakers.
7. Steven is wearing a scarf.
8. Steven and Pablo are wearing hats.

B

2. No, they aren't. / No, they're not. They're wearing jackets.
3. No, she isn't. / No, she's not. She's wearing jeans.
4. No, she isn't. / No, she's not. She's wearing a dress.
5. No, they aren't. / No, they're not. They're wearing blouses.
6. No, they aren't. / No, they're not. They're wearing pants.

Exercise 7

1. My name's Jamie. I*'m wearing* a T-shirt and shorts. I'm wearing sneakers, too. It's raining, but I'm not wearing a raincoat.
2. It's winter, so Maria's not wearing / isn't wearing high heels – she's wearing boots. She's wearing a scarf, but she's not wearing / isn't wearing a hat.
3. It's very hot. Richard and Meg aren't wearing sweaters today. They're wearing T-shirts. It's warm, so Meg's wearing light pants, and Richard's wearing shorts.
4. Ed's wearing a suit. He's not wearing / isn't wearing a scarf, but he's wearing a tie. He's wearing shoes and socks. It's very windy.

Exercise 8

2. It's very cold outside, but I'm not wearing a coat.
3. Her skirt is blue, and her blouse is blue, too.
4. It's raining, so I need an umbrella.
5. He's wearing an expensive suit, but he's wearing sneakers.
6. It's summer and it's very sunny, so it's hot.

5 What time is it?

Exercise 1

2. It's seven o'clock in the morning.
3. It's a quarter to three in the afternoon. / It's two forty-five in the afternoon.
4. It's nine-twenty in the morning. / It's twenty after nine in the morning.
5. It's a quarter after six in the evening. / It's six-fifteen in the evening.
6. It's eleven o'clock at night.
7. It's three-thirty in the morning.
8. It's twelve o'clock in the afternoon. / It's noon.

Exercise 2

2. It's 11:00 A.M. in Phoenix. It's eleven o'clock in the morning.
3. It's 12:00 P.M. in Mexico City. It's noon. / It's twelve o'clock in the afternoon.
4. It's 1:00 P.M. in Lima. It's one o'clock in the afternoon.
5. It's 2:00 P.M. in La Paz. It's two o'clock in the afternoon.
6. It's 3:00 P.M. in Montevideo. It's three o'clock in the afternoon.

Exercise 3

2. It's twelve o'clock.
3. It's nine-oh-three.
4. It's a quarter to two.
5. It's four-thirty.
6. It's ten after eight.

Exercise 4

2. It's 10:00 P.M. It's ten at night.
3. It's 5:15. It's five-fifteen.
4. It's 7:00 P.M. It's seven in the evening.
5. It's 4:30. It's four-thirty.
6. It's 8:00 A.M. It's eight in the morning.
7. It's twelve P.M. It's noon.
8. It's 2:00 P.M. It's two in the afternoon.
9. It's twelve A.M. It's midnight.
10. It's 6:45. It's a quarter to seven.
11. It's 11:15. It's a quarter after eleven.

Exercise 5

2. He's working.
3. She's riding a bike.
4. They're watching a movie.
5. He's driving.
6. He's shopping.
7. They're having breakfast.
8. They're taking a walk.
9. She's calling a friend.

Exercise 6

3. No, he's not. He's swimming.
4. No, he's not. He's cooking.
5. No, they're not. They're running.
6. No, she's not. She's sleeping.
7. No, he's not. He's reading.
8. No, they're not. They're playing basketball.

Exercise 7

2. A: Is Bob drinking soda?
B: Yes, he is.
3. A: Are Jason and Beth watching a movie?
B: No, they're not. They're dancing.
4. A: Is Adriana wearing jeans?
B: No, she's not. She's wearing a skirt.
5. A: Are Amy and Gabriela chatting online?
B: No, they're not. They're eating pizza.
6. A: Is Daniel talking to Adriana?
B: Yes, he is.
7. A: Is Bob wearing shorts?
B: No, he's not. He's wearing pants.
8. A: Is Min talking on the phone?
B: Yes, she is.

Exercise 8

3. A: What are Tom and Donna doing?
B: They're visiting friends.
4. A: What is Sandra doing?
B: She's getting up.
5. A: What are you and Isabella doing?
B: We're riding bikes.
6. A: What are Diego and Patricia doing?
B: They're working.
7. A: What is Tim doing?
B: He's listening to music.
8. A: What are you doing?
B: I'm studying English. / We're studying English.
9. A: What are Sonya and Annie doing?
B: They're having dinner.
10. A: What am I doing?
B: You're finishing this exercise.

Exercise 9

Answers will vary.

6 I ride my bike to school.

Exercise 1

A

1. Alice and Larry are my *parents*. Alice is my mother, and Larry is my father.
2. Nick is my husband. I'm his wife.
3. Ethan, Avery, and Bella are our children. Avery and Bella are our daughters, and Ethan is our son. Avery is Bella's sister, and Ethan is her brother.

B

Answers will vary.

Exercise 2

Christine: So, do you live downtown, Sarah?
Sarah: Yes, I *live* with my brother. He has an apartment near here.
Christine: Oh, so you walk to work.
Sarah: Actually, I don't walk to work in the morning. I take the bus to work, and then I walk home at night. What about you?
Christine: Well, my husband and I have a house in the suburbs now, so I drive to work. My husband doesn't work downtown. He works in the suburbs near our house, so he goes to work by bus.

Exercise 3

A

3. goes
4. has
5. lives
6. rides
7. sleeps
8. studies
9. takes
10. uses
11. walks
12. watches

B

s = /s/	s = /z/	(e)s = /ɪz/	*irregular*
sleeps	studies	dances	does
takes	lives	uses	goes
walks	rides	watches	has

Exercise 4

A

Answers will vary.

B

Answers will vary.

Exercise 5

2. She goes to work at 8:00 every day.
3. She has lunch at 11:00 every day.
4. She takes a walk at 2:00 every day.
5. She finishes work at 5:00 every day.
6. She plays basketball at 6:00 on Mondays.
7. She goes to class at 6:00 on Tuesdays and Thursdays.
8. She watches a movie at 6:00 on Fridays.

Exercise 6

Answers will vary.

2. I . . . on Tuesdays. I don't . . . on Tuesdays.
3. I . . . on Wednesdays. I don't . . . on Wednesdays.
4. I . . . on Thursdays. I don't . . . on Thursdays.
5. I . . . on Fridays. I don't . . . on Fridays.
6. I . . . on Saturdays. I don't . . . on Saturdays.
7. I . . . on Sundays. I don't . . . on Sundays.

Exercise 7

1. A: Do you go to bed Ø late *on* weekends?
   B: Yes, I do. I go to bed at midnight. But I go to bed Ø early on weekdays.
2. A: Do you study in the afternoon?
   B: No, I study in the morning on weekends, and I study in the evening on Mondays and Wednesdays.
3. A: What time do you get up in the morning on weekdays?
   B: I get up at 6:00 Ø every day.
4. A: Do you have English class in the morning?
   B: No, I have English at 3:30 in the afternoon on Tuesdays and Thursdays. On Mondays, Wednesdays, and Fridays, our class is at 5:00.

Exercise 8

2. A: Do you and your family watch television in the afternoon?
   B: Yes, my family and I watch television in the afternoon.
3. A: Do you get up early on Fridays?
   B: Yes, I get up early on Fridays.
   A: What time do you get up?
   B: I get up at 5:30.
4. A: Does your sister drive to work?
   B: No, my sister doesn't drive to work.
   A: Does she take the bus?
   B: No, she doesn't take the bus. She takes the train.
5. A: Does your dad work on weekends?
   B: No, my dad doesn't work on weekends.
   A: When does he work?
   B: He works on weekdays.
6. A: Does your mom work in the city?
   B: Yes, my mom works in the city. She's a restaurant manager.
   A: Does she use public transportation?
   B: No, she doesn't use public transportation. She drives to work.
7. A: Do you have a big lunch on Sundays?
   B: Yes, we have a big lunch on Sundays.
   A: What time do you have lunch?
   B: We have lunch at 1:00.

Exercise 9

2. We don't live in the suburbs.
3. We take the bus, the train, or the subway.
4. He goes to work before noon.
5. I don't work far from here.
6. She doesn't get up early on Sundays.

Exercise 10

Answers will vary.

1. I . . . on weekdays.
2. I . . . on weekends.
3. I . . . on Friday nights.
4. I . . . on Sunday mornings.

7 Does it have a view?

Exercise 1

2. bathroom
3. kitchen
4. dining room
5. living room
6. garage
7. yard
8. closet

Exercise 2

Ji-hye: Do you live in a house, Fernanda?
Fernanda: No, I live in an apartment.
Ji-hye: Well, is it very big?
Fernanda: Yes, it has three bedrooms.
Ji-hye: Does it have a view?
Fernanda: Yes, it has a great view of the city.
Ji-hye: Oh, that's great! And do you live alone?
Fernanda: No, I don't. I live with my sisters.

Exercise 3

Al: Do you live near here, Brandon?
Brandon: Yes, I do. My wife and I live on Main Street.
Al: Oh, do you live in an apartment?
Brandon: No, we don't. We have a house.
Al: Oh, great! Do you have children?
Brandon: No, we don't. But my mother lives with us.
Al: Really? Does she do a lot of work at home?
Brandon: Yes, she does. In fact, she cooks dinner every night!
Al: You're lucky! I live alone, and I cook my own dinner.

Exercise 4

Answers will vary.
2. Yes, I do. / No, I don't.
3. Yes, I do. / No, I don't.
4. Yes, it does. / No, it doesn't.
5. Yes, s/he does. / No, s/he doesn't.
6. Yes, we do. / No, we don't.
7. Yes, we do. / No, we don't.
8. Yes, it does. / No, it doesn't.
9. Yes, it does. / No, it doesn't.
10. Yes, it does. / No, it doesn't.

Exercise 5

A

2. A: Do they need a table?
B: Yes, they do.
3. A: Do they have chairs?
B: No, they don't.
4. A: Do they need a dresser?
B: No, they don't.
5. A: Do they have a mirror?
B: No, they don't.
6. A: Do they have curtains?
B: Yes, they do.
7. A: Does he have a bookcase?
B: Yes, he does.
8. A: Does he need curtains?
B: Yes, he does.
9. A: Does he need a sofa?
B: No, he doesn't.
10. A: Does he have a chair?
B: No, he doesn't.
11. A: Does he have a lamp?
B: Yes, he does.
12. A: Does he need pictures?
B: No, he doesn't.

B

Answers will vary.
1–4. I have . . . / I need . . .

Exercise 6

In Martin's apartment, there's a big living room. There are two bedrooms and two bathrooms. There's no elevator, but there are stairs. He has a lot of books, so there are bookcases in the living room and bedrooms. There aren't any chairs in the kitchen, but there's a big table with chairs in the dining room. There's no coffee maker in the kitchen, but there's a microwave oven. There are two televisions in Martin's apartment – there's one television in the living room, and there's one television in the bedroom.

Exercise 7

Answers will vary. Possible answers:
2. Yes, there's a stove in my kitchen. / No, there isn't a stove. / No, there's no stove.
3. Yes, there's a sofa in my living room. / No, there isn't a sofa. / No, there's no sofa.
4. Yes, there are some bookcases in my living room. / Yes, there's one bookcase in my living room. / No, there aren't any bookcases in my living room. / No, there are no bookcases in my living room.
5. Yes, there's a clock in my bathroom. / No, there isn't a clock in my bathroom. / No, there's no clock in my bathroom.
6. Yes, there are some pictures in my bedroom. / Yes, there's one picture in my bedroom. / No, there aren't any pictures in my bedroom. / No, there are no pictures in my bedroom.
7. Yes, there's a closet in my bedroom. / No, there isn't a closet in my bedroom. / No, there's no closet in my bedroom.

Exercise 8

A

2. There aren't any chairs in the dining room. / There are no chairs in the dining room.
3. There's a stove in the living room.
4. There's a refrigerator in the bedroom.
5. There's no bed in the bedroom. / There isn't a bed in the bedroom.
6. There are armchairs in the bathroom.
7. There's a bed in the kitchen.
8. There aren't any bookcases in the living room. / There are no bookcases in the living room.

B

Answers will vary.

Exercise 9

2. A: Do you need living room furniture?
B: Yes, I do. I need a sofa and a coffee table.
3. A: I really need a new desk.
B: So let's go shopping this weekend.
4. A: Do you have chairs in your kitchen?
B: Yes, I do. I have six chairs.

Exercise 10

Answers will vary.

8 Where do you work?

Exercise 1

2. f
3. b
4. a
5. i
6. h
7. j
8. e
9. d
10. g

Exercise 2

Answers will vary. Possible answers:

2. He's a vendor. He handles money. He handles food. He stands all day. He works outside.
3. She's/He's a firefighter. She/He helps people. She/He works hard.
4. She's a chef. She works in a restaurant. She handles food. She stands all day.
5. He's a taxi driver. He handles money. He sits all day. He helps people.
6. She's a teacher. She works in a school. She helps students. She works hard.

Exercise 3

2. A: What do Victoria and Jon do?
   B: Victoria and Jon are nurses. And they work together, too.
   A: Where do they work?
   B: At Springfield Hospital.
3. A: Where does your daughter work?
   B: My daughter works in an office.
   A: What does she do?
   B: She's an accountant.
4. A: What do you and Don do?
   B: Don and I? We're software engineers.
   A: How do you like it?
   B: We like it a lot!

Exercise 4

1. A: *Do* you *have* a job?
   B: Yes, I do.
   A: Oh, what do you do?
   B: I'm / am a graphic designer.
   A: Where do you work?
   B: I work at home.
   A: Oh, wow! How do you like your job?
   B: I really like it. It's a great job!
   A: What time do you start work?
   B: I start work at 8:00 A.M., and I finish at 3:00 P.M.
2. A: My brother has a new job.
   B: Really? Where does he work?
   A: He works at the Town Center Mall.
   B: What does he do there?
   A: He's / is a security guard.
   B: How does he like his job?
   A: Oh, I guess he likes it.
   B: What time does he start work?
   A: He starts work at 10:00 A.M., and he finishes at 6:00 P.M.

Exercise 5

A

2. b
3. a
4. c

B

Answers will vary. Possible answers:

2. A security guard's job is boring. A security guard doesn't have an exciting job. A security guard's job isn't exciting.
3. Paul has a dangerous job. Paul doesn't have a safe job. Paul's job isn't safe.
4. A front desk clerk has a stressful job. A front desk clerk doesn't have a relaxing job. A front desk clerk's job isn't relaxing.
5. Amanda's apartment is small. Amanda doesn't have a big apartment. Amanda's apartment isn't big.
6. Cristina has a big house. Cristina doesn't have a small house. Cristina's house isn't small.
7. Brenda's brother is talkative. Brenda doesn't have a quiet brother. Brenda's brother isn't quiet.
8. I have an easy job. I don't have a hard job. My job isn't hard.

Exercise 6

Answers will vary.

2. A mechanic has . . . / A mechanic's job . . .
3. An artist has . . . / An artist's job . . .
4. A scientist has . . . / A scientist's job . . .
5. A plumber has . . . / A plumber's job . . .
6. A reporter has . . . / A reporter's job . . .

Exercise 7

Answers will vary.

9 I always eat breakfast.

Exercise 1

Fruit
2. oranges
3. apples
4. bananas
Vegetables
5. lettuce
6. broccoli
7. potatoes
8. carrots
Grains
9. rice
10. cereal
11. bread
12. crackers
Dairy
13. milk
14. cheese
Fats and oils
15. butter
16. oil
Meat and other proteins
17. chicken
18. beans
19. nuts
20. fish

Exercise 2

2. This is Ø yogurt.
3. This is a potato.
4. This is an egg.
5. This is an onion.
6. This is Ø rice.

Exercise 3

Answers will vary.

Exercise 4

1. A: What do you eat for lunch?
B: Well, I usually have *some* noodles in broth.
A: That sounds good. Do you have any vegetables?
B: No, I don't eat any vegetables for lunch.
A: Really? Do you have anything else?
B: Well, I usually have some fruit – grapes or strawberries, but I don't eat any dessert.
A: Do you drink anything with your lunch?
B: I always have some water and coffee. I don't put any milk in my coffee, but I like some sugar in it.

2. A: What do you want for dinner?
B: Let's make some chicken soup.
A: Good idea. Do we have any chicken?
B: Yes, we have some chicken, but we don't have any vegetables. Let's get some celery and onions.
A: OK. Do we need any pasta for the soup?
B: Yes, let's get some pasta. Oh, and some garlic, too.
A: Great. We have some salt and pepper, so we don't need any spices.
B: Yeah, but let's get some bread. And some crackers, too.

Exercise 5

Answers will vary. Possible answers:
2. You need some lettuce, tomatoes, onions, and carrots. You don't need any . . .
3. You need some pasta, tomatoes, onions, and cheese. You don't need any . . .
4. You need some fish, bread, lettuce, and a tomato. You don't need any . . .
5. You need some apples, oranges, bananas, and blueberries. You don't need any . . .
6. You need some . . . You don't need any . . .

Exercise 6

A

2. In Canada, people hardly ever have salad for breakfast.
3. Some people in South Korea always eat pickled vegetables for breakfast.
4. Americans often put cream in their coffee.
5. Brazilians often make drinks with fruit.
6. In England, people usually put milk in their tea.
7. Some people in Mexico never eat pasta.
8. In China, people hardly ever put sugar in their tea.

B

Answers will vary.

Exercise 7

Answers will vary. Possible answers:
2. I never/hardly ever/sometimes/often/usually/always have pasta for lunch.
3. I never/hardly ever/sometimes/often/usually/always have coffee for lunch.
4. I never/hardly ever/sometimes/often/usually/always have eggs for lunch.
5. I never/hardly ever/sometimes/often/usually/always have beef for lunch.
6. I never/hardly ever/sometimes/often/usually/always have rice for lunch.
7. I never/hardly ever/sometimes/often/usually/always have beans for lunch.
8. I never/hardly ever/sometimes/often/usually/always have salad for lunch.

Exercise 8

Answers will vary.
1. My favorite restaurant is . . .
2. I usually have . . . for dinner.
3. Yes, I sometimes / often cook. / No, I hardly ever / never cook.
4. My favorite kind of food is . . .
5. My favorite snack is . . .

10 What sports do you like?

Exercise 1

A

2. f
3. h
4. d
5. g
6. a
7. j
8. i
9. e
10. c

B

go		play		
bike riding	ice-skating	*hockey*	baseball	golf
swimming	hiking	basketball	soccer	football

Exercise 2

Katie: *What do you do on the weekends?*
Isabela: I like to play sports.
Katie: Really? What sports do you like?
Isabela: Well, I love to go snowboarding.
Katie: Does your husband go snowboarding, too?
Isabela: No, he doesn't like cold weather. He likes to play basketball.
Katie: What do you like to do in the summer?
Isabela: I like to play tennis when the weather is warm.
Katie: Who do you practice with?
Isabela: I practice with my sister. She loves tennis, too.

Exercise 3

Answers will vary.

2. What sports do you watch? I watch . . .
3. What sports do you play? I play . . .
4. How often do you go swimming? I . . .
5. Who do you play sports with? I play sports with . . .

Exercise 4

2. Can Doug ride a horse? No, he can't.
3. Can Mariana bake cookies? No, she can't.
4. Can Felipe and Ken skateboard? Yes, they can.
5. Can George play hockey? Yes, he can.
6. Can Ana and Debbie play tennis? Yes, they can.

Exercise 5

Answers may vary. Possible answers:

2. He can do math in his head, but he can't fix a computer.
3. She can play chess, but she can't play soccer.
4. She can build a robot, but she can't sing.

Exercise 6

2. A: Who do you go bike riding with?
   B: My friends from school.
3. A: Who can play the piano?
   B: Marco can.
4. A: Where do you go hiking?
   B: In the mountains.

Exercise 7

A

Answers will vary.

B

Answers will vary.

Exercise 8

2. He can play sports well.
3. She has many talents.
4. I love it.
5. He can't dance at all.
6. She tells good jokes.

Exercise 9

Answers will vary.

1. Yes, I can. / No, I can't.
2. Yes, I can. / No, I can't.
3. Yes, I can. / No, I can't.
4. Yes, I am. / No, I'm not.
5. Yes, I am. / No, I'm not.
6. Yes, I do. / No, I don't.
7. Yes, I can. / No, I can't.
8. Yes, I do. / No, I don't.
9. Yes, I do. / No, I don't.
10. Yes, I can. / No, I can't.

Exercise 10

Answers will vary.

11 I'm going to have a party.

Exercise 1

A

2. February
3. March
4. April
5. May
6. June
7. July
8. August
9. September
10. October
11. November
12. December

B

Answers will vary.

C

2. March fifteenth
3. November first
4. August sixteenth
5. July twenty-fourth
6. May tenth
7. February second
8. December twenty-seventh

Exercise 2

2. Liz is going to be thirty-three on October sixth.
3. Ruth and Sharon are going to be sixty-nine on September twenty-first.
4. I am going to be . . . on . . .

Exercise 3

2. On August sixth, he's going to play tennis after work.
3. On August eighth, he's going to drive to the beach with Melissa.
4. On August tenth, he's going to go shopping after work.
5. On August twelfth, he's going to work late.
6. On August thirteenth, he's going to meet Melissa for dinner.
7. On August fifteenth, he's going to go to a museum with Livia.
8. On August nineteenth, he's going to buy Kenta's birthday present.
9. On August twentieth, he's going to go to Kenta's birthday party.
10. On August twenty-eighth, he's going to see a movie with friends.

Exercise 4

2. On Friday, my friend Joe and I <u>are going to see</u> a movie. After the movie, we <u>are going to eat</u> dinner at our favorite Mexican restaurant.
3. On Saturday morning, my parents <u>are going to visit</u>. They <u>are going to drive</u> into the city, and we <u>are going to go</u> to the art museum. I think my mother <u>is going to love</u> it, but my father <u>isn't going to like</u> it. Later, we <u>are going to watch</u> a baseball game on TV. My parents <u>are going to go</u> home after dinner.
4. On Sunday, I <u>am going to get up</u> early. Then I <u>am going to take</u> a walk. On Sunday afternoon, I <u>am going to do</u> yoga. In the evening, my friend Eve and I <u>are going to study</u> together.

Exercise 5

1. *Eric:* <u>*What are you going to do this weekend?*</u>
Alex: This weekend? I'm going to go to the city with my son.
Eric: That's nice. <u>Where are you going to stay?</u>
Alex: We're going to stay at my sister's apartment. She lives there.
Eric: Really? <u>What are you going to do? / Where are you going to go?</u>
Alex: I think we're going to go to a museum.
Eric: <u>Is your sister going to go with you?</u>
Alex: No, my sister isn't going to go with us. She's going to go bike riding.

2. *Scott:* I'm going to have a birthday party for Ben next Saturday. Can you come?
Emily: Sure. <u>Where is it going to be?</u>
Scott: It's going to be at my house. Do you have the address?
Emily: Yes, I do. And <u>when is it going to start? / what time is it going to start?</u>
Scott: It's going to start at seven o'clock.
Emily: <u>Is Bob going to be there?</u>
Scott: No, Bob isn't going to be there.
Emily: That's too bad. <u>Are you going to bake a cake?</u>
Scott: No, I'm not going to bake a cake. I can't bake! I'm going to buy one.
Emily: OK. Sounds good. See you on Saturday.

Exercise 6

A

2. They're going to play soccer.
3. She's going to play the piano.
4. They're going to go shopping.
5. He's going to study.
6. They're going to play chess.
7. They're going to see a movie.
8. They're going to bake cookies.
9. He's going to ride a horse.

B

Answers will vary.

Exercise 7

Answers will vary.

12 How do you feel?

Exercise 1

2. mouth
3. neck
4. stomach
5. fingers
6. leg
7. toes
8. hair
9. ear
10. nose
11. teeth
12. shoulder
13. elbow
14. arm
15. hand
16. foot

Exercise 2

2. She has a sore throat.
3. He has an earache.
4. He has a stomachache.
5. She has a headache.
6. She has a backache.

Exercise 3

1. *Jake:* Hi, Camila. How are you?
Camila: *I'm fine, thanks. How about you?*
Jake: Not so good. Actually, I feel really awful.
Camila: What's wrong?
Jake: I think I have the flu.
Camila: That's too bad. Are you going to see a doctor?
Jake: No, I'm going to go home now.
Camila: OK. Get some rest.
Jake: OK. Thanks.

2. *Camila:* How do you feel today?
Jake: I feel much better.
Camila: I'm glad to hear that.
Jake: Thanks.
Camila: So, are you going to go to the meeting this afternoon?
Jake: Yes, I am.
Camila: Great. See you later.

Exercise 4

2. I have a horrible cold, so I'm going to buy some cold medicine.
3. Your eyes look red and tired. Get some eye drops.
4. Alan has a stomachache, so he's going to get some antacid.
5. I have a terrible headache. I need some aspirin.
6. Mandy's cough sounds awful. I'm going to give her some cough syrup.

Exercise 5

2. What's wrong?
3. I'm very tired.
4. I'm sorry to hear that.
5. I'm glad to hear that.
6. My head feels terrible.
7. I have a stomachache.
8. I have a sore throat.

Exercise 6

2. Go home early.
3. Drink some water.
4. Go to the grocery store.
5. Don't stay up late.
6. Have a hot drink.
7. Don't lift heavy things.
8. Don't work too hard.

Exercise 7

Answers will vary.

Exercise 8

A

Answers will vary.

B

Answers will vary.

13 How do I get there?

Exercise 1

A

2. I'm going to go to the bank. I need a new debit card.
3. My car is almost out of gasoline. Is there a gas station near here?
4. Are you going to the post office? I need some stamps.
5. On Sundays, I buy food for my family at the supermarket.
6. We're going to have an espresso at the coffee shop before class.
7. Anita is going to get some medicine at the drugstore.
8. My son is going to school next week. We're going to the department store downtown to buy him a backpack.

B

Top row: 2, 6, 3, 1
Bottom row: 8, 4, 5, 7

Exercise 2

2. The hospital is behind the bank.
3. The bookstore is on the corner of Fox Street and Second Avenue.
4. The Chinese restaurant is on West Street, between the coffee shop and the supermarket.
5. The shoe store is next to the drugstore.
6. The Mexican restaurant is across from the park.

Exercise 3

A

Answers will vary.

B

Answers will vary.

Exercise 4

Tom: Excuse me. Can you help me?
Woman: Sure.
Tom: Is there a restroom around here?
Woman: Yes, there is. It's in the supermarket on West Street.
Tom: Where on West Street?
Woman: It's on the corner of West Street and Third Avenue.
Tom: Next to the Chinese restaurant?
Woman: Yes, that's right. It's right next to the Chinese restaurant.
Tom: Thanks a lot.
Woman: You're welcome.

Exercise 5

2. The Empire State Building is far from here, but Central Park is near here. You can walk there.
3. Don't walk down Columbus Avenue. Walk up Columbus Avenue.
4. The New London Hotel isn't in front of the bank. It's behind it.
5. Don't turn left on Sixteenth Street. Turn right.

Exercise 6

Answers will vary. Possible answers:

2. Go up Fourth Street. Turn left on West Street. Walk to Second Avenue. It's on the right, between the coffee shop and the supermarket.
3. Walk down Second Avenue. Turn left on Harris Street. Walk to Fourth Avenue. It's on the left, across from the park.
4. Walk up Third Avenue. Turn left on West Street. Turn right on Second Avenue. It's on the right, next to the coffee shop.

Exercise 7

Answers will vary.

14 I had a good time.

Exercise 1

A

2. He answered email.
3. They exercised.
4. He cleaned the house.
5. She did laundry.
6. She studied.
7. He washed the car.
8. She went grocery shopping.

B

Answers will vary.

Exercise 2

Kim: It was really busy. I *worked* on Friday, then I invited friends over after work. I cooked dinner for them. We listened to music and talked about work, but they didn't stay very late.
Kim: I got up early on Saturday because I played basketball with Angela. Then I visited relatives. We walked downtown and ate dinner. Oh, and we saw a movie. On Sunday, I studied for my math test with my friends. I did laundry on Sunday afternoon, too.
Alisha: Wow! That was a busy weekend! I didn't do much this weekend. I answered email on Friday night and I watched TV, too. On Saturday, I didn't get up early. I cleaned the house and I went grocery shopping. I didn't do anything on Sunday!

Exercise 3

2. Hiro went to a museum. Claudia didn't go to a museum.
3. Claudia rode a bicycle. Hiro didn't ride a bicycle.
4. Claudia and Hiro cooked.
5. Hiro studied. Claudia didn't study.
6. Claudia shopped. Hiro didn't shop.
7. Hiro played tennis. Claudia didn't play tennis.

Exercise 4

Present	*Past*	*Present*	*Past*
buy	*bought*	go	went
come	came	have	had
do	did	read	read
eat	ate	ride	rode
feel	felt	see	saw
meet	met	sit	sat

Exercise 5

Aaron: So, Beth, *did* you *have* a good summer?
Beth: Well, I had an interesting summer. My sister and her family came to visit for two weeks.
Aaron: That's nice.
Beth: Yes and no. My sister didn't feel well, so she sat on the sofa and watched TV. She hardly ever got up.
Aaron: Oh, well. Did her husband and kids have a good time?
Beth: I think so. They played volleyball and rode their bikes every day.
Aaron: Did you go out to any restaurants?
Beth: No, I cooked breakfast, lunch, and dinner every day. They ate a lot of food, but they didn't wash any dishes.
Aaron: That's too bad. Did you relax at all last summer?
Beth: Yes. My sister and her family finally went home, and then I relaxed. I just read some books and listened to music.

Exercise 6

Answers will vary.

2. A: Did you go anywhere interesting?
B: Yes, I did. . . . / No, I didn't. . . .
3. A: Did you take any pictures?
B: Yes, I did. . . . / No, I didn't. . . .
4. A: Did you buy anything interesting?
B: Yes, I did. . . . / No, I didn't. . . .
5. A: Did you eat any new foods?
B: Yes, I did. . . . / No, I didn't. . . .
6. A: Did you play any games?
B: Yes, I did. . . . / No, I didn't. . . .
7. A: Did you play any sports?
B: Yes, I did. . . . / No, I didn't. . . .
8. A: Did you meet any interesting people?
B: Yes, I did. . . . / No, I didn't. . . .
9. A: Did you see any good movies?
B: Yes, I did. . . . / No, I didn't. . . .

Exercise 7

A

Answers may vary.

2. They had a barbecue.
3. They went hiking.
4. They ate pizza.
5. They played golf.
6. They read books.
7. They saw a movie. / They watched a movie. / They went to the movie theater.
8. They went to New York.

B

Answers will vary.

15 Where were you born?

Exercise 1

Jason: Were you born here in the U.S., Marie?
Marie: No, I wasn't. I was born in Europe.
Jason: Oh, were you born in France?
Marie: No, I'm from Belgium.
Jason: Really? What city were you born in?
Marie: I was born in Brussels.
Jason: Were your parents born in Brussels, too?
Marie: Yes, they were. We were all born there.
Jason: And why did you come to the U.S.?
Marie: We came here for my father's job.
Jason: So when did you move here?
Marie: We moved here in 2009.
Jason: Really? How old were you then?
Marie: I was sixteen.
Jason: Was it scary?
Marie: No, it wasn't. I loved it!

Exercise 2

1. *Sandra:* Were you born in the U.S., Ivan?
Ivan: Yes, I was. My brother and I were born here in Miami.
Sandra: I was born here, too. What about your parents? Were they born here?
Ivan: Well, my father wasn't. He was born in Cuba, but my mother was born in the U.S. – in Detroit.
Sandra: Detroit? Really? My parents were born in Detroit, too!

2. *Kristin:* I called you on Saturday, but you weren't home.
Jennifer: No, I wasn't. I was at the beach all weekend.
Kristin: That's nice. How was the weather there?
Jennifer: It was beautiful.
Kristin: Were your parents there?
Jennifer: No, they weren't. I was with my sister. It was great!

3. *Mindy:* Were you in college last year, Alan?
Alan: No, I wasn't. I graduated from college two years ago.
Mindy: So where were you last year?
Alan: I was in Japan.
Mindy: Oh! Were you in Tokyo?
Alan: No, I wasn't. I was in Osaka. I had a job there.
Mindy: What was the job?
Alan: I was an English teacher.

Exercise 3

Answers will vary.

Exercise 4

2. A: Who was your favorite teacher?
B: My art teacher, Mrs. Heintz.
3. A: When did you graduate from high school?
B: In 2006.
4. A: Where did you go to college?
B: I went to Duke University.
5. A: Why did you study physics?
B: Because I wanted to become an astronaut!
6. A: How were your professors in college?
B: They were great.
7. A: How old were you when you graduated?
B: I was 22 years old.

Exercise 5

2. True.
3. False. Students often/usually/always eat lunch in the cafeteria.
4. False. Physical education classes are never/almost never in an auditorium.
5. True.

Exercise 6

1. A: *How was your first day of school?*
B: (Answers will vary.)
2. A: Who was your favorite teacher?
B: (Answers will vary.)
3. A: What was your favorite class?
B: (Answers will vary.)
4. A: Who were your best friends?
B: (Answers will vary.)
5. A: Where did you spend your free time?
B: (Answers will vary.)
6. A: When did you leave elementary school?
B: (Answers will vary.)

Exercise 7

A

2. A: Did you grow up in a big city?
B: Yes, I did. / No, I didn't.
3. A: Did you play sports?
B: Yes, I did. / No, I didn't.
4. A: Was your home near your school?
B: Yes, it was. / No, it wasn't.
5. A: Did you ride a bus to school?
B: Yes, I did. / No, I didn't.
6. A: Were you a good student?
B: Yes, I was. / No, I wasn't.
7. A: Were your teachers nice?
B: Yes, they were. / No, they weren't.
8. A: Did you have a lot of friends?
B: Yes, I did. / No, I didn't.
9. A: Did your grandparents live near you?
B: Yes, they did. / No, they didn't.
10. A: Did both your parents work?
B: Yes, they did. / No, they didn't.

B

Answers will vary.

16 Can I take a message?

Exercise 1

Receptionist: Good morning, Oceanside Medical.
Mr. Jones: Good morning. Is Dr. Silva there?
Receptionist: I'm sorry, but Dr. Silva is in a meeting.
Mr. Jones: Oh.
Receptionist: Can I take a message?
Mr. Jones: Yes. This is Brian Jones. Please ask her to call me.
Receptionist: Does Dr. Silva have your number?
Mr. Jones: I don't think so. It's (604) 555-0662.
Receptionist: (604) 555-0662. I'll give her your message.
Mr. Jones: Thank you very much.
Receptionist: You're welcome. Good-bye.
Mr. Jones: Good-bye.

Exercise 2

2. *Jay:* Hello?
Kate: Hey, Jay. It's –
Jay: Kate. Sorry, can you call me in the morning? I'm in bed

3. *Marcela:* Hello?
Kate: Hi, Marcela. It's Kate. Do you want to see a movie tonight?
Marcela: I'd love to, but I can't. I'm on vacation with my parents.

4. *Bob:* Hello?
Kate: Hi, Bob. It's Kate. You know, you sound terrible. Are you OK?
Bob: Not really. I'm in/at the hospital. I broke my leg!

5. *Angie:* Hello?
Kate: Hello, Angie? It's Kate. Why are you whispering? Where are you?
Angie: Oh, I'm at the library.

6. *Pedro:* Hello?
Kate: Hey, Pedro. Do you have a minute?
Pedro: Not really. I'm at work. Call me tonight.

Exercise 3

2. Can I help you?
3. They gave her the book.
4. Do you remember me?
5. I missed his call yesterday.
6. We visited them last weekend.

Exercise 4

Ann's message
Hello, Miss Anderson. This is Ann Lopez. *I* work at First City Bank. You left your wallet here this morning. Please call me at (808) 555-1247. I'd like to give it back to you before we close today.

Jim's message
Hey, Heidi. It's Jim. I'm sorry I missed your call yesterday. Listen, my friends and I are going to go out for coffee tomorrow morning. We're meeting at my house at 9:00. Would you like to join us? Give me a call!

Sarah's message
Hi, Heidi. It's Sarah. Did you see Marco today? He's having a birthday party on Friday. Do you want to go with me? I'm going to buy him a present later. Call me! Thanks!

Exercise 5

Allison: Hello?
Evan: Hello. Can I speak to Roberta, please?
Allison: I'm sorry, but she's in a meeting. Can I give her a message?
Evan: Yes. This is Evan Martin. Please ask her to call me. I'm at work.
Allison: Does she have your number?
Evan: Yes, she does.

Exercise 6

Answers will vary.

Exercise 7

Answers will vary.

Exercise 8

1. A: Would you *like to* go to Bill's party on Thursday night?
B: I'd like to / love to go, but I have to study. I have a test on Friday.
2. A: Do you want to play tennis after work?
B: I'd like to / love to, but I have to work late.
3. A: Would you like to have dinner at our house?
B: Yes, I'd love to!
4. A: Do you want to visit the science museum tomorrow?
B: I'd like to / love to go, but I already have plans.
5. A: Would you like to go to the movies tonight?
B: Yes, but I don't want to see Horror House 3. I don't like scary movies!
6. A: Do you want to leave a message?
B: Yes, please tell Dr. O'Brien that I'd like to speak with her about our meeting.

Exercise 9

Answers will vary.
2. I like to . . .
3. I need to . . .
4. I want to meet . . .
5. I like to eat . . .
6. I want to . . .
7. I like to . . .
8. I like to go . . .

CREDITS

The authors and publishers acknowledge the following sources of copyright material and are grateful for the permissions granted. While every effort has been made, it has not always been possible to identify the sources of all the material used, or to trace all copyright holders. If any omissions are brought to our notice, we will be happy to include the appropriate acknowledgements on reprinting and in the next update to the digital edition, as applicable.

Texts

The Roxbury Hotel for the adapted text on p. 49. Reproduced with kind permission; Attrap'Rêves for the adapted text on p. 49. Reproduced with kind permission.

Key: B = Below, BL = Below Left, BC = Below Centre, BR = Below Right, B/G = Background, C = Centre, CL = Centre Left, CR = Centre Right, Ex = Exercise, TC = Top Centre, T = Top, TL = Top Left, TR = Top Right.

Illustrations

337 Jon (KJA Artists): 24, 29, 85; **Mark Duffin:** 15, 12(T), 31(T), 44(T), 47, 115, 121; **Thomas Girard** (Good Illustration): 3, 11, 13, 23, 25, 36, 37, 50, 79(T), 89, 100, 102; **Dusan Lakicevic** (Beehive Illustration): 21, 41, 87; **Quino Marin** (The Organisation): 26, 31(B), 79(B); **Gavin Reece** (New Division): 27, 44(B), 45, 101**; Gary Venn** (Lemonade Illustration): 56, 88, 90, 91, 127, 128; **Paul Williams** (Sylvie Poggio Artists): 9, 30, 119.

Photos

Back cover (woman with whiteboard): Jenny Acheson/Stockbyte/GettyImages; Back cover (whiteboard): Nemida/GettyImages; Back cover (man using phone): Betsie Van Der Meer/Taxi/GettyImages; Back cover (woman smiling): PeopleImages.com/DigitalVision/GettyImages; Back cover (name tag): Tetra Images/GettyImages; Back cover (handshake): David Lees/Taxi/GettyImages; p. x: Betsie Van Der Meer/Taxi/GettyImages; p. x: PeopleImages.com/DigitalVision/ GettyImages; screenshots on p. xi, xii, xiii, xiv from Interchange 5e Student's Book Intro, Jack C. Richards; p. xv: Betsie Van Der Meer/Taxi/GettyImages; p. xvi: PeopleImages.com/DigitalVision/GettyImages; screenshot on p. xvi (B) from Interchange 5e Games, Jack C. Richards; screenshot on p. xvii from Interchange 5e Workbook Intro, Jack C. Richards; screenshot on p. xviii from Interchange 5e Teacher's Edition Intro & Complete Assessment Program, Jack C. Richards; p. xix (woman): Jenny Acheson/Stockbyte/GettyImages; p. xix: Nemida/GettyImages; screenshots on p. xx from Interchange 5e Intro Teacher's Resource Worksheets & Supplementary Resources Overview; p. xxiii: PhotoAlto/Sigrid Olsson/ GettyImages; p. 2 (header), p. iv (unit 1): Paul Bradbury/OJO Images; p. 2 (CR): Paul Bradbury/Caiaimage/GettyImages; p. 2 (BL): Stefania D'Alessandro/ WireImage/GettyImages; p. 2 (BR): Steve Granitz/WireImage/GettyImages; p. 4 (Ex 7.1): Ariel Skelley/Blend Images/GettyImages; p. 4 (Ex 7.2): Design Pics/Ron Nickel/GettyImages; p. 4 (Ex 7.3): Dan Dalton/Caiaimage/GettyImages; p. 4 (Ex 7.4): Squaredpixels/E+/GettyImages; p. 5 (T): Fabrice LEROUGE/ONOKY/ GettyImages; p. 5 (C): Erik Dreyer/The Image Bank/GettyImages; p. 5 (B): theboone/E+/GettyImages; p. 6: Maskot/Maskot/GettyImages; p. 7 (T): Peter Dazeley/Photographer's Choice/GettyImages; p. 7 (Ex 14.1): Klaus Vedfelt/ DigitalVision/GettyImages; p. 7 (Ex 14.2): Tim Robberts/The Image Bank/ GettyImages; p. 7 (Ex 14.3): Ariel Skelley/Blend Images/GettyImages; p. 7 (Ex 14.4): Nicolas McComber/E+/GettyImages; p. 8 (header), p. iv (unit 2): John Slater/ Stockbyte/GettyImages; p. 8 (backpack): igor terekhov/iStock/GettyImagesPlus; p. 8 (cellphone): Peter Dazeley/Photographer's Choice/GettyImages; p. 8 (hairbrush): slobo/E+/GettyImages; p. 8 (sunglasses): Fodor90/iStock/GettyImages; p. 8 (wallet): bibikoff/E+/GettyImages; p. 8 (keys): Floortje/E+/GettyImages; p. 8 (umbrella): Picheat Suviyanond/iStock/GettyImages; p. 8 (energy bar): Juanmonino/iStock/Getty Images Plus/GettyImages; p. 8 (book): Image Source/ Image Source/GettyImages; p. 8 (notebook): kyoshino/E+/GettyImages; p. 8 (pen): Ann Flanigan/EyeEm/Fuse/GettyImages; p. 8 (eraser): subjug/iStock/GettyImages; p. 8 (clock): GoodGnom/DigitalVision Vectors/GettyImages; p. 9 (tablet): daboost/ iStock/Getty Images Plus/GettyImages; p. 9 (box): Guy Crittenden/Photographer's Choice/GettyImages; p. 9 (phone case): Jeffrey Coolidge/DigitalVision/ GettyImages; p. 9 (television): Cobalt88/iStock/GettyImages; p. 9 (newspaper): -Oxford-/E+/GettyImages; p. 9 (Id): Daniel Ernst/iStock/Getty Images Plus/ GettyImages; p. 9 (clip): Steven von Niederhausern/E+/GettyImages; p. 9 (ticket): Gediminas Zalgevicius/Hemera/GettyImages; p. 9 (purse): Stramyk/iStock/ GettyImages; p 10 (flash drive): zentilia/iStock/Getty Images Plus/GettyImages; p. 10 (laptop): Coprid/iStock/Getty Images Plus/GettyImages; p. 10 (laptops.): karandaev/iStock/GettyImages; p. 10 (keys): krungchingpixs/iStock/GettyImages; p. 10 (backpacks): pavila/iStock/GettyImages; p. 10 (umbrella): Kais Tolmats/E+/ GettyImages; p. 10 (sunglasses): Zaharia_Bogdan/iStock/GettyImages; p. 10 (wallet): malerapaso/iStock/GettyImages; p. 10 (window): beright/iStock/ GettyImages; p. 10 (credit card): freestylephoto/iStock/GettyImages; p. 10 (headphones): tiler84/iStock/GettyImages; p. 12 (backpack): JulNichols/E+/ GettyImages; p. 12 (flash drive): Garsya/iStock/GettyImages; p. 12 (laptop): Creative Crop/Photodisc/GettyImages; p. 12 (newspaper): goir/iStock/ GettyImages; p. 12 (computer): AlexLMX/iStock/GettyImages; p. 12 (chair): urfinguss/iStock/GettyImages; p. 12 (wallet): pioneer111/iStock/GettyImages; p. 12 (notebook): drpnncpp/iStock/GettyImages; p. 12 (tv): selensergen/iStock/ GettyImages; p. 12 (glasses): bonetta/iStock/GettyImages; p. 15 (cellphone): Manuel Faba Ortega/iStock/GettyImages; p. 15 (cellphones): sunnycircle/iStock/ GettyImages; p. 15 (purse): penguenstok/E+/GettyImages; p. 15 (purses): iulianvalentin/iStock/GettyImages; p. 15 (wallet): Nyo09/iStock/GettyImages; p. 15 (wallets): alarich/iStock/GettyImages; p. 16 (header), p. iv (unit 3): stock_colors/ iStock/Getty Images Plus/GettyImages; p. 16 (T): Photography by ZhangXun/ Moment/GettyImages; p. 16 (BR): Roberto Westbrook/Blend Images/GettyImages; p. 17 (T): Robert Frerck/The Image Bank/GettyImages; p. 17 (B): Jane Sweeney/The Image Bank/GettyImages; p. 18 (Ex 5.1): Dan MacMedan/WireImage/GettyImages; p. 18 (Ex 5.2): Steve Granitz/WireImage/GettyImages; p. 18 (Ex 5.3): Clasos/CON/ LatinContent Editorial/GettyImages; p. 18 (Ex 5.4): Koki Nagahama/Getty Images AsiaPac/GettyImages; p. 18 (Ex 5.5): Jeff Spicer/Getty Images Entertainment/ GettyImages; p. 19 (TR): SolStock/E+/GettyImages; p. 19 (cellphone): Peter Dazeley/Photographer's Choice/GettyImages; p. 19 (Ben): Hero Images/Hero Images/GettyImage; p. 19 (Nadia): Portra Images/DigitalVision/GettyImages; p. 19 (Ex 7.c.a): Fuse/Corbis/GettyImages; p. 19 (Ex 7.c.b): Purestock/GettyImages; p. 19 (Ex 7.c.c): Lucy Lambriex/Moment/GettyImages; p. 19 (Ex 7.c.d): James Woodson/ Photodisc/GettyImages; p. 19 (Ex 7.c.e): Fuse/Corbis/GettyImages; p. 20 (Ex 8.a.1): Alex Barlow/Moment/GettyImages; p. 20 (Ex 8.a.2): Jupiterimages/Stockbyte/ GettyImages; p. 20 (Ex 8.a.3): PhotoAlto/Frederic Cirou/PhotoAlto Agency RF Collections/GettyImages; p. 20 (Ex 8.a.4): Hill Street Studios/Blend Images/ GettyImages; p. 22 (header), p. iv (unit 4): Sam Edwards/Caiaimage/GettyImages; p. 22 (formal man): Spiderstock/E+/GettyImages; p. 22 (formal woman): Grady Reese/E+/GettyImages; p. 22 (rain coat): EdnaM/iStock/Getty Images Plus/ GettyImages; p. 22 (coat): DonNichols/E+/GettyImages; p. 22 (dress): ARSELA/E+/ GettyImages; p. 22 (casual woman): BLOOM image/BLOOMimage/GettyImages; p. 22 (pajamas): madtwinsis/E+/GettyImages; p. 22 (swimwear): dendong/iStock/ Getty Images Plus/GettyImages; p. 22 (shorts): 487387674/iStock/Getty Images Plus/GettyImages; p. 22 (cap): Steve Zmina/DigitalVision Vectors/GettyImages; p. 25 (brazilian flag): Image Source/Image Source/GettyImages; p. 25 (japanese flag): Jim Ballard/Photographer's Choice/GettyImages; p. 25 (american flag): NirdalArt/iStock/GettyImages; p. 25 (canadian flag): Encyclopaedia Britannica/UIG/ Universal Images Group/GettyImages; p. 25 (TL): Andrea Pistolesi/Photolibrary/ GettyImages; p. 25 (TR): Photograph by Kangheewan/Moment Open/ GettyImages; p. 25 (BL): Bruce Leighty/Photolibrary/GettyImages; p. 25 (BR): EschCollection/Photonica/GettyImages; p. 25 (thermometer): Burke/Triolo Productions/Stockbyte/GettyImages; p. 29: PeopleImages.com/DigitalVision/ GettyImages; p. 30 (header), p. iv (unit 5): Driendl Group/Photographer's Choice/ GettyImages; p. 30 (Brian): Daniel Grill/GettyImages; p. 30 (Amar): Peter Cade/The Image Bank/GettyImages; p. 31 (Ex 3.a.1): Raimund Koch/The Image Bank/ GettyImages; p. 31 (Ex 3.a.2): Science Photo Library/Science Photo Library/ GettyImages; p. 31 (Ex 3.a.3): Paul Bricknell/Dorling Kindersley/GettyImages; p. 31 (Ex 3.a.4): SergeiKorolko/iStock/GettyImages; p. 31 (Ex 3.a.5): pagadesign/iStock/ GettyImages; p. 31 (Ex 3.a.6): scanrail/iStock/GettyImages; p. 32 (T): Plume Creative/DigitalVision/GettyImages; p. 32 (BR): B. Sporrer/J.Skowronek/StockFood Creative/GettyImages; p. 32 (Jay): B. Sporrer/J.Skowronek/StockFood Creative/ GettyImages; p. 32 (Kate): Rafael Elias/Moment Open/GettyImages; p. 33 (TL): Tetra Images/Brand X Pictures/GettyImages; p. 33 (TC): Hola Images/GettyImages; p. 33 (TR): Tim Robberts/The Image Bank; p. 33 (CL): annebaek/iStock/Getty Images Plus/GettyImages; p. 33 (C): Stockbyte/Stockbyte/GettyImages; p. 33 (CR): Caiaimage/Tom Merton/Caiaimage/GettyImages; p. 33 (BL): LWA/Sharie Kennedy/ Blend Images/GettyImages; p. 33 (BC): sot/DigitalVision/GettyImages; p. 33 (BR): David Crunelle/EyeEm/EyeEm/GettyImages; p. 34 (dance): Blend Images - Ariel Skelley/GettyImages; p. 34 (drive): Westend61/Westend61/GettyImages; p. 34 (music): Hero Images/Hero Images/GettyImages; p. 34 (basketball): Daniel Grill/ Tetra images/GettyImages; p. 34 (read): Peathegee Inc/Blend Images/ GettyImages; p. 34 (bycycle): Daniel Milchev/The Image Bank/GettyImages; p. 34 (run): Ty Milford/Aurora Open/GettyImages; p. 34 (shop): BJI/Blue Jean Images/ blue jean images/GettyImages; p. 34 (study): JAG IMAGES/DigitalVision/ GettyImages; p. 34 (swim): J J D/Cultura/GettyImages; p. 34 (walk): Dougal Waters/ Photographer's Choice RF/GettyImages; p. 34 (movie): Blend Images/Andres Rodriguez/Blend Images/GettyImages; p. 35 (Eva35): Sebastian Doerken/fStop/ GettyImages; p. 35 (PamL): Denis Schneider/EyeEm/EyeEm/GettyImages; p. 35 (TL): Hero Images/Hero Images/GettyImages; p. 35 (BR): Betsie Van Der Meer/Taxi/ GettyImages; p. 36 (header), p. iv (unit 6): Enrique Díaz/7cero/Moment/ GettyImages; p. 36 (Ex 1.1): Image Source/DigitalVision/GettyImages; p. 36 (Ex 1.2): Kentaroo Tryman/Maskot/GettyImages; p. 36 (Ex 1.3): Susanne Kronholm/ Johner Images Royalty-Free/GettyImages; p. 36 (Ex 1.4): Eternity in an Instant/The Image Bank/GettyImages; p. 36 (Ex 1.5): Marilyn Nieves/iStock/GettyImages; p. 36 (Ex 1.6): Matt Dutile/Image Source/GettyImages; p. 36 (Ex 1.7): Ciaran Griffin/ Stockbyte/GettyImages; p. 36 (Ex 1.8): Maria Teijeiro/DigitalVision/GettyImages; p. 38: Robert Daly/Caiaimage/GettyImages; p. 39: Michael Berman/DigitalVision/ GettyImages; p. 40: Frank van Delft/Cultura/GettyImages; p. 41: vadimguzhva/ iStock/GettyImages; p. 42 (man): James Whitaker/DigitalVision/GettyImages; p. 42 (woman): Tyler Stableford/The Image Bank/GettyImage; p. 43: Pingebat/ DigitalVision Vectors; p. 44 (header), p. iv (unit 7): Peter Adams/Photolibrary; p. 45 (lobby): piovesempre/iStock/GettyImages; p. 45 (apartment): Joe_Potato/iStock/ GettyImages; p. 45 (house): Ron Evans/Photolibrary/GettyImages; p. 45 (kitchen): ttatty/iStock/GettyImages; p. 46 (armchair): xiaoke ma/E+/GettyImages; p. 46 (stove): taist/iStock/GettyImages; p. 46 (curtains): darksite/iStock/GettyImages; p. 46 (pictures): Glow Decor/Glow/GettyImages; p. 46 (bed): Emevil/iStock/ GettyImages; p. 46 (coffee maker): GeorgePeters/E+/GettyImages; p. 46 (table): EdnaM/iStock/GettyImages; p. 46 (coffee table): DonNichols/E+/GettyImages; p. 46 (oven): mbbirdy/E+/GettyImages; p. 46 (refrigerator): JazzIRT/E+/ GettyImages; p. 46 (lamps1): Creative Crop/DigitalVision/GettyImages; p. 46 (lamps2): stuartbur/E+/GettyImages; p. 46 (sofa): AnnaDavy/iStock/GettyImages; p. 46 (desk): Hemera Technologies/PhotoObjects.net/GettyImages; p. 46 (bookcase): DonNichols/iStock/GettyImages; p. 46 (dresser): Hemera Technologies/PhotoObjects.net/GettyImages; p. 46 (chairs): Firmafotografen/ iStock/Getty Images Plus/GettyImages; p. 46 (mirror): Omer Yurdakul Gundogdu/ E+/GettyImages; p. 46 (rug): DEA/G. CIGOLINI/De Agostini Picture Library/ GettyImages; p. 46 (cupboards): ChoochartSansong/iStock/GettyImages; p. 47: Marco Baass/GettyImages; p. 48 (loft): Martin Barraud/OJO Images/GettyImages; p. 48 (mountains): Barrett & MacKay/All Canada Photos/GettyImages; p. 48 (villa): Maremagnum/Photolibrary/GettyImages; p. 48 (beach house): catnap72/E+/ GettyImages; p. 49 (T): BERTHIER Emmanuel/hemis.fr/hemis.fr/GettyImages; p. 49 (B): Michael Marquand/Lonely Planet Images/GettyImages; p. 50 (header), p. iv (unit 8): iStock/Getty Images Plus/GettyImages; p. 51 (hospital): Vincent Hazat/ PhotoAlto Agency RF Collections/GettyImages; p. 51 (office): Peopleimages/E+/ GettyImages; p. 51 (store): Maskot/Maskot/GettyImages; p. 51 (hotel): DAJ/amana images/GettyImages; p. 51 (BR): Nevena1987/iStock/GettyImages; p. 51 (Jorden): Sam Edwards/OJO Images/GettyImages; p. 51 (Alicia): Philipp Nemenz/Cultura/ GettyImages; p. 52 (BL): Digital Vision./DigitalVision/GettyImages; p. 52 (BC): PeopleImages/DigitalVision/GettyImages; p. 52 (BR): Glow Images, Inc/Glow/ GettyImages; p. 53 (lawyer): rubberball/GettyImages; p. 53 (pilot): Katja Kircher/ Maskot/GettyImages; p. 53 (photographer): stock_colors/E+/GettyImages; p. 53 (engineer): Thomas Barwick/Iconica/GettyImages; p. 53 (BR): Rubberball/Mike Kemp/Brand X Pictures/GettyImages; p. 53 (Paula): Marc Romanelli/Blend Images/

GettyImages; p. 54 (T): Hero Images/Hero Images/GettyImages; p. 54 (B): Jetta Productions/Stone/GettyImages; p. 55 (B): Australian Scenics/Photolibrary/GettyImages; p. 55 (T): Eugenio Marongiu/Cultura/GettyImages; p. 57 (veterinarian): fotoedu/iStock/GettyImages; p. 57 (dentist): XiXinXing/XiXinXing/GettyImages; p. 57 (architect): John Lund/Marc Romanelli/Blend Images/GettyImages; p. 57 (hairstylst): Glow Images, Inc/Glow/GettyImages; p. 58 (header), p. vi (unit 9): Johner Images/GettyImages; p. 58 (apples): Maximilian Stock Ltd/Photolibrary/GettyImages; p. 58 (lemons): osoznaniejizni/iStock/GettyImages; p. 58 (bananas): Burazin/Photographer's Choice/GettyImages; p. 58 (kiwis): serebryakova/iStock/GettyImages; p. 58 (blueberries): Richard Coombs/EyeEm/EyeEm/GettyImages; p. 58 (oranges): David Marsden/Photolibrary/GettyImages; p. 58 (tomatoes): James A. Guilliam/Photolibrary/GettyImages; p. 58 (onions): Joff Lee/StockFood Creative/GettyImages; p. 58 (lettuce): Richard Clark/Photolibrary/GettyImages; p. 58 (carrots): Maximilian Stock Ltd./Photolibrary/GettyImages; p. 58 (potatoes): SvetlanaK/iStock/GettyImages; p. 58 (broccoli): Tsuji/E+/GettyImages; p. 58 (pasta): Dave King Dorling Kindersley/Dorling Kindersley/GettyImages; p. 58 (noodles): Yoyochow23/iStock/GettyImages; p. 58 (rice): Maximilian Stock Ltd/Photolibrary/GettyImages; p. 58 (crackers): Richard Griffin/iStock/GettyImages; p. 58 (bread): Pavlo_K/iStock/GettyImages; p. 58 (cereal): Graham Day/Photolibrary/GettyImages; p. 58 (butter): DustyPixel/E+/GettyImages; p. 58 (mayonnaise): Suzifoo/E+/GettyImages; p. 58 (oil): John E. Kelly/Photolibrary/GettyImages; p. 58 (cheese): jjwithers/E+/GettyImages; p. 58 (milk): PhotoObjects.net/PhotoObjects.net/GettyImages; p. 58 (cream): malerapaso/E+/GettyImages; p. 58 (yogurt): Science Photo Library/Science Photo Library/GettyImages; p. 58 (beans): malerapaso/iStock/GettyImages; p. 58 (nuts): Maximilian Stock Ltd./Photographer's Choice/GettyImages; p. 58 (eggs): ermingut/E+/GettyImages; p. 58 (beef): Lew Robertson/StockFood Creative/GettyImages; p. 58 (chicken): Andrea Bricco/StockFood Creative/GettyImages; p. 58 (fish): angorius/iStock/GettyImages; p. 59 (TR): RyanJLane/E+/GettyImages; p. 59 (potato salad): JFsPic/iStock/GettyImages; p. 59 (potato): -massmedia-/iStock/Getty Images Plus/GettyImages; p. 59 (celery): anna1311/iStock/GettyImages; p. 59 (onions): prwstd/iStock/GettyImages; p. 59 (mayonnaise): BWFolsom/iStock/GettyImages; p. 59 (apple): Raimondas/iStock/GettyImages; p. 60 (oranges): JannHuizenga/iStock/Getty Images Plus/GettyImages; p. 60 (apples): joanek/iStock/GettyImages; p. 60 (lettuce): Foodcollection RF/GettyImages; p. 60 (potatoes): RBOZUK/iStock/GettyImages; p. 60 (tomatoes): S847/iStock/Getty Images Plus/GettyImages; p. 60 (celery): Stefano Oppo/Stockbyte/GettyImages; p. 60 (bananas): PavlinaGab/iStock/GettyImages; p. 60 (kiwis): nullplus/iStock/Getty Images Plus/GettyImages; p. 60 (lemons): Michael Paul/StockFood Creative/GettyImages; p. 60 (carrots): RBOZUK/iStock/GettyImages; p. 60 (onions): IJdema/iStock/GettyImages; p. 60 (broccoli): Marco Vacca/Photographer's Choice RF/GettyImages; p. 60 (blueberries): billnoll/iStock/Getty Images Plus/GettyImages; p. 60 (BL): Rohit Seth/iStock/GettyImages; p. 60 (BC): MIXA/GettyImages; p. 60 (BR): Alberto Coto/Photodisc/GettyImages; p. 61 (TR): artparadigm/Taxi Japan/GettyImages; p. 61 (BR): Luis Alvarez/Taxi/GettyImages; p. 62: LiudmylaSupynska/iStock/Getty Images Plus/GettyImages; p. 63 (CR): Mardis Coers/Moment/GettyImages; p. 63 (TL): BIEL ALINO/AFP/GettyImages; p. 63 (CL): gnomeandi/iStock/GettyImages; p. 63 (BR): Danita Delimont/Gallo Images/GettyImages; p. 64 (header), p. vi (unit 10): Mike Powell/Allsport Concepts/GettyImages; p. 64 (racket): Arijuhani/iStock/Getty Images Plus/GettyImages; p. 64 (volleyball): Burazin/Photographer's Choice/GettyImages; p. 64 (goggles): Image Source/Image Source/GettyImages; p. 64 (football): Image Source/Image Source/GettyImages; p. 64 (hockey): C Squared Studios/Photodisc/GettyImages; p. 64 (baseball): PhotoObjects.net/PhotoObjects.net/GettyImages; p. 64 (basketball): Andrew Dernie/Stockbyte/GettyImages; p. 64 (skates): RedKoalaDesign/iStock/GettyImages; p. 64 (snowboard): Stockbyte/Stockbyte/GettyImages; p. 64 (bike): hamurishi/iStock/GettyImages; p. 64 (hiking boots): Don Bayley/E+/GettyImages; p. 64 (soccer): Lazi & Mellenthin/Westend61/GettyImages; p. 64 (BR): Blend Images - Jose Luis Pelaez Inc/Brand X Pictures/GettyImages; p. 64 (Victor): Blend Images - Jose Luis Pelaez Inc/Brand X Pictures/GettyImages; p. 64 (Tara): Tom Merton/Caiaimage/GettyImages; p. 65 (T): Michael DeYoung/Design Pics/First Light/GettyImages; p. 65 (B): Lewis Mulatero/Taxi/GettyImages; p. 66 (T): Jupiterimages/Stone/GettyImages; p. 66 (B): shaunl/iStock/Getty Images Plus/GettyImages; p. 67 (Ex 7.a.1): Alexander Rhind/Stone/GettyImages; p. 67 (Ex 7.a.2): leaf/iStock/Getty Images Plus/GettyImages; p. 67 (Ex 7.a.3): innovatedcaptures/iStock/Getty Images Plus/GettyImages; p. 67 (Ex 7.a.4): Spaces Images/Blend Images/GettyImages; p. 67 (Ex 7.a.5): alfalfa126/Moment/GettyImages; p. 67 (Ex 7.a.6): Gazimal/The Image Bank/GettyImages; p. 68 (Ex 9.1): Nicola Tree/Taxi/GettyImages; p. 68 (Ex 9.2): Westend61/Westend61/GettyImages; p. 68 (Ex 9.3): MarioGuti/iStock/GettyImages; p. 68 (Ex 9.4): Kyle Monk/Blend Images/GettyImages; p. 68 (Ex 9.5): Chad Springer/Image Source/GettyImages; p. 68 (Ex 9.6): olegkalina/iStock/GettyImages; p. 68 (Ex 9.7): Roberto Cerruti/Hemera/GettyImages; p. 68 (Ex 9.8): Tatomm/iStock/GettyImages; p. 69 (TL): Carlos Osorio/Toronto Star/GettyImages; p. 69 (Centre): SAM PANTHAKY/AFP/GettyImages; p. 69 (TR): Raul Sifuentes/Guiness World Records/Newscom; p. 71 (chef): Jetta Productions/Iconica/GettyImages; p. 71 (mechanic): Tanya Constantine/Blend Images/GettyImages; p. 71 (artist): Lisa Stirling/The Image Bank/GettyImages; p. 71 (musician): Hill Street Studios/Blend Images/GettyImages; p. 72 (header), p. vi (unit 11): Caiaimage/Tom Merton/Caiaimage/GettyImages; p. 72 (BR): Dorling Kindersley/Dorling Kindersley/GettyImages; p. 72 (Ava): LWA/Larry Williams/Blend Images/GettyImages; p. 72 (Martin): Marcos Ferro/GettyImages; p. 73 (Ex 3.a.1): Dave and Les Jacobs/Lloyd Dobbie/Blend Images/GettyImages; p. 73 (Ex 3.a.2): Mike Svoboda/DigitalVision/GettyImages; p. 73 (Ex 3.a.3): Kathrin Ziegler/Taxi/GettyImages; p. 73 (Ex 3.a.4): UpperCut Images/UpperCut Images/GettyImages; p. 73 (Ex 3.a.5): Jetta Productions/Iconica/GettyImages; p. 73 (Ex 3.a.6): Caiaimage/Paul Bradbury/OJO+/GettyImages; p. 73 (Ex 3.a.7): Nicolas McComber/E+/GettyImages; p. 73 (Ex 3.a.8): John Eder/The Image Bank/GettyImages; p. 74 (Morgan): Image Source/Image Source/GettyImage; p. 74 (Issac): T.T./Iconica/GettyImages; p. 74 (Lauren): PeopleImages/DigitalVision/GettyImages; p. 74 (Brian): Eugenio Marongiu/Cultura/GettyImages; p. 74 (Ex 7: photo1): tiridifilm/E+/GettyImages; p. 74 (Ex 7: photo2): Gail Shumway/Photographer's Choice/GettyImages; p. 74 (Ex 7: photo3): Zeb Andrews/Moment/GettyImages; p. 74 (Ex 7: photo4): PeopleImages.com/DigitalVision/GettyImages; p. 74 (Ex 7: photo5): Tetra Images/Tetra images/GettyImages; p. 74 (Ex 7: photo6): Rudi Von Briel/Photolibrary/GettyImages; p. 75 (Allie): Louise Morgan/Moment/Getty Images; p. 75 (Jim): Louise Morgan/Moment/Getty Images; p. 75 (TR): Vegar Abelsnes Photography/Photodisc/GettyImages; p. 76 (special cloth): William Tang/Design Pics/Perspectives/GettyImages; p. 76 (food): Ronnie Kaufman/Larry Hirshowitz/Blend Images/GettyImages; p. 76 (decorate): Photo by Glenn Waters in Japan/Moment/GettyImages; p. 76 (give gifts): Fastrum/iStock/GettyImages; p. 76 (play music): Derek E. Rothchild/Photolibrary/GettyImages; p. 76 (parade): Oliver Strewe/Lonely Planet Images/GettyImages; p. 76 (picnic): uniquely india/photosindia/GettyImages; p. 76 (fireworks): Ichiro Murakami/EyeEm/EyeEm/GettyImages; p. 76 (blossom festival): Bohistock/Moment/GettyImages; p. 76 (carnival): Yadid Levy/robertharding/robertharding/GettyImages; p. 77 (TL): Foodcollection RF/Foodcollection/GettyImages; p. 77 (CR): Emilia Krysztofiak Rua Photography/Moment/GettyImages; p. 77 (BL): Thomas Fricke/First Light/GettyImages; p. 77 (BR): Kelly Cheng Travel Photography/Moment Open/GettyImages; p. 78 (header), p. vi (unit 12): Mark Alcarez/Photolibrary/GettyImages; p. 78 (man): Eric Audras/ONOKY/GettyImages; p. 78 (holding volleyball): Stockbyte/GettyImages; p. 80 (Ex 4.a.1): Predrag Vuckovic/iStock/GettyImages; p. 80 (Ex 4.a.2): Ghislain & Marie David de Lossy/Cultura/GettyImages; p. 80 (Ex 4.a.3): Lawren/Moment/GettyImages; p. 80 (Ex 4.a.4): g-stockstudio/iStock/GettyImages; p. 80 (chamomile tea): Maximilian Stock Ltd./Photographer's Choice/GettyImages; p. 80 (cough syrup): Comstock/Stockbyte/GettyImages; p. 80 (chicken soup): Shawn Gearhart/E+/GettyImages; p. 80 (cold medicine): MakiEni's photo/Moment Open/GettyImages; p. 80 (eye drops): BananaStock/BananaStock/GettyImages; p. 80 (aspirin): Diane Macdonald/Photographer's Choice RF/GettyImages; p. 80 (antacid): STEVE HORRELL/SPL/Science Photo Library/GettyImages; p. 80 (nasal spray): hamikus/iStock/GettyImages; p. 80 (ice pack): Hero Images/Hero Images/GettyImages; p. 81: Chad Baker/Jason Reed/Ryan McVay/Photodisc/GettyImages; p. 82 (Ex 10.a.1): diego_cervo/iStock/GettyImages; p. 82 (Ex 10.a.2): BSIP/UIG/Universal Images Group/GettyImages; p. 82 (Ex 10.a.3): Garry Wade/The Image Bank/GettyImages; p. 82 (Ex 10.a.4): ViewStock/View Stock/GettyImages; p. 83: pixologicstudio/iStock/Getty Images Plus/GettyImages; p. 85 (TL): Paul Bradbury/OJO Images/GettyImages; p. 85 (TC): BartekSzewczyk/iStock/GettyImages; p. 85 (TR): Image Source/Photodisc/GettyImages; p. 85 (BL): baona/iStock/GettyImages; p. 85 (BC): Manuel Faba Ortega/iStock/GettyImages; p. 85 (BR): Jamie Grill/The Image Bank/GettyImages; p. 86 (header), p. vi (unit 13): Andy Ryan/Stone/GettyImages; p. 86 (Ex 1.a.a): Tetra Images/Tetra images/GettyImages; p. 86 (Ex 1.a.b): Musketeer/DigitalVision/GettyImages; p. 86 (Ex 1.a.c): PhotoAlto/James Hardy/Brand X Pictures/GettyImages; p. 86 (Ex 1.a.d): Bloomberg/Bloomberg/GettyImages; p. 86 (Ex 1.a.e): Deborah Cheramie/iStock/GettyImages; p. 86 (Ex 1.a.f): Jetta Productions/The Image Bank/GettyImages; p. 86 (Ex 1.a.g): Inti St Clair/Blend Images/GettyImages; p. 86 (Ex 1.a.h): David Nevala/Aurora/GettyImages; p. 89 (TL): David Henderson/Caiaimage/GettyImages; p. 89 (TC): Chris Mellor/Lonely Planet Images/GettyImages; p. 89 (TR): Medioimages/Photodisc/Photodisc/GettyImages; p. 89 (BL): Cultura RM Exclusive/Christoffer Askman/Cultura Exclusive/GettyImages; p. 89 (BC): STAN HONDA/AFP Creative/GettyImages; p. 89 (BR): Chris Mellor/Lonely Planet Images/GettyImages; p. 91 (TL): Fandrade/Moment/GettyImages; p. 91 (TC): Anton Petrus/Moment/GettyImages; p. 91 (TR): Karina Vera/Moment/GettyImages; p. 91 (CL): Rebeca Mello/Moment Open/GettyImages; p. 91 (BL): Bettmann/Bettmann/GettyImages; p. 91 (BR): Alfredo Herms/STR/LatinContent WO/GettyImages; p. 92 (header), p. vi (unit 14): Adam Burton/robertharding/GettyImages; p. 92 (Ex 1: photo 1): Caiaimage/Paul Bradbury/Riser/GettyImages; p. 92 (Ex 1: photo 2): Maskot/GettyImages; p. 92 (Ex 1: photo 3): Fabrice LEROUGE/ONOKY/GettyImages; p. 92 (Ex 1: photo 4): Holger Mette/iStock/Getty Images Plus/GettyImages; p. 92 (Ex 1: photo 5): Ariel Skelley/Blend Images/GettyImages; p. 92 (Ex 1: photo 6): David Jakle/Image Source/GettyImages; p. 92 (Ex 1: photo 7): Andersen Ross/Blend Images/GettyImages; p. 92 (Ex 1: photo 8): Hero Images/GettyImages; p. 92 (BR): Absodels/ABSODELS/GettyImages; p. 93: A. Chederros/ONOKY/GettyImages; p. 94 (TL): Djura Topalov/iStock/Getty Images Plus/GettyImages; p. 94 (TC): JGI/Jamie Grill/Blend Images/GettyImages; p. 94 (TR): KNSY/Picture Press/GettyImages; p. 94 (CL): svetikd/E+/GettyImages; p. 94 (C): Ghislain & Marie David de Lossy/Cultura/GettyImages; p. 94 (CR): Kevin Kozicki/Image Source/GettyImages; p. 95 (TR): Greg Elms/Lonely Planet Images/GettyImages; p. 95 (Kim): Sam Edwards/Caiaimage/GettyImages; p. 95 (Martin): Jetta Productions/Blend Images/GettyImages; p. 95 (BR): Thomas Barwick/Taxi/GettyImages; p. 96: Matthew Micah Wright/Lonely Planet Images/GettyImages; p. 97 (Nick): William King/The Image Bank/GettyImages; p. 97 (Jessie): Caiaimage/Sam Edwards/OJO+/GettyImages; p. 97 (Armando): Daniel Ernst/iStock/Getty Images Plus/GettyImages; p. 97 (Juliette): Robert Daly/Caiaimage; p. 99 (T): David Wall Photo/Lonely Planet Images/GettyImages; p. 99 (C): Emma Innocenti/Taxi/GettyImages; p. 99 (B): Robert Deutschman/DigitalVision/GettyImages; p. 100 (header), p. vi (unit 15): David Oliver/The Image Bank/GettyImages; p. 100 (Ex 1.1): Jeff Kravitz/FilmMagic, Inc/GettyImages; p. 100 (Ex 1.2): Gary Gershoff/WireImage/GettyImages; p. 100 (Ex 1.3): Bruce Glikas/FilmMagic/GettyImages; p. 100 (Ex 1.4): G Fiume/Getty Images Sport/GettyImages; p. 100 (Ex 1.5): Kevork Djansezian/Getty Images News/GettyImages; p. 102 (TR): John Eder/The Image Bank/GettyImages; p. 104: Ridofranz/iStock/GettyImages; p. 105 (map): Richard Sharrocks/iStock/Getty Images Plus/GettyImages; p. 105 (boy): Tim Kitchen/DigitalVision/GettyImages; p. 105 (B/G): Mark Miller Photos/Photolibrary/GettyImages; p. 106 (header), p. vi (unit 16): Lumina Images/Blend Images; p. 106 (CL): PhotoAlto/Frederic Cirou/PhotoAlto Agency RF Collections/GettyImages; p. 106 (CR): Caiaimage/Sam Edwards/Caiaimage/GettyImages; p. 106 (BL): REB Images/Blend Images/GettyImages; p. 106 (BR): Gary Burchell/Taxi/GettyImages; p. 106 (BR): Cultura RM Exclusive/Gary John Norman/Cultura Exclusive/GettyImages; p. 107: Marc Romanelli/Blend Images/GettyImages; p. 108 (camping): Hero Images/Hero Images/GettyImages; p. 108 (amusement park): Joe McBride/Iconica/GettyImages; p. 108 (street fair): Patti McConville/Photographer's Choice/GettyImages; p. 108 (concert): PeopleImages.com/DigitalVision/GettyImages; p. 108 (barbecue): Hero Images/Hero Images/GettyImages; p. 108 (play): Caiaimage/Robert Daly/OJO+/GettyImages; p. 108 (Nathan): Ezra Bailey/Taxi/GettyImages; p. 108 (Julie): Mike Chick/Stone/GettyImages; p. 108 (BR): Image Source/Image Source/GettyImages; p. 109: NT Photography/Image Source/GettyImages; p. 110 (TR): B Busco/Photographer's Choice/GettyImages; p. 110 (BR): monkeybusinessimages/iStock/GettyImages; p. 111 (T): Cooper Neill/Getty Images Entertainment/GettyImages; p. 112 (Audrey Hepburn): Michael Ochs Archives/Moviepix/GettyImages; p. 112 (Nelson Mandela): Per-Anders Pettersson/Hulton Archive/GettyImages; p. 112 (Paul Walker): Jason Merritt/FilmMagic/GettyImages; p. 113: PeopleImages/DigitalVision/GettyImages; screenshots on p. T-114–131 from Interchange 5e Student's book Intro, Jack C. Richards.

Video still on p. xv (B) by Nesson Media Boston Inc.